Insurgent Collective Action and Civil War in El Salvador

Widespread support among rural people for the leftist insurgency during the civil war in El Salvador challenges conventional interpretations of collective action. Those who supplied tortillas, information, and other aid to guerrillas took mortal risks and yet stood to gain no more than those who did not. Wood's rich tapestry of explanation is based on oral histories gathered from peasants who supported the insurgency and those who did not over a period of many years during and immediately following the war, and interviews with military commanders of both sides. Peasants supported the FMLN, Wood found, not for any material gain that was contingent on their participation, but rather for moral and emotional reasons. In supporting the insurgency they not only defied state violence, they also affirmed their dignity and autonomy after generations of contempt by the landed elite. And as their successes mounted, others joined in to participate in writing a page in the history of their locality. Wood's alternative model places emotions and morals, as well as conventional interests, at the heart of collective action.

Elisabeth Jean Wood is Associate Professor of Politics at New York University and Visiting Research Professor at the Sante Fe Institute. She is the author of *Forging Democracy from Below* (Cambridge 2000) and other works in comparative politics and political economy.

to Sam

Cambridge Studies in Comparative Politics

General Editor
Margaret Levi   *University of Washington, Seattle*

Associate Editors
Robert H. Bates   *Harvard University*
Peter Hall   *Harvard University*
Stephen Hanson   *University of Washington, Seattle*
Peter Lange   *Duke University*
Helen Milner   *Columbia University*
Frances Rosenbluth   *Yale University*
Susan Stokes   *University of Chicago*
Sidney Tarrow   *Cornell University*

Other Books in the Series

Continued on the page following the index.

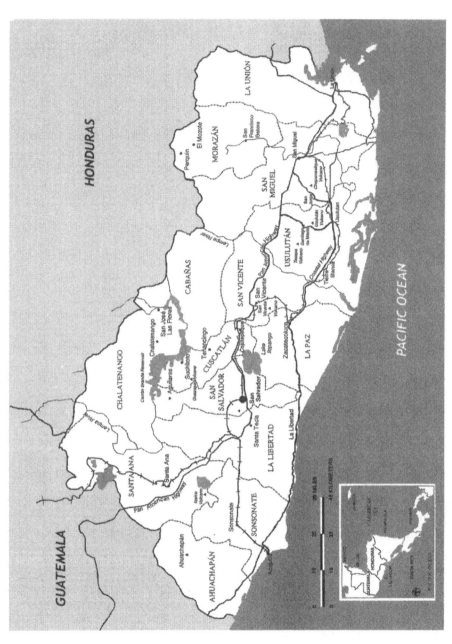

Map of El Salvador. By Carolyn Resnicke

Insurgent Collective Action and Civil War in El Salvador

ELISABETH JEAN WOOD

New York University

CAMBRIDGE
UNIVERSITY PRESS

CAMBRIDGE UNIVERSITY PRESS
Cambridge, New York, Melbourne, Madrid, Cape Town, Singapore,
São Paulo, Delhi, Dubai, Tokyo

Cambridge University Press
The Edinburgh Building, Cambridge CB2 8RU, UK

Published in the United States of America by Cambridge University Press, New York

www.cambridge.org
Information on this title: www.cambridge.org/9780521010504

First published 2003

A catalogue record for this publication is available from the British Library

ISBN 978-0-521-81175-0 Hardback
ISBN 978-0-521-01050-4 Paperback

Transferred to digital printing 2010

Contents

Illustrations and Tables

Illustrations

Illustrations and Tables

Table

Preface and Acknowledgments

El Salvador drew my interest beginning in the early 1980s when I worked as a volunteer paralegal and translator helping Salvadoran refugees prepare applications for political asylum. I was disturbed by their accounts of political violence and inspired by their resilience in the face of danger and hardship. I was less impressed with U.S. accounts – both official and oppositional – of the civil war. I eventually decided to resign my position teaching physics in order to devote myself full time to social science research in general and to research on the origins and resolution of civil wars in particular.

I first went to El Salvador in 1987 to study an unprecedented agreement negotiated by officials of the Catholic Church with representatives of the Salvadoran military and of the insurgent guerrilla forces. Under the terms of the agreement, the residents of Tenancingo, who had fled the town when its history of intense conflict culminated in its bombing in 1983, could return there regardless of their past political involvement, and Tenancingo would be an "unarmed zone." The agreement was sharply contested on the ground and in the pages of national newspapers, but those who returned were able to plant corn fields, rebuild houses, and participate in an experiment unlikely in the midst of a civil war: a representative town council. In later years, I continued to visit Tenancingo to follow the evolution of a community that had been bitterly divided during the war yet reunited to some extent around the idea of a local peace.

In September 1991, I began eighteen months of field research on the origin and consequences of rural collective action and civil war. I chose to concentrate my work on the conflicted but wealthy province of Usulután, as its history promised to illustrate both the civil war and its aftermath. My interviews took place in the fields and villages of southwestern, central, and eastern Usulután and in the towns of Tierra Blanca, Jiquilisco,

San Francisco Javier, and Santiago de María. I traveled frequently to San Salvador, not only for respite from the demands of research in a war-torn countryside still occupied by opposing armed camps, but also to interview various other sources crucial for documenting the roots of the civil war and its negotiated settlement. After returning to the United States, I continued to visit El Salvador frequently.

This research resulted in two books. The first, *Forging Democracy from Below: Insurgent Transitions in South Africa and El Salvador* (Cambridge University Press, 2000), is a study of democratization in societies where an oligarchic alliance of privileged economic elites and powerful state elites long maintained exclusionary political regimes and unequal distributions of wealth. I explain why, in these two unlikely cases, a transition to democracy and a durable resolution of civil conflict occurred. I show that sustained insurgency by the less well-off disrupted and eventually transformed the economic interests of key sectors of economic elites. As a result, business elites pressed for negotiations with insurgent representatives, changing the balance of power between regime hard-liners and moderates.

Forging Democracy from Below addressed political change at the national level. In contrast, this book is a local exploration of what Barrington Moore, Jr., calls the "social bases of revolt" (1978). In exploring the trajectory of insurrection in El Salvador, I focus on why, despite the extraordinarily high risks of doing so, many peasants supported opposition organizations, including the guerrilla army waging war against the state. I trace the evolving form of peasant collective action from the mid-1970s, when rural organizations worked closely with urban organizations in a mass social movement, to the scattered but vital covert support for the insurgent army in the early 1980s to the construction of a vibrant civil society under the shadow of the military stalemate that emerged in 1984. I compare patterns of participation in the insurgency across five case-study areas, drawing on interviews with *campesinos* who supported the insurgency and with those who did not, as well as interviews with guerrilla and military commanders, landlords, and other sources. While material grievances, principally the unequal distribution of land, played a role in motivating rebellion, I show that emotional and moral reasons were essential to the emergence and consolidation of insurgent collective action in the areas I studied.

I believe that what I found is relevant to other situations where poor people are excluded from social and political participation, where an emerging social movement challenges that exclusion and makes claims on the state and the well-to-do, and where the response of the state is repression rather than accommodation.

Acknowledgments

One accumulates many debts in fifteen years of research. I am deeply grateful to the residents of the field sites in El Salvador for their willingness to tell me their history and that of their communities through the years of the civil war. I deeply wish I could thank them all by name.

Fieldwork in conflicted areas during and just after civil war is difficult, and made possible only by the support of many people. I am especially grateful to the shelter and counsel provided by Sister Elena Jaramillo of the parish of Jiquilisco, by Ana Karlslund in Santiago de María, and by Sister Ivonne de Groot and the staff members of the Salvadoran Foundation for Development and Low-Income Housing in Tenancingo (FUNDASAL). Their experience and wisdom saved me from many an error. The staff of the several opposition political organizations in Usulután (the National Confederation of Federations of the Salvadoran Agrarian Reform, United Communities of Usulután, the National Federation of Agrarian Cooperatives, and the Coordinator for the Development of the Coast) answered endless questions and facilitated my meetings with individual members. I am grateful for their accommodating the curiosity of an academic interloper.

I am also grateful to the many persons interviewed in San Salvador and other urban areas, particularly the landlords of Usulután and Tenancingo for sharing their experiences and perceptions of the war. My thanks go as well to government officials in the various reconstruction, land reform, and land transfer agencies; to several officers of the Salvadoran Armed Forces; to the field commanders of the People's Revolutionary Army (the guerrilla faction active in Usulután) and of the Popular Liberation Forces (the faction active in Tenancingo); to the members and staff of the Farabundo Martí Front for National Liberation (the guerrilla force) working on land transfer and reconstruction; to the staff members of the United Nations mission to El Salvador; to Michael Wise, Ana Luz de Mena, and María Latino of the United States Agency for International Development; and to the directors and staff of FUNDASAL.

Many of the individuals interviewed chose to share their perceptions and histories with an academic researcher because they wanted to contribute to a work that would document and analyze a troubled period of their local and national histories. I can only hope this book proves worthy of their trust. While I do not presume to have "given voice to the voiceless" – most of whom speak out for themselves and their communities just fine – I hope I have accurately conveyed to a wider audience something of their experiences and perceptions of the civil war.

My heartfelt thanks go as well to the many colleagues and friends who read and commented on the entire manuscript: William Barnes, Amrita Basu, Leigh Binford, Cynthia McClintock, Philippe Bourgois, Samuel Bowles, David Smilde, Jack Hammond, Mark Kesselman, Vincent McElhinny, Christopher Nicholson, Jillian Nicholson, Kenneth Roberts, Gay Seidman, David Smilde, Jack Spence, Charles Tilly, George Vickers, Timothy Wickham-Crowley, and Richard Wood, as well as anonymous reviewers of the manuscript.

I also thank those who commented on related articles or individual chapters: Javier Auyero, Vincent Boudreau, John Brentlinger, Ethel Brooks, Michael Chwe, Alex Downes, George Downs, Mitchell Duneier, Richard Fagen, Ann Ferguson, Adam Flint, Michael Foley, Jeffrey Goodwin, Russell Hardin, David Hunt, Allen Hunter, James Jasper, Courtney Jung, Stathis Kalyvas, Terry Karl, Jackie Klopp, David Laitin, Murray Last, Aldo Lauria-Santiago, Roy Licklider, John Markoff, Mieke Meurs, David Meyer, John Miller, Christopher Mitchell, Tommie Sue Montgomery, Barrington Moore, Jr., Kevin Murray, Jeffrey Olick, Bertell Ollman, Paule Ollman, Francesca Polletta, Daniel Posner, Adam Przeworski, Philippe Schmitter, Mitchell Seligson, Susan Stokes, Sidney Tarrow, Michael Watts, Steven Wilkinson, Pete Wolfe, and Marilyn Young. Discussions with members of workshops and seminars at the University of Chicago, Columbia University, the Laboratory in Comparative Ethnic Processes, the University of New Mexico, and New York University also helped shape the final manuscript. Comments of those above corrected errors, clarified the argument, and improved its presentation. My revisions have perhaps done justice to some of the challenges and criticisms, but certainly not all.

It has been my very good fortune to work with Lewis Bateman, Senior Politics Editor of Cambridge University Press. His intellectual judgment and ongoing advice greatly contributed to this book. I also thank Margaret Levi for inclusion of this book in the Comparative Politics series.

I am grateful to Antonio Alvarez, Ever Amaya, Elena Castro ("Carmelo"), Margarita Flores, Vincent McElhinny, Mitchell Seligson, Jack Spence, William Stanley, and staff members of the Salvadoran Institute of the Agrarian Reform, the Ministry of Agriculture, the U.S. Agency for International Development, FUNDASAL, and the United Nations

Preface and Acknowledgments

Observer Mission in El Salvador for providing landholding, electoral, and other data.

I also express my appreciation to the members of the Institute for Economic and Social Research of the José Simeón Cañas Central American University, which provided institutional support during my field work in Usulután, to the staff members of FUNDASAL for logistical and other help during my fieldwork in Tenancingo, and to the University of Siena and the Santa Fe Institute for inspiring settings that facilitated the writing of this book.

Carolyn Resnicke of the Santa Fe Institute digitally restored the images of the maps drawn by *campesinos* to something remarkably close to their original vibrant colors, working from color photographs of the original maps taken for me by journalist Tom Gibb. Color versions of the maps appear on the Web site us.cambridge.org/features/wood. She also drew three other maps for this book and with Samuel Bowles designed the cover. The majority of the photographs are by Jeremy Bigwood, a photojournalist who worked in the contested areas of El Salvador to document the course and consequences of the civil war. Research assistance from Mary Bellman, Bridget Longridge, and Christina Schatzman was invaluable.

Funding for this research project came from the United States Institute of Peace, the Harvard Academy for International and Area Studies of Harvard University, the MacArthur Foundation through the Stanford Center for Arms Control, the Tinker Foundation, the Institute for the Study of World Politics, and New York University. I am grateful to all of them for their support.

Finally, to Sam for his excellent criticism, constant support, and wonderful companionship during the writing of this book – a most heartfelt thank you. It is much the better book for his comments and for his never-faltering belief in the project.

List of Abbreviations

ARENA Alianza Republicana Nacional (National Republican Alliance)

BPR Bloque Popular Revolucionario (Popular Revolutionary Block)

CODECOSTA Coordinadora para el Desarrollo de la Costa (Coordinator for the Development of the Coast)

COMUS Comunidades Unidas de Usulután (United Communities of Usulután)

CONFRAS Confederación Nacional de Federaciones de la Reforma Agraria Salvadoreña (National Confederation of Federations of the Salvadoran Agrarian Reform)

ERP Ejército Revolucionario del Pueblo (Revolutionary Army of the People)

FECCAS Federación Cristiana de Campesinos Salvadoreños (Christian Federation of Salvadoran Campesinos)

FENACOA Federación Nacional de Cooperativas Agrarias (National Federation of Agrarian Cooperatives)

FMLN Frente Farabundo Martí para la Liberación Nacional (Farabundo Martí Front for National Liberation)

FPL Fuerzas Populares de Liberación Farabundo Martí (Farabundo Martí Popular Liberation Forces)

FUNDASAL Fundación Salvadoreña de Desarrollo y Vivienda Mínima (Salvadoran Foundation for Development and Low-Income Housing)

ORDEN Organización Democrática Nacionalista (Democratic Nationalist Organization)

1

The Puzzle of Insurgent Collective Action

This is what I think: what was the war for? For the solution to the land problem. We feel something already, and we're sure that we will be free – that is a point of the war that we have won. Higher incomes? Who knows? But that we not be seen as slaves, that we've won.

Member, Land Defense Committee, Las Marías, 1992[1]

Before the civil war in El Salvador, almost everyone in Tierra Blanca worked on the Hacienda California, a giant farm stretching from the edge of town across the fertile coastal plain to the Bay of Jiquilisco ten kilometers to the south. From their small houses in town or their shacks along the railway and roadways, every morning the workers walked past the hacienda's security post, past the gun ports of the fortified bunker, and through the gated entrance. They continued past the hacienda compound and the soldiers' quarters, past the barracks that housed the migrant workers during the harvest, and on toward the vast cotton fields, pastures, and salt flats beyond.

Before the war, the children of this town in southwestern Usulután had little reason to doubt that when they grew up, they would join their parents tending cotton and cattle and processing salt on the Palomo family's vast and well-guarded estate.

But in the mid- and late 1970s, some residents of Tierra Blanca joined in local protests and strikes, a few marched in the capital, San Salvador, and a very few collaborated with guerrilla organizations that would become the Frente Farabundo Martí para la Liberación Nacional (Farabundo Martí

---

[1] Unless otherwise indicated, all quotations are from interviews carried out in Spanish by the author.

1

Front for National Liberation, or FMLN). Unrest and violence deepened after 1976 when a coalition of landlords and military hard-liners brutally derailed a reformist government's attempt at a limited agrarian reform along the coastal plain. In 1979, workers struck for higher wages on the Hacienda California, their last attempt to better working conditions through what in many other countries would be considered normal forms of worker collective action. National Guard troops billeted on the farm responded with growing violence. As the country lurched toward civil war at the end of the 1970s, brutalized corpses of activists, relatives of activists, and suspected activists appeared overnight where the coastal highway meets the roads going north to the towns of San Francisco Javier and San Agustín. Many residents fled the area for the relative safety of the town of Jiquilisco, San Salvador, and the United States. In 1980, the besieged government expropriated several farms in the area as part of an agrarian reform intended to quell the insurgency. Like many large holdings, the Hacienda California was not included, as the Palomo family had preemptively subdivided the legal ownership of the property into nine parcels owned by different family members (although it was worked as a single enterprise). But as violence deepened in the area, a few residents joined the FMLN. Many began covertly supporting the insurgent organization. The Palomo family retreated to San Salvador and no longer visited or actively worked the farm. "It was bad luck for the Palomo family," one elderly resident of Tierra Blanca (1992) told me; "in 1979, the people rose up against all this injustice – the origins of the war lie in the holding of land in the hands of a few."

What accounts for the emergence of a powerful insurgent movement in an area where quiescence had long been the response of the rural poor to social injustice? Why did many poor people run extraordinarily high risks to support the insurgency? Why did others decline to do so? This book addresses the puzzle of insurgent collective action in the high-risk circumstances of severe repression and civil war. While material grievances, principally inadequate access to land, played a role, I show that emotional and moral motives were essential to the emergence and consolidation of insurgent collective action in the areas I studied. Like the land defense committee member I quote above, insurgent *campesinos* in interviews repeatedly stressed the importance of motives such as "that we not be seen as slaves."

Largely as a result of *campesino* support, the FMLN expanded in the early years of the war. For the next decade, both the FMLN and government troops maintained a presence in the region, the FMLN in small encampments in the rough terrain both north and south of Tierra Blanca and the government in bases in Tierra Blanca and the nearby towns of Jiquilisco and San Marcos Lempa. Minor fire fights were frequent. Occasionally, one side or the other would mount a major offensive beyond their bases, leading to renewed flight from neighboring hamlets to Tierra Blanca and the town of Jiquilisco.

In 1983 residents began to cultivate the Hacienda California and neighboring properties, planting corn and some beans to sustain their families. At first they did so surreptitiously. After government control of Tierra Blanca was stabilized in the following years, representatives of the Palomo family were intermittently present in the area and residents paid rent for use of the land. In 1987, a few dozen tenants formed a cooperative to strengthen their tenancy; they continued to pay rent to the Palomos. In 1990, militant activists were elected to lead the cooperative. According to a cooperative member, "We felt that it was unjust: many people had died, yet the Palomos still received their rent and a few people still controlled the land. So we made some new rules" (interview, Tierra Blanca, 1992). The new leadership affiliated the cooperative with a national organization with close ties to the FMLN.

On May 5, 1991, cooperative members took over the hacienda, claiming it as the property of their organization, the Cooperativa California. The Palomo family responded by leasing it to a powerful commercial farmer, Francisco Guirola, but when he attempted to enter the property, cooperative members blocked the entrance. He returned two days later accompanied by the National Guard, but cooperative members again blocked the entrance as journalists called in by the national organization documented the confrontation. Emboldened by their success, a few months later the cooperative took over the Palomos' lucrative salt flats along the coast. In defense of these and other occupations in the area, members of the Cooperative California and neighboring cooperatives blocked the coastal highway in September 1991, actions made less risky by the presence of journalists and observers from the United Nations who had been alerted by federation leaders (see photographs in Chapter 6).

After representatives of the Salvadoran government and the FMLN signed an interim agreement on September 25, 1991, in Mexico City sketching the terms of the final peace agreement that would end the civil war, members of the Cooperativa California began fencing the boundaries of the estate in a renewed and explicit expression of the de facto transfer of property rights. In anticipation of the settlement, both parties to the civil war attempted to preemptively settle supporters as claimants to the rich coastal area. On January 28, 1992 – twelve days after the signing of the peace agreement and a few days before the beginning of the formal cease-fire that would confine government forces to their barracks – the National Guard and the army's Sixth Brigade evicted those attempting to occupy the nearby Hacienda Concordia, another property leased by Guirola, and arrested several activists. The eviction sent two people to the hospital in San Salvador as a result of what U.N. observers judged excessive force. On January 30, the president and vice president of the Cooperativa California were also arrested. In response to the arrests, local FMLN commanders suspended the movement of their forces to the designated cease-fire areas, an action that briefly endangered the peace process, until the activists were released. Cooperative members eventually won title to a portion of the Hacienda California under the terms of the peace agreement.

The civil war thus transformed the political, economic, and social landscape of the Jiquilisco coast. Rather than the large estates protected by state security forces that dominated the area before the civil war, in its aftermath new organizations played powerful roles. Cooperatives controlled land, federations of cooperatives articulated their needs nationally as well as locally, and the FMLN – now an opposition political party in an unprecedently competitive political party system – sought to represent their interests politically. In 1997 and again in 2000, the FMLN candidate won the municipal election in Jiquilisco.

Some of these changes of the Jiquilisco landscape are captured in Figures 1.1 and 1.2, maps drawn for me by members of the Cooperativa La Normandía over the course of two days in 1992. Color versions of the two maps are available online at us.cambridge.org/features/wood. Figure 1.1 shows the Hacienda La Normandía, a very large property (1,500 hectares) similar to the Hacienda California that lies along its eastern border, extending from the coastal highway to the Bay of Jiquilisco. Before the war, the farm was owned by the Del'Pech family, a major coffee-producing family. Cotton was the principal crop, as indicated by the lollipop symbol. The cow figures along the lower edge, teasingly called *cucarachas* (cockroaches) by kibbitzing members of the cooperative, indicate the raising of cattle near the mangrove thickets along the bay. Toward the upper left-hand corner of the map, the barracks of the National Guard (three or four members were always billeted on the farm) and the airstrip are indicated. The permanent workers lived in the *cantón* La Cruzadilla just above the map's center.

The farm was expropriated in 1980 as part of the agrarian reform and a cooperative of former employees was named by the military officer present. But the counterinsurgency intent of the reform was not realized: some members of the cooperative continued to covertly assist the FMLN, and the cooperative later joined an opposition organization. As shown in Figure 1.2, at the close of the war the approximately 175 cooperative members cultivated individual plots of corn, sesame, and, near the old farmhouse, chile; many cooperative members raised a few head of cattle as well. Notably, the National Guard post was gone. (The grid of properties – colored pink on the website version of the map – along the right-hand edge of the map indicates property lost in 1989 as a result of a conflict with the government.) For cooperative members, this was a way of life far different from their lives before the war. Such profound changes were not limited to the Jiquilisco coast, as we see below.

The *campesinos* who recounted to me the taking of the Hacienda California, those who drew for me maps of the lands they occupied in Jiquilisco and elsewhere, and others like them throughout El Salvador redrew the boundaries of class and reshaped political culture as the civil war raged around them.[2] Few of them had ever engaged in politics of any kind. Just a decade earlier the idea that they would write a chapter in the history of their country would have seemed a cruel joke.

Insurgent Collective Action in El Salvador

The *campesinos* in Usulután and throughout El Salvador who participated in land occupations and marches and provided logistical support to the guerrillas ran mortal risks in doing so. Many paid the ultimate price. Just before and during much of the war, covert death squads and regular military forces carried out assassinations and disappearances with impunity throughout the contested areas. In interview after interview during and immediately after the civil war, my respondents described the loss of family members, friends,

---

[2] In referring to the poor rural residents of El Salvador as *"campesinos"* (literally, of the countryside, *campo*), I follow their own usage. The word is not well translated by "peasants" as many, indeed most, of those who refer to themselves as *"campesinos"* are not owners of small-holdings but merely aspire to be. Throughout this book, *campesino* refers to a person who engages in agricultural activities (except of course owners of properties who hire significant numbers of wage laborers) or, as an adjective, to refer to organizations in which *campesinos* participate. Thus a *campesino* may be a landless day laborer, a permanent wage employee, or a farmer working a small holding. When distinctions between these different types of agriculturalists are necessary for the argument, I make them explicitly.

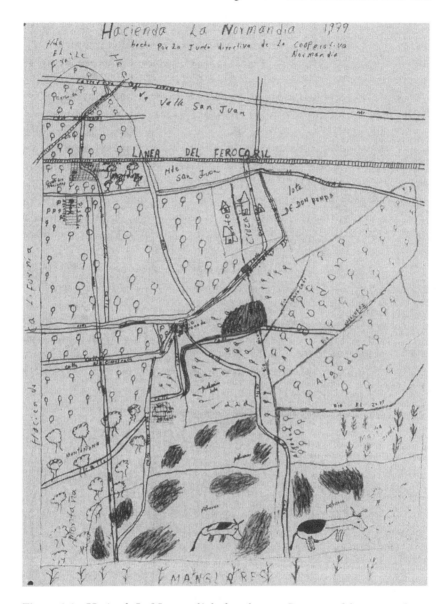

Figure 1.1 Hacienda La Normandía before the war. Courtesy of the map-makers. A color version of this map can be see online at us.cambridge.org/features/wood.

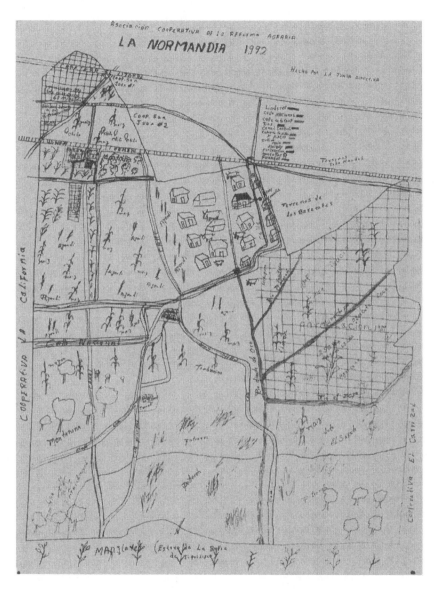

Figure 1.2 Cooperative La Normandía. Courtesy of the map-makers. A color version of this map can be see online at us.cambridge.org/features/wood.

and fellow participants. One young woman, a resident of the hamlet of La Peña north of Jiquilisco, told me,

Some armed themselves, others fled. We [those who stayed in the area] were all seen as guerrillas. Every time we went to the coast, we were searched at the intersection. 1982 was a year of desperation, almost everyone left. My brother disappeared in 1982, one of hundreds who disappeared in 1982 and 1983 – every day there were two or three bodies at the intersection. After all these years of war, the dead weigh heavily. (1992)

While her count at the intersection is higher than other sources suggest, multiple sources document the large numbers of Salvadorans who died during the civil war. More than 75,000 people (in a country of five million people) were killed during the war, about one in 56 Salvadorans (1.8 percent), a figure comparable to that of the United States during the American Civil War (one in 55) and of Britain in World War I (one in 57), and somewhat less than the figure for the Guatemalan civil wars (about one in 40).[3] The death rate of civilians in El Salvador was 28 times greater than that of civilians under the military regimes of Argentina and Chile, where human rights activists were said to run high risks.[4]

According to the Truth Commission for El Salvador (1993), the U.N.-sponsored organization authorized by the peace agreement to document human rights violations during the civil war, the vast majority (more than 85 percent) of the serious acts of violence analyzed by the commission were carried out by state agents or those acting under the direction of state agents against alleged supporters of opposition organizations. In contrast to much of the violence in Argentina and Brazil, the violence often occurred in public or the results were displayed in public places.[5] Activists did not

---

[3] Seligson and McElhinny (1996: table 3). Seligson and McElhinny compared more than twenty sources of statistics on war-related deaths in El Salvador, including those of the Salvadoran military, the U.S. Embassy, and various human rights organizations. They argue that the best estimate of total civilian and military related deaths in the Salvadoran civil war is between 80,000 and 94,000, of which 50,000 to 60,000 were civilians (ibid.: 224). So the standard estimate of 75,000 deaths is a conservative one. The *World Handbook of Political and Social Indicators*, the standard cross-national source for statistics on political violence, seriously underestimates the level of violence in Central America (see Brockett 1992 for a critique).

[4] Calculated from Loveman 1998: table A1.

[5] It was not always the case that deaths were publicly displayed; clandestine cemeteries were occasionally discovered. For example, a cemetery containing more than 150 bodies was uncovered on May 24, 1982, at the Puerta del Diablo near the indigenous community of Panchimalco, a dozen kilometers south of San Salvador (Comisión Interamericana de Derechos Humanos 1982: 1151).

have to be guerrillas or to work with the guerrillas to run the risk of being "disappeared" or killed. The Truth Commission found that "any organization in a position to promote opposing ideas that questioned official policy was automatically labeled as working for the guerrillas. To belong to such an organization meant being branded a subversive" (Truth Commission 1993: 311). *Campesinos* were frequent victims of the violence: the human rights agency of the Archdiocese of San Salvador recorded 12,501 political murders in 1981; of the 6,718 whose profession was known, 76 percent were *campesinos* (Americas Watch and the ACLU 1982: 278–9).

The degree of risk of course varied from place to place and month to month. Violence against politically active or suspect *campesinos* was most extensive and arbitrary before and in the early years of the war (from about 1979 to 1983), after which it declined significantly (in part a response to the conditioning of U.S. assistance to the government on its human rights record). This decline is evident in Figure 1.3, which traces maximum and minimum estimates of war-related deaths (both civilian and military, including disappearances) each year. Nonetheless, *campesino* activists were killed throughout the war; leaders of land occupations were particularly vulnerable. Extensive and egregious violence recurred when the regime

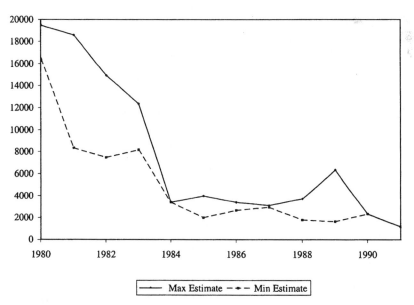

Figure 1.3 War-related deaths, 1980–91. *Source:* Seligson and McElhinny (1996: table 1).

9

felt threatened, as during the FMLN's November 1989 offensive, when the government's Atlacatl Battalion, on the order of the High Command, executed six Jesuit scholars, their housekeeper, and her daughter, and the Air Force bombed civilian neighborhoods of San Salvador.

It appears that some participants in high-risk activism weigh the likely costs and benefits carefully. Participants in the 1964 Freedom Summer campaign in the U.S. South ran high risks of bodily harm in challenging the long-standing practices of racial exclusion in Mississippi. After hearing reports of severe violence against initial volunteers in the campaign, one young American, a white Northerner, in the course of deciding whether or not to join Freedom Summer, wrote in his journal:

What are my personal chances? There are 200 COFO volunteers who have been working in the state a week, and three of them have already been killed. I shall be working in Forrest County, which is reputedly less violent than Nesoba County. But I shall be working on voter registration, which is more dangerous than work in Freedom Schools or Community Centers. There are other factors which must be considered too – age, sex, experience, and common sense. All considered, I think my chances of being killed are 2%, or one in fifty. (McAdam 1988: 70–1)

Whether or not many Salvadoran *campesinos* engaged in such grim reckoning, the risks of participation in the insurgency were evident in the patterns of widespread disappearances of purported activists and the subsequent reappearance of many of their tortured bodies.

Despite the high risk of insurgent activism, support by many – but far from all – poor rural residents was an essential element of the FMLN's military and political capacity throughout the war, according to a wide range of analyses, including that of U.S. military officers.[6] What explains insurgent participation in this context of high risk? The relevant literatures on revolutions, collective action, and social movements provide some guidance but not adequate answers to the puzzle of high-risk collective action in the Salvadoran context.[7]

---

[6] Bacevich, Hallums, White, and Young (1988). See also the analyses by three U.S. congressmen (Hatfield, Leach, and Miller, 1987) and RAND's National Defense Research Institute (Schwarz 1991).

[7] What accounts for revolutionary mobilization should be distinguished from what accounts for regimes that succumb to such mobilization (such that a "revolutionary situation" leads to a "revolutionary outcome"; Tilly 1978, 1993: 8–10). Scholars who address this second question argue that less institutionalized regimes, termed *personalistic, sultanistic,* or *neopatrimonial,* are vulnerable to revolutionary overflow (Goodwin and Skocpol 1989; Wickham-Crowley 1989; Foran 1993; Goodwin 1994a, 2001); agrarian bureaucratic states are also vulnerable

The Puzzle of Insurgent Collective Action

Some analysts of revolutions and peasant rebellions suggest that class conflict forms the basis of revolutionary mobilization. Karl Marx, for example, argued that the shared experience of exploitation on the part of the industrial proletariat would lead to socialist mobilization and revolution. Marx was of course mistaken in his identification of the likely bearer of revolutions: poor rural working people played essential roles in most social revolutions, while the industrial proletariat mobilized for revolution in only a few. Which particular type of poor rural resident played the preponderant role in various revolutions is much debated in the literature, whether it was the peasant, strictly speaking, or landless rural workers, and so forth. In an analysis of agrarian revolutions, Jeffrey Paige (1975) analyzes which configurations of landlords and cultivators result in which kinds of rural protests. He concludes that peasants participate in revolution (as opposed to isolated agrarian revolts) where landlords largely depend on income from land and thus can make few concessions and peasants depend on wages and are thus less dependent on particular landlords for access to land.

Paige's emphasis on the underlying conflict between cultivators and landlords and the latter's willingness to compromise (or not) certainly illuminates the Salvadoran case. The Salvadoran civil war was, at the macro level, a struggle between classes. The long-standing oligarchic alliance of the economic elite and the military led to a highly unequal society in which the great majority of Salvadorans were excluded from all but the most meager life opportunities. The response of this oligarchic alliance to the social movements of the 1970s and their demands for economic reform and political inclusion was repression, not compromise. Very few of those who owned coffee estates, agroexport firms, or other elite enterprises supported the insurgency. Few urban professionals did so; the dozen urban intellectuals who led the FMLN were the rare exceptions.[8] Support for the FMLN was much more likely on the part of poor Salvadorans than middle- and upper-class people. The vast majority of insurgent combatants were from poor rural backgrounds (McClintock 1998: 266–7).

(Skocpol 1979). The Salvadoran regime was significantly institutionalized, reflecting the long-standing convergence of the interests of economic and military elites. Thanks to U.S. assistance, the regime had sufficient resources to stave off insurgent military victory.

[8] With the exceptions of Salvador Cayetano Carpio and Facundo Guardado of the FPL, the top leaders of all five FMLN factions were university students or professionals who embraced revolutionary politics in the early 1970s (Wickham-Crowley 1992: 337–8; McClintock 1998: 251–60). The emergence of revolutionary leadership, while a necessary condition for sustained insurgency, is hardly sufficient, however. In many Latin American countries such revolutionary vanguard groups failed to foment rural rebellion.

But rural class position – either in the narrow sense as defined by access (or not) to land or other assets or in a wider sense of relative income – does not adequately explain participation in the Salvadoran insurgency. Before the war, El Salvador's rural poor were highly heterogeneous in terms of their livelihoods. Class differences among the *campesinos* of the case-study areas do not explain differences in their participation. The evidence presented here from the case-study areas shows that participants in the insurgency came from a variety of poor rural class backgrounds. The many *campesinos* who joined government networks and civil patrols or served as government informants came from equally diverse economic backgrounds.

The "high risk activism" underlying the Salvadoran insurgency is puzzling not just because the likely costs were so great, but also because the apparent benefits were so limited. As Mancur Olson (1965) pointed out in his critique of Marx's approach, collective action of the type studied here yields benefits (when successful) that are public goods – their enjoyment does not depend on one's having contributed to their provision. In these cases, Olson famously concluded, forms of collective action that are costly to individuals will not be sustained except where participation is coerced or motivated voluntarily through the provision of "selective incentives" available *only* to those participating. Extending Olson's approach, Samuel Popkin in *The Rational Peasant* (1979) argued that revolutionaries offer such individual incentives (for Popkin, exclusively material benefits) to peasants contingent on their participation, thereby possibly overcoming the free-rider problem.

This selective incentive argument does not appear to hold for the case-study areas, however. Before the war, few material benefits were won; the immediate consequence of mobilization was violence rather than material gain (Chapter 4). Early in the civil war, the insurgents offered very few benefits to civilian supporters. From about 1984 to the end of the war, it was possible for *campesinos* in contested areas to remain in the vicinity and farm abandoned land whether or not they participated in the insurgency (Chapter 5). During that period, the material benefits of the insurgency in the case-study areas – access to abandoned land and a degree of autonomy from the daily authority of landlords and the security forces – were available to *everyone* (nonparticipants as well as participants) who remained in these contested areas *whenever* they were available to participants, and thus did not have the requisite selective structure required to overcome the obstacles to collective action. In short, "free-riding" on the insurgency was possible – indeed, most peasants in the case-study areas (about two-thirds of them) took advantage of this possibility and did not actively support the insurgents.

In contrast to Popkin, some scholars note that guerrillas often offer peasants collective, rather than selective, goods, much as a state might do (Skocpol 1982; Wickham-Crowley 1987, 1991; Goodwin and Skocpol 1989). Doing so, they argue, is an essential element of the consolidation of revolutionary movements: guerrillas offer land and other subsistence goods in areas under their control as an incentive to joining or supporting insurgent forces. But how the provision of collective goods in itself motivates individual participation in insurgent collective action, thereby squaring the Olsonian circle, is not evident. The FMLN did indeed become an alternative governing authority to some extent in some of the case-study areas and did provide some collective goods. But *campesinos* in the contested areas could enjoy these few goods without directly supporting the FMLN.

Some scholars emphasize the provision of protection from government forces as a material benefit extended by revolutionary forces. Protection, or the hope of some degree of it, motivates participation in insurgency particularly when government violence does not target insurgents but is indiscriminate; in that case, joining the insurgents would at least not increase the chance of government violence against the insurgent and his family (Mason and Krane 1989). In extreme form, state violence leaves "no other way out" than joining the insurgency (Goodwin 2001). In the case examined here, protection motivated some *campesinos* to flee advancing government forces with guerrilla units during the early years of the worst and most arbitrary government violence. While some subsequently joined the ranks of supporters, many others made their way back to their homes when the situation was calmer or sought refuge in urban areas without further supporting the insurgents. More important, during most of the war, the FMLN offered little protection from government forces in the case-study areas. Even in their strongholds of northern Morazán and Chalatenango, the FMLN could not protect residents from aerial bombardment and many civilians went to refugee camps until the late 1980s (Bourgois 1982, 2001; Pearce 1986). Thus, protection per se does not explain the ongoing participation of those who continued to support the insurgency.

Another approach to the puzzle of collective action suggests that preexisting social networks and a shared collective identity might provide frequent and multifaceted contact based on shared norms. Some close-knit communities have a high capacity for collective action due to their cultural homogeneity and the "generalized reciprocity" among their members; in

this context of repeated, ongoing interactions, participants impose sufficiently high costs on nonparticipants to ensure widespread participation
(Taylor 1988). A classic example of social networks comprising strong communities comes from the U.S. South where the activism on the part of local
civil rights protesters was supported by the strong social networks and significant resources of the African American churches and colleges (Morris
1984). Peasant communities with strong horizontal networks are necessary
for revolutionary mobilization, according to Barrington Moore (1966). In
contrast, James Scott (1976) emphasized the erosion of vertical relations:
marginal community members rebel when reciprocal relations with landlords (the "moral economy") are threatened by the expansion of markets or
increased demands for resources by the state.

But long before El Salvador's descent into civil war, its traditional peasant communities had been disrupted by migration and the concentration
of land in the hands of the wealthy landlords. The displacement of Indians
from indigenous communities occurred from the late nineteenth century
through the first decades of the twentieth as coffee cultivation expanded
rapidly as a result of increasing restrictions on communal forms of property.
Indigenous culture in El Salvador virtually disappeared after the brutal repression of indigenous rebellions, including the uprising of 1932 after which
tens of thousands of indigenous people were killed. Traditional patron-
client relationships on estates were gradually replaced by highly coercive
wage-labor relationships as cattle-raising and the cultivation of cotton and
sugar expanded in the aftermath of World War II. Local social ties were
increasingly weakened as increasingly land-poor *campesinos* sought work in
distant labor markets. Thus the breakup of the traditional peasant communities occurred too early to explain the mobilization beginning in the
1970s.

Moreover, there is little evidence that preexisting social networks before
the mobilization of the 1970s in El Salvador were sufficiently strong or
that the norms political culture and collective identity of rural communities were sufficiently robust to enforce participation in a context of such
high risk. Based on a 1973 survey of *campesinos*, Jesuit sociologist Segundo
Montes (1986: 144–5) characterized the rural poor as fatally resigned to
poverty and misery, as venerating both civil and military authority, and
with little potential for class consciousness. Religious practices such as the
veneration of particular saints by lay societies generally reinforced this fatalism (Cabarrús 1983: 144). Compared with the communities Scott studied
in Southeast Asia, there was little social solidarity and little evidence of

a "moral economy" of close reciprocal ties immediately before the 1970s mobilization. Competition for land and jobs rather than solidarity characterized relations between peasants before the war.

That a widespread social movement and later an agrarian insurgency did emerge in El Salvador suggests, nonetheless, that a "hidden transcript" of discontent and resistance (Scott 1990), in contrast to the public performance of deference and conformity, may have been available to be tapped, despite the absence of strong communities or social networks. Many landlords were willing to pay for the billeting of members of the National Guard on their estates, a more draconian solution to ordinary problems of social order than most societies provide, which suggests landlords did not discount the possibility of collective action on the part of their work force. To some extent, songs and legends kept alive the memory of the heroes of past rebellions (Boland 2000). In interviews, a few *campesinos* mentioned smuggling small amounts of coffee beans from the coffee estates before the war, but many more mentioned the severe punishment such forms of resistance to landlords (termed "weapons of the weak" by James Scott; Scott 1985) incurred.

Social networks of radicalized catechists and members of guerrilla groups did play a role in insurgent collective action, coordinating local protest into a national movement in the 1970s. But these networks were not based on strong antecedent communities but instead emerged in the mid-1970s as a result of the new pastoral practices on the part of some Catholic priests and organizations, on the one hand, and initial organizing efforts by the then-tiny guerrilla organizations, on the other (Chapter 4). The latter were initially outsiders; only as the government's repression intensified in the late 1970s did local residents join.[9] That the values, beliefs, social norms, and political identities of these new networks could outweigh the risk of disappearance, torture, and death is of course at the heart of the puzzle of Salvadoran insurgency.

In another approach to political mobilization, a necessary condition for the emergence of social movements is the widening of political opportunity (McAdam 1982; Kitschelt 1986). As political opportunity increases, as when elite alliances weaken or relevant legal provisions change, the potential benefits of collective action increase or the costs decrease, or both.

---

[9] An alternative network, that of the Christian Democratic Party, played a role in the 1970s mobilization nationally but was weak in the case-study areas and supported the government after the party joined the government in 1980.

More precisely, movement organizers may seize such changes in political opportunity to reframe perceptions on the part of potential participants to encourage their joining. The challenge for this perspective is to specify changes in political opportunity nontautologically; that is, the observation of political mobilization cannot itself count as evidence of the widening of political opportunity (Goodwin and Jasper 1999).

There is no question that on some occasions, political mobilization in El Salvador responded to variation in political opportunity. Marches and demonstrations disappeared in the early 1980s at the height of repression. A vibrant rural civil society emerged during the military stalemate of the mid- to late 1980s, spreading outward from guerrilla strongholds as activists observed the success of neighboring cooperatives in occupying land and acted on the perception of widened political opportunity to form their own cooperatives (Chapter 6).

But other aspects of the insurgency are puzzling from this standpoint. Political mobilization *increased* in El Salvador in the late 1970s despite the *narrowing* of what would seem essential components of political opportunity. Election results were increasingly controlled, efforts at land reform by a reformist president were defeated by hard-line military officers, and repression by state security forces was rapidly intensifying. Severe repression did not quell political mobilization but resulted in significant numbers of erstwhile protestors becoming guerrilla members or supporters, thereby deepening the conflict. President Jimmy Carter's emphasis on human rights in U.S. foreign policy and the Sandinista revolution in nearby Nicaragua may have comprised a widening of political opportunity for international alliances in the late 1970s, but it is difficult to see how that would outweigh in the eyes of ordinary people the immediate experience of rising state violence. Equally puzzling from the political opportunity perspective is the fact that the widening of political opportunity since the signing of the peace accord and the democratization of the political regime has been associated with a considerable reduction in political mobilization despite significant enduring grievances.

In short, classic explanations of revolutionary mobilization – class struggle, widening political opportunity, solidary peasant communities, preexisting social networks, and selective benefits – do not adequately account for patterns of insurgent collective action in El Salvador. Even as extended with these classic explanations, Olson's canonical framework appears, at best, to account for the majority of Salvadorans who did *not* participate in the insurgency. It provides little illumination about those who *did*.

The Puzzle of Insurgent Collective Action

In addressing this puzzle, I focus on civilian supporters of the insurgency. By *support for the insurgency*, I mean the provision to the insurgents of information and supplies beyond the contribution necessary to remain in contested areas, and the refusal to give information and supplies to government forces beyond the necessary contribution. (Everyone in the case-study areas felt they had to supply food and water to combatants of either side when asked to do so.) Some civilian supporters also participated in local insurgent militia. I distinguish civilian supporters, whom I term *insurgent campesinos*, from those who did not make such contributions (whatever their sympathies), the noninsurgents or nonparticipants, and from the full-time members of the guerrilla army, the insurgent combatants. (Some insurgent *campesinos* at some point also served as combatants.) Roger Petersen (2001: 8–9) distinguishes three levels of support for insurgent forces: a first level of unarmed and unorganized opposition to the regime, a second level of direct support of or participation in a local armed organization, and membership in a mobile armed organization. My analysis focuses on insurgent collective action at the second level while tracing the processes that moved supporters between the first and second and between the second and third levels (Petersen's "triggering mechanisms") and the processes that maintained collective action at the second level (an instance of his "sustaining mechanisms"; ibid.: 13–15).

A satisfactory explanation of insurgent participation in the war will have to account for several patterns in the insurgent collective action I observed in the case-study areas of the municipality of Tenancingo, in the department of Cuscatlán, and of several municipalities in Usulután (Chapters 4 to 6). First, on the basis of my interviews and observations of meetings of *campesino* organizations, I show that participation was voluntary (with a few exceptions). Second, participation was also widespread: my necessarily rough estimate is that about a third of *campesinos* who stayed in the case-study areas actively supported the guerrilla forces by providing intelligence, moving ordnance, and serving in part-time militias. Third, the form of insurgent collective action evolved over time, from Bible study groups based on the teaching of liberation theology in some areas of Usulután and from covert guerrilla cells in others to strikes, marches, and demonstrations typical of labor and social movements to covert support for the guerrilla organizations to participation in opposition organizations overtly allied to the FMLN. Fourth, individuals supported the insurgency in different ways, and many moved in and out of various forms and degrees of participation for a variety of personal and political reasons. While some *campesinos* participated throughout

17

the insurgency and in a variety of forms of collective action, others joined only during the military stalemate of the mid- and late 1980s. Fifth, the end of the civil war did not return political culture in Usulután and Tenancingo to the status quo ante. Its legacy included new values, norms, practices, beliefs, and memories that comprised a new political identity and culture among insurgent supporters, reflecting the fact that once-quiescent *campesinos* had for over a decade contested the authoritarian practices of landlords and the state and asserted unprecedented claims to citizenship.

Given that two-thirds of residents of the case-study areas chose not to support the insurgency, what explains the insurgent collective action of the other third? Why did people so similarly situated in terms of their economic circumstances before the war act so differently? And why did people in quite different circumstances sometimes act so similarly? What accounts for these patterns of participation and nonparticipation?

I sought an answer in interviews with approximately 200 *campesinos*, participants as well as nonparticipants, which I carried out in militarily contested areas of El Salvador between 1987 and 1996. My insurgent informants made it clear to me that moral commitments and emotional engagements were principal reasons for their insurgent collective action during the civil war. Before the war, many participated in a social movement calling for economic reform and political inclusion. Many did so because they had become convinced that social justice was God's will and that to act righteously was to participate. As government violence deepened, some *campesinos* supported the armed insurgency. They did so as an act of defiance of long-resented authorities and a repudiation of perceived injustices (particularly the brutal and arbitrary violence by security forces). Participation per se expressed outrage and defiance; its force was not negated by the fact that victory was unlikely and in any case was not contingent on one's participation. Through rebelling, insurgent *campesinos* asserted, and thereby constituted in their own eyes, their dignity in the face of condescension, repression, and indifference. As state terror decreased, insurgent collective action spread across most of the case-study areas once more as *campesinos* occupied properties and claimed land for insurgent cooperatives. They did so despite their already having access to abandoned land because they took pride, indeed pleasure, in the successful assertion of their interests and identity, what I term here the *pleasure of agency*. To occupy and claim properties was to assert a new identity of social equality, to claim rights to land and self-determination, and to refute condescending elite perceptions of one's incapacities. In short, insurgent *campesinos* were motivated in part by the value they put on being part of the making of history.[10]

The reasons advanced here thus differ in two ways from those emphasized in conventional accounts of collective action. First, participant motivations were not limited to canonical self-regarding preferences, such as material benefits, defined over the consequences of one's actions. To be sure, the desire for land is part of the story: landlessness initially motivated some *campesinos*; recalcitrant opposition to land redistribution motivated state repression; access to abandoned land provided the autonomy that made possible insurgent collective action for many; and moral outrage at the injustice of landlessness and the brutal measures taken to ensure it fueled mobilization. But during the war, insurgent *campesinos* did not act because they were confident they would receive land as a result of their own participation. Rather, reasons for which participants acted referred irreducibly to the well-being of others as well as oneself, and to processes, not just outcomes. Second, political culture – the values, norms, practices, beliefs, and collective identity of insurgents – was not fixed but evolved in response to the experiences of the conflict itself, namely, previous rebellious actions, repression, and the ongoing interpretation of events by the participants themselves.[11]

I marshal various kinds of evidence to support my interpretation of insurgent collective action. The primary evidence for my interpretation is interviews with nearly 200 supporters of the insurgency, the vast majority *campesinos* but also including mid-level FMLN commanders (most from *campesino* families), and with nonparticipants, including *campesinos*, military officers, and landlords. Nearly all of these interviews were lengthy; I interviewed some of the respondents on various occasions over several years. I also use maps drawn for me by insurgent *campesinos* in the Usulután case-study areas. I evaluate (and discount) alternative interpretations by

---

[10] The exercise of insurgent agency of course had its negative legacy as well, particularly for those who participated in acts of violence in the context of civil war where the policing of internal loyalty takes on paramount value. Philippe Bourgois (2001) argues that some FMLN combatants came to the difficult postwar judgment that not all their acts of violence were justified, particularly those against supposed informers. In contrast, judging by my interviews, the positive aspects of collective action appeared to have dominated the experience of insurgent *campesinos*, few of whom served as full-time members of the guerrilla army.

[11] On the endogeneity of preferences generally, see Bowles (1998); of class consciousness, see Przeworski (1985).

19

comparing the pattern of insurgent participation across five case-study areas, and by comparing the life-histories, values, and beliefs of participating and nonparticipating *campesinos*. In addition to various published and unpublished documents, I analyze databases of electoral results and of the evolution of agrarian property rights. Finally, I illustrate the central argument of the book with a formal model (Appendix).

The argument presented here thus draws on literatures – on peasant rebellion, revolution, social movements, and collective action – often treated in isolation (but see McAdam, Tarrow, and Tilly 2001). The origin of a revolutionary peasant rebellion is traced to an antecedent social movement, and the resolution of the puzzle of collective action depends on emotional processes, moral perceptions, and shifting political culture as well as on the emergence of insurgent social networks and widening political opportunity. The account centers on the local political processes of insurgency, such as the path-dependent consequences of political violence and the assertion of agency by long subordinate people, and treats changes in political culture as not just consequences but causes of further insurgency.

I now turn to the history of El Salvador and the civil war for those unfamiliar with the country. A short chronology is included at the end of the book.

Overview of the Civil War in El Salvador

The roots of the civil war in El Salvador lie in the country's long-standing patterns of economic, political, and social exclusion. As elsewhere in Central America the colonial period saw the gradual encroachment of haciendas and estates on indigenous lands and intensifying attempts to direct indigenous labor toward Spanish enterprises. Unlike in other Latin American countries, the expansion of coffee production in the late nineteenth century occurred in areas where indigenous communities were highly concentrated (Roseberry 1991), a pattern that had dramatic consequences for the country's subsequent development.[12] The geography of coffee cultivation put commercial and government elites in competition with indigenous communities for land and indigenous labor. It also intensified conflicts within indigenous communities as some members welcomed opportunities for commercial production where others feared the infringement of cultural

---

[12] This brief history of El Salvador draws on Browning (1971), Lindo-Fuentes (1990), Stanley (1996), and Williams (1986, 1994).

prerogatives (Lauria-Santiago 1999). Legal and economic reforms introduced in the 1880s made it increasingly difficult for indigenous communities to retain communal landholdings. While some community members benefited directly by varied processes of privatization, most beneficiaries were middle-class professionals, including some military officers, well positioned to take advantage of their understanding of the complicated legal procedures to obtain private title and credit for cultivation.

Key features of the country's political economy at the outbreak of civil war in the late 1970s were already in place by the 1930s. The best agricultural land was increasingly concentrated in the hands of a small group of coffee plantation owners, and the processing of coffee was also controlled by a small group (whose membership overlapped to some extent with the former but which also included significant numbers of recent immigrants). Together the two groups comprised a classic oligarchy that largely controlled coffee production, processing, export, and finance. The high demand for labor on coffee plantations was met by the combination of a permanent, unfree labor force living on the estates under highly restrictive conditions (including restrictions on movement without the permission of the landlord and debt peonage) and the massive migration of poor people from across El Salvador to the estates during the months of the harvest.

Some indigenous groups resisted the expansion of private and state prerogatives, occasionally through armed uprisings. But the suppression of these revolts and the control of the labor force was ensured by the founding of the National Guard and other security forces to enforce private property rights; a close local relationship between landlords and government forces endured for decades. In 1932, approximately 17,000 indigenous people were killed by state forces in the aftermath of a failed uprising organized by the fledgling Communist Party, an event that seared elite memories and solidified elite opposition to political reform (Anderson 1971; Paige 1997). The massacre profoundly undermined indigenous culture as the threat of renewed state violence led to the abandonment of traditional dress, language, and many other indigenous practices.

La matanza (the massacre) and the subsequent years of General Maximiliano Hernández Martínez's regime forged an enduring alliance between the oligarchy and the military. Though riven by divergent interests on some issues, this oligarchic alliance agreed on the bottom line: the maintenance of the country's rigid class structure and its exclusionary political regime. Military officers ruled (with a brief exception in the 1940s), usually through a veneer of tightly controlled elections always won by the official party,

21

while economic elites controlled key economic ministries. The majority of Salvadorans labored for little pay with little access to education or medical services, enduring extraordinary poverty and social exclusion, even by Latin American standards.

The development of cotton, sugar, and cattle production after World War II did little to diversify the economic elites who controlled the cultivation, export, and processing of the new crops as well as the old. Economic power remained extremely concentrated as these families controlled the financial sector, the export agricultural sector, and the slowly expanding manufacturing sector (Colindres 1976, 1977; Sevilla 1985; Paige 1987). The oligarchic alliance continued to patrol the bottom line. Rural labor unions remained illegal, National Guardsmen were billeted on the largest estates, and government economic policy did not encroach on elite prerogatives.

The result of this pattern of economic exclusion was a highly unequal distribution of land (Fig. 1.4). Farms of larger than 100 hectares constituted less than 1 percent of all farms (0.7 percent), but they constituted over a third of the land (38.7 percent). In contrast, half of the farms (48.9 percent) were smaller than a hectare but together comprised less than 5 percent of farmland. These figures substantially underestimate the inequality of

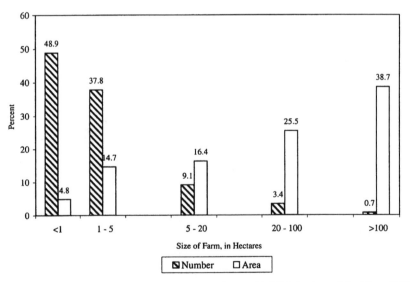

Figure 1.4 Farmland distribution, 1971. *Source*: DGEC (1974: tables II and III, pp. xxx–xxxi).

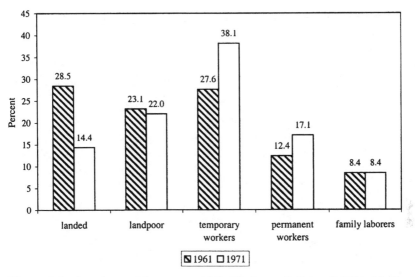

Figure 1.5 Agrarian social structure, 1961–71. *Source*: Seligson (1995: table 5).

access to land, moreover, for two reasons. First, this distribution, the only one available, counts farms, not families. As wealthy families tended to own more than one farm, the concentration of farmland by family was significantly higher than by farm. Second, landless families are not included in the distribution of farms. This is very significant as agricultural workers, temporary or permanent, comprised more than half of the economically active agrarian population in 1971 (see Fig. 1.5). One indication of how inequality affected the living standards of the very poor before the war in El Salvador is a comparison of its infant mortality rate in 1977 with similar Latin American countries. El Salvador's extraordinary rate of 95 deaths per 1,000 live births was about 15 deaths above the level of countries with similar per capita incomes.[13]

Moreover, poverty and landlessness intensified in the decades preceding the civil war. As shown in Figure 1.5, temporary day workers increased from 27.6 percent of the economically active agrarian population in 1961 to 38.1 percent in 1971. Permanent wage workers increased from 12.4 percent to 17.1 over the same period. The landed fraction of

[13] This crude estimate is based on the residuals from a linear regression of infant mortality rates on per capita incomes (purchasing power parity values from the Penn World Tables) in the mid-1970s for Latin American countries of similar per capita incomes (the Caribbean countries, Mexico, Argentina, Chile, Uruguay, and Venezuela were excluded).

the economically active agrarian population meanwhile decreased from 28.5 percent to 14.4 percent. Two factors contributed to this rapid increase in landlessness: the return of more than 100,000 land-poor *campesinos* from Honduras after the 1969 "soccer war" led to their expulsion from that country (Durham 1979) and the modernization of some agrarian labor practices, particularly the increasing emphasis on wage labor. For poor rural residents, these changes were dire. According to the Economic Commission for Latin America (1984: 61–2), in 1980, 76.4 percent of rural residents lived in poverty, without income sufficient to meet their basic needs, and 55.4 percent lived in extreme poverty, without the income to pay for a minimum shopping-basket of food.

One result of this unequal distribution of land, income, and opportunity and its maintenance by coercive labor practices was an acquiescent *campesino* political culture in which overt resistance was extremely muted. Ignacio Martín-Baró, Segundo Montes, and other scholars noted pervasive attitudes of self-deprecation, fatalism, conformism, and individualism among Salvadoran *campesinos*. Martín-Baró traced this culture to the poverty, dependency, and insecurity of the landless, land-poor, and those permanent employees who lived in clientelistic relationship to patrons (1973: 482–9). Clients lived in complete dependence on the *patrón*, as the cost of deviance was to lose everything: work, food, and home. Frequent unemployment left landless day laborers dependent on wages earned as a result of migration. In their access to their own small landholdings, the land-poor had a degree of autonomy and security, which, although limited, they deeply valued. Given the immediate repression of attempts to organize workers in the countryside, *campesinos* had little reason to expect any change in life circumstances; fatalism and conformism reinforced each other. Schooling provided little opportunity for social mobility, as few rural children attended school past the first or second grade, as indicated by the 63 percent illiteracy rate in 1971 (Montes 1986: 98).

On the eve of the civil war, the political culture of economic elites combined paternalistic condescension with virulent anticommunism (Paige 1997). Elites understood any unrest as subversion of order rather than bargaining over terms of work, an ideology readily exploited by the military in a long-standing "protection racket" whereby military privileges and prerogatives were accepted by economic elites as necessary for the maintenance of order (Stanley 1996). Nor were such attitudes limited to the coffee elite. Despite their involvement in a crop whose cultivation depended on wage labor and modern technology – namely, cotton – the attitudes of landlords along the Pacific coast toward workers were little different. For example, the wife of an Usulután landlord recalled her good works of the bygone days with nostalgia:

We lived on the property, unlike so many others. The social relations were intimate, we were appreciated. I helped with birth control projects, through the Demographic Association. The Cotton Producers Association lent us two cars to travel around to give talks. Children were dying from pure ignorance; women were dying in labor. It was hard work. I brought some women here for the operation – sterilization. There are other methods but the truth is that they were so ignorant that you had to sterilize them. It was a nice project. With my friends from the other haciendas, I traveled around. We had equipment, nurses; we took down names, physical data. (Interview, San Salvador, 1992)

While reformist factions of the military occasionally attempted to reform land tenure and labor relations, the core alliance of landlords and military hard-liners defeated such attempts in 1944, 1960, 1972, and 1976 (Walter and Williams 1993; Stanley 1996). Economic modernization did not lead to political modernization, but beginning in the 1960s the military regime allowed a degree of political participation, including contested municipal elections in the 1960s. This controlled political liberalization came to a dramatic halt in 1972. The government had allowed a Christian Democrat candidate to run in the presidential election for the first time, but when José Napoleón Duarte, the popular Christian Democrat mayor of San Salvador, won, the military quickly overruled the results.

Together, enduring economic exclusion and the renewed political closure in the 1970s fueled political mobilization both in urban areas, where Christian Democrats had built networks among the small middle class and workers in manufacturing, and in the countryside. The new teachings of liberation theology, increasingly practiced by some Roman Catholic priests and nuns had profound consequences in some areas of the countryside, as rural poor people in small groups discussed biblical and church teachings on social justice (Chapter 4). By the mid-1970s, covert guerrilla groups were active in San Salvador and very limited areas of the countryside. The Fuerzas Populares de Liberación Farabundo Martí (Farabundo Martí Popular Liberation Forces, or FPL), founded in 1970 after a split in the Communist Party over the potential for armed struggle, organized cadres in covert cells in San Salvador, Santa Ana, and north-central El Salvador. A rival organization, the Ejército Revolucionario del Pueblo (Revolutionary Army of the People, or ERP), was founded a few years later. By the late 1970s,

25

five such guerrilla organizations were recruiting university and secondary school students in urban areas and *campesinos* in rural areas.

Political mobilization rapidly expanded in the mid-1970s. The response of the government was repression rather than compromise. In 1975, a march protesting the extravagance of the Miss Universe pageant was machine-gunned by security forces, leaving at least fifteen marchers dead. When President Arturo Molina announced a limited but symbolically important measure of agrarian reform in 1976, a renewed coalition of military hard-liners and economic elites brought it to a swift end. Military hard-liners strengthened the control of the military and security forces over key infrastructures such as the telephone system. The regime also poured resources into paramilitary organizations in the countryside, drawing on veterans and reserve members of the military as well as patron-client networks of powerful agrarian elites. Major Roberto d'Aubuisson, later to be infamous as the director of death squads, played an important role, compiling intelligence files and building covert networks of hard-liners within the military.

Confronted with a massive social movement and a growing (though still small) guerrilla organization, divisions within the military deepened, culminating in a coup by young officers in October 1979. The reformist officers were quickly displaced by a group of senior officers, however. Far from ending repression, the new junta oversaw its dramatic deepening. In response to the largest demonstration in Salvadoran history on January 22, 1980, the regime killed twenty people and wounded about 200. Forced to leave the military as part of the compromises between the young and senior officers, d'Aubuisson nonetheless continued to coordinate death squad units working out of the intelligence services in various military units, the National Police, and the Treasury Police. In 1980, the number of those killed in political violence exceeded 1,000 a month, decimating the leadership of many opposition organizations. Any possibility of a broad revolutionary alliance including centrist political forces was eliminated in November 1980 when government forces kidnapped and executed six leaders of the Frente Democrático Revolucionario (Democratic Revolutionary Front), a center-left alliance of urban and rural groups led by urban professionals.

While repression discouraged many from participating in opposition organizations, it galvanized others (Chapters 4 and 7). Some joined the guerrilla organizations after the March 1980 assassination of Archbishop Oscar Romero, who was killed the day after he called for soldiers to refuse to obey orders. As was widely believed at the time, d'Aubuisson had ordered his assassination, according to the Truth Commission (1993: 354–7).

As the country descended toward civil war, four guerrilla organizations (later joined by the fifth) founded the FMLN in November 1980 to better coordinate their efforts. Their "final offensive" of January 1981 failed, however, and the guerrilla organizations withdrew to the countryside to reorganize their forces for a longer struggle.

While the junior officer coup did not end repression, it did smooth the way for a new governing alliance. When the initial junta members found they could neither curb the growing violence by paramilitary and government forces against popular organizations nor in fact decide state policy, several members resigned, prompting a search for a new governing coalition. As part of its conditions for extending military assistance to the beleaguered regime, the United States insisted that the Christian Democratic Party be brought into the government, and that agrarian reform be carried out and competitive elections held. Even hard-line leaders of the military recognized the usefulness of the international legitimacy to be gained by governing in a broader coalition (Stanley 1996: 180–3). Beginning in March 1980, the government carried out a significant agrarian reform. Nonetheless, the inability of the second junta to control the violence led to a split in the Christian Democratic Party as several ministers and officials resigned and left the country, a split that deepened after the assassination of Archbishop Romero.

The response of economic elites to the new governing alliance and the agrarian and other reforms was threefold. First, many exported massive amounts of capital to Guatemala, Mexico, and the United States.[14] Some resettled in other countries. Second, some hard-line elites based in Miami and Guatemala financed d'Aubuisson's "death squads" (Truth Commission 1993; Joint Group 1994; Stanley 1996), groups of civilians and members of the military and security forces that carried out well-publicized acts of violence in urban areas. Third, some helped d'Aubuisson found a new rightist political party, the Alianza Republicana Nacional (National Republican Alliance, or ARENA), to contest for power in elections.

Despite severe losses, the FMLN gradually forced landlords and security forces to retreat from significant areas of the countryside. During this initial

---

[14] According to one estimate (Funkhauser 1992: 136), 6.3 percent of GDP in 1979 and 11.4 percent in 1980 was sent out of the country.

period of the war, the FMLN's strategy emphasized large-scale attacks on military and infrastructure targets. In 1983, the FMLN significantly extended its control of territory, a trend that was halted by increased U.S. military assistance.

Intensifying efforts by U.S. citizens to draw attention to state violence against civilians and the U.S. role in training and arming the military led U.S. government officials in late 1983 to convince Salvadoran military leaders to rein in the military's human rights abuses (recall the rapid decline in war-related deaths beginning in 1984 in Fig. 1.3; Smith 1996; Peceny 1999). While the warning did not lead to the dismantling of military networks responsible for the violence, violence decreased as the military reluctantly embraced counterinsurgency measures that emphasized winning the "hearts and minds" of civilians.

The change in government strategy soon led to a change in insurgent strategy as well. The FMLN reorganized its forces into small, more mobile and autonomous groups. The FMLN's new strategy soon proved effective and the insurgents slowly extended their covert presence in both rural and urban areas, carrying out brief sorties against military forces and intensifying economic sabotage. In some areas, *campesinos* began founding cooperatives and taking over abandoned land. By the mid-1980s, some analysts described the military situation as a stalemate. Others, misjudging the new FMLN strategy as declining military capability, foresaw a slow winding down of the war.

Another consequence of the shift in regime strategy away from violence against civilians was a shift within the ARENA party away from the leadership of d'Aubuisson toward new, more moderate leaders in order to appeal to a wider constituency. The shift within the party also reflected the shift in elite economic interests as export agriculture continued to decline and as remittances fueled a boom in services and commerce; economic elites with more diversified economic interests tended to be more moderate politically than those with interests narrowly in agro-export production (Paige 1997; Wood 2000). This shift in electoral strategy soon bore fruit: ARENA candidate Alfredo Cristiani defeated the Christian Democrat candidate in the 1989 presidential elections, as voters registered dissatisfaction with government corruption and Duarte's failure to end the war. Desultory efforts at negotiation between the rebels and the Cristiani government soon broke down.

In November 1989, the FMLN launched an unprecedented offensive in San Salvador and several other major cities. Guerrilla forces succeeded in occupying some working-class neighborhoods of San Salvador for several days despite the absence of a general insurrection by the population. The panicked High Command ordered the Atlacatl Battalion to assassinate the six Jesuits, a measure that brought an end to the effectively unconditional U.S. congressional support for aid to the Salvadoran government (Whitfield 1994). FMLN forces occupied the wealthy suburbs of San Benito and Escalón, for the first time bringing the war into the homes of the privileged. The offensive soon fizzled and the FMLN withdrew.

The offensive led to the negotiations that ended the civil war. In its wake, both the U.S. and Salvadoran governments were forced to the unwelcome realization that change in the Soviet Union and the declining popularity of the Sandinistas in Nicaragua had not eroded FMLN military capability. No longer relying for their income on disciplining of agrarian labor by the security forces, the moderate economic elites in control of the ARENA party could afford compromises unthinkable a decade earlier, principally the inclusion of the left in the political party system and the transfer of policing from the military to a new civilian force. Of course, the end of the Cold War also contributed to the negotiated resolution of the war, strengthening those more inclined to compromise within both the FMLN and the government. U.S. support for negotiations brought the Salvadoran military to the bargaining table. Indeed, a potential coup attempt by a hard-line general was defused when the United States, Mexico, and Venezuela all assured the conspirators that no oil would be forthcoming in the aftermath of a military takeover.

Serious negotiations to end the war began under U.N. mediation in 1990, culminating in the signing of the final peace agreement on January 16, 1992, in Mexico. Key government concessions included limiting the mandate of the military to defense, the disbanding of the security forces, the founding of a new civilian police force that would include ex-combatants of the FMLN, and the strengthening of the judicial and electoral systems. The FMLN agreed to disarm, to enter the now-inclusive election system as a legally constituted political party, and to accept the terms of the 1983 constitution, including provisions protecting private property rights. In addition, the parties agreed that land would be transferred to ex-combatants of both sides as well as to FMLN supporters occupying land not their own. (Rumors of this provision fueled a last-ditch land grab at the close of the war, but do not explain land takeovers that occurred earlier.) Detailed annexes to the agreements defined a chronology of steps to be taken by both sides over the course of the cease-fire; their staggered sequence would assure each party that the other was complying with the agreement. In addition, both parties agreed that a U.N. mission would monitor human rights violations during the cease-fire.

The subsequent cease-fire proceeded relatively smoothly. While some delays occurred, no shots were exchanged as the two forces separated to distinct geographical areas under U.N. monitoring for the nine months of the cease-fire. Ongoing mediation by the U.N. mission contributed to the successful resolution of a series of crises, including ongoing land occupations, the reluctance of the military to demobilize the security forces, government suspicion that the FMLN had failed to turn over significant numbers of arms (subsequently proven correct when an arms cache in Managua, Nicaragua, exploded in 1993), and ongoing difficulties in implementing reforms to the electoral system in time for the first postwar elections. In April 1994, the first inclusive elections were held. The ARENA candidate won the presidency, after a runoff election between the candidate of a coalition of leftist parties including the FMLN. The FMLN won a respectable 21 out of 84 seats in the legislature.

Thus insurgency forged democracy in El Salvador by laying the political and economic bases of compromise after mobilization for economic and political inclusion was met with state violence. After the 1989 offensive, even government officials recognized that the FMLN had become what I elsewhere term "an insurgent counter-elite" (Wood 2000), a group with which the government had to come to terms if the war was to end. This is the story of how the willingness of tens of thousands of poor rural residents to act together for social change, despite the high risks of doing so, led to the emergence of the FMLN as a group that had to be dealt with and thus opened the doors to democracy in El Salvador.

2

Ethnographic Research in the Shadow of Civil War

We feel a great patience. If we forget what we have suffered, it will come again. We want to press for change, we can't forget all we've suffered.

Campesina, Tenancingo, 1987

We have lived the deepest truth of the war.

Cooperativist, Los Horcones, 1992

To explore why some *campesinos* rebelled in contested areas of El Salvador before and during the civil war, my principal research strategy was to ask participants in the insurgency why they supported it, and to ask others why they did not. For revolutionary social movements, this is not usually done; the scholarly analysis of peasant rebellions, revolutions, civil wars, and even some social movements often relies on official or elite sources. In particular, as Nancy Bermeo (1986) and Nora Kriger (1992) argue, the study of peasant insurgency often relies not on the accounts of peasants themselves but on the memoirs of elite revolutionary leaders who are usually from a different class or on macro level data.[1] One reason of course is that peasant actors are often illiterate or semi-literate and leave few written accounts of their actions, although oral sources in the form of stories and songs may be very rich. Participant accounts, be they elite memoirs, the few biographies of peasant participants available (which were often dictated to journalists or other literate interlocutors), or other accounts based on oral histories,

---

[1] This characterization of the literature on peasant rebellion as relying on elite sources loses much of its force if such rebellions are seen as the outgrowth of social movements, many of which have been extensively studied using participant accounts.

rarely address social science concerns of how representative the narrator is or whether alternative accounts better explain available evidence.

In the absence of participant accounts, one alternative in studying historical instances is to infer the logic of insurgency from the "prose of counterinsurgency" (Guha 1983b): the records of judicial, colonial, and other governmental authorities are read for insight into subaltern motives and beliefs. Not all states engaged in counterinsurgency produce the kind of records that facilitate such a rereading of official sources, however. Before and during El Salvador's civil war, those suspected of subversion by government agents were only in extraordinary circumstances processed by courts or other judicial bodies. Police and other security forces left few records of detentions, torture, or disappearances. (Nor were records of the Salvadoran military detailing particular operations available at the time of the writing of this book.) Of the few such records that existed, many were destroyed in order to render postwar investigation of human rights violations and other abuses of power more difficult. While human rights organizations kept records of violations as best they could, their records of rural events are very incomplete. Given conditions in the countryside, records exist only for those events that occurred where witnesses willing to report abuses resided. Such witnesses (often local priests or nuns) would have to run the risk of reporting an abuse by telephone and then meeting a human rights investigator locally, or of traveling to human rights offices in San Salvador. As a result, most violent events in the case-study areas went unrecorded.[2]

Nor does survey data provide much help in analyzing the course of the civil war. While a few surveys of households in contested areas were done by government agencies or other researchers for various reasons toward the end of the war, they usually gathered data on the composition of households, whether homes had access to potable water and schools, and the sources of income. In any case, residents' willingness to respond to questions concerning the history of the war in their own community and their own participation or not in political violence depends on a relationship with the researcher that is more personal than is possible in survey research.

The civil war in El Salvador offers the opportunity to analyze grass-roots accounts of revolutionary participation using methods similar to those frequently used in the study of ordinary social movements. This book draws

---

[2] While the report of the Truth Commission contains much information on certain high-profile human rights cases and lists thousands more in the annexes to the report, the coverage of Usulután is strikingly poor, apparently because the ERP did little to encourage residents to report violations to the Commission.

principally on open-ended interviews with rural residents, both participants and nonparticipants in the insurgency, in the Tenancingo and Usulután case-study areas. (I defer detailed discussion of the criteria for their selection to the following chapter.) In this chapter I discuss the challenges of ethnographic research in areas of political violence and the strategies I pursued to meet them as well as possible.

Social Processes of Memory Formation

> *Non tutto quello che si racconta in questo libra è vero; ma tutto è stato*
> *veramente raccontato.* [Not all that is recounted in this book is true,
> but everything truly was so recounted.]
> Alessandro Portelli, *Biografia di una Città* (1985: 18)

For this book, I asked *campesinos*, participants and nonparticipants alike, landlords, and military officers questions concerning local conditions before the war, the local history of the war, including violence by both sides, and the emergence of new local organizations. That this analysis relies principally on open-ended interviews of course raises difficult issues of interpretation. The responses to my questions were shaped by three factors: the accuracy and intensity of the respondent's initial memories, the subsequent shaping of those memories through social and cultural processes, and the respondents' objectives in the ethnographic setting of the interview itself. I discuss each in turn.

First, recent laboratory studies that test for accuracy of recall of images and events that vary in intensity ("arousal" in the language of this literature) and pleasantness or unpleasantness ("valence") have found that images and events that rank as highly intense (in a variety of cognitive and biological measures) tend to be better remembered in both the short and long term than less intense images and events.[3] This appears to be true whether or not the stimuli are pleasant or unpleasant; there is some additional but debated evidence that unpleasant stimuli are better remembered than pleasant stimuli of the same intensity. What these laboratory studies suggest (but of course do not show, given the many differences between the laboratory and actual settings) is that the violent events frequently witnessed or participated in during civil war are the type – highly intense and most often very

---

[3] See the reviews by Margaret M. Bradley (1994) and Charlotte van Oyen Witvliet (1997). My attention was first brought to this literature by an analysis of narratives told by Lithuanians of the violence there during and after World War II by Roger Petersen (n.d.).

unpleasant – that are most likely to be well remembered.[4] For example, in one experiment, two groups of subjects were shown films that were identical except that one version contained a violent event midway through, while the other contained a parallel but nonviolent event (Bornstein, Liebel and Scarberry 1998). The subjects shown the violent version had better recall of the middle scene than subjects shown the nonviolent version, but had less recall of what came before and after. This is not of course surprising: those who suffer from post-traumatic stress disorder are haunted by intrusive memories and nightmares – they often remember too much of their past experience, not too little.

Second, memories of political events, however well they are initially remembered, may be later reshaped by social and cultural processes that affect which memories were retained, which emphasized, and which forgotten.[5] An example of the shaping of memory by subsequent experience is Leigh Binford's finding that witnesses in northern Morazán a decade later blamed the government's Atlacatl Battalion – notorious in the area for having killed more than a thousand people in 1981 at El Mozote – for several killings of *campesinos* that occurred *before* the battalion was even founded (1996: 105). Another example comes from Italy. Alessandro Portelli (1991) compared oral history accounts of the death of the worker Luigi Trastulli at the hands of a special police force in Terni, an industrial town in central Italy, with other sources. Workers he interviewed decades later remembered that during a protest against layoffs in 1953, Trastulli had been shot high against a stone wall with arms outstretched in a Christ-like position. The militant labor movement, they recalled, had fought all the harder after his death. According to contemporary judicial and journalistic accounts, however, Trastulli was shot in 1949 at street level with no memorable pose and there was little labor mobilization in response. Portelli argues that the labor movement's quiescent response to Trastulli's death was not consonant with the movement's culture, requiring the translation of the event in memory to circumstances in which the movement was more militant. Cultural norms may thus result in the suppression of some memories or

---

[4] A distinction should be made between memories of past political *attitudes* and of intense political *events*. While memories of political attitudes appear to be particularly malleable, those of former political protests are more reliable (Markus 1986: 40–41).

[5] The literature on social memory and narrative is vast. I have found the following particularly helpful: Portelli (1991, 1997), Halbwachs (1992), Passerini (1992), Jelin (1996), Polletta (1998a, 1998b, 1999), and Auyero (1999). See Olick and Robbins (1998) for a recent review of the literature.

expressions as unacceptable. In Sultanpuri, a neighborhood of Delhi, Veena Das (1990: 390) found distinct patterns of mourning by surviving relatives of communal violence: for example, younger widows were not allowed to mourn at all. She suggests that social structures intervene in the way that emotions such as guilt and sorrow are formed, "the way in which the world can be reformulated," and therefore how narratives can be told. In particular, memories of wartime events may be shaped by postwar outcomes, for example, by disappointment in the failure of a postwar government to deliver on redistributive goals promised in negotiated peace settlements.[6]

Third, the telling of personal and community histories in an ethnographic setting is also shaped by the respondent's personal and family trajectories through the war, by his or her present political loyalties, beliefs concerning the likely consequences of participating in the interview and of expressing particular views, and present personal objectives – all as informed by his or her understanding of the purpose of the interview. Political opinions may be systematically misrepresented out of security considerations, particularly in the context of civil war. Narratives may reflect self-aggrandizing motives as respondents tell stories in which their roles are exaggerated or indeed entirely recast. Claimed motivations may be reconstructions that attribute a post hoc coherence to events by placing them in relation to a presumed goal (Markoff 1996: 603). Portelli (1997) points out that while oral history interviews are a personal exchange between the interviewer and interviewee, they are also testimonies intended as public statements and thus involve interpreting and legitimizing past actions and perceptions.

Moreover, because the telling of stories of past injustice and resistance shapes *present* propensities for mobilization and political identities, they may be told for precisely that purpose, rather than to convey accurate accounts of events as remembered. One result may be erroneous stories of origin, as in the case of Rigoberta Menchú, whose life history recounted in her *I, Rigoberta Menchú* to a Venezuelan anthropologist was not literally true although certainly representative of the violence during that period in the Guatemalan highlands (Stoll 1999). Another example comes from the U.S. civil rights movement, whose stories of origin (Polletta 1998a, 1998b) often

---

[6] Leigh Binford (2002) argues, for example, that some of the disillusionment expressed by some former FMLN guerrillas may reflect such disappointment. Nora Kriger's finding (1992) that Zimbabwean peasants were coerced into supporting the liberation forces may reflect such disillusionment (her interviews were conducted several years after the end of the war).

overlooked the previous activism and training in civil disobedience of Rosa Parks before she initiated the Montgomery, Alabama, bus boycott of 1955 by refusing to move to the back of the bus. Those stories also frequently and erroneously claimed that the occupation of luncheon counters to protest segregation were spontaneous rather than organized activities.

Divergent memories of events of the Salvadoran civil war, I found, sometimes reflected these processes of memory formation. The bombing of Tenancingo in September 1983 provides a dramatic example. The FMLN attacked the municipal center despite the presence there of the well-trained and heavily armed Jaguar Battalion, commanded by a Captain Calvo. After his troops were trapped in the town, the town was bombed for several hours by government aircraft, an action that Americas Watch (1986: 157) at the time described as the "war's single most devastating attack" that left at least 75 civilians dead.[7] In interviews four years later, all respondents recalled the event with horror – and profound fear that the same thing might happen again – but the particular tale told appeared to reflect the political loyalties of the teller.

Survivors supportive of the FMLN reported that, when faced with imminent defeat, Calvo

locked himself and approximately forty soldiers into the Church. He called in the Air Force, saying that he was lost and that all those moving around the church were guerrillas. But they weren't just guerrillas, but civilians running crazy through the streets. The Green Cross [the domestic equivalent of the Red Cross] wanted to take the civilian population from the town, but a guerrilla stopped them, warning them that they would be bombed. They didn't try it, but another group of civilians did, fleeing down the road. A plane bombed them – children, women, and men. They bombed houses, streets, everything. All this didn't stop the FMLN – they captured Calvo and the forty soldiers from the church and spent the night in the town. . . . We later learned that the soldiers were freed some months later. (Interview with resident, Tenancingo, 1987)

Several Tenancingo residents told similar versions with varying degrees of apparent trauma.

One person, whom I came to consider one of my most informed and reliable respondents in Tenancingo, told me that he had later heard over

[7] Reputable human rights sources disagree about the number killed during the attack and response. Americas Watch (1986: 79) claimed in 1986 that approximately 100 had been killed but later revised that number to 75 killed (1991: 53). In both documents, Americas Watch states that 35 civilians were killed when a plane dropped a bomb on the group retreating with the Green Cross. Tutela Legal, the human rights organization of the Archdiocese of San Salvador, estimated the number of dead at 175 (cited in Pearce 1986: 201).

the radio an audio tape of a pilot circling over Tenancingo calling his base for instructions, stating that those he saw on the streets looked like civilians. The response of his commander was to order him to bomb whomever he saw moving. As the likely source for the airing of the tape was one of the FMLN radio stations, I was skeptical. (I did not ask whether that was in fact the case, as it would implicate him politically in a way inappropriate at that time. I later came to believe that was indeed the source.) However, Jesuit scholar Ignacio Martín-Baró reported much the same thing:

I remember hearing a recording of a conversation between the pilot of a Salvadoran bomber and his commanding officer at the base. The pilot, who was flying over the town of Tenancingo, saw a group of people in a state of panic seeking cover in the local church and transmitted to the officer that they were civilians so he could not bomb them. But, from the command post, the officer insisted that "anything that moves is the enemy," that they were nothing but "subversives" and, therefore, that the pilot must bomb. (Martín-Baró 1988: 338)

A Belgian journalist who worked with the ERP for three years in Usulután states explicitly that she heard the tape on Radio Venceremos (Lievens 1988: 87–8). Whether the tape was in fact a recording of radio transmissions between the pilot and the base (which I judge likely, as Martín-Baró would have been skeptical), the conversation is etched in the memory of some Salvadorans, among them some Tenancingo residents.

Some interpretations emphasized the heroism of guerrilla forces in Tenancingo; one bordered on the mythical. According to a written, apparently eyewitness, account that circulated soon after the bombing and that was shown to me in 1987, the members of the Green Cross did retreat with the group and

with megaphones called to the pilot to stop the bombing, but he didn't and dropped a bomb on them, killing eighteen persons there alone. My aunt, my cousin, and their sons died there; another cousin [would have died] inside [her pregnant mother], who fell dead from the shrapnel. But a passing female guerrilla that might have been a nurse said she had to save the life of the baby. She took out a knife and opened my cousin's side and took out the daughter. She cut the umbilical cord and gave her to another aunt to take to Cojutepeque where she was cared for. And by a miracle of God she is safe and well.[8]

---

[8] "Narración sobre los sucesos que pasaron en Tenancingo" (Narration of events that occurred in Tenancingo), an eyewitness testimony signed "un hijo de Tenancingo," undated but apparently written soon after the bombing, which was given to me in 1987 by a Tenancingo resident.

In this account, not only did the Air Force overlook the presence of civilians in the town, but a guerrilla fighter literally produced life out of the suffering endured. Another Tenancingo resident reported in a 1989 interview that an entire family was killed except for a fetus who was saved. His repeating this story was particularly interesting, as he was not an insurgent supporter. Perhaps he had read this account and believed it; in any case he reported it as something he knew to be true. Still another resident stated in a 1989 interview that an entire family, including a pregnant woman, had been killed, but did not mention the saving of a fetus.

"Memories" held by members of the Tenancingo elite – none were in fact present at the time of the bombing – tended to be very different. For example, one wealthier resident claimed – and seemed to sincerely believe – that guerrilla combatants captured Calvo and forced him to call in the Air Force to bomb the town, thus attributing moral responsibility to the FMLN while admitting the Air Force had bombed the town (the FMLN did not have planes or helicopters). Such beliefs persisted despite the long-standing acceptance of responsibility for the bombing on the part of the military itself. Colonel Domingo Monterrosa, the commander of the Atlacatl Battalion that moved into the area soon after the attack, was reported to have said to the surviving residents of Tenancingo, "Here we all lost, we lost and you lost, but you must understand that it was an exception and that the bombing occurred because the lives of the soldiers were in danger."[9] General Adolfo Blandón, Armed Forces Chief of Staff at the time, reiterated to me the military's responsibility in a 1987 interview:

It was my fate to be commander of the army when the worse that could happen to a town happened.... [After the first attack] we were able to arrange things a bit... and things were going forward when there was another confrontation. There was also an aerial action. It was an error.

Thus both government and insurgent supporters told narratives consonant with their political beliefs and loyalties.

As evident in these varied memories of the bombing of Tenancingo, processes of the social construction of memory are very salient in war narratives, particularly when storytellers participated in or supported political violence. Statements of past motivation may reflect present ambivalence concerning the justification of violence (Portelli 1997: 138). Statements in

---

[9] According to a newspaper report published in the Nicaraguan newspaper *Barricada*, September 30, 1983.

interviews with supporters of the insurgency concerning motivation for actions carried out some years earlier may be particularly subject to interim processes of both individual and social selection as ongoing dialogue within families, organizations, and communities reshapes initial impressions into social memories. Motivations claimed in interviews may be ex-post rationales for participation, whose real reasons lie elsewhere.

Moreover, silences in interviews may be as significant as the events related. When Kay Warren returned to the village in highland Guatemala where she had done ethnographic research before the civil war, she was struck by the "strategic ambiguities" in narratives concerning the local history of violence (e.g., "they burned, they killed . . ." with the identity of "they" left unrevealed; 1998: 110). Those who could not understand the implication of such ambiguities were "by definition strangers with whom it was not wise to share information" (ibid.: 94). Villagers were reluctant to discuss the violence in any detail, offering generalizations in response to questions. The violence of the civil war had riven families and communities, with the result that her respondents lived in a world of betrayal and existential dilemmas captured in phrases such as "we don't know who is listening" and "one did not know who was who" (ibid.: 107–8). Such silences may be particularly important for the ethnographer, as when villagers in the northern highlands of Peru proudly told how a group of purported thieves had been beaten and stabbed to death but neglected to say that one had been a young teenager (Starn 1999: 82–85), or when Chinese villagers who were displaced by a hydroelectric dam in central China were silent about traumatic village events during the Cultural Revolution (Jing 1996: 56). Moreover, silences in narratives may evoke corresponding silences by ethnographers. Linda Green did not feel free to pursue certain topics with the Maya war widows she interviewed; in particular, she could not ask widows whose husbands were killed by the army about the photograph on the wall of a son in an army uniform: "I would give them the opportunity to say something, but I felt morally unable to pursue the topic" (Green 1995: 112–3). Thus the usual tension in the interpretation of oral history interviews – between the need to reconstruct events and the need to understand respondents' representations of those events – is sharpened in the aftermath of conflict and violence (Portelli 1997: 146).

There is an additional danger in relying on what Charles Tilly calls "standard stories," those frequently told by participants in a social movement (Tilly 1999). Such reliance may result in the analyst's neglect of causal mechanisms such as structural and demographic factors that may not be well captured in the personal narratives of histories of individuals and communities. Nonetheless, the choice to participate in a movement or not to do so rests on the perceptions and interpretations of structures and processes by individuals (shaped, to be sure, by their participation in organizations). Scholarly analysis of such perceptions and interpretations necessarily relies in part on the reports of potential participants in interviews, memoirs, and similar sources.

Research Method

My interviews took place during the Salvadoran civil war and the subsequent, initially precarious, cease-fire in politically polarized areas that suffered severe political violence. The interviews addressed the very issues of political opinion and participation that generated and reinforced that violence. The interviews and associated fieldwork thus required "certain precautions and incredible delicacy" (Adler 1992: 229). Among other things, such fieldwork raises challenging issues of personal security (for those interviewed but also for the researcher) and the confidentiality of interview records. As Linda Green (1995, 1999) explores in her work on war-torn areas of Guatemala, violence and terror often leave behind a legacy of silence, fear, and uncertainty that can be deeply corrosive of self-confidence, trust, and hope. These field conditions made necessary research procedures – in particular, for informed consent to participation in the research – that emphasized the voluntary nature of participation in interviews and the confidentiality of informant identities.[10] These concerns are not unusual in ethnographic research, of course, but their importance is much deepened in the context of research on civil war and political violence. For example, I informed all respondents that I was interviewing people across the political spectrum. I did so because I judged that knowledge important for their informed consent as well as their decisions about what to say and what not to say. Moreover, respondents' understanding that I was doing so would protect me from misunderstanding should participants with one side see me interviewing adherents of the other. Of course, my interviews with both sides were undoubtably shaped by this knowledge.

---

[10] Research was carried out under protocols approved by the human subjects research review committees of the University of California at Berkeley, Stanford University, and New York University.

Ethnographic Research and Civil War

Despite these difficulties, approximately 200 *campesinos* were interviewed at length, many repeatedly over a period of four or five years in a variety of settings, both individual and collective. Initial interviews with insurgent supporters in a particular area usually occurred with a small group of leaders of the principal local organization (a federation of cooperatives or a land defense committee). They usually started with an introduction by a person known to them (typically a representative of a nongovernmental organization with longstanding contacts in the area).[11] This initial interview, usually a long discussion of the purpose of the project and of issues of security and confidentiality, was essentially a vetting of my research project by these local leaders.[12] In all cases, these local representatives agreed that their organizations would participate in the research project, and arrangements for interviews with members were made.

Subsequent interviews were usually extended conversations with small groups of activists concerning the history of their community during the civil war, the founding of local organizations, and their perceptions of contemporary political issues. Local leaders preferred that initial encounters be group rather than individual interviews, a process I understood as a further vetting of me and the project, a further assessment of its likely consequences, and an assertion of their control over the process. I later interviewed many members individually (and some repeatedly) in private settings; no obstacles or conditions were imposed on these interviews by anyone to my knowledge. Given the substantial degree of violence, political tension, and uncertainty around the themes of this study in the recent past, I promised I would not reveal the identity of those with whom I spoke (except in the case of a few political elites). While from the present vantage point this may seem an unnecessary precaution, it is a pledge which I have honored. For this reason, I characterize interviews only by the role of the interviewee (*campesino*, landlord, ERP commander, and so on) and the year and location in which it occurred.

However, one disadvantage of my reliance on local opposition organizations for initial contacts with insurgent *campesinos* was that I interviewed

---

[11] I usually succeeded in persuading the person who introduced me to leave after doing so. I was the only outsider present at all subsequent interviews. While this entailed my traveling alone through the case-study areas, that was preferable to the uncertainty that the presence of another outsider would introduce into the interview setting.

[12] See Adler (1992) and Sluka (1995) for discussion of vetting processes in the contexts of ethnographic research with trade unionists in South Africa and nationalists in Northern Ireland, respectively.

fewer women than men: while many women participated in the organizations, they tended to be less active than their male counterparts, and few were leaders. In group interviews I did my best to ensure their speaking, but they were often interrupted repeatedly. I also interviewed at length a dozen women in private settings about their experiences during the war, but because I particularly sought to know the history of the emergence of insurgent organizations, I inevitably rely more on men.

In these circumstances of recent political violence and enduring political polarization, I did not attempt to construct representative samples of local respondents. I did, however, interview the members of a wide range of organizations. Of the ten cooperatives established by the government as part of the 1980 counterinsurgency agrarian reform in the Usulután case-study areas, members of six were interviewed. Of more than forty insurgent (as opposed to agrarian reform) cooperatives in the those areas, members of thirty-two were interviewed. Representatives of nearly all other *campesino* political organizations active in the Usulután case-study areas, including those founded by the government in the aftermath of the agrarian reform, were interviewed. In Tenancingo, leaders and members of a variety of organizations were interviewed, in both group and individual settings. Dozens of meetings of organizations in both Usulután and Tenancingo were also observed.[13]

Nor did I attempt to conduct field research in an area where insurgent activities were entirely absent (which would have been the ideal research design, as it would have added a clearly contrasting case). Ethnographic research on such politically sensitive questions during the civil war in areas of uncontested government and landlord control would have been dangerous for those interviewed. That I could carry out such research in contested areas was an achievement of the insurgency: rebellion had carved out a political "space" of relative autonomy (Adler 1992).

In the case-study areas, I interviewed *campesinos* who did not participate in the insurgency where and when I could. As nonparticipants generally did not belong to organizations (except small evangelical sects in some cases), it was more difficult to obtain introductions that they would trust. As a result, most of my interviews with twenty-four nonparticipants took place in small

---

[13] Observing meetings of insurgent organizations took up much more of my time in the case-study areas than the reader would infer from their relative absence from these pages. They were, however, very important for my credibility with insurgent interviewees and for my sense of relations between leaders and members.

towns such as Tierra Blanca, Tenancingo, and Santiago de María, where I stayed with individuals trusted by many nonparticipants (in two cases local Catholic nuns, in one case a European development expert). These interviews usually took place in private, one-on-one settings in the case of *campesinos*; in official, sometimes group, settings in the case of mayors and other officials; and in private homes and offices in San Salvador and other cities in the case of landlords. I also interviewed residents of two types of sites of likely nonparticipation: government-sponsored repopulated towns in Suchitoto and agrarian reform cooperatives in western El Salvador.

Interviews across this range of political allegiances during a bitter civil war proved possible for various reasons. International attention on the reconstruction of Tenancingo, which included significant European funding and press coverage, may have raised the costs to both the FMLN and the government of hostility to an academic researcher. That the researcher conducting it was not from El Salvador but from the United States may also have contributed to its feasibility, particularly given the importance of U.S. funding to the government and the attention given to harassment (by either side) of U.S. and European citizens. That the cease-fire was in place during much of the Usulután research made travel to those areas less precarious than it would have been earlier. Finally, with a few minor exceptions, I had excellent luck: I was never caught in the wrong place at the wrong time. Such luck is a not-to-be-underappreciated aspect of fieldwork in settings of political violence (Sluka 1995).

I believe my research in contested areas was possible for a more profound reason. My inquiries met with the enthusiastic collaboration of many residents of contested zones (and of nearly all those approached in San Salvador as well), irrespective of class, occupation, or political affiliation. Residents acted on a willingness (perhaps even a need in some sense) to discuss with an outside researcher their own history and that of their families and communities.[14] Perhaps this willingness is a measure of the trauma and change brought by the war. Those interviewed frequently expressed a desire for their story to be told, that some account (or accounting) be made of the local history of the civil war. For example, one Tenancingo resident not allied with any political faction told me in 1987, "The people here are suffocating

---

[14] Some of those interviewed might have been initially motivated by some hope that collaboration with the research might bring some material benefit. I did my best to discount such hopes in the informed-consent procedure that I went through, though of course I cannot know that I succeeded. In any case, no such benefits materialized; those I approached for a subsequent interview nonetheless appeared ready to participate again.

from the cries and shouts that we cannot speak. It suffocates. It does me good to talk to someone – I can't speak to people here about these things." One leader of the Land Defense Committee of Las Marías, a longtime insurgent activist whose involvement began with his training as a catechist in the mid-1970s, remarked:

Just a comment on your project: I understand that you are asking us to consider participating in the construction of what we might call a history of the war in the conflicted zones. [pause] There are no more hidden things. We have suffered so; it would be right that there be such a history. What a period we have lived through! The *campesino* does not have the capacity to do it; you engage with such things more there [in the U.S., in U.S. universities]. But it is something we have lived and we are still living. I don't know where to start. . . .

This willingness of many residents of contested areas to talk about their personal and community histories at length with a researcher is common to many other ethnographies of civil wars. Green found that many of the Maya war widows she interviewed, including some she came to know very well, would tell her their stories over and over (1995: 115). In her analysis of the civil war in Mozambique after independence, Carolyn Nordstrom suggests that because the experience of violence is profoundly personal and linked to processes of self-identity and personhood, narratives of political violence are also attempts to find a meaningful way to deal with experience and to organize experience after the fact, and thus respondents exhibit what appears to be a "need to talk and talk" (1997: 3–4, 21–22, 79). Das suggests that survivors of communal violence in Sultanpuri agreed to interviews because "[a]ll this signified the fact that their lives held a meaning, and that their suffering would not go untold" (1990: 395). Marcelo Suárez-Orozco argues that narratives of political violence, known in Latin American literature as *testimonios* (testimonies) are rituals "of both healing and a condemnation of injustice – the concept of testimony contains both connotations of something subjective and private and something objective, judicial, and political" (1992: 367).

Yet the statements that Salvadoran insurgent *campesinos* made in interviews were concerned not only with violence. While most stories they told began as histories of injustice, violence, suffering, and loss, many continued as proudly told stories of the achievements of opposition organizations during the conflict – of land occupied and defended, of new organizations founded, and of new identities asserted. The *campesinos* recounted these achievements with enthusiasm, interrupting each other to cap the last story with the next. With groups I interviewed repeatedly over months and sometimes years, support for this project was particularly evident on my return after an absence. I would often be met with shouted greetings such as, "Well, Elisabeth, do we have something to tell you!" or (to each other), "What did we say we should remember to tell Elisabeth?" These assertions of pride contrast sharply with those gathered in many ethnographies of civil war and political violence.

Redrawing Boundaries: The Mapmaking Workshops

A place on the map is also a place in history.

Adrienne Rich (1986: 212)

At the level of open defiance, the mapping of revolution and riot is a reminder of the contingent nature of sovereign authority and the controverted character of sovereign power. By directing attention to issues of social distribution, mapping can also open the politically charged question of social justice.

Jeremy Black (1997: 77)

In analyzing the course of the civil war in the case-study areas, I rely in part on the maps drawn for this study in 1992 by a dozen teams of *campesinos* from across Usulután in three workshops I convened in 1992. I asked representatives of a dozen cooperatives to draw with marker pens on large sheets of butcher paper maps of their localities showing property boundaries and land use before and after the civil war. Drawn collaboratively by at least two and usually several members in a process interspersed with much discussion of the history of the area as well as gossip, jokes, and teasing of one another (and of me), the resulting maps document how *campesino* collective action literally redrew the boundaries of class relationships through their depiction of changes in de facto property rights and patterns of land use in the case study areas during the war. The accuracy of the claims by these cooperative leaders to occupy extensive areas of land in 1992 was confirmed by my own travel and observation in the case-study areas and by examination of the archives of landholding and land claims data maintained by the FMLN, the government, and the United Nations during the postwar process of adjusting property titles.[15]

[15] I also attempted to compare the maps to aerial photographs taken before the war by the Ministry of Agriculture. Approximately two dozen of the properties photographed fall in

These maps are therefore quite different in origin and purpose from most maps, which are usually the product of efforts on the part of expanding empires or consolidating states to centralize power, define frontiers, and regulate property rights (Harley 1988; Black 1997). The security interests of the U.S. Department of Defense in El Salvador, for example, led to the production of a number of maps of El Salvador, including one map of Usulután on which the many hacienda airstrips were carefully marked. In particular, cadastral maps (maps of properties, often linked to a property register for tax purposes) reemerged in Renaissance Europe, as maps of private estates proved useful to asserting land claims or settling property disputes. They were later deployed by states to plan land reclamation (as in the Netherlands), collect taxes, manage state resources such as royal forests, and to distribute land to settlers in colonies (Kain and Baigent 1992). Such maps were of course used to the advantage of some against the interests of others and in "portraying one reality, as in the settlement of the New World or in India" helped obliterate the old (ibid.: 344). Indeed, Michael Biggs argues that the development of modern cartography contributed to the concept of the modern state as a *territory* over which the state held a monopoly of violence: the development of maps reshaped state lands into territory, a homogenous and uniform space with boundaries (1999: 385). In short, maps are not just strategic but also cultural constructions. Maps not only reflect cultural practices of their producers, revealed by analyzing what is included and excluded (for example, whether or not places important to subordinate but not dominant social groups are named, how images are presented in relation to one another, and so forth); they may also have enduring cultural consequences.

Maps are not always produced in the service of the powerful. Sometimes (as here) they are produced by subordinate social actors or by civil society organizations contesting dominant values (as in many environmental maps; Black 1997). Among the Beaver tribe of northeastern British Columbia, for example, some elders draw "dream maps" that indicate not only hunting trails and territories but routes to heaven (Brody 1982). When mapping is

the Usulután case-study areas, of which eight were claimed by cooperatives at the end of the war. Of these eight, two were drawn for me by cooperative members. Unfortunately, due to the poor resolution of the original ministry photographs (or perhaps the quality of copying of those photographs since), only the general shapes of properties were more or less recognizable, and detailed comparisons with the mapmakers maps were not possible. The *campesino*-drawn maps were roughly similar to the aerial photographs of these two properties.

a consistent cultural practice, anthropologists sometimes try to account for that fact. Robert Rundstrom (1990) argued that the Inuit of northwestern Canada and Alaska produce accurate and detailed maps, not because they need them for hunting more than other societies that do not produce them, but because mimicry is a prime cultural value that runs throughout their culture. Map-making by indigenous or peasant actors often occurs in the course of conflict with state authorities over land or other resources, as in the case of conflict over reed beds in Lake Titicaca (Orlove 1991, 1993) or over the consequences of the Alaska Highway natural gas pipeline for the traditional hunting territories of the Beaver (Brody 1982).

In this case, the willingness of insurgent *campesinos* to draw the maps reflected their assertion of contested property rights at the end of the civil war. Drawing such maps involved considerable sacrifice of work time on the part of individuals (with no recompense except, in some cases, a meal of beans and tortillas) and forgone opportunities on the part of the *campesino* organizations: each pair of maps took two full days to draw, given the unfamiliarity of the task. Despite this time commitment, cooperative members participated with remarkable enthusiasm; only one of twelve pairs of maps was not completed. Perhaps the process evoked what Dolores Hayden (1995: 9) calls "the power of place," the power of ordinary landscapes to "nurture citizens' public memory." Moreover, for all participants the process required a willingness to engage in the challenging task of conceptualizing familiar terrain in entirely new terms. For the many semi-literate and illiterate participants, the map-making workshops were the scene of difficult – and public – struggles with unfamiliar tools. One elderly map-maker, the president of a cooperative in northeastern Usulután unaccustomed to holding a pencil, traced an elaborate tapestry of small and medium holdings with his forefinger; his grandson carefully drew a line in its wake. While I promised that the maps would be returned to the communities, which may have provided some incentive, my impression was that the map-makers were motivated primarily by their commitment to recounting their history.

Map-making was thus not an existing cultural practice but an artifact of my research.[16] A few of the map-makers were familiar with maps, particularly those who worked closely with local FMLN commanders whom I observed to use fine-scale topographic maps (usually much creased and

[16] While a form of map making appears to have been practiced in pre-Columbian times in Mesoamerica (Harley 1992: 524–6), I am unaware of any evidence that rural communities retained the practice in the late twentieth century in what is now El Salvador.

held together by layers of tape). Most certainly appeared to be natural cartographers; indeed, one developed an innovative projection in his maps (see Chapter 7). But map-making was not something any of them had previously attempted.

Nonetheless, the maps reveal much about the history of the case-study areas, particularly the patterns of land occupation and use (Chapter 3), and also the perceptions and values of their makers (Chapter 7). Honoring an often-regretted but ethnographically correct pledge, I returned the maps to the map-makers out of respect for their insight, gratitude for their taking the time, and hope that they might prove useful. What are reproduced in black and white here are photographs of the original maps (tacks pinning the maps to the wall are visible on some maps) that were then digitally restored to a quality close to the original maps. Color versions may be seen online at the website us.cambridge.org/features/wood.

This willingness to collaborate in interviews and workshops reflected in part the isolation of many of these communities during the war. In interviews with members of organizations in San Salvador that frequently hosted international visitors, there was often a distinctly professional tenor to testimonials offered, as if a script were being played once again. In contrast, Usulután had been little visited by journalists, and to my knowledge, sustained research concerning the history of the war had not been carried out there. Few of the landlords interviewed had ever been approached for their opinions. Tenancingo, the site of a unique reconstruction project supported by European donors, had been visited by journalists, development specialists, and diplomats in the first few years of the project, but few lingered long enough to interview residents other than a few members of the community council. While my initial interviews with community leaders had the feel of an oft-told story, in subsequent interviews this initial script was abandoned and more complicated stories were told (e.g., patterns of violence were more convoluted in later narratives).

Conclusion

Clearly, the interviews and maps that this book is based on must be interpreted carefully. This is particularly true for interviews concerning the history of the contested areas of Usulután, which is largely constructed from interviews carried out just before the end of the war. While some of the salient events had occurred quite recently, others dated back to before the war or to its early years. That the intervening years and experiences reshaped perceptions of earlier events is true of Tenancingo as well. Although interviews began there in 1987, the history of the early years of the war relied on the memory of interviewees (but to a significantly lesser extent, given the greater availability of human rights records for events there). And interviews were inevitably affected by the political context in which the interview occurred. Some interviews that I conducted with insurgent *campesinos* in the first few months of 1992, for example, clearly reflected the spirit of euphoria and victory prevalent throughout the case-study areas in the first weeks of the cease-fire. Later interviews with the same informants reflected a more sober and considered assessment of the achievements of the insurgency.

A possibly mitigating factor is that many interviewees claimed to have never told the story of their community before, which would suggest that explicitly social processes of memory formation had not been particularly strong in the case-study areas. On the other hand, because some interviews were with groups of *campesinos*, the interview itself was an instance of the process of the social construction of memory and political identity. The map-making workshops were explicit exercises in social memory as participants recalled events of the civil war and discussed and celebrated its legacy as they drew. The maps, like all maps, "act as a form of memory" (Black 1997: 93).

To the extent possible, the oral testimonies gathered were compared with one another and discrepancies were explored in subsequent interviews. Because interviews with key respondents in both Tenancingo and Usulután were repeated over several years, it was possible to construct histories of both areas that were less shaped by immediate political processes than histories relying on interviews gathered during a single period would have been, and to later fill in some of what had initially been silences.

I also draw on other sources, including interviews with landlords of properties in the contested areas (11 of them, of which seven were landlords of large properties in the case-study areas), pastoral agents of local parishes, FMLN commanders (16 of them, including 12 mid-level ERP commanders in Usulután, five of whom I interviewed on several occasions), Salvadoran military officers (three colonels responsible for government forces in the case-study areas and two generals), staff of several nongovernmental organizations, officials of the Salvadoran government and of the U.S. Agency for International Development, and staff of the U.N. Observer Mission in El Salvador. Corroboration was also sought in documents produced by human rights organizations (principally, Americas Watch and El Rescate, a

U.S. solidarity and human rights organization that compiled data gathered by Salvadoran human rights organizations, particularly the human rights office of the Archdiocese of San Salvador, and reports appearing in the press), Salvadoran and foreign nongovernmental organizations, including the publications of the Universidad Centroamericána José Simeón Cañas, the national press, the United Nations, the Salvadoran government, and the U.S. Agency for International Development.[17] I also analyze a rural household survey carried out at the end of war, the results of postwar elections, and databases documenting evolving agrarian property rights during and after the war. Finally, I illustrate the central argument of the book with a formal model (Appendix).

So whether the reasons for participating in collective action expressed by many insurgent *campesinos* in interviews (and inferred from interviews by me) comprised an essential part of their reasons for participation at the time of the actions cannot be directly inferred given the intervening processes of social construction of memory. Yet memories do not evolve randomly; the deviation of memory from what was in fact the case illuminates values and beliefs. The retrospective nature of some interviews and the coloring of accounts of the past by the perceptions of the present are not just inevitable complications of my reliance on interviews, but also provide direct evidence of one legacy of the civil war, the reshaping of political culture in the contested areas of El Salvador. According to Luisa Passerini (1980: 10), "[O]ral sources are to be considered, not as factual narratives, but as forms of culture and testimonies of the changes of these forms over time." I return in the final chapter to these issues of interpretation and show that the reasons for insurgent collective action evident in retrospective interviews reflected emotional and moral reasons for rebellion earlier in the war.

---

[17] For example, the history of Tenancingo after 1986 is documented by a wider range of sources thanks to the resettlement project and the resulting attention of nongovernmental and international agencies to the district.

3

Redrawing the Boundaries of Class and Citizenship

> We felt the poverty in our own flesh. The pain that we are now
> suffering in our bodies is the labor of the birth of something new.
>
> *Campesina*, Tierra Blanca, 1992

On January 16, 1992, the Plaza Cívica in downtown San Salvador over-
flowed with a festive crowd, many carrying FMLN flags or wearing FMLN
bandanas or headbands. Enormous banners proclaiming support for the
FMLN and other insurgent organizations hung from the National Palace
and the cathedral. At noon the cathedral bells tolled in the peace, shortly
before the signing in Mexico of the agreement that ended more than a
decade of war. One of the FMLN's clandestine radio stations broadcast the
speeches and music from the cathedral. Many in the plaza, including some
members of the FMLN's General Command and several regional commanders, had not been seen in the capital for more than a decade. I saw a
number of reunions of people separated by the vagaries of the war, including
one in which both had believed the other dead for years. Between blaring
dance numbers, speakers celebrated the peace agreement as an insurgent
victory, reiterating the theme that the FMLN had forced the government
to negotiate a transition to democracy, allowing political participation of
the left for the first time.

Two blocks away in the Parque de la Libertad, the governing ARENA
party celebrated its own interpretation of the signing, lauding the contributions of President Alfredo Cristiani to freedom, peace, and the successful
defense of the country from communism. Distinctly absent from the government celebration was the Salvadoran military, which lost long-standing
prerogatives under the terms of the agreement. One of the most striking
things I observed that day was that many people walked back and forth

51

between the two rallies, listening to the speakers and dancing to the bands of both.

In the optimism of the moment, the twin celebrations heralded a future of electoral rather than armed competition for political power. No one could have imagined these events just a few years earlier. Even after the signing of several interim agreements beginning in 1990, most observers had remained skeptical. Unlike many Latin American countries where a recent transition to democracy was a return to democratic rule, the transition to democracy in El Salvador – forged in the fire of a decade-long civil war – was unprecedented. A socialist guerrilla group and its associated social movement organizations had forced the once virulently undemocratic elites of El Salvador to agree to an inclusive political regime.

The civil war that eventually brought these political actors to downtown San Salvador took place in the countryside (with the notable exception of the November 1989 offensive). The FMLN's military and political capacity that undergirded the eventual stalemate was largely rural: neither side could defeat the other in the countryside, in large part because of the willingness of many *campesinos* to provide supplies and intelligence to the insurgents. The evolution of the principal economic interests of the elite away from export agrarian property toward other sources of income as a result of insurgency and counterinsurgency shaped the compromise that ended the civil war.

The changes wrought during the civil war in some of the case-study areas were no less profound. By the war's end, dozens of insurgent *campesino* organizations occupied properties and claimed them under the terms of the peace agreement. Through their ties to each other and to national and international organizations, these new political actors articulated hitherto unheard grievances and claims. Thus de facto agrarian property rights, land use, and civil society had been transformed in some areas. Yet in other areas, continuity rather than change was the dominant pattern. In this chapter I document these patterns of change and continuity across the case-study areas. I first discuss the criteria for the case-study areas and show that together the five case-study areas met those criteria. Using the maps drawn by insurgent *campesinos*, I then describe each in detail. (Color versions of the maps can be found at us.cambridge.org/features/wood.)

The Case-Study Areas

To address the central questions of this book, the case-study areas had to meet four criteria. First and obviously, the areas had to be accessible to the researcher, a far from trivial requirement during and just after civil war. Second and relatedly, because the central issue is that of support for an insurgency, the case-study areas had to be contested regions where both supporters and nonsupporters were present. This meant that areas where one side or the other generally maintained control would not serve, as that meant, in the Salvadoran context, that only supporters of the controlling party would be visible to the researcher (whatever their private preferences).

This criterion ruled out regions sometimes referred to as the FMLN's "controlled zones" along the northern and northeastern rim of the country.[1] These controlled zones were generally deserted early in the war. The FMLN forced government supporters from the area, and major sweeps by government forces left many civilians dead, as at El Mozote in 1981 and the Río Sumpul in 1980 when more than 300 noncombatants were trapped and killed by government forces (Truth Commission 1993: 347–53; Binford 1996). The areas were extensively bombed as well (Americas Watch 1984). As a result, almost all residents fled to refugee camps in Honduras and Nicaragua or to shanty towns at the margins of Salvadoran cities. Although slowly repopulated beginning in the mid-1980s, access to these northern areas was usually difficult and travel too dangerous for sustained research until the return of many refugees from the camps to resettlement communities funded by international development agencies in the late 1980s. While research was then possible in those communities, their experience reflected years in closed refugee camps and an unusually high degree of FMLN hegemony (Argüello Sibrian 1990; Cagan and Cagan 1991; Edwards and Tovar Siebentritt 1991), which suggested that findings based on research there would not be readily generalizable to other cases of insurgent collective action.

Of course that there even existed zones "controlled" by the FMLN was hotly denied by government and military officials. Even at the close of the war when negotiators were defining the areas where the FMLN would live during the cease-fire, one official, an ex-military officer, told me, "Here you don't find controlled zones. The army goes where it wants to go" (San Salvador, 1991). He continued in a telling afterthought, "But to remain there is something else. We don't have the capacity to project ourselves everywhere [at once]." Similarly, a lieutenant colonel reported that when he inaugurated a school near an agrarian reform cooperative, he told the

[1] The "controlled zones" were, roughly, the northern regions of the north-central and north-eastern departments of Chalatenango, Cabañas, San Miguel, and Morazán.

assembly that "tomorrow perhaps the guerrillas may arrive to destroy it." He added, "It took them two weeks to arrive; they couldn't enter earlier due to our security" (Zacatecoluca, 1987). So while the army could enter and secure areas at will, it could not do so widely at the same time, the classic pattern of irregular warfare.

Nor were areas of sustained government control appropriate sites for this research. Where government forces were rarely challenged by the FMLN (e.g., most of southwestern El Salvador), landlords and security forces retained tight control over the rural population, which made sustained interviews concerning political events and opinions dangerous to respondents. Research there would also have been less fruitful for the purposes of this research, given that few had any opportunity to support the insurgency and those who had done so had generally left the area.

To avoid introducing unwarranted assumptions concerning who participated in the agrarian insurgency, the third criterion for the case-study areas was that they comprise a variety of agrarian economies, including both subsistence and agro-export crops, diverse forms of property rights including various forms of tenancy and scales of production, and various forms of agrarian livelihoods including landless laborers, harvest workers, the unemployed, wage laborers, smallholders, and commercial farmers. Many areas that saw sustained conflict during the civil war (including the FMLN-controlled zones) were regions of marginal farmlands of little commercial value and lacked this diversity.

Finally, the case-study areas had to be manageable politically. Maintaining a research profile acceptable to the principal political actors in a civil war is a difficult enterprise, particularly when one intends to move between the contending parties interviewing both supporters and nonsupporters, *campesinos* and landlords, and FMLN commanders and military officers. In the Salvadoran setting, the often fraught relations among the five factions of the FMLN could significantly complicate this balancing act as suspicions between factions concerning outsiders could sometimes rival those between the armed parties to the war. This meant that the case-study areas should not involve more than one or two guerrilla factions.[2]

---

[2] In retrospect, this might have been an exaggerated consideration. Throughout 1992, I found FMLN members responsible for the transfer of land to ex-combatants and insurgent supporters to be uniformly helpful regardless of their factional ties. However, those officers tended to be among the most politically sophisticated. Most commanders still in the field might not have been as cooperative as they were if I had attempted to interview members of more than two guerrilla factions.

The areas analyzed in this book, the municipality of Tenancingo in the department of Cuscatlán and four case-study areas in the department of Usulután, together met these criteria. (A municipality corresponds roughly to a U.S. county but governs all settlements within its borders; a department is something like a U.S. state but with little autonomy from the central government.)

Tenancingo is in many ways typical of the northern and north-central departments of El Salvador. Tenancingo lies in the outer folds of the Guazapa volcano in north-central El Salvador. Before the war, *campesinos* grew corn, sorghum, and beans on small holdings in outlying areas for their own consumption, with few modern inputs, technology, or services. Medium-scale commercial farmers produced eggs, fruit, and tobacco in the fertile areas near the municipal seat, the Villa of Tenancingo, for national and regional consumption. The average farm size in Tenancingo in 1971 was only 2.8 hectares, compared with the national average of 5.4 hectares (calculated from DGEC 1974: tables 1 and 2, pp. 1–13). Reflecting the importance of small holdings in the department of Cuscatlán (where Tenancingo is one of several municipalities), farms of less than 10 hectares cultivated 46.7 percent of farmland in Cuscatlán in 1971, compared with the national level of 27.1 percent. In Cuscatlán, the fraction of farms worked by the owner was 57 percent compared with 39.9 percent in El Salvador generally. Cuscatlán had lower illiteracy rates than the national average before the war (while the rural illiteracy rate in 1971 was 53 percent, it was nonetheless lower than the average for rural El Salvador of 59 percent; DGEC 1977: table 11, pp. 107–14). Prewar social conditions were documented in detail by William Durham (1979), which provided an additional incentive to conduct research in Tenancingo.

The municipality was deeply divided before and during the civil war. Nearly a fifth of the FMLN combatant deaths reported to the Truth Commission occurred in this small municipality in the four years between 1979 to 1983.[3] Cuscatlán was the department with the highest proportion

---

[3] However, this figure is based on a dubious source, Annex 9 of the report of the Truth Commission (1993). The reporting of war casualties and human rights violations to the commission appears to have been extremely uneven across geographical regions. The reasons are not clear, but probably include differences in the effort made by regional organizations affiliated with the FMLN to mobilize residents to report violations, as well as the different accessibility of regions during the war itself. (The report draws on various sources, including violations directly reported to the commission and those compiled by human rights organizations during the war.) The annexes are not useful for research on Usulután, as the

of respondents in a postwar survey reporting a death of a family member as a result of the war (72.5 percent compared with 54.5 percent in Chalatenango, the next highest; Seligson and McElhinny 1996: 230). Tenancingo was conflicted in large part because of its proximity to the broken terrain of the Guazapa volcano, which was an important strategic gateway from the northern controlled zones to San Salvador for the FMLN and the site of numerous military campaigns to dislodge insurgent forces. According to the colonel responsible for part of the Guazapa area at the time, "Guazapa is like a knife in the heart of the capital, a fundamentally strategic point. That's why the guerillas don't want to lose Tenancingo" (Zacatecoluca, 1987). General Blandón, head of the Armed Forces, stressed the propaganda value of the FMLN's presence on and near Guazapa, quoting to me in an interview a newspaper headline "'Combat in Guazapa – 14 kilometers from the Capital'" (San Salvador, 1987).

Despite the similarities among the *cantones* of the municipality, violence occurred unevenly across Tenancingo. The northern *cantones* (areas that together comprised a municipality) were deserted by 1980 because of political violence, as was the municipal seat after its 1983 bombing. In contrast, the southern *cantones* remained populated and formed civil defense patrols in coordination with the military detachment in the department capital. After the town of Tenancingo was resettled in 1986, research was once again feasible in the municipality in part because of its high profile as the site of a unique and important reconstruction project. From that time, the FPL was the FMLN faction most present in the area. The area remained extremely conflicted.

The case-study areas of Usulután complement the small-scale agriculture of Tenancingo: they were among the few regions of significant agroexport production that were contested during the war.[4] Shaped by the various agro-export booms that punctuated El Salvador's history, Usulután's pattern of land tenure, land use, and social relations were typical of the nation as a whole. Inequality of landholdings before the civil war was extremely high: the Gini coefficient for land inequality in Usulután in 1971 was 0.83, slightly higher than the national level of 0.81 (McElhinny 2001:

underreporting there was severe. Nor are the annexes yet available in electronic form, which further complicates their scholarly use.

[4] Other areas of export agriculture that were contested during the war were the neighboring department of San Vicente, small areas planted in coffee in northern Usulután (not contiguous with the coffee highlands studied here) and northern San Miguel, and the coastal plain of the departments of La Paz, San Miguel, and La Unión.

table A1). Before the war, Usulután was one of the most productive departments of El Salvador, generating 34 percent of the nation's cotton and 10 percent of its coffee as well as a substantial fraction of basic grains (DGEC 1974: tables 20 and 29). Reflecting the importance of export agriculture in the department, the distribution of farmland in Usulután was even more concentrated than in El Salvador generally. In 1971, farms of more than 100 hectares comprised 0.7 percent of farms and cultivated 38.7 percent of farmland in El Salvador; in Usulután, such farms comprised 0.9 percent of farms and cultivated 46.9 percent of farmland (ibid.: tables II, III, and 7, pp. xxx, xxxi, and 40). Male rural unemployment was almost 50 percent higher in Usulután than El Salvador generally (DGEC 1977: table 3, pp. 14–22).

On the eve of the civil war, extensive cotton and cattle farms such as the Haciendas California and La Normandía dominated the fertile coastal plain, while coffee estates covered the mountainous highlands that rise sharply from the Rio Lempa at the department's western border to the Volcán Chaparrastique across its eastern border (Fig. 3.1). Sandwiched between the

Figure 3.1   Map of Usulután. By Carolyn Resnicke.

coastal plain and the coffee highlands was a narrow belt of small family farms on land too low for coffee cultivation and too hilly for cotton cultivation.

Labor relations and general living conditions in Usulután also reflected those of El Salvador generally. Some *campesinos*, particularly in the coffee area, lived on estates, providing labor and guarding property in exchange for access to a simple house and permission to plant a cornfield. But most were landless or nearly so, living along railways and roadsides, as well as in village settlements scattered throughout the department. During the harvest, landless workers, smallholders, and most other adult family members migrated or commuted to the coastal farms and to the coffee estates. As was typical in El Salvador before the war, the presence of the National Guard on the major farms and in the towns was complemented by village patrols and networks of military reservists that reported suspicious activity. Although the expansion into cotton and cattle diversified production after World War II, land remained highly concentrated and labor relations highly coercive.

Several areas of Usulután were deeply contested during the civil war as guerrilla units, government forces, Catholic activists, civil defense units, death squads, nongovernmental organizations, and national federations of cooperatives all competed for rural political loyalties. These groups were representative of the range of social actors in El Salvador before and during the civil war, with the exception that urban unions played little role in these areas. While at different times all five FMLN factions were active in Usulután, by the war's end only two, the ERP and the FPL, maintained a significant presence there. At the war's end, approximately a quarter of the land occupied by insurgent cooperatives in El Salvador fell in Usulután. And of the 644 schools destroyed during the war, 17 percent were in Usulután (Ministry of Education, *Diario de Hoy*, January 27, 1992).

For the Usulután case-study areas, I decided to focus on the areas where the ERP was present because these included the highly conflicted Jiquilisco coast as well as an extensive area in the coffee highlands.[5] Because of the proximity of these areas to major roads (the coastal highway,

[5] An additional reason is that nearly all scholars of the civil war study events at the national level with little sustained local or regional focus, study repatriated refugee communities, or study regions where the FPL was the dominant FMLN faction, particularly Chalatenango. One reason for the focus on the FPL might be that during the war the ERP had the reputation of being more militaristic or "maximalist" than the FPL with generally less good relations with civilians. Another reason might be that the FPL developed and maintained stronger international contacts, which might have facilitated work on FPL areas by foreign scholars. Jenny Pearce's book (1986) on Chalatenango; the work of Vincent McElhinny (n.d.) on

the Pan American highway, and the paved road connecting the two through Santiago de María), access via my small pickup truck was possible to all but the most outlying parts of these areas except during the height of the rainy season. Specifically, the four case-study areas in Usulután are (shown as shaded areas in Fig. 3.1, from left to right): western Jiquilisco (the municipality of Jiquilisco west of the road from the coastal highway to the town of Jiquilisco), the area around the town of San Francisco Javier (the municipalities of San Francisco Javier, Ozatlán, and the eastern part of San Agustín), the municipality of Santiago de María, and the area known as "Las Marías" (the southern part of the municipality of Jucuapa, the northern part of Santa Elena, and the municipalities of Chinameca and San Jorge in the department of San Miguel, just east of Usulután, included because memberships and affiliations of *campesino* organizations there overlapped with those of the rest of Las Marías at the close of the war). The Usulután case-study areas include three contested towns (Tierra Blanca, San Francisco Javier, and San Jorge) as well as Santiago de María, a town high in the coffee area that was less contested.

While the Tenancingo and Usulután case-study areas met these four criteria, their selection was a more complicated process than the above account might suggest. I originally studied Tenancingo for a different reason: its resettlement took place under the terms of a unique agreement by the FMLN and the government that it would be rebuilt as an unarmed zone not subject to conflict in the midst of a sharply contested area. The result was far from an unarmed zone. During my research there (three months in 1987 and at least annual shorter visits through the end of the war), both sides carried arms through the area, mortars frequently boomed overhead, and there were occasional battles on its streets or outskirts that resulted in the deaths of a few residents. To visit Tenancingo, I frequently had to travel through armed roadblocks set up by one or the other armed force and sometimes by both. Nonetheless, civilian supporters of both sides returned to live in the town, and research on the municipality's political history and evolution proved possible. Fortunately, much of the data I gathered for the analysis of the reconstruction project proved equally relevant for this project as well.

The choice of the case-study areas in Usulután reflected a different and soon-abandoned research agenda. When I began a new period of sustained research in El Salvador in September 1991, I planned to compare forms of

San Vicente, a little studied FPL area; and Leigh Binford's work (1996, 1997, 1999, 2003) on Morazán (another ERP area) are three exceptions to the pattern of national-level analysis.

peasant organization across different political economies, that is, how opposition peasant organizations differed in areas of cotton production with large wage-labor forces, areas of coffee production with a diversity of labor relations, and areas where small holdings predominated. I decided to work on Usulután, as all these political economies had been present before the war. After a few trips there, however, it became evident that far from varying, the forms of peasant organization were quite similar. There appeared to be a number of possible explanations: the traditional mobility of agrarian labor may have undermined the potential political heterogeneity of organizations in different areas; the departure of landlords and government security forces may have disrupted prewar class relationships and identities and made possible almost universal access to at least some land for those *campesinos* that remained; and guerrilla organizations may have exerted a strong homogenizing influence on *campesino* organization. Moreover, throughout the Usulután case-study areas, participants in the insurgency ranged from skilled mechanics to autonomous peasant farmers to landless laborers to artisans. So I abandoned that research agenda, which in retrospect seems strikingly economistic, for the present inquiry. Field research in Usulután continued through December 1992, which included the months of the cease-fire, and on short annual visits until 1996.

I now turn to the individual case-study areas, briefly describing prewar social relations and land tenure patterns as well as the changes wrought during the civil war.

Western Jiquilisco

The coastal plain in the municipality of Jiquilisco in southwestern Usulután was one of the areas of the country most affected by the 1980 agrarian reform, and western Jiquilisco was of the most hotly contested coastal areas during the war. By the war's end the area was a complex quilt of cooperatives of various origins, with a few medium-sized properties still cultivated by landlords or their tenants.

From the late 1930s through the 1960s, Jiquilisco was one of the principal sites of the rapid expansion of cotton in El Salvador, particularly after the completion of the coastal highway in 1962. Between 1961 and 1971, the area planted in cotton in Usulután increased by 39.8 percent and production by 61.1 percent (DGEC 1974: vol. 1, table 4). By 1971, some 42 percent of Jiquilisco was planted in cotton and the municipality produced 14.1 percent of the nation's cotton (ibid.: tables 3 and 20, pp. 19 and 140). The result was a highly concentrated distribution of farmland: in 1971, the average farm size in the municipality was 10.4 hectares, compared with the national average of 5.4 (calculated from ibid.: tables 1 and 2, pp. 1–13). The largest producers controlled the processing and marketing of cotton through their control of the national marketing board. The sizable permanent work force, largely skilled laborers such as mechanics, drivers, and pilots (cotton cultivation can require as many as forty applications of pesticides per year), lived in the towns of Tierra Blanca, Jiquilisco itself, and smaller villages along the highway. Subsistence cultivators displaced by the expansion of cotton and cattle production retreated to scattered settlements on national property along the railways and public roadways. The harvesting of cotton was extremely labor-intensive. Tens of thousands of workers migrated to the area from elsewhere in Usulután and from the northern departments to supplement the local work force. The National Guard and the Treasury Police maintained a strong presence in the municipality, with posts in San Marcos Lempa, Tierra Blanca, Jiquilisco, and several *cantones* near the coast, in addition to the National Guardsmen billeted on individual farms.

By the 1970s, large cotton and cattle farms such as the Haciendas California and La Normandía (recall Fig. 1.1) dominated the social landscape of the Jiquilisco coastal plain. According to the last agricultural census, carried out in 1971, in Usulután 0.7 percent of farms (those over 500 hectares) that produced some cotton occupied 36.8 percent of the area planted in cotton. The 2.6 percent of farms (those between 100 and 500 hectares) that produced some cotton planted an additional 49.4 percent of the crop area (ibid.: vol. 2, table 18, p. 110). (This high proportion of cotton planted in farms of the latter size suggests that the aborted second phase of the 1980 agrarian reform would have had a substantial impact on cotton as well as coffee.) As the census takes farms, not landowners, as its unit of analysis, this underestimates the concentration of income and wealth in the sector, as landlords often owned more than one farm.

The Jiquilisco coastal plain was to have been an important site for President Molina's 1976 agrarian reform initiative, a response to increasing demands for land reform on the part of the Catholic Church and emerging *campesino* organizations. The reform declared an area of 58,744 hectares in San Miguel and Usulután, including Jiquilisco, subject to a new ceiling on landholding of 35 hectares (Montes 1986: 148). The program targeted the highly concentrated cotton sector: 34 percent of the affected region was cultivated in cotton; of the 236 affected landlords, the twelve largest controlled 31.6 percent of the affected area, and the top 102 controlled 61.0 percent

(Gordon 1989: 191–2). Despite assurances of compensation by the U.S. Agency for International Development, significant additional funding by Sweden, and the backing of the Organization of American States, the private sector swiftly and nearly unanimously opposed the project (Brockett 1990: 148). The landlords joined the national business associations to unleash a campaign that combined vitriolic rhetoric in the national press, lobbying of the government, and intimidation of prospective beneficiaries along the coast. The government soon backed down via a compromise (no land would be forcibly sold or expropriated) that effectively ended the initiative (McClintock 1985: 177).

When the military carried out the 1980 agrarian reform, Usulután generally, and Jiquilisco in particular, were among the areas most affected by the first phase, under which approximately 15 percent of the nation's agricultural land was transferred to cooperatives formed of former estate workers, as in the case of the Cooperativa La Normandía. Because of ongoing conflict in the area, most landlords whose properties had not been expropriated gradually abandoned them. Sabotage of the cotton harvest further contributed to the exodus, but a few medium-sized farms bordering the coastal highway continued to cultivate some cotton as well as sesame and other commercial crops (as did the very few reform cooperatives that continued to receive credit). Other reform cooperatives were abandoned due to the ongoing violence; some, such as the Normandía, never received formal title to the cooperative property.

Despite their access to land through the agrarian reform, some members of reform cooperatives in western Jiquilisco continued covertly to support the FMLN. Several Jiquilisco cooperatives, including the Cooperativa La Normandía, affiliated formally with a leftist organization of Phase I cooperatives. The western Jiquilisco cooperatives were a crucial element of the organization, as a number of national leaders were members of local cooperatives, including its long-term president, Miguel Alemán, a member of the Cooperativa La Maroma, located a few kilometers to the west of the Hacienda California.

In the wake of the landlords' retreat, the decline of many cooperatives, and the absence of state authorities, local *campesinos* planted corn, and those who could afford to grazed cattle as well. The planting of corn not only secured the family's subsistence, but perhaps also symbolized their reclaiming of land previously given over to agro-export crops. On properties that had not been expropriated, as in the case of the Hacienda California, some *campesinos* organized insurgent cooperatives, occupied abandoned properties, and claimed them at the close of the war under the terms of the peace agreement.

Las Marías

From the coastal plain, the Usulután landscape rises sharply to the coffee highlands that stretch north from San Francisco Javier toward Berlín, and east across the department to the town of San Jorge in the department of San Miguel. The distribution of land planted in coffee was highly concentrated before the war. While there were many small farms in Usulután – the average farm planted with some coffee occupied only 8.6 hectares – the 41 farms with more than 100 hectares planted in coffee (1.9 percent of the farms with some area planted in coffee) farmed 45 percent of the land planted in coffee (DGEC 1975: table 30, pp. 182–3). This figure again significantly underestimates the concentration of wealth, as a wealthy landlord typically owned more than one and sometimes several coffee estates, called *fincas*. A hundred hectares in coffee was a source of significant wealth: the owner of more than 70 hectares typically owned a mill, possibly controlled an export firm, and certainly wielded substantial local power (Paige 1987: 156).

The Finca Las Conchas was typical of the larger coffee estates of the highlands of Usulután,[6] with 280 hectares (400 *manzanas*). (An area the size of a hectare, if square, measures 100 meters on each side. A *manzana* is approximately 70 percent of a hectare. In this chapter I give areas in both *manzanas* and hectares as it may help the reader interpret the maps.) The *finca* was planted almost entirely in coffee except for its areas of highly developed infrastructure, which included warehouses, water tanks, shacks for short-term storage of green coffee beans, two playing fields, tree hedges planted as windbreaks, and an office for armed private guards. The remnants of the infrastructure can be seen in Fig. 3.2, a map representing the estate at the end of the war. A few houses of *colonos* (permanent farm employees who lived in small houses and were usually allowed to plant a small cornfield in exchange for providing labor and security) were scattered at the periphery of the property, but the majority of the labor force was drawn from nearby villages, particularly the *cantón* San Lorenzo, shown on the upper left-hand corner of the map, near the town Berlín. (Distances at the edge of this map are severely distorted; the distance between the estate and Berlín, as well as

---

[6] Finca Las Conchas lies in the case-study area of San Francisco Javier, but I include it here because the map well illustrates large coffee estates before the war.

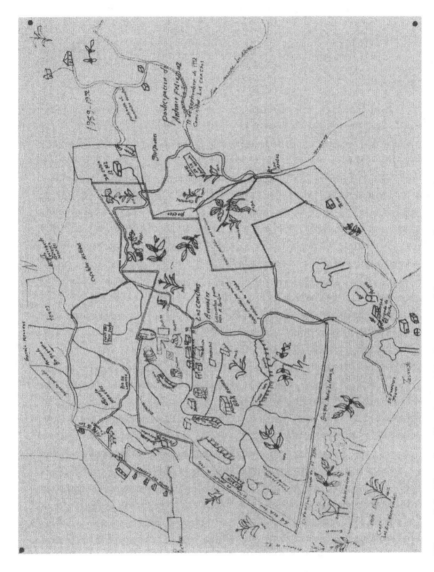

Figure 3.2 Finca Las Conchas, 1992. Courtesy of the map-makers. A color version of this map can be seen online at us.cambridge.org/features/wood.

that between the estate and San Francisco Javier at the lower edge of the map, are much greater than the map implies.) During the war, the estate was abandoned, and *campesinos* planted some corn within its boundaries, as indicated by the scattered corn stalks on the map. At the war's end, a group of *campesinos* claimed the estate under the peace agreement. The map-makers, led by Antonio Félix Díaz, as noted on the map, estimated that the coffee trees were about 50 percent "ruined" (see the notation to the left of the map's center); presumably, they expected yields to be half of prewar yields. They claimed to have occupied the estate since 1989 (note the date toward the upper right-hand corner). As the group had not yet been legally recognized as a cooperative, the map-makers refer to the occupying organization along the right-hand edge of the map as Comunidad Las Conchas, rather than Cooperativa Las Conchas. In 1991, they succeeded for the first time in marketing some of the estate's coffee. The *campesinos* continued to occupy the property at the war's end, despite the landlady's response, "forty lawyers and three chains across the gates," according to a local organizer.

To the east of Las Conchas lies the town of Santiago de María. Between Santiago and the next town to the east, Chinameca (in the department of San Miguel), Mount El Tigre juts sharply upward. The area between El Tigre, Chinameca, Jucuapa, and Santa Elena was known by the FMLN and supporters as "Las Marías" after the hamlet at its center. In the Las Marías area, estates were generally smaller than Finca Las Conchas, ranging from small holdings of four hectares to estates of more than 100 and occasionally more than 300 hectares. The larger estates had several outbuildings, including patios for the drying of coffee. In the hamlet Las Marías, there was a coffee mill that processed some of the coffee produced in the local area; most was transported to the large mills in Santiago de María or to smaller ones in Jucuapa. Jucuapa, a municipality of almost 19,000 people before the war, supplied a substantial fraction of the harvest labor to the estates in the surrounding area.

The Las Marías area was one of the most constantly contested areas of the entire department, particularly after 1985. The existence of an FMLN force so close to Santiago de María was intended as a thorn in the side of the Santiago elites, according to local ERP commanders. Ongoing efforts were made to dislodge the guerrilla units. Despite intense conflict, many *campesinos* remained in the area throughout the war, planting corn and learning "to dive for the edge of the cornfield" when firing broke out and, "after a time, to begin again," according to one resident (Las Marías, 1992). Beginning in the late 1980s, residents organized insurgent cooperatives with the legal help and political tutelage of an FMLN-affiliated federation of co-operatives. By the war's end, some two dozen cooperatives in the area near Las Marías worked closely together as the Comite de Defensa de Tierra (Land Defense Committee), with ongoing support from the federation and the ERP.

The *cantón* Los Arenales, which lies south of the village of Las Marías approximately halfway between Santa Elena and Jucuapa, is typical of the area (Fig. 3.3). The largest coffee farm in the *cantón* was the Finca Leonor, a small but well-capitalized farm of 38.5 hectares (55 *manzanas*), which may be seen in the map's center, just inside the upper left-hand curve as it bends to the right. The Finca Leonor had a well-developed infrastructure of water tanks, storehouses, and patios for drying coffee, as I was able to confirm when I visited the now-dilapidated property in 1992. Other properties high above the main road (indicated by arrows along what would be the center line if it was paved), were also planted in coffee, as indicated on the map by the branch with fairly straight leaves and berries close to the branch. In the lower altitudes other crops were cultivated, including oranges and maguey.

The map-maker who drew this and the following figures, a long-standing leader in the area, was one of the most literate and articulate of the *campesinos* I interviewed. Coached by two kibitzing fellow cooperative members, he numbered each plot and listed the corresponding owners down the lower left-hand margin of the map. The workers mostly lived in the village of Los Arenales, to the right of the main road; a few before the war had lived as *colonos*.[7]

As shown by the cornstalks drawn on the postwar map of the area (Fig. 3.4), during the war residents cultivated corn on the properties clos-est to the roadway. The map-maker, a very religious person, marked with crosses the sites where two *campesinos* died at the hand of the Atonal Battalion in 1983, and where Comandante "Miriam" of the armed wing of the Communist Party (shown by its acronym "FAL") died in 1984, as can be seen in the legend in the lower left-hand corner, which includes the names of the dead. In 1987, the map-makers, the two kibitzers, and other local residents founded the Cooperativa San Pedro Los Arenales. The map title midway down the left-hand side of the map, "Mapa de las Propiedades de la Asociación Cooperativa San Pedro Los Arenales, de Responsibilidad Limitada" ("Map of the Properties of the Cooperative Association San

---

[7] While the *colono* form of labor bound to landlords by tradition and dependency to had been legally abolished in 1965, the practice continued in many areas.

Pedro Los Arenas of Limited Responsibility," the latter phrase the Salvador equivalent of "Incorporated"), includes the formal name of the cooperative as a way of emphasizing the cooperative's legal claim. The members of the cooperative all lived close together at the very southern end of the town, an unusually tight clustering of members (in the color version on the website, members are distinguished by green dots). The cooperative gradually occupied ten local estates, including the Finca Leonor, which are listed by landlord and area in on the left-hand legend. Not all the properties in the area were occupied; a few are visible within the cooperative boundary. Cooperative members stated that they targeted abandoned farms or those with "uncooperative" owners. Three of the properties (numbers 1, 6, and 10) exceeded 35 hectares (50 *manzanas*), a significant holding if planted in coffee. The total of 330 *manzanas* (231 hectares) is inscribed in large notation. The cooperative claimed all these properties in 1992 under the terms of the peace agreement. This is one of the smaller land claims by insurgent cooperatives in terms of area, but one with significant economic potential. (For example, the cooperative Los Tres Postes, typical of the larger insurgent cooperatives, claimed 700 hectares just to the southwest of Los Arenales.)

Figures 3.5 and 3.6 illustrate the changes wrought in the landscape near the town of San Jorge to the east of Las Marías. San Jorge lies high on the northwest shoulder of the Volcán Chaparrastique, just beyond the departmental boundary. Before the war, the area north of San Jorge was largely planted in medium-size coffee estates, as shown in Figure 3.5, a map drawn for me in 1992 by members of the Cooperativa Candelaria, un Nuevo Amanecer (Candelaria, a New Dawn). The town is shown at the lower edge of the map. Each field and grove is labeled with the name of the owner and the crop indicated with symbols. The area north of town included several estates exceeding 70 hectares (100 *manzanas*). The wealth of the largest property, 280 hectares (400 *manzanas*), is symbolized by the large house shown. The symbol for coffee varies significantly across the map, perhaps depicting the size and power of the estates. The caption along the right-hand edge reads (literally translated): "This is how it was in the year 1970, the place of the lands where the Cooperativa Candelaria a New Dawn was born."

Figure 3.6 is the cooperativists' representation of the landscape after the civil war. By the end of the war, the abandoned coffee estates (shown at the top of the figure) were more forest than farm, as indicated by the serpent toward the upper right corner, the broken coffee branches toward

Figure 3.3 Cantón Los Arenales, 1980. Courtesy of the map-makers. A color version of this map can be seen online at us.cambridge.org/features/wood.

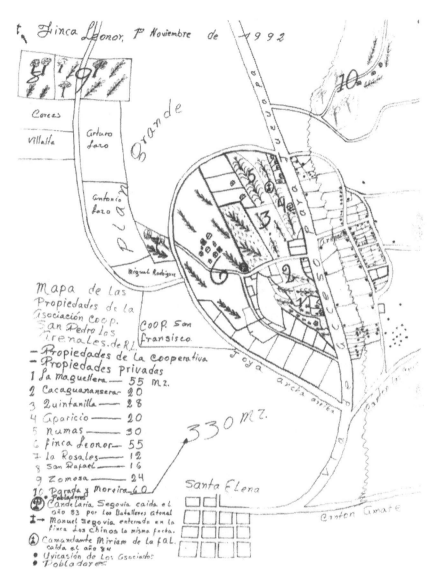

Figure 3.4 Cooperativa San Pedro Los Arenales, 1992. Courtesy of the map-makers. A color version of this map can be seen online at us.cambridge.org/features/wood.

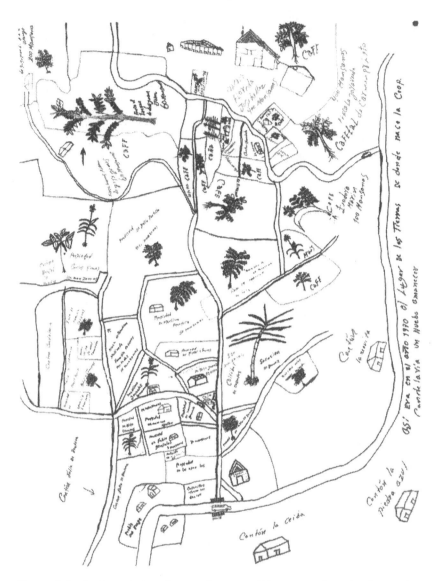

Figure 3.5 San Jorge before the war. Courtesy of the map-makers. A color version of this map can be seen online at us.cambridge.org/features/wood.

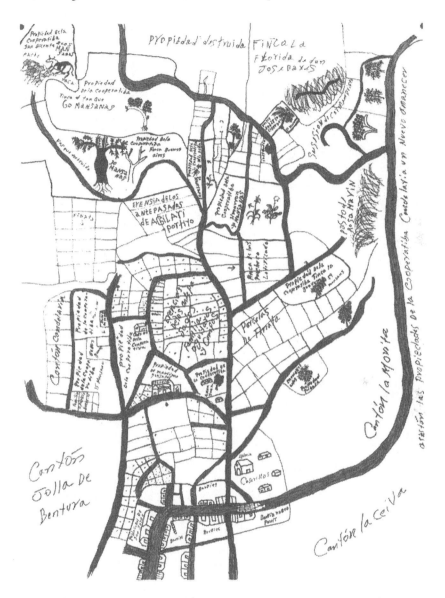

Figure 3.6 Cooperative Candelaria, un Nuevo Amanecer. Courtesy of the map-makers. A color version of this map can be seen online at us.cambridge.org/features/wood.

the upper left one, and notations such as "*propiedad destruida*" (destroyed property) and "*vosque destruido*" [*sic*] (destroyed forest). As elsewhere, corn was more widely planted (not evident in Fig. 3.6, but easily noted when I visited the cooperative). In the late 1980s, militant *campesinos* founded the cooperative and claimed 322 hectares of the now-rundown coffee estates in 1992. On the map, several properties, including a significant fraction of the coffee estates north of town, are labeled "*propiedad de la cooperativa*" ("property of the cooperative") and the acreage of each is given.

Other processes also contributed to the changed landscape. Closer to town, a number of properties were broken up into small holdings, evident if one compares the two maps. Two properties were distributed to residents in the early 1980s under the "land-to-the-tiller" phase of the agrarian reform; one is labeled "parcelas de FINATA," and the other simply "FINATA," which refers to the acronym of the administering agency. Others were subdivided into lots when landlords who found themselves unable to cultivate or market coffee sold land to pay off accumulating debts. Some families could afford to buy land for housing or a small holding as a result of cash transfers from relatives in San Salvador, provincial towns, or the United States. (Remittances from the United States were substantial inflows in some areas of El Salvador, fueling an unprecedented land market around towns even in contested municipalities.) The subdivision of property among heirs also contributed to the proliferation of small holdings.

Santiago de María

Most coffee produced in the highlands of Usulután was processed by one of the several large mills in Santiago de Maria, a beautiful town nestled high in the volcanic highlands that epitomized the hierarchical social relationships of rural El Salvador before the war. In sharp contrast to the occupation of properties, the emergence of cooperatives, and the founding of new organizations in contested areas of Usulután, continuity rather than change characterized the evolution of social relations in the municipality through the years of the civil war. Before the war, the politics and economy of the town and the surrounding area were dominated by a handful of elite families that developed highly productive coffee estates and built modern mills, including one of the largest and most modern in the country, the Llach family's Oromontique mill. Reflecting the high value of land planted in coffee, in the municipality owners worked 96.6 percent of the farms, compared with the national average of 39.9 percent; the average farm size was

11.4 hectares, compared with the national average of 5.4 hectares; and illiteracy among producers was only 40.7 percent, compared with 60.0 percent nationally (DGEC 1974: tables 1, 2 and 4, pp. 1–13, 21–4). In interviews, *campesinos* sometimes referred to the town as the *cuña de la oligarquía* ("the cradle of the oligarchy"). Santiago was indeed central to the interests of two oligarchic families, the Llach Schonenberg and the Homberger families, as well as a host of less wealthy second-tier families.[8] In the early 1970s, the Llach Schonenberg family ranked third among families in El Salvador in coffee production and eighth in coffee exports; the family also produced a substantial fraction of the nation's cotton, ranking eleventh (Williams 1986: 202; Williams 1994: 282). A member of the family served on the national cotton-marketing board in the early 1970s and was one of three private sector directors of the central bank in the early 1970s (a Homberger was one of the other two; Johnson 1993: 47).

Although there was little employment other than coffee, about 20,000 people inhabited the municipality of Santiago at the beginning of the war. More than half lived in the town itself, walking to work in the estates lying in all directions or to the Oromontique mill at the southern edge of town. Two banks had agencies in the town; the National Police and the National Guard both quartered troops in the town.

The war did bring some change to the outlying areas of the municipality. Some landlords found in the early 1980s that they could no longer safely manage their properties. In their absence, those lands were occupied by insurgent cooperatives. Landlords of properties located nearer to Santiago were forced to pay "war taxes" to the FMLN during some years of the war under the threat of extortion and sabotage, such as the burning of tens of thousands of seedlings belonging to the Llach family in the late 1980s, according to interviews with FMLN commanders. The response of the landlords was to harvest the coffee beans over a shorter period to minimize their exposure to insurgent threats and to pay the war taxes.

However, the political economy of the town and its immediate environs was relatively untouched by the forces that transformed the other case-study areas. There were three principal reasons. First, a death squad decimated circles of local activists in the late 1970s and early 1980s, as we see in the next chapter. Second, properties continued to be held by the traditional landlords throughout the war, with the exception of the expropriation of four estates

---

[8] Based on Johnson's analysis (1993: 58), both families qualify as oligarchic, with major investments in at least three of the dominant agro-export rubrics.

on which agrarian reform cooperatives were founded, two atop Mount El Tigre and two south of Santiago. The reform did not encroach more significantly on the privileges of Santiago elites because most properties were legally held by a number of family members, and so each individual plot was less than the threshold for expropriation. At the war's end the Llach family, whose heiresses included then-President Alfredo Cristiani's wife, appeared to be *expanding* their holdings in the area with the purchase of an additional estate in 1992. Third, during the coffee harvest when landlords were most vulnerable, troops from the Sixth Brigade moved from their base in the city of Usulután to Santiago to safeguard the harvest.

San Francisco Javier

To the southwest of Santiago de María and to the north of Tierra Blanca lies the contested town of San Francisco Javier, just above the transition zone between the coastal plain and the coffee highlands. Before the war, the National Guard maintained a post in the town, but I was not told of troops residing on particular farms. An American immigrant, Billy Moore, dominated the town as owner of eight coffee estates and a cattle ranch in the town's outskirts, as well as the municipality's sole coffee mill. Two other families also had large landholdings: the Vidaurre family owned a coffee estate and a sizable property south of the town, and the Del 'Pech family, owners of the Hacienda La Normandía, also owned a farm near San Francisco Javier. Workers lived in the town and in the surrounding *cantones* and had very limited access to land.

By the end of the civil war, the pattern of land tenure and land use in the immediate area of San Francisco Javier (Fig. 3.7) had been transformed. The map shows the town itself (the small shapes are homes) as well as the surrounding area. As indicated by the crosses scattered around the town (not just in the cemetery in the lower right-hand side of the map), the war had claimed a significant number of lives. The town's infrastructure had been destroyed; Figure 3.8 shows children collecting water from the river for household use. The most obvious change in the landscape is the planting of corn north of the town; before the war it had been entirely coffee groves. Not all land was planted, however, as indicated by the plots labeled "*bosque*" (forest) to the left of the road running from the top to the bottom of the map; that land had all been coffee as well. As part of the land-to-the-tiller component of the 1980 land reform, two of Moore's properties had been subdivided and titled to individual campesinos. Those who benefited

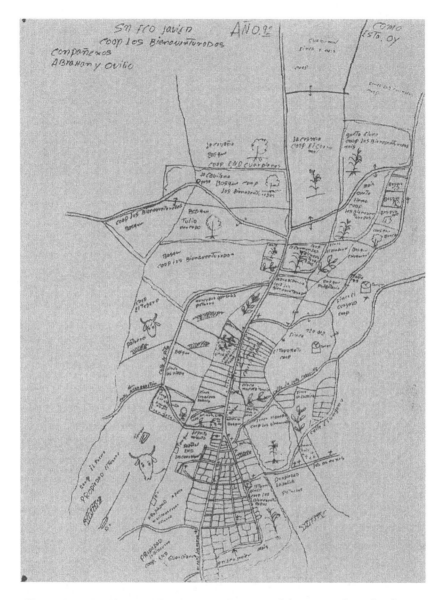

Figure 3.7 San Francisco Javier, 1992. Courtesy of the map-makers. A color version of this map can be seen online at us.cambridge.org/features/wood.

Figure 3.8   Children collecting water with oxen, San Francisco Javier, 1987. Photograph by Jeremy Bigwood.

subsequently formed service cooperatives (through which they could in principal pool the buying of inputs, but held individual titles, in contrast to the production cooperatives of Phase I properties). Among them were the Cooperative El Tesoro, which raised cattle as well as corn, shown on the lower left-hand corner across the river from the town, and the Cooperativa El Cuarumal, which farmed the two properties along the right-hand edge of the main road leading northward out of town. Two other land-to-the-tiller service cooperatives are also shown, the Cooperativa El Taburete and the Cooperativa El Guayava.

Two extensive land claims by insurgent cooperatives are also evident on the map, indicated by lines around occupied properties (pink on the website version of the map) and by the name of the cooperative on each occupied plot. The Cooperativa Bienaventurados ("the fortunate ones," a reference to the Beatitudes) occupied several farms to the north of the town as well as a few in the town's immediate outskirts. The Cooperativa Los Guardianos ("the guardians"), formed by a group of combatants of the ERP based at the ruined coffee mill during the cease-fire, claimed the "*bosque*" property, the coffee mill and its remaining infrastructure, and the Vidaurre property south of town. Both cooperatives pursued legal title

76

for the occupied properties under the terms of the peace agreement and provided significant leadership to other cooperatives in the area.

The occupation of these and many other properties in the area around San Francisco Javier was coordinated by another FMLN-allied organization of insurgent cooperatives and communities. In several meetings that I observed, activists under the leadership of the organization's staff members and the regional political officer of the ERP identified candidate properties for occupation, recruited prospective cooperative members, wrote threatening letters to landlords, and hosted visits by representatives of a few foreign organizations that supported projects such as the extension of agricultural credit and training on a small scale to some affiliates. Even the El Tesoro and Cuarumal cooperatives, formed under the counterinsurgency land-to-the-tiller program, were members; the agrarian reform had evidently failed to win their "hearts and minds."

Between the coastal plain and the coffee highlands of Usulután runs a belt of small holdings. This belt cuts across the southern edge of the municipality of San Francisco Javier south of the town. Some of these small holdings, originally part of the two largest Jiquilisco estates, were distributed to families in two of the very rare instances of land distribution in El Salvador before the war. In the 1930s, the Palomo family allowed the northern part of what was then a single gigantic estate, the Hacienda California, to be subdivided for family farms as part of General Maximiliano Martínez Hernández's "Mejoramiento Social" (social betterment) policy (Stanley 1996: 60–1). The northern part of the Hacienda Nancuchiname was subdivided in the early 1970s to help settle Salvadorans expelled from Honduras in the aftermath of the 1969 "soccer war."

Before the civil war, the peasant families who owned these properties mostly cultivated basic grains and vegetables and raised chickens for their own subsistence. Many landless families lived in villages in the area. During the cotton and coffee harvests, they migrated south to the coastal plain or north to the highlands to earn wages that played a significant part in the family's annual cash flow. While most residents fled the area during the early 1980s, many began to return around 1983, as conflict lessened. At the close of the war, the presence of several Pentecostal churches was a notable feature of the small-holding belt. Few members of these churches participated in insurgent organizations, but those living close to the coffee highlands paid war taxes in the form of tortillas and water to the FMLN (and also to government troops when they passed through).

At the end of the 1980s, some of these small holdings were occupied by insurgent cooperatives. One such cooperative was the Cooperativa La Joya del Pilar ("Jewel of Pilar"), a cooperative of mostly landless residents that occupied several small holdings in the hamlet of La Joya (Fig. 3.9). Along the northern and eastern edge of the map the occupied properties are indicated by the crosshatching around their borders (red in the website version). Most of the small holdings were planted in corn, but the three in the upper right-hand corner were used for cattle. When I asked why some small holdings but not others had been occupied, local leaders responded that those properties occupied had been abandoned or were owned by people who had not "cooperated" during the civil war. (The inclusion of such small holdings in the first list of occupied properties presented by the FMLN in the negotiations over land during the 1992 cease-fire occasioned a significant debate, one in which the FMLN was politically vulnerable as it appeared to be displacing poor smallholders as well as wealthy landlords. The FMLN subsequently presented a list in which many such small holdings had been deleted.)

Tenancingo

Tenancingo lies northeast of Usulután in the steep hills southeast of the Guazapa volcano, an FMLN stronghold during the civil war. In Tenancingo before the war, an impoverished and marginalized peasantry subsisted in the ten *cantones* of the municipality, while commercial farmers and traders lived and worked in the Villa, which is how residents refer to the town of Tenancingo. In contrast to much of El Salvador, prewar patterns of land tenure, household income, and social structures in Tenancingo are well documented, thanks to William Durham's classic study (1979). The following account draws on Durham's study as well as interviews conducted in Tenancingo with residents and in San Salvador with prosperous families displaced by the civil war.

The presence of extensive small holdings in Tenancingo dates back to the collapse of indigo cultivation in the nineteenth century. As elsewhere in El Salvador, assimilation of the indigenous culture began in the late seventeenth century, in part due to the marriage of the local leader and the daughter of one of the prominent Spanish families, according to local tradition. The expansion of indigo cultivation on several haciendas displaced some of the indigenous population; their conversion to landless laborers further contributed to their acculturation. After indigo's collapse, the

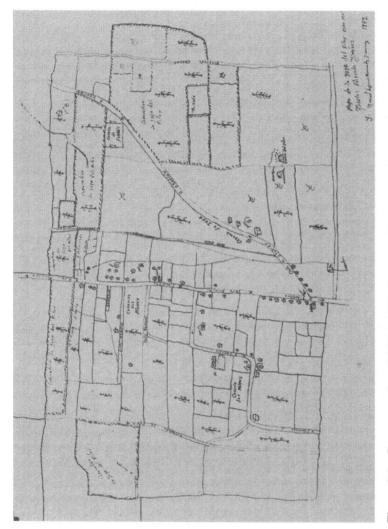

Figure 3.9 Cooperativa Joya del Pilar, 1990. Courtesy of the map-makers. A color version of this map can be seen online at us.cambridge.org/features/wood.

haciendas were divided into small holdings. By the 1970s, land was scarce in Tenancingo: in spite of the poor soil and its unsuitability for intense cultivation, nearly all land that could be farmed was farmed. Durham reported and photographed the signs of land scarcity – and the resulting erosion – everywhere. According to the 1971 census (cited in Durham 1979: 64), 45.2 percent of the land was dedicated to annual nonexport crops, 37.5 percent to pasture, 2.6 percent to perennial crops, 8.3 percent to woodland and scrub, and only 2.0 percent to export crops – in sharp contrast to Usulután.

Since colonial times, the local economy also included the production of hats made from braided palm leaves (Durham 1979: 74–5). Palm leaves were brought from the Salvadoran and Guatemalan coasts to Tenancingo, where they were dried, split, and then braided into long strands by women and children, a source of cash income – although an extremely limited one – for *campesino* families. In the hat factories of the Villa, the strands were then sown together into palm hats, pressed into shape, and bleached in ovens. The hats were sold in San Salvador, other cities of Central America, and even Texas. A few individual households also produced hats.

Before the war, the great majority of Tenancingo's inhabitants lived in houses dispersed throughout the *cantones* (Fig. 3.10). Only rarely were houses clustered with others at the intersection of foot trails. At the time of Durham's study, only the three villages along the main road were accessible by vehicle; none had electricity or running water; several had elementary schools. Males (including male children) worked the fields, and women generally managed the household (preparing food, bringing water, and caring for children) and braided palm leaves. Because the gender division of labor in rural El Salvador was not as rigid as in other Central American countries, women also cultivated some crops.[9] Residents of the *cantones* went to the Villa to purchase manufactured items and medicines. Social life in the *cantones* revolved around the cycle of religious festivals, especially the celebrations of the patron saints of the *cantones* and the Villa.

Durham (1979: chapter 3) examined the relations among access to land, migration, and various socioeconomic indicators based on his 1975 survey of 258 representative families. He found that 43.4 percent of the households farmed land they owned, 34.5 percent were tenants, 13.2 percent

---

[9] According to Jesuit anthropologist Rafael Cabarrús, who studied a similar area to the northeast of Guazapa, "Customary [gendered] practices exist but breaking them does not imply any recrimination" (1983: 125). Tenancingo has had several women mayors in the last fifteen years; all were members of wealthy Villa families. Toward the end of the war, several women without adult male family members worked corn and bean fields themselves.

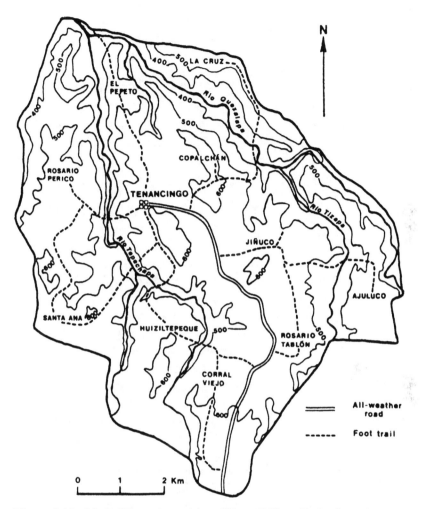

Figure 3.10 Map of Tenancingo. Adapted from William H. Durham, *Scarcity and Survival in Central America: Ecological Origins of the Soccer War*, figure 3.1, p. 65. Copyright © 1979 by the Board of Trustees of the Leland Stanford Jr. University. Reprinted with the permission of Stanford University Press, www.sup.org.

farmed land lent to them by relatives, 5.0 percent were *colonos*, and 3.9 percent wholly landless. The vast majority of the families were very poor: the average holding of those who owned land was 1.6 hectares; tenants farmed an average of 0.75 hectares. Of those families farming 1.5 hectares or less, 97 percent used all their harvest of corn, beans, and sorghum for family consumption (ibid.: 84). He documented a nearly exponential dependence of family income on access to land; that is, income more than doubled when landholding doubled. Child mortality decreased with access to land, but was higher for tenants than for landowning families. Given the critical importance of access to land (whether owned or rented) for the family's well-being, the decline in that access to land between generations (from an average of 1.43 hectares for the past generation to 1.10 for the current one; ibid:. 81) meant a substantial deterioration of the ability of the *campesino* families to obtain even a minimal self-subsistence.

According to the 1971 census, 1,600 of the 10,000 inhabitants of Tenancingo lived in the Villa. The village elites were far from wealthy by the standards of the oligarchy, but they were moderately prosperous. Some of the landlords of the larger properties were traditional (although small-scale) *hacendados* who divided their land among land-poor *campesinos* for rent or sharecropping. Others were commercial farmers who produced tobacco (not of export quality), oranges, and eggs for sale in the departmental capital Cojutepeque and San Salvador. Others combined features of both traditional and capitalist agriculture, for example, letting some land for sharecropping and grazing cattle on the rest. The scale of the Villa enterprises can perhaps be conveyed by the size of their work force: the two largest hat factories each employed approximately 100 employees, the egg farm 50, and the largest cattle farm 15 to 20. The landowners and hat-factory owners were wealthy enough to maintain second homes in Cojutepeque or San Salvador, where their children went to school. There were also eleven stores, two bakeries, and two pharmacies in the Villa before the war. Typically the men managed the agricultural enterprises and the women ran the family store or pharmacy.

These relatively wealthy individuals formed an interlocking locally dominant class linked by marriage and other family relations. These families controlled the political and social structures of the municipality. For many years, the mayor was the owner of the largest store in the Villa and one of the larger landowners. Being mayor was a powerful position, as the slate of the winning candidate becomes the entire municipal council. He was succeeded by his daughter, the wife of one of the most successful commercial farmers, Antonio Vargas (pseudonym). She was succeeded by another of the largest landowners, who was succeeded by one of the store owners, whose husband was one of the largest tobacco farmers and processors. The local commander of the National Guard was related to both of the hat factory–owning families. For many years, the Caja de Crédito (the equivalent of a local savings and loan) was run by Antonio Vargas and a partner. Vargas linked the local elite to national political and commercial interests through his ties to the ruling party.

Relations between the wealthier families and the poor families of Tenancingo were classic examples of the patron/client pattern, mediated by local institutions of godparenting, marriage, and patron saint celebrations. Antonio Vargas was typical of these patrons. He began his career as a money collector for one of the truck owners, but after his marriage to the daughter of the mayor, he founded one of the most successful commercial farms in the region. Vargas described himself as a small-scale, innovative entrepreneur – a figure of both substantive and symbolic importance in Tenancingo as well as El Salvador – who built a small empire from loans. He claimed to have more than 500 godchildren; his wife was godmother to more than 100 children. Through these godparenting relationships, some families approached Vargas for help in emergencies, but most found his wife more approachable. Vargas provided much of the financial backing for the traditional fiestas of the town, yet paid his workers "peons' wages," according to interviews with residents.

Members of wealthy families generally viewed their employees as inferior; similarly, the employees looked down on the *campesinos*. For example, one landlord disparagingly stated that 40 percent of the Tenancingo people were illiterate (actually a significant underestimate), that those who could read and write didn't think, and that they all needed a bit of order, or *orden*, a play on words since "orden" is also the acronym of a locally active right-wing paramilitary organization responsible for significant violence in the *cantones* of Tenancingo. Figure 3.11 shows a Tenancingo landlord and a tenant, with a child looking on. As the landlord approached the home of the tenant, he made sure that the gun in his belt was visible, according to Durham, who took the photograph in the mid-1970s.

The wealthier families did not return to Tenancingo during the reconstruction project, nor did they participate in the unprecedented experiment in local democratic governance there. As in the case-study areas of Usulután, insurgent cooperatives claimed property under the terms of the peace agreement.

Conclusion

By the end of the civil war, new patterns of land tenure, land use, social organization, and rural authority had been forged in some of the case-study areas. Scores of insurgent cooperatives in Usulután and Tenancingo first

Figure 3.11 Tenancingo landlord and tenant before the war. Photograph by William Durham. Used with permission.

occupied land and then claimed it under the terms of the peace agreement. Some cooperatives formed during the agrarian reform were, by the war's end, affiliated to opposition federations of cooperatives. While most families remained desperately poor – indeed, with the collapse of government services, patron-client relations, and a sustained fall in real wages, their situation was worse at war's end despite increased access to land – social relations in the case-study areas were nevertheless transformed in two dramatic and obvious ways: the de facto transferral of agrarian property rights and the presence of *campesino* political organizations.

The best measure of the extent of land occupation by insurgent cooperatives at the end of the war is the June 1992 FMLN inventory of occupied private properties, a detailed list accepted by the commission negotiating the postwar land settlement.[10] According to that inventory, 18.5 percent of

---

[10] The peace agreement did little more than sketch the terms or scope of the land transfer to ex-combatant and FMLN supporters occupying properties. A process of bargaining between the FMLN and the government mediated by the United Nations (and, nominally, a multiparty commission set up by the agreement for the purpose) gradually defined a set of compromises (Wood 1995: chapters 5 and 6). Successive versions of the inventory were intensively debated until the commission and the government accepted the one presented

Table 3.1 *Insurgent Land Occupation at the End of the Civil War, by Department*

Department	Number of properties occupied (% of inventory properties)	Area occupied (% of inventory area)
Usulután	10.3	25.3
Chalatenango	21.2	17
San Vicente	5.4	11.7
San Miguel	7.2	11.3
Cuscatlán	10.7	8
Morazán	5.8	6.4
San Salvador	3.4	5.8
Santa Ana	0.6	4.3
Cabañas	5.7	3.3
La Paz	1.4	2.6
La Unión	0.2	1.8
La Libertad	0.4	1.8
TOTALS	4,666 properties	268,451 hectares

Note: The percentages do not sum to 100 percent, because the table excludes occupied housing sites ("human settlements") in Chalatenango and Morazán and departments with negligible occupations.

Source: Calculated from the June 1992 FMLN inventory of occupied private properties (FMLN 1992).

the nation's farmland was occupied by insurgent cooperatives at the end of the war.[11] This scale of land occupation is similar to the seizure of land in Portugal (23 percent of farmland in 12 months) by landless agrarian workers in the early 1970s (Bermeo 1986: 4). Usulután was the leading department in terms of its share of the occupied land (Table 3.1). The average size of occupied properties was significantly greater in the department than in others (with the exception of La Unión and La Libertad, where very few properties were occupied, but those few were very large). It was also the leading department in terms of the fraction of departmental area occupied, with more than double that of other departments.

The presence of the network of insurgent *campesino* organizations marked a profound change in political organization and authority from

by the FMLN in June 1992. Because the process was one of log-rolling compromises across various other issues, it is not an ideal measure. My interviews and observations in the Usulután case-study areas suggest, however, that it is in fact a fair estimate of occupied land.

[11] Calculated as a percent of 1971 farmland (from DGEC 1974: xxii).

before the war. *Campesinos*, with or without their collaborators – sometimes the FMLN, sometimes national *campesino* organizations of varying political ties – built dozens of organizations, particularly insurgent cooperatives that by late 1980s occupied tens of thousands of hectares of prime agricultural land. In these organizations, *campesinos* articulated local interests and negotiated strategies for the assertion of property rights. In sharp contrast to the prewar domination of rural social relations by a small elite and their allied security forces, *campesinos* came to lead as well as participate in *campesino* organizations, political parties, and cooperatives, an unprecedented degree of representation of and participation by a previously excluded sector. In none of the case-study areas had any such organizations existed before the civil war; yet at war's end, in some areas they comprised a vibrant local civil society. The consequences for political authority and legitimacy were profound: the local alliance of landlord and security forces that had dominated these areas no longer existed, and popular organizations contested the authority and legitimacy of those landlords and government authorities that did remain.

But contrasts across the case-study areas are equally striking. In some areas such as the northern *cantones* of Tenancingo, the Las Marías area, southwestern Jiquilisco, and north of San Francisco Javier, many *campesinos* supported insurgent organizations. In many other areas they did not, as in Santiago de María, the southern *cantones* of Tenancingo, and in much of the Usulután smallholding belt. In some areas, nonparticipation in the insurgency took the form of active support for the government, in others that of a studied neutrality. This diversity of political loyalties occurred across both smallholding areas and across agro-export areas. In some towns such as San Francisco Javier residents largely supported the FMLN; in others such as Santiago de María residents remained loyal to the government; in still others such as Tenancingo residents held widely divergent loyalties throughout the war; in yet others such as Tierra Blanca civilian supporters of either side maintained an uneasy truce.

How these dramatic changes and distinct outcomes were wrought on the landscapes of the case-study areas is the subject of the next chapters.

4

From Political Mobilization to Armed Insurgency

> Let's see why the war emerged. Perhaps – the majority say so
> anyway – because the Catholic Church gave a certain orientation.
> Perhaps the words of the Bible connected with a very deep injustice –
> they treated us like animals, it was slavery. In the Word of God,
> there was something that would touch you. In truth, we had been
> living as though the Word was in the air, when it was something to
> live within ourselves. I am grateful that there were such people,
> many of them now dead.
>
> Leader, Cooperativa El Carrizal, 1992

In response to intensifying political mobilization by *campesinos* and coffee
mill workers for access to land and higher wages in Santiago de María
in the late 1970s, Héctor Antonio Regalado, a local landlord and dentist,
began to recruit young men to what appeared to be a Boy Scout troop.
Members, who on one account may have numbered as many as a hundred,
wore uniforms in marches through town. Rather than the usual scouting
activities, however, members of Regalado's troop killed dozens of activists
and suspected activists, including teachers, unionists, cooperativists, and
students, not only in Santiago de María but in the cities of Usulután, Berlín,
Alegría, Jucuapa, Villa El Triunfo, and Chinameca. In interviews at the end
of the war, townspeople told stories of cadavers appearing at the edge of
town, of a decapitated head found in a ditch, and other public displays of
extreme violence. Like others that soon emerged throughout El Salvador,
Regalado's death squad operated with the cooperation of elements of the
Salvadoran military. The scouts were occasionally ferried around eastern
El Salvador in Army helicopters. According to two participants who worked
with him in Santiago de María, Regalado was in close touch with Roberto

d'Aubuisson, the director of death squad operations in San Salvador.[1] After d'Aubuisson's arrest for plotting an aborted coup in May 1980, Regalado fled to Guatemala and subsequently ordered the killing of his scouts, apparently fearing they knew too much. On December 27, 1980, ten were killed in Santiago.[2]

In response to the death squad's assassinations, local activists either left the area or abandoned their political activities. Throughout the 1980s, the town of Santiago was less contested than other towns in the case-study areas. The FMLN usually targeted Santiago and nearby coffee mills only during major offensives. Fighting impinged on the town only occasionally, as on October 18, 1988, when the FMLN occupied the town for several hours and destroyed three coffee mills, killing three policemen and wounding several soldiers in the process, and on March 9 and 10, 1990, when FMLN forces attacked the city, destroying one mill and causing several civilian and government casualties (Gruson 1988; El Rescate Human Rights Chronology). Nonetheless, the landlords of Santiago, including the powerful Llach and Homberger families, continued to grow coffee on nearby estates. During the harvest (when coffee wealth was at its most vulnerable to sabotage and theft) and when necessary during the rest of the year, Sixth Brigade troops occupied the town. Perhaps because of the earlier violence, there was apparently little effort to organize the workers of the coffee mills in Santiago even when the union of coffee-mill workers renewed their activities elsewhere in El Salvador in the mid-1980s.

Nonetheless, the processes of the civil war were at work in the municipality. According to interviews in the area, many landlords came under strong guerrilla pressure despite the brigade's frequent presence. Many paid war taxes to the FMLN and a few reduced their employees' hours of work in

---

[1] This history of Regalado and his death squad relies on two investigative articles by Doug Farah (1988a, 1988b), an unpublished manuscript by Tom Gibb and Farah (1989), an unpublished book manuscript by Gibb (2000), as well as my own interviews with townspeople.

[2] Regalado resurfaced in 1982 after d'Aubuisson's election to the Constituent Assembly. As head of security for the subsequent Legislative Assembly, Regalado directed death squads in San Salvador until a group of businessmen complained to d'Aubuisson that he might be killing too many people. Regalado briefly appeared on the U.S. Embassy payroll as a shooting instructor for the Drug Enforcement Agency in 1987. Gibb and Farah (1989) began their investigation after rumors circulated that d'Aubuisson and Regalado were again rebuilding the death squads after ARENA's legislative victories in 1988. See also Americas Watch (1991: 24) and the report of the Truth Commission (1993: 359 and 408, nn. 412 and 413).

response to FMLN efforts to regulate working conditions. The FMLN prohibited some from selling their land, claiming it as "land of the people." The presence of reform cooperatives just east and south of the town was a constant reminder of the government's 1980 expropriations. The wealthy families of Santiago de María spent much less time in their residences there than before the war, preferring their San Salvador residences to the difficulties of travel on often insecure roads. And just over the El Tigre ridge from Santiago, the Las Marías area became a center of military activity; landlords there abandoned their farms entirely.

Repression in Santiago had the intended consequence of suppressing political mobilization in the town's mills and streets. A similar degree of state violence occurred throughout the case-study areas. Elsewhere in the case-study areas, however, repression had more complicated consequences. While repression everywhere ended political mobilization in the form of strikes and demonstrations for many years, many activists joined the armed insurgency. By 1983, their numbers throughout El Salvador were sufficient that FMLN forces controlled approximately a fifth of national territory, a "revolutionary situation" (Tilly 1993: 10) of contested or even dual sovereignty in El Salvador. Despite subsequent strategic and tactical innovations on the part of both the Salvadoran military and the FMLN, the military stalemate continued until the end of the civil war. In this chapter, I document the course of the civil war in the case-study areas, from the its origins in prewar political mobilization to the emergence of the military stalemate.

Political Mobilization in Tenancingo

The organizing began in 1976, a mix of young adults and elders.
It was Biblical study that made people conscious, a process
that eventually took another form. By means of the Bible it all
began.

Campesina, Tenancingo, 1987

It was like a plague that kept advancing, because they obtained the support of the Tenancingo parish priest. That's where the god of the poor and the god of the rich were born.

Tenancingo businessman, 1987

The history of the civil war in the municipality of Tenancingo was one of profound divisions: divisions within *cantones*, within the town, and between the northern and southern *cantones*.[3] Some residents of the northern *cantones* who became participants in the insurgency began by joining Bible study groups organized by Catholic priests and catechists, which seem to have been fairly widespread in the northern part of the municipality. Residents recall that while some catechists were from the local parish, others were from outside Tenancingo. While it is difficult to recreate the pattern or content of the meetings (residents' memories of later violence against group members appeared stronger than memories of what the study groups actually did), the catechists met at least occasionally with the brothers José Inocencio Alas and Higinio Alas, activist priests of the parish of Suchitoto, the municipality bordering Tenancingo to the north.[4]

The Alas brothers were part of the liberation theology movement that fundamentally reshaped the Latin American Catholic Church in the late 1960s and 1970s. In light of the call from the meeting of the world's bishops known as Vatican II (1962–4) for renewal of the Church through a more direct engagement with "the world," as well as their own growing concern about the enduring poverty in Latin America, many Latin American priests, nuns, lay theologians, and activists reevaluated their pastoral and spiritual practices in order to deepen their involvement with issues of social justice (Smith 1991). Because representatives of this movement dominated a meeting of Latin American bishops held in Medellín in 1968, the conference called for the Latin American Church to make a "preferential option for the poor." This was understood as a fundamental reorientation of religious faith that emphasized the presence of God in the lives of the poor and that required a radical concentration of services and resources in poor neighborhoods and villages (Gutiérrez 1973; CELAM 1978; Ellacuría and Sobrino 1991). As many nuns and priests abandoned their middle-class schools and hospitals for the poor villages of the countryside and the desperate shantytowns of the urban periphery, deep divisions emerged within the Church across Latin America. In answer to the Pope's call for missionaries in Latin America, many North American and European priests and nuns joined them in their new ministry.

---

[3] This history of the civil war in Tenancingo is based on interviews conducted in 1987, 1988, 1989, and 1991 with residents, FMLN and military officers, and landlords displaced from the municipality, as well as secondary evidence.

[4] I could not find any of the Tenancingo catechists to interview. They apparently had been killed, were with the guerrillas, or were still displaced from the area.

The Alas brothers were key figures in the spread of both liberation theology practices and opposition organizations in north-central El Salvador. Beginning in 1969, José Inocencio Alas organized base Christian communities, small groups of perhaps a dozen or two people who met weekly to reflect on biblical readings and local events (Pearce 1986: 102–3; Montgomery 1995: 97–9). The process included visits to *cantones* and individual homes and the training of community representatives as catechists. The Suchitoto parish was one of thirteen parishes in the Archdiocese of San Salvador in which priests were applying liberation theology teachings (as were twenty communities of nuns in the diocese; Rivera Damas 1977: 810). In 1974, the Alas brothers called a national meeting of *campesino* organizations, university groups, and trade unions in Suchitoto to protest the high cost of living and the imminent displacement of hundreds of families due to the construction of the Cerrón Grande dam.

Among the participants were representatives of the Federación Cristiana de Campesinos Salvadoreños (the Christian Federation of Salvadoran Campesinos, or FECCAS) from the town of Aguilares, twenty kilometers northwest of Tenancingo. In Aguilares, a group of Jesuits was particularly effective in implementing the new pastoral practices of liberation theology. The Jesuits and their team of catechists and seminarians began their work in 1972, living for two weeks in each *cantón* of the parish, visiting and eating with families and recruiting catechists who participated in short training courses that emphasized group reflection on the structures of sin, violence, and oppression.

According to Carlos Rafael Cabarrús, a Guatemalan Jesuit and anthropologist who was part of the Aguilares pastoral team, this new style of pastoral work with its emphasis on history and liberation caused an "unblocking" of traditional *campesino* fatalism (Cabarrús 1985: 135). Another Jesuit analyst of the Aguilares experience observed that catechists and some other parishioners "realized that it was not the will of God that things continue unchanged. In effect, the mission's preaching had lowered God from the clouds and presented him as Yahweh, God of history" (Cardenal 1985: 259). As a result, many actively committed themselves to work for justice and peace, even if it meant giving their lives: "[T]he absolute 'No' of God toward injustice demanded as well a 'Yes' toward justice and peace" (ibid.: 261). The priests explicitly denounced injustices from the pulpit and recorded the abusive harvest practices of local landlords. As parishioners increasingly identified with "Jesús Rebelde" (Rebel

91

Jesus), their gathering refusal "to accept present inequality in exchange for equality after death" broke the dominant ideology (ibid.: 272). Participants began to develop a new confidence in themselves as they discovered their ability to develop and express opinions in public and a new solidarity among themselves in place of their traditional identification with the *patrón*.

The existence of a network of active intermediaries (the catechists) linking the *cantones* and the parish facilitated the entry of FECCAS organizers into the *cantones*. However, the draining of delegates from parish work toward more political work caused increasing tension among the parish team, who struggled to find ways of supporting the organization without identifying the parish with it (Cardenal 1985: 472–4).

This tension deepened after the FPL changed its strategy in 1974 to emphasize the building of an alliance between workers and *campesinos*, particularly agricultural workers and those small holders who depended on wages as well as farm production (Pearce 1986: chapter 4; Harnecker 1993: 109–10). The strategy emphasized the development of mass organizations in which mobilized workers and *campesinos* would fight for their needs; through the process of so doing, they would come to recognize the need for armed struggle. By 1975, FECCAS was "under the guidance" of the FPL (Harnecker 1993: 126–7) and began to recruit party cadres in the Aguilares area. The fast growth of the FPL in this period is probably due more to the close ties between the FPL and progressive Catholic priests than the worker-peasant alliance per se (Gibb 2000: 47). According to Cabarrús, similarities between liberation theology and revolutionary ideology contributed to the FPL's appeal: both emphasized structural injustice and the need for a new social order, and both drew on a central faith and demanded passionate commitment to a shared creed.

The Suchitoto meeting in 1974 was one of the first national meetings attended by both rural and urban organizations. Coordination across organizations deepened in the following months.[5] After several university students on a march in San Salvador were killed by security forces on July 30, 1975, several organizations occupied the San Salvador cathedral and founded the Bloque Popular Revolucionario (Popular Revolutionary Block, or BPR), a coalition of rural and urban organizations. The BPR was soon the largest popular organization in the country, capable of mobilizing

---

[5] At the 1974 Suchitoto meeting, the Frente de Acción Popular (Front for Popular Action) was founded, the first opposition organization uniting rural and urban groups.

tens of thousands of Salvadorans, even, on occasion, hundreds of thousands. From its founding, several leaders were in contact with the FPL (and a few key leaders were party members).

This mobilization of *campesinos*, workers, and students met with increasing repression on the part of the state security forces. Particularly targeted were those elements of the Church that were seen as having encouraged *campesino* mobilization, especially after the Church opposed the suspension of the 1976 agrarian reform (Cardenal 1985: 509). In 1977, Rutilio Grande, a Salvadoran Jesuit and the parish priest of Aguilares, was killed as part of a rightist campaign in which more than thirty priests were jailed, tortured, expelled, or assassinated (Cabarrús 1983: 285). Aguilares itself was occupied for a month by the military in response to a series of land occupations in the surrounding area. In the same year, the government expelled the Alas brothers from the country. But this campaign against the liberation church backfired. Rather than deepening fear, it appeared to have invoked the 2,000-year history of Christian martyrdom (Gibb 2000: 63). In the aftermath of this violence, several of the opposition organizations created closer ties with the as yet-tiny revolutionary groups. By 1979, the BPR was closely tied to the FPL.

Tenancingo's proximity to the Suchitoto parish contributed to the founding of Bible study groups in the poor northern *cantones*: Rosario Périco, Santa Anita, and La Cruz. No doubt their isolation from municipal life centered in the Villa was another factor. The residents of the Villa became aware of the extent of the organizing in the northern *cantones* when a series of marches and rallies took place in the Villa in 1979 and 1980. Marchers, both people from the *cantones* and Villa teenagers, carried posters through the streets to the central square, an unprecedented display of dissent. They briefly took over the church before returning to the *cantones*. One well-off woman fearfully recalled her reaction: "It scared me. They spoke of injustices, of class struggle. They were influencing people of little schooling with such things" (San Salvador, 1987).

In interviews, well-off former residents of Tenancingo stressed the presence of two teenagers from "outside" who gave political talks and organized meetings under the cover of holding services of a gnostic sect. One emphasized the role of the parish priest, perhaps because the priest had invited him to a meeting where the priest discussed the agrarian reform of 1976, an action sufficient to label anyone an activist regardless of their actual organizational ties. The priest does not appear to have played a significant role; other Villa residents did not mention his involvement. Those interviewed tended to see the Catholic Church in general, and the Alas brothers in particular, as the catalysts for the unrest. One Tenancingo landlord told me:

I understood them [the Alas brothers] to be revolutionary; they had studied outside the country. It was such priests who spoke of social injustice, who organized the Federation. It began in Medellín where a group of young Latin American priests started a theology of two gods – they were with the poor, not the rich. (San Salvador, 1987)

He paused, and then continued, "I only know one god." The only explanation for the unrest advanced by Villa elites was the proximity of those *cantones* to Suchitoto and the "*ideologías comunistas*" of the Alas brothers; the poverty of the *cantones* did not figure as a factor. Their memories of the Villa evoked nostalgia for a better past, "How beautiful it was, a town of commerce."

The response of the authorities to the growth of these groups was severe. According to a *campesina* who was a child at the time of the initial violence in Rosario Périco,

I, my mother and father, and my little brother all left. We left because of the persecution of the army. We hadn't committed any crime – we had only tried to participate in the movement of Jesus Christ and Monseñor Romero. The Armed Forces came to the house, asked questions, and threatened Papa with a pistol to the head and a machine gun to the neck, wounding him four times. They took him and my three brothers prisoner and held him in Cojutepeque for a year. (Interview, Tenancingo, 1987)

She continued, "They forced me to point out people and then shot them. We left when my father returned from prison." After describing this incident, she continued:

They burned the houses and fields, they poisoned the water and killed whomever they saw. They took people out at night and disappeared them. During each invasion people were killed; perhaps a majority of the people died – pregnant mothers, kids, all and everyone. It was a time of great hunger and we hid in the mountains. The Red Cross took us from the *cantón* to a refugee camp.

This first wave of violence took place in 1976 in Rosario Périco. Other waves soon followed in this most conflicted of *cantones*. Her story is typical of those told by participants in the early mobilization: repression followed hard on the heels of the emergence of base Christian communities, particularly after members participated in political meetings. Some families fled to "the mountains" where they attempted to join with FPL forces, others to refugee camps or to the anonymity of urban shantytowns.

In light of her overall testimony, I believe this second, more general denunciation is a "community memory" of repressive events, many of which took place in Périco *after* she and her family had left for the refugee camp. What is clear from her testimony is that the distinction is for her unimportant; she appeared to understand the repression as having been directed against and suffered by an entire community for whom she is the voice. This role parallels that of Rigoberta Menchú, who misrepresented some violent events and ignored others in telling her life story, apparently representing the experiences of the indigenous people of Guatemala, rather than her own individual experience (Stoll 1999).

Some of the violence against the activists of the northern *cantones* was carried out by local members of the Organización Democrática Nationalista (Democratic Nationalist Organization, or ORDEN, which means "order" in Spanish), essentially a national civilian auxiliary of the National Guard. ORDEN was present in virtually every *cantón* of Tenancingo at least as early as 1975.[6] According to a Villa landlord, there were approximately thirty members of ORDEN in the municipality. Incentives to join ORDEN included access to farming supplies, health care, education, jobs, and protection from repression by the National Guard (Cabarrús 1983; Pearce 1986). The Christian Democrat mayor from 1980 to 1982 confirmed to me ORDEN's presence during that period and stated, "They mistreated people: people were killed simply because ORDEN did not like them." She linked ORDEN with the local military reserve force (*escolta militar*):

In every *canton*, there was an *escolta militar* with a commander and eleven members. Beginning in 1975 or 1976, the Federation [FECCAS] was organizing in some places. By 1978 the violence was tremendous here. An informer, usually a member of the *escolta militar* and of ORDEN, would advise the National Guard and soon the troops would arrive. (Interview, San Salvador, 1987)

One well-to-do landlord stated that the repression against Périco and El Pepeto was particularly brutal because those *cantones* had voted for the Christian Democratic candidate in municipal elections.

The surrounding area was convulsed as well. In the nearby town of San Pedro Perulapán, a series of violent encounters between mobilized campesinos and ORDEN members culminated in the execution of five ORDEN members by the FPL (Pearce 1986: 176). On March 30,

---

[6] Interview with William and Kathleen Durham, Stanford, California, April 1988.

1978, the Treasury Police, the National Guard, the National Police, and ORDEN mounted a major military operation in the area southwest of Tenancingo. Centered on San Pedro Perulapán, the sweep of a thousand-square-kilometer area left 68 disappeared, six dead, and 14 wounded (Cabarrús 1983: 301). Activists fled to neighboring municipalities, including Tenancingo, where they were again confronted by military troops and armed ORDEN members.

By 1979, the FPL had established a permanent presence in the Tenancingo area. According to an FPL member from Tenancingo, their first activity in the northern *cantones* was the execution of several people (most of them ORDEN members) believed by local activists to have been government informers. They also extorted "war taxes" from people who still had stores or other vulnerable enterprises north of the Villa. They strengthened their presence significantly when the National Guard withdrew from the Villa during most of 1980 and part of 1981, as part of a brief national policy of concentrating troops in regional headquarters. On January 24, 1980, the guerrillas took over the town, calling everyone to a meeting in the park. They demanded that the assembled population make a spontaneous judgment of ORDEN members and the Christian Democratic mayor. The population supported the mayor, who was released. The guerrillas then locked the ORDEN members in the church and destroyed the guard post, the mayor's office, and the community center. The FPL continued this campaign against the town elites, for example, by burning the tobacco ovens belonging to the mayor's husband and stealing fifty-seven cows. No one was killed, but elite families began to leave the Villa. The mayor, who stated she did not know who was responsible, left the Villa with her family for San Salvador within a few months. She remarked with sadness, "A lifetime's work was destroyed in a few days" (San Salvador, 1987).

Government forces soon responded. On March 22, 1980, the military attacked the *cantón* of Rosario Périco in force. According to one resident,

We suffered a lot from the violence. My father died, the Armed Forces killed him during the first invasion, it was 1980. I felt crazy; I still feel desperate sometimes; I feel traumatized. We watched his death. They really messed him up. An uncle was also killed. They had participated in the Bible studies. (Tenancingo, 1987)

The attack left nine residents dead. The remaining population fled the *cantón*, some to refugee camps, others to join the guerrillas in hidden camps, others to the Villa. Some of the families of other northern *cantones* began sleeping in the Villa in order to avoid being denounced as guerrilla supporters, equivalent to a death sentence at the time. After the post was reestablished in the Villa in 1981, the National Guard began making more frequent forays into the *cantones*, particularly El Pepeto, where they attacked families whose younger members had joined the guerrillas.

It is difficult to establish the precise relationship in the northern *cantones* between the Bible study groups, the opposition organizations, and the FPL in this period (1979–80). They appeared to have been mutually supportive. Many members of the base Christian communities welcomed the FPL and facilitated their presence in the area. In any case, the security forces made few distinctions between liberationist pastoral workers, politically active *campesinos*, and the FPL guerrillas. One Villa woman recalled:

The Guard killed three teenagers. The families all had to leave. Women bringing in food were accused of supplying the guerrillas. They [the guardsmen] threatened church-goers. People continued going to church, but fearfully. Even the priest was questioned by the soldiers. (Tenancingo, 1987)

As a result of the intensifying conflict, by 1981, El Périco, La Cruz, and Copalchán were deserted, and El Pepeto nearly so.

While these government measures effectively suppressed ordinary political mobilization for many years, they merely redirected the insurgency. One of the most astute local observers dates the taking up of arms on the part of many of the residents of the northern *cantones* to the 1980 attack on *cantón* Rosario Périco. One women recalled several teenagers who subsequently left the Villa to join the guerrilla forces, including one who did so after being forced by the guard to watch the killing of his father. During subsequent guerrilla attacks, townspeople recognized five guerrillas as former residents of the municipality.

Similar acts of repression took place across El Salvador in late 1979 and early 1980 as violence deepened in the aftermath of the coup by junior officers. By late 1980, the guerrilla organizations, particularly the FPL as a result of its stronger political organizations, had far more volunteers than they had arms (Gibb 2000: 103).

In contrast to the devastated and depopulated *cantones* north of Tenancingo, the southern *cantones* – Santa Anita, Hacienda Nueva, Ajuluco, Corral Viejo, and Rosario Tablón – were not abandoned. While a few residents may have participated in Bible study groups, most did not. Some adult males joined civil defense patrols in Santa Anita, Hacienda Nueva, and Ajuluco and received arms and training from the military detachment in Cojutepeque. The FMLN occasionally attacked the patrols, but in general there was much less mobilization and significantly less violence in the southern *cantones*. Typically, some family members left with the children for the safety of San Martín, Cojutepeque, or San Salvador during periods of fighting, while others remained behind to cultivate their small holdings.

In 1983, the FMLN twice attacked government forces and civil defense patrols in the Villa. During both attacks, the FMLN forced the National Guard and civil defense forces to retreat and then briefly occupied the central buildings. The first attack occurred on July 3. According to a well-informed local source, the attack resulted in thirty to fifty deaths, of which ten to twenty were members of the civil defense patrols. Most of the Villa residents left the town for Santa Cruz Michapa (the nearest town) and Cojutepeque. After a meeting of regional civilian and military authorities, the Cojutepeque army commander insisted the families return to the Villa and provided a dozen trucks for the trip from Cojutepeque to Tenancingo. The few remaining well-off families who were present at the time of the first attack did not return.

On September 24, the FMLN again attacked the town, despite the presence of hundreds of soldiers of the Jaguar Battalion. It was during this attack that the bombing of the town described in Chapter 2 occurred. Residents of the Villa fled to Santa Cruz Michapa, where the local nun, Madre Ivonne de Groot, helped with food and medicine. Some then went to the outskirts of the nearby towns of San Martín and Cojutepeque. A few went on to San Salvador and a very few to the United States. The town itself was completely deserted. The last hundred residents – the poorest, who had returned to the town after the bombing – were evacuated for fear of an epidemic due to the presence of unburied corpses (Americas Watch 1986: 79). The battle left deep emotional scars on residents, particularly those who lost family members. One resident whose grandmother and two aunts were killed during the battle reflected years later, "The Day of the Dead is quite difficult: there are only mass graves and we did not even hold a wake" (Tenancingo, 1991).

For those displaced to shantytowns, the difficulties of obtaining cash for firewood, food, and rent were only partially alleviated by help from Madre Ivonne, charities, or government agencies. Those interviewed after their return to Tenancingo told of their suffering as exiles from their town or *cantón*, including frequent moves from one place to another, family separations induced by alcoholism (often made worse by displacement from home), and the difficulty of obtaining food without cash.

In contrast, life in exile for elite families of the Villa was challenging, but most rebuilt some degree of prosperity through loans and connections. The hat-factory owners took advantage of marketing contacts in San Salvador to resettle there; one established a new factory, another began with just a few sewing machines, a third marketed hats. The large landowners settled in Cojutepeque or San Salvador, occasionally traveling to the southern *cantones* to manage farms in relatively safe areas. Antonio Vargas, the entrepreneurial businessman introduced in the previous chapter, became a member of the national savings and loan association. One son became an engineer in the United States, the other, a treasurer of a principal national business organization. Not all did so well. The Christian Democrat mayor and her husband lived in a small San Salvador apartment, which was all they could afford on his salary as a minor civil servant. She commented, "It is hard to be an employee after being your own boss, with your own business. It would be nice to have even a little house" (San Salvador, 1987).

Mobilization in Usulután

As in Tenancingo, new pastoral practices on the part of the Catholic Church played a significant role in the emergence of political mobilization in Usulután in the early and mid-1970s.[7] Several activists, when I asked how the war emerged in the area, began their history with the arrival of catechists: "Catechists arrived in the area with courses on how to improve the community. That's how the orientation began, in a language you could understand: as human beings, we are of value" (Cooperativa Mate de Pina, 1992). One leader of the 1970s mobilization in Tierra Blanca recalled: "It was a language which you could understand, for example, how was land distributed in the time of Jesus Christ? As a consequence, it was clear that we have rights as human persons. That's how it captivated so many people" (San Marcos Lempa, 1992). The "orientation" described in the opening quote of this chapter was conveyed in part by local priests (some of whose names were explicitly recalled in interviews), but more frequently by lay catechists. Several residents who eventually became local insurgent leaders became

---

[7] This section relies principally on the recollections of *campesinos* resident in the area at the time but draws also on interviews with landlords and pastoral workers of the Catholic Church. In contrast to Tenancingo, there are few other sources of information on the civil war in Usulután.

catechists after attending training courses at one of the *centros de formación campesina* (*campesino* training centers) sponsored by the Catholic Church in Jiquilisco and in Chirilagua, San Miguel (just across the border).[8] These two centers offered month-long courses that emphasized the development of *campesino* leaders committed to organizing for social justice (Peterson 1997: 55–8; Binford 2003). One resident of Tierra Blanca described to me his training during this period:

I studied pastoral work for several months at the centers and went to seminars in Jiquilisco, San Marcos Lempa, El Triunfo, and Coyolito. I worked as a catechist for ten years. But the rich were killing the people so I joined the BPR in 1976 as a way to fight back. (Tierra Blanca, 1992)

Many more residents attended events sponsored by the centers throughout the province. An ERP commander who held various command positions in Usulután throughout the war emphasized to me the contribution of the catechists:

It all began with the *concientización* [consciousness-raising] through small Christian groups who eventually began to carry out revolutionary work. For the first years, it was all religious activity and protests, only later was it demonstrations. (Las Marías, September 1992)

One elderly resident recalled, "The Bloque Popular came to the churches, and that's how it began – only afterward did they come to the *cantones* and the towns."

However, the influence of new pastoral practices appears to have been less important in the Usulután field sites than in Suchitoto, Aguilares, or Tenancingo. In contrast to the sustained and geographically focused work of the Jesuit team in Aguilares, efforts in Usulután were more diffuse. A few priests were supportive of liberation theology and base Christian communities, but most were not. Some activists shrugged off the contribution of religious agents in their locality with remarks such as "Yes, there were some efforts like that here, they tried to get people to believe in the possibility of economic and social change, but there was nothing concrete, there were no Christian base communities or anything like that" (San Francisco Javier,

---

[8] Leigh Binford (2003) points out that analysis of the impact of liberation theology in El Salvador has overemphasized the role of prominent priests, neglecting the significant role played by the "army of lay peasant and worker catechists" trained at the centers.

1992). One activist emphasized the use of training in religious centers as a cover for political organizing:

Here there were people working for the emergence of the Frente [FMLN]. It is correct to mention the Catholic Church and the university of the *campesinos*. Strategically, they [the *campesino* training centers] taught with the Bible in hand, but in truth the purpose was to orient us to our own reality. These people moved about under the cover of the church itself; they were the beginnings of the FMLN. (Las Marías, 1992)

In contrast to interviews in Tenancingo, most activists interviewed in the Usulután case-study areas emphasized the role of the popular organizations in the mobilization of the 1970s, rather than that of catechists, as in this statement by a long-term Tierra Blanca activist (1991):

From 1975 on, the popular organizations appeared, a whole series of unarmed popular organizations demanding better wages, agrarian reform, and a just distribution of land. Although the Christian Democrats decreed the agrarian reform to calm the people, the organizations went on creating structures, of which one was the Frente. Many decided to join the struggle as members of the FMLN, taking up arms for precisely this, the just distribution of land.

In some areas, the trajectory to mobilization and insurgency was mixed. According to a long-term activist with *campesino* organizations, a working-class resident of Santiago de María before the war and later a member of the ERP,

We in Santiago de María got involved with Christian Democracy, the only political expression in Santiago before 1974, through the Catholic Church. Then from 1974 to 1978, many of those *compañeros* joined – we joined – the struggle via clandestine organizations and semi-clandestine organizations. From there some of us joined the FMLN. (San Francisco Javier, 1992)

Despite the relative absence of activist priests and nuns in Usulután, the seminars and courses appeared to have an enduring impact on many *campesinos*, reflecting the power of the new practices and ideas under the prevailing conditions of poverty and uncertainty. The physical location in Jiquilisco of one of the most important training centers probably contributed. In contrast to northern Morazán, where most catechists were from smallholding families and thus more able to afford to miss work during the long training courses held far away at the coastal centers (Binford 2003), catechists in Usulután appeared have been quite heterogeneous and included significant numbers of landless workers, perhaps because it was easier to combine attendance with work when living nearby.

According to locals involved at the time, urban student activists arrived in 1972. But they found the well-controlled rural areas of Usulután difficult to organize. A few years later, the BPR began to organize along the Jiquilisco coast and soon proved significantly more successful than the students had been. By the late 1970s, the Ligas Populares "28 de febrero" (February 28 Popular Leagues), an opposition organization founded in 1976 by the ERP as an above-ground political organization with covert ties to the party, was also active in Usulután, particularly in San Agustín, Santa Elena, the Las Marías area, and Jucuarán.

Overt political unrest along the Jiquilisco coastal plain initially took the form of labor mobilization under the auspices of the BPR. In the late 1970s, some workers participated in strikes for higher wages and shorter workdays on farms south of the coastal highway. On one or two occasions, workers struck with enough support to blockade the coastal highway during the harvest period, winning a wage increase. Particularly effective during a strike on the Hacienda California and the La Maroma farm south of Tierra Blanca was the refusal to harvest cotton until concessions were made. A few acts of large-scale sabotage were also carried out, such as the burning of some properties planted in cotton in 1979 and 1980. As a result of these unprecedented activities, workers in the immediate area gained sufficient confidence to institute a shorter workday by simply refusing to work past a certain hour.

Guerrilla groups began organizing clandestinely in the southwestern Jiquilisco area in the mid-1970s. Despite the widespread presence of paramilitary networks (including ORDEN), several small cells of committed participants were formed by the FPL and the ERP. According to one commander native to the area who joined the ERP early on, while some cells were developed south of the coastal highway, the most fertile initial organizing grounds were the smallholding communities north of the highway, where many families farmed their own land but also relied on wage labor. Recruitment to the guerrilla cells was an extremely clandestine activity that put a premium on insurgent security, a contrast to the pattern in Morazán where recruitment was a more open process, with members recruiting a certain quota from their extended families (Binford 1997).

The ERP had been founded in 1972 by a heterogenous group of students influenced by Marxism and by progressive Christianity, which included some members of evangelical churches.[9] After carrying out a series of urban actions such as demonstrations and strikes in San Salvador and San Miguel, the group decided to focus their efforts in Morazán, in part because they could build on the pastoral work of Father Miguel Ventura, a radical priest influential there despite the hostility of other priests and the local bishop (Raudales and Medrano 1994: 67). The ERP at first exclusively emphasized the development of military organizations, in contrast to the FPL's dual emphasis on building relatively autonomous political organizations as well as military cells. In 1975, the ERP moderated its militaristic vision after its leaders murdered one of its most prestigious members, well-known poet Roque Dalton, having incorrectly suspected him of being a CIA spy. This catastrophic event resulted in the split of the ERP and the exit of many of the more moderate intellectuals to found a rival guerrilla organization, the National Resistance. The ERP's Morazán army grew quickly in the late 1970s and early 1980s and became one of the most militarily effective guerrilla forces.

The response by the security forces to overt mobilization and covert organizing along the Usulután coast was severe, and it intensified as unrest continued. The military began arming the military reserve forces in the *cantones* of southwestern Jiquilisco as early as 1975. As elsewhere in El Salvador, the security forces did not discriminate between those who participated in the armed insurgency and those involved in the labor organizing efforts. Family members were frequently considered targets equal to the activists themselves. In 1975, after activists occupied the coastal highway near San Marcos Lempa and then retreated northward toward the *cantón* of Tres Calles, members of the National Guard killed all but one of the members of the Otorga family in their home in the *cantón*, including one twelve-year-old boy, although the activist members of the household were not present.[10] This was one of the earliest and most public acts by security forces in the coastal area. The frequency with which residents told the story (with varying dates) suggests it remained a traumatic memory for many, one probably reinforced by its role as a rallying cry for opposition organizations. The Tres Calles attack was far from an isolated event. Residents of the Usulután case-study areas consistently described the late 1970s and early

---

[9] On the history of the ERP, see Raudales and Medrano (1994), Montgomery (1995: 101–25), Binford (1997, 1999), and Gibb (2000).

[10] The Tres Calles attack was denounced by *campesino* organizations at the time (see Amnesty International 1977: 3) and in testimony to the U.S. Congress by William L. Wipfler (1976).

1980s as a period of extreme violence by government forces, sometimes on the heels of a guerrilla incursion or assassination but often not. Residents of a *cantón* near San Francisco Javier described a rising tide of state violence between 1979 and 1984 that began with detentions and beatings, escalated to disappearances of leaders and the mass rape of eight women by the local civil defense force, and culminated in the assassination of several residents who had participated in marches and strikes. A woman who lived in Tierra Blanca recalled:

During the war, there were nights when no one slept – explosions first on one side, then the other. Every day in 1980 trucks left the town, carrying away yet more families. From 14 de Julio [a town north of the coastal highway] to here are buried rows of dead men and women, who knows exactly where! To go forward to claim formally the dead – they would punish you as well. So people were just buried in the field, alongside the road. In Tierra Blanca, some are buried in front of the school and three are buried in our yard. (Interview, Tierra Blanca, 1992)

By 1980, many activists throughout Usulután no longer slept at home, preferring the discomfort of sleeping outdoors to the threat of unwelcome midnight visitors. Following a successful strike on a coastal farm, the BPR organizer of the strike was killed. According to a participant, the farm administrator was an ex-military man who "had his friends." As state violence deepened throughout El Salvador in early 1980, it reached new levels in Usulután as well. The National Guard burned two people alive near Tierra Blanca in February 1980, according to the brother of one of the victims. One activist who lived just north of the coastal highway recalled, "At the beginning, the army would arrive so infuriated, so bitter, that before they even know who you were, they would shoot. They did not respect either color or size. We were so fearful at nightfall that we would not sleep. Miraculously we survived, but many did not" (Los Horcones, 1992).

Violence and terror also spread in the highlands as Regalado's death squad carried out dozens of murders in late 1979 and early 1980 in Santiago de María and surrounding areas. One resident of the Las Marías area remarked on the consequences of participation in opposition activity with a gruesome pun on the dentist's name using the word *regalados*, which refers to an object given as a gift: "The popular organizations were very militant by 1980 but they were neutralized by the large scale of the repression. It was tragic to see the *compañeros* taken from their houses and *regalados* in the streets" (resident, Las Marías, 1992). A middle-class Christian Democrat who lived through the war in Santiago stated simply,

"It was not possible to denounce the killings. The local judge was himself killed by unknown men. Out of fear, we all stayed in a single bedroom. We still never visit other people, or have people over" (Santiago de María, 1992).

As elsewhere in El Salvador, the assassination of Archbishop Romero in 1980 led many hitherto nonviolent activists to join or actively to support the guerrillas. Many were familiar with Romero because he had served as bishop of Santiago de María for several years before his appointment as Archbishop of San Salvador in 1977. Many of the former catechists interviewed noted that his pastoral leadership in the earlier period was conservative, which was difficult to square with his later role as spokesman against the violence of the late 1970s. One *campesino*, a teenager in the mid-1970s, described Romero's influence on his emergence as an activist as follows:

I grew up with my grandparents. There was already talk of movements but my grandmother said to me that it was the beginning of communism. They [landlords, local authorities] painted a false hell for us: even as they exploited us, they taught us that it was the poor who were thieves and the rich who were the good people. And it was the poor who were sent to jail.

He continued,

But there was one who saw the necessities of the people: Archbishop Romero. He formed a *campesino* school and many priests supported it. Then I liked going to Mass, they spoke of politics. He was bishop of Santiago de María, at the time still soft-spoken, not yet with his later confidence. Injustice had not yet grabbed him. I never did learn the mentality of the rich; I left home rather than listen. (San Pedro Arenales, 1992)

But this attribution to Romero of an important early role in the formation of *campesino* centers was not true. Indeed, at one point he closed down one of them and allowed its reopening only after the murder of five catechists (Gibb 2000: 56–7). Some *campesinos* believed that until he became archbishop, Romero was afraid to speak out, that it was his later exposure to the militant urban movements of San Salvador that gave him courage. Others saw his lack of overt militancy as strategic; conditions were not yet ripe. In any case, a number of insurgent *campesinos* explicitly traced their decision to support the FMLN to his assassination: "When they killed the bishop, that's when it began. It was necessary to give a response, and there weren't any other ideas really but to do what was called 'organizing', organizing ourselves in cells of two or three people committed to social change" (Cooperative Tesoro, 1992).

Agrarian Reform in Usulután

How the agrarian reform was designed was one thing; it was
something else how it happened.

Leader, Cooperativa La Maroma, 1992

Repression was not the sole response of the state to political mobilization.
On March 6 and 7, 1980, technicians from the Instituto Salvadoreño para
Transformación Agraria (Salvadoran Institute for Agrarian Transformation)
arrived at almost a hundred of the largest haciendas of El Salvador, accompanied by truckloads of soldiers. They announced that the properties were
now the property of a cooperative to be formed immediately; the soldiers
assured the listeners that the intervention had the support of the military.
According to a leader of a reform cooperative in Jiquilisco, Cooperative
Nancuchiname (San Marcos Lempa, 1992), "The troops arrived and took
over the property from one night to the next day. We didn't know what
'agrarian reform' meant. 'This is yours now,' they said, 'and you'll have to
pay for it.'" Another leader added, "They just arrived at the hacienda, never
had they given any notice or education. They didn't explain a thing. They
gave us the land, but with the intention of wiping out the movement." Another remembered the event as threatening: "They just said to the people:
sign up here! And gave out a form. Some did not want to join because of
fear. We still have people who are not members, who prefer not to join for
that reason."

The affected haciendas were believed to exceed the new ceiling of
500 hectares for landholding.[11] According to the reform legislation, the affected landlords would be compensated and the reform beneficiaries would
assume a debt to the state under significantly subsidized terms (the assessed
value of the property was to be paid to the state over thirty years at an
interest rate of 6 percent). Those eligible to become members of the new
cooperative were the salaried employees, the tenants, and the *colonos* resident on the estate. The members elected leaders and generally continued to
work the properties as before under the tutelage of government technicians
(many of whom were former managers of the farm retained by the agrarian
reform agency). By December 1982, the number of farms affected by what
was termed "Phase I" of the agrarian reform had risen to 328 and by 1990

[11] More precisely, if the total area owned by an individual, perhaps comprised by a number
of separate farms, exceeded 500 hectares, the farms were subject to expropriation with the
exception of a "reserve right" of 100 to 150 hectares.

From Political Mobilization to Armed Insurgency

Figure 4.1 Agrarian reform cooperatives in Usulután. Based on a wall map in the Usulután office of the Eastern Region of the Institute Salvadoreña de Transformación Agraria. Courtesy of the Regional Director.

to 477 properties, comprising 13.1 percent of land suitable for agriculture and forestry in El Salvador (calculated from PERA 1991: 4).

Usulután was the department most affected by this phase of the agrarian reform. Approximately 15 percent of the area appropriated was in Usulután. An impression of its extent can be seen in Figure 4.1, based on a tracing I made in 1991 of a map hanging on a wall of the regional office of the Phase I implementing agency.[12] Jiquilisco itself was among the municipalities most affected. More than 18,000 hectares were distributed

---

[12] In addition to the area being greatest, more properties were affected in Usulután than anywhere else (PERA 1989: Anexo I; PERA 1991: Anexo I). La Libertad was nearly as affected; but after the deletion of reserve rights and natural reserves, the area assigned to cooperatives was highest in Usulután.

to eleven cooperatives, of which eight fell in the case-study area of western Jiquilisco.[13] Two cooperatives were founded in Santiago de María, and several in the nearby municipalities of Tecapán, Berlín, and Ozatlán.

A few months later, the government announced the third phase of the agrarian reform, whereby tenants could become owners of their rented plots. (The second phase, which would have seen the expropriation of properties between 100 and 500 hectares – and therefore of a significant fraction of coffee holdings – was never implemented). U.S. advisers had insisted on this "land-to-the-tiller" program as key to counterinsurgency efforts and conditioned U.S. economic and military assistance on it.[14] Under the program, renters and sharecroppers would gain individual title to land they worked. Land reform in general and land-to-the-tiller in particular would undermine rural mobilization by delivering concrete benefits the insurgents could only promise.[15] In contrast to the first phase's reliance on military intervention, the measure was supposed to be "self-implementing," as claims were to be initiated by beneficiaries. According to the decree, those who rented or sharecropped up to seven hectares had to register their claim with the implementing agency, which would negotiate the transfer price with the owners. The beneficiaries would then repay the agency on terms similar to those of the first phase. Estimates of the potential impact of the land-to-the-tiller program varied widely. The most credible puts the figure at 17 percent of the nation's farmland and 117,000 beneficiaries (Wise 1986: 53).

The implementation of the agrarian reform left a legacy of extreme violence in its wake. A state of emergency was announced the day after the agrarian reform, and was renewed monthly. Under the cover of the state of siege and the turmoil occasioned by the expropriation of properties, violence escalated as government forces targeted *campesino* activists. The legal

---

[13] There were no Phase I cooperatives founded in Tenancingo, an area of smallholdings and medium-sized farms.

[14] According to William Stanley's detailed analysis of intramilitary politics, whether U.S.-advocated measures were implemented depended on whether they coincided with the interests of the high command. Where they did, as with the land reform that "augmented the power of the military, placated reformist officers, pleased the United States, and served the counterinsurgency project," U.S. recommendations were followed (Stanley 1996: 180–1). Where they did not, as with policies to reduce violence by the state, they were not.

[15] Roy Prosterman, a key architect of the land-to-the-tiller phase and an adviser to the American Institute for Free Labor Development and the Salvadoran Comunal Union, argues that land reform in South Vietnam cut recruitment by the Vietcong in the South from 7,000 men per month to 1,000 (Prosterman 1982: 21).

aid office of the Archdiocese of San Salvador recorded the following increase in killings of noncombatants in 1980: 234 in February, 487 in March, approximately 1,000 in June, and over 10,000 for the year as a whole (cited in McClintock 1985: 270). The same office reported that 12,501 civilians were killed in 1981, of which over 40 percent were *campesinos* (cited in Strasma, Gore, Nash, and Rochin 1983: 61). The newly elected leaders of reform cooperatives were sometimes targeted by the state; participation in the state-sponsored reform was no protection from the growing violence.[16] In the judgment of U.S. sources, most of the violence against cooperative members was by agents of the state. According to a memo by the American Institute for Free Labor Development (a U.S. organization working with Christian Democrat organizations) dated November 12, 1980, 133 of the 184 deaths of campesinos, government employees, and others associated with the land reform were known to have been carried out by government and paramilitary forces (cited in Bonner 1984: 201).

It was in this context of extreme state violence that Archbishop Romero called for soldiers to refuse to obey orders; he was assassinated the next day on the orders of Roberto d'Aubuisson by a death squad that included two Armed Forces captains (Truth Commission 1993: 354–7). By December 1981, a *campesino* organization affiliated with the Christian Democratic Party,[17] reported that at least ninety officials and promoters of similarly affiliated *campesino* organizations had been killed or disappeared and estimated that more than 25,000 tenant families had been evicted to prevent transfer of land to them under the third phase (UCS-AIFLD 1981: 1–2).[18]

The third phase of the reform distributed land to only 36 percent of the potential beneficiaries. In Tenancingo, 139 families benefited as 172 hectares of land changed hands. Usulután accounted for a mere 9 percent of the area transferred under the third phase and for only 6 percent of the beneficiaries, a disproportionately low fraction given its size, probably due both to the department's extreme level of violence in the early 1980s

---

[16] In addition to the sources cited in the text, see Americas Watch and the ACLU (1982) and the report of the Truth Commission (1993).

[17] The Unión Comunal Salvadoreña (Salvadoran Communal Union).

[18] Much of the violence surrounded the land-to-the-tiller program. The original legislation did not specify a threshold of landholding size above which a landlord would be affected by the third phase of the agrarian reform. As a result, a wave of claims against owners of small amounts of land were made, and significant violence occurred between smallholding owners and their tenants. To address this problem, a "widows and orphans" ruling that limited claims against those holding less than seven hectares themselves was added to the implementing regulations.

and to its lower incidence of tenancy.[19] In Santiago de María, where tenancy was particularly infrequent and violence extreme, only five families benefited. Other case-study areas saw some land transfer under the third phase.

Campesinos were not the only targets of violence. On January 4, 1981, top army intelligence officers ordered the killing of Rodolfo Viera, head of the Phase I implementing agency and a leader of the Salvadoran Comunal Union; killed with him were two American advisers from the American Institute for Free Labor Development. Viera's second-in-command, Leonel Gómez, was spirited out of a hospital by U.S. Agency for International Development personnel after he was wounded in a different attack by National Guardsmen that left more than a dozen members of an agrarian reform cooperative dead. Later granted asylum in the United States, Gómez testified to the House Subcommittee on Inter-American Affairs that between March and December 1980, some 240 leaders of agrarian reform cooperatives had been killed, 80 percent of them by government forces, 2 percent by guerrillas, and the rest by persons unknown (cited in Bonner 1984: 200). Between 1980 and 1983, approximately 260 local and national leaders of the Christian Democratic Party were killed, including thirty-five mayors, most by ORDEN members (Pyes 1983: 8).

After the decimation of the FMLN's urban networks in 1980 and the failure of its 1981 offensive – an effort one ERP commander characterized as a disaster due to their lack of arms and experience – the guerrillas turned to the countryside. Based on their analysis of the agrarian reform as primarily a government counterinsurgency effort, they increasingly targeted the infrastructure and harvests of the reform cooperatives, particularly the vulnerable crop-dusting planes essential to cotton production. As violence intensified throughout 1980 and 1982, a number of reform cooperatives were abandoned, some for the duration of the war. By December 1981, nineteen of the expropriated farms had been abandoned; by September 1982, the figure had risen to twenty-eight farms (Checchi and Company 1981: 66; Strasma et al. 1983: 62). Some properties distributed under the land-to-the-tiller component of the reform were also abandoned, but disproportionately fewer, perhaps because *campesinos* who benefited under that rubric were more motivated to stay on the property (other things being equal) since they claimed individual title, not collective title in the name of the cooperative, as in the case of the agrarian reform cooperatives.

---

[19] Calculated from the database of transferred properties of the land-to-the-tiller implementing agency.

Violence was particularly severe in Usulután. Members of agrarian reform cooperatives mentioned several deaths of reform cooperative leaders by government forces in this period. As a result of the violence by both sides, several reform cooperatives in Usulután were abandoned, and many members fled the area, leaving all cooperatives weakened. In Jiquilisco, the reform cooperatives La Canoa and El Marillo were abandoned until the last months of the war, as were the small "traditional" cooperatives (founded before 1980) of San Antonio Potrerillo, Lempamar, La Salinera, Montemaría, and Nancuchiname, a small traditional cooperative distinct from the Phase I cooperative of the same name (ISTA 1991: Annex 4 and 5).

Civil War in Usulután, 1980–1984

This war has left us many memories.
Member, Cooperativa Luz en el Horizonte, 1992

Overt military conflict between the FMLN and government forces intensified in Usulután in 1981 as the ERP expanded its activities from Morazán into Usulután and San Miguel. By mid-1982, Usulután and the neighboring department of San Vicente were among the most conflicted departments. In the three months of July, August, and September 1982, between 10 and 15 percent of FMLN actions and 16 percent of government casualties (a rate second only to that of San Vicente) occurred in Usulután (CUDI 1982: 912–17). In part, the expansion of conflict in Usulután reflected a new emphasis on the part of the Salvadoran military on consolidating its control of economically vital areas, as well as its increased efforts to intercept the increasing influx of arms along the Usulután coast. In response, the FMLN in Usulután carried out ambushes on advancing troops and sabotage on economic targets. During an FMLN offensive between October and December 1982, the highest number of government casualties occurred in Usulután (17 percent, closely followed by Chalatenango); major insurgent actions occurred most frequently in San Vicente and next most frequently in Usulután (16 percent); Usulután also ranked second in the frequency of insurgent sabotage (21 percent, after San Salvador with 25 percent; CUDI 1983: 43–8). By the end of the offensive, political analysts affiliated with the Central American University noted that the observed level of military activity and sabotage suggested that certain areas of Usulután were under the "solid control of the FMLN" (ibid.: 44). The offensive also demonstrated a new level of coordination across the five guerrilla factions and between the newly differentiated insurgent forces (regular army, guerrilla, and militia units).

FMLN forces blew up the bridge across the Rio Lempa along the coastal plain in 1983, making travel and communication between the Usulután coast and the capital still more difficult. Until 1982, there was a National Guard base and a civil defense patrol in San Francisco Javier. The FMLN attacked the base several times, killing eleven soldiers in 1982 and forcing the base out of the area by 1985. The mayors of San Francisco Javier, Jucuapa, Santa Elena, and San Agustín retreated to nearby towns (Jiquilisco, Santiago de María, Usulután, and Jiquilisco, respectively). As in Tenancingo, landlords in the more conflicted areas of Usulután abandoned their farms, taking with them what machinery and furniture they could. Between 1980 and 1983, nearly all remaining private properties south of the coastal highway (those that had not been nationalized under the agrarian reform) in western Jiquilisco were effectively abandoned (in the sense that no commercial production took place, although on a few estates *campesinos* paid rent to the landlord's agent, as on the Hacienda California). The coffee estates in San Francisco Javier and the Las Marías areas were abandoned by 1985.

The area west of the road connecting the coastal highway and San Agustín, known as the Tres Calles area, became the principal rearguard for the guerrilla forces in western Usulután. In the early years of the war, four of the five FMLN factions maintained troops in the area and smaller forces along the coast. Occasional territorial disputes and ambushes of one another's forces by mistake led to a 1985 agreement that the ERP would remain in the coastal area, while the small groups of other troops were pulled out to reinforce their forces elsewhere. Both the FPL and the ERP were active in the mountains north of San Francisco Javier; the ERP was the sole group in the Las Marías area.

According to the commander of the ERP forces in southwestern Usulután, the department had a particular political importance for the FMLN. The FMLN's presence in an area of such high economic value and substantial population was a statement that the insurgent forces could not be confined to the marginal northern departments of Chalatenango and Morazán. He stated,

For the enemy, this was a political problem that provoked much more intense levels of conflict here [than in the northern FMLN-controlled zones], not in the sense of great battles, but in the frequency of combat, sometimes three or four times a week, sometimes even three or four times a day. The north might go even a year without the enemy crossing the river [the Torola River, an informal border between FMLN and government territories in Morazán]. Here, the enemy had a military and political commitment that they had to keep. (San Francisco Javier, 1992)

While emphasizing the political importance of Usulután for the FMLN, the commander downplayed the importance of the Jiquilisco coast as a site of significant arms flows from Nicaragua. While some arms arrived through Jucuarán, a hilly municipality along the eastern border of the department, the terrain along the Jiquilisco coast was not advantageous for that purpose, he claimed. Moreover, after initially abandoning key parts of the Jiquilisco coastline, government forces recovered significant territory, posting troops and creating civil defense forces along the coast to deter landings of arms. The ERP retreated, dismantling significant infrastructure but maintaining a few small patrols in the area. U.S. and Salvadoran officials had a different view, arguing that arms flows did occur along the length of the Usulután coast in general and through the Bay of Jiquilisco in particular.[20] Indeed, General Blandón stated in a 1987 interview that the government chose Usulután as the site for a major repopulation project for that reason (a project that was never carried out). While the Jucuarán coast was clearly an important corridor for arms coming by sea from Nicaragua (Raudales and Medrano 1994: 159–61; Partido Demócrata 1997: 336), I could not determine the extent of arms flows through the Jiquilisco Bay. While local *campesinos* reported occasionally moving arms and other supplies up from the coast, my impression was that it was substantially smaller than the Jucuarán inflows. In any case, both sides increasingly saw Usulután as strategically central to their war efforts.

As conflict intensified in the department, it became increasingly difficult for residents to remain in many of the case-study areas, particularly the isolated outlying *cantones*. Nonetheless, many stayed, some because they sought to safeguard their houses or small holdings, others because they had no resources to leave and nowhere better to go. With evident exaggeration

---

[20] The source of FMLN arms was a much debated topic during the civil war (see, e.g., Montgomery 1995: 117–18). During the war, the FMLN claimed that many arms were captured or purchased from corrupt army officers in El Salvador and Honduras. Juan Ramón Medrano, an ERP commander who worked in Jucuarán for several years during the war, states in his autobiography that the majority of the FMLN's arms arrived by sea to the Jucuarán coast from Nicaragua, particularly in 1975, 1979–80, and 1982 (Raudales and Medrano 1994: 161).

one told me: "We passed entire days underneath the bed, sometimes a week. Airplanes, soldiers, guerrilleros – a great confusion." Key crossroads and towns were militarized as the Sixth Brigade expanded its presence in the early 1980s, to some extent taking over from the security forces. One resident of a village just north of the city of Usulután recalled,

There were days when you would see no one at all. All the houses were closed, the store and pharmacy were closed. The fear was greatest from 6 o'clock in the afternoon and after. You wouldn't even dare to take someone ill to the hospital as you would have to pass through difficult military checkpoints on the road. (Santa Elena, 1992)

One resident of a hamlet halfway between Santa Elena and Las Marías recalled an incident that took place, he said, on March 15, 1982: "They [the army] called a meeting where cloaked figures picked out certain people. About forty people were taken to the other side of the village. By the third day, most were dead and we went searching for their bodies" (Cooperative 13 de Junio, 1992). The use of local residents to point out insurgent activists was reported in many interviews. The practice was, of course, an ideal opportunity to name personal enemies as well as suspected insurgents, which added to the terror.

By 1983, outlying *cantones* and villages had been abandoned in western Jiquilisco, the northern part of San Francisco Javier, and the higher altitudes of the Las Marías area (with the exception of San Jorge). The pattern of displacement in southwestern Usulután was very similar to that in Tenancingo. While some families left the area entirely, the majority retreated to the relative safety of local towns or built shacks along railways and roads close to the coastal highway. Despite the influx, the population of the towns of Jiquilisco, San Francisco Javier, and Las Marías declined as many more residents fled the violence. The populations of Tierra Blanca, Santa Elena, and Santiago de María did not change significantly. Some families and individuals left, but many others came to these towns from surrounding villages.

During these initial years of violence and conflict, much of the land in the outlying areas was not planted; rural enterprises such as the salt patios along the Bay of Jiquilisco and the coffee mills in San Francisco Javier and Las Marías did not function; and there was little commerce or travel along the coastal and Pacific highways. Many families subsisted on food distributed by charities and agencies in major towns or received funds sent occasionally by family members from the cities or the United States. After conflict lessened in the mid-1980s, many families planted crops on abandoned land and some earned income from selling food and drinks along highways as commerce and travel resumed to a limited extent.

Some residents of the Usulután case-study municipalities, however, did not retreat from political activity or from the area but joined the FMLN or actively supported it in the wake of violence against family members and neighbors. As in Tenancingo, repression by government forces appears to have been the best recruiter for insurgent forces throughout Usulután. Prior to the period of extreme violence, only a few *campesinos* had joined the guerrilla forces, although many had some degree of contact with them. The widespread, extreme, and frequently arbitrary violence by government forces from 1978 to about 1983 led to the suppression of the nonmilitary popular organizations; the unintended consequence was that discontent was channeled more directly to the FMLN.[21] As one resident of a *canton* near San Francisco Javier (1990) expressed it, "Some armed themselves, others fled. Thirty out of a hundred stayed." One *campesino* described his decision to join the ERP (he later left to be a local cooperative leader):

In 1982, a *compañero* arrived here to help form a [insurgent] cooperative. He was killed, and all our efforts ended. We could not even respond. Out of love for my friends, I took up arms. It came to this extreme: taking up arms, our right. I am who I am, fighting still. (San Jorge, 1992)

Indeed, sometimes entire hamlets became supporters in the aftermath of local violence. One insurgent cooperative leader who had been an active catechist emphasized that increased but entirely covert support for the FMLN was the direct consequence of repression: "Thanks to persecution, the *campesinos* had to be quiet. It was necessary to always coordinate with the armed [guerrilla] forces, as a guarantee. The foundational work of liberation could not be expressed" (Las Marías, May 1992). Another resident of the Jiquilisco area who became an ERP political cadre suggested that "[r]epression itself formed networks of information, defensive groups of *campesinos*. Because of repression, there were groups – fifty people at a time – that could not live in their houses and were obliged to move about" (San Salvador, 1992). The commander of ERP forces in southwestern Usulután, himself a native of the area, reflected: "As the repression grew, rather than containing the mobilization, the hatred grew still more. People wanted to confront the security forces with only a machete. It had become a

[21] Binford (1999: 7–8) documents a similar process in northern Morazán.

115

situation of hate, people said, 'If only we had arms' " (San Francisco Javier, 1992). While someone in his position would probably perceive and no doubt report this pattern of growing polarization and hatred, it was confirmed in many interviews with insurgent *campesinos*.

Shifting Forms of Collective Action

There appear to have been two distinct effects of state violence that led some activists to support the armed insurgency. First, some activists who had been denounced to government forces, together with nonparticipants who had merely been denounced as insurgents by grudge-bearing enemies, faced difficult choices of fleeing the area (as many did) or of joining the insurgency (as some did). One reason to do so was that the FMLN as an organized armed force might provide protection from government forces (Goodwin 2001: 162).

However, protection in the sense of immediate shelter does not appear to explain sustained collaboration with the insurgents on the part of civilian supporters, for two reasons. As civilians, they continued to be exposed to government forces given the contested nature of the area. In Usulután, the dispersed guerrilla forces made few efforts to take civilian supporters with them when they retreated, unlike the pattern in Chalatenango, San Vicente, and Morazán during this period. Insurgent forces were too dispersed, government attacks too frequent, and there was no extensive rearguard to which such combined groups could attempt to retreat. As a result, civilian supporters were left exposed to the army. Also, some residents, fearful of identification as activists, fled government advances with guerrilla troops, but subsequently went to urban peripheries rather than stay in contested areas. In short, they took advantage of insurgent protection in the short run without assuming the long-run commitment of ongoing participation.

Second, the government's arbitrary and brutal repression reinforced and deepened the insurgents' framing of the government as a profoundly unjust authority. State violence deployed against unarmed civilians and sometimes against uninvolved family members or other residents legitimated the choice to rebel against the state, and to use arms in doing so.

ERP leaders and local *campesinos* shared other experiences that also contributed to the willingness of some *campesinos* to support the insurgent forces in the case-study areas in this period. Most of the ERP midlevel commanders I interviewed were from *campesino* families themselves. Some were from local villages, several others were from Morazán. While most had joined the ERP as young teenagers and thus had little experience themselves as farmers other than helping their parents as children, they nonetheless shared elements of local *campesino* culture that probably contributed to the spread of insurgency.

My interviews made it clear that *campesino* support for the insurgents in this period also reflected years of clandestine political work by the ERP and other guerrilla groups with local residents. While it was not easy to reconstruct the content of that early political work, it appeared to consist in large part as framing historical patterns of land tenure, labor relations, and governance as unjust, thus building on the work of catechists and other organizers before the war. Another important theme was the unprovoked brutality of government repression, which was held to justify the use of violence. Another aspect emphasized strict adherence to guerrilla authority, discipline, and norms as necessary to the struggle. Thus the content of this political work in Usulután appears to be similar to that which the ERP conducted in Morazán, which emphasized the "profound coincidence" between the Christian emphasis on love of neighbor and the socialist fight for the common good; economic analysis of agrarian structure, particularly the accumulation of land on the part of elites; the history of campesino uprisings; and the historical necessity for guerrilla struggle, according to ERP commander Juan Ramón Medrano (Raudales and Medrano 1994: 70–1). In Usulután, much of this political work was done by political cadres who worked closely with insurgent *campesinos* and organized local militias. Figure 4.2 shows an ERP political officer active in the area around San Francisco Javier. He was from a large family in Morazán that worked a small holding. As a young teenager he was already an activist with *campesino* organizations. First arrested when he was fifteen years old, he escaped after his second arrest and joined the ERP, abandoning his wife and children.

To attract and consolidate support, ERP commanders also attempted to demonstrate the advantages of the future society they proposed. One midlevel commander emphasized the importance of concrete benefits that the guerrilla forces brought for the development of an insurgent political base in northern Usulután. After describing the abuse with which one landlord treated his workers, he continued,

So when we began the struggle here in 1981 and 1982, we found quite a receptive response, and quite a lot of participation. One of the fundamental reasons was the unjust distribution of land, very evident here in Usulután where there had been a

Figure 4.2 ERP commander "Eric," San Francisco Javier, 1991. Eric was a political officer, now deceased, with responsibility for southwestern Usulután. Photograph by Jeremy Bigwood.

forceful expropriation by the oligarchy with the resulting profound poverty. These resentments couldn't be expressed until guerrilla units appeared, making proposals for change. So a call to revolution was *heard*. We insisted that the *tarea* [area of the coffee estate assigned to a worker to weed and prune] be decreased. [As a result], it would have been impossible to arrest the wave of support for us. (Las Marías, 1992)

Another commander said that the ERP also negotiated and enforced higher wages. In November 1986, for example, FMLN troops occupied the Hacienda Nueva near Santiago de María and informed the 360 coffee pickers that the FMLN had decreed a new minimum wage (*El Diario de Hoy*, November 4, 1986). The workers were told to go and not return until the owner complied.

The first commander argued that this improvement of working and living conditions was the direct result of the FMLN's presence:

Before, nothing was possible: on every hacienda there was a National Guard post which enforced the total authoritarian power of the landlord. The guardsmen would arrest, beat, and throw in jail any worker who was said to have stolen firewood or fruit. This scheme was broken when the armed struggle began in 1981 and 1982.

The landlords were the first to depart, leaving behind their administrators. The National Guard left as well, in order to avoid combat and because while the state paid their monthly salary, the landlords no longer paid the expected additional wages. (Las Marías, 1992)

Campesinos confirmed that the length of their workdays decreased, but the campaign for increased wages was not successful.

Two factors suggest that these benefits did not themselves motivate participation in insurgency. First, they were not "selective" in the sense that they were enjoyed only by insurgent supporters. Rather, all workers in the area benefited, irrespective of their political loyalty. Second, such benefits did not necessarily outweigh the likely costs. Such claims by insurgent commanders fail to mention the costs subsequently paid by civilians in areas where the FMLN had pushed out security forces. One insurgent *campesino* remarked ruefully, after discussing the benefits of shorter working days and increased wages, "But afterward, as *campesinos* we suffered worse. We were the target of the Armed Forces." Nonetheless, he went on to describe his clandestine insurgent activities in the area.

Conclusion

For some insurgent *campesinos*, a trajectory of political mobilization began with their involvement in Bible study groups. For others, it began with conventional efforts at labor organization. For still others, it began with covert collaboration with guerrilla organizations. And others joined only late in the war. While active support for the insurgents was widespread, it was not the choice of most *campesinos* in the case-study areas. Many residents openly opposed the left. Some participated in paramilitary groups, particularly in southern Tenancingo, and a few in Regalado's death squad in Santiago de María. Others fled the violence. Still others participated in centrist alternatives, such as the Christian Democratic Party.

The reiterated references to the work of catechists in interviews suggest that the growth of political organizations before the war depended significantly on the ideological work of liberation theology, even in areas where that work was relatively weak. For many poor residents of the case-study areas, the practices and teaching of liberation theology awoke in them a vision that a more just social landscape was possible because it was God's will and that bringing it about required their own efforts, with the help of God's other agents. One ERP political officer summarized his analysis of the relationship between religious and leftist organizing as follows: "Through the work of the Church, the *campesino* raised his consciousness, and afterward took up the struggle in his own hands, as his own work and knowing his rights" (Usulután, 1992). The guerrilla organizations shaped *campesinos'* understanding of liberationist teachings through their ideological work, interpreting state violence as making armed insurgency necessary if liberationist aspirations were to be realized.

Thus overlapping networks – of religious activists and covert leftist collaborators – played a role in the rising trajectory of political mobilization and the emergence of armed insurgency in Tenancingo and Usulután. But those networks were formed early on in that trajectory with the explicit purpose of furthering political mobilization. In contrast to the African American churches and colleges that played such an important role in the emergence of the civil rights movement in the U.S. South, the networks in El Salvador were not preexisting organizations whose membership and resources formed the basis of recruitment and organizing into the movement. Rather, the networks were built in the course of mobilization, as in some other social movements (Polletta and Jasper 2001: 291). As Binford (2003) argues for the case of Morazán, the catechists built up the sense of community, lacking since the violence of 1932, that was a necessary condition for development of organized resistance in El Salvador (Kincaid 1987).

Some scholars argue that severe repression may forge armed insurgency from political mobilization because civilians seek guerrilla protection (Mason and Krane 1989; Goodwin 2001). However, the wide variety of patterns of participation across individuals and across time suggests that in El Salvador, activists, and civilians generally, had more choices than this suggests: they could take advantage of guerrilla protection in the short run without making long-run commitments, or they could flee the area. In any case, the Salvadoran guerrillas offered precious little protection in the early years of the war. Rather, repression forged insurgency because it reinforced the framing of the government as a profoundly unjust authority, an ongoing demonstration constantly interpreted as such by insurgent organizers. Thus, as we see in more detail in the following chapters, most civilian insurgents appeared to support the guerrilla forces not out of an illusory desire for protection but out of their deepening conviction that the government no longer merited their loyalty or acquiescence.

5

The Political Foundations of Dual Sovereignty

> Now we have seen a new dawn. We did it all despite the great
> pressure of the army. Where I live, sixteen *campesinos* were killed,
> and not a single *guerrillero*. They were killed just as you might kill
> whatever little animal. For us, this has been quite a history.
> > *Campesino* leader, Cooperativa La Conciencia, 1992

In the early 1980s, some of the *campesinos* who had been active in the
1970s mobilization allied with guerrilla forces in Usulután, Tenancingo,
and other contested areas of the countryside. A few, mostly younger men,
became full-time fighters; others gave logistical and intelligence support.
Together their support was sufficient to undergird the FMLN's expansion
from strongholds in Morazán and Chalatenango to a broad swath of national territory, including significant areas of Usulután, by the end of 1983.
While the provision of supplies and the movement of ordnance were important, the provision of military intelligence concerning the movement
of government forces was the essential *campesino* contribution to this expansion and thus to the emergence of a military stalemate by the end of
1983. As a result, large areas of the countryside exhibited dual sovereignty
by the mid-1980s. In some, state authority had been effectively replaced
by novel insurgent institutions. In others, government and insurgent forces
contested the authority to rule.

As insurgent forces expanded their activities in 1982 and 1983, the government changed its strategy toward winning the "hearts and minds" of
residents of contested areas while intensifying the use of force in FMLN
"controlled" areas. The FMLN successfully reorganized its forces on this
new political and military terrain. In particular, the FMLN maintained
its strong advantage in military intelligence, thanks to enduring political

loyalty on the part of insurgent *campesinos* and the apparent absence of counterparts providing similarly effective intelligence to government forces. As
a result, the military stalemate continued. Despite the weakening of the
FMLN's main international supporters (Cuba and Nicaragua) in the late
1980s, the FMLN's undiminished military capacity – brought home to all
during the FMLN's 1989 offensive – together with structural changes in
the economy brought recalcitrant Salvadoran elites to the negotiating table
to end the civil war.

In this chapter I analyze the political foundations and processes of the
military stalemate. I first describe *campesino* contributions to the emergence
of the stalemate in Usulután. I document the changing military strategies
of both armies, in particular the new emphasis by both sides on building
civilian loyalties, as they sought vainly to break the stalemate. I then analyze the repopulation of Tenancingo, an initiative that depended on that
emphasis. I describe the civil war and *campesino* life in the Usulután case-
study areas under the stalemate (1984 to early 1991) and analyze variations
among individuals in support for the ERP. A key point emerges from this
history: insurgent military capacity rested in large part on the political support voluntarily provided by many *campesinos*.

Campesino Contributions to Armed Insurgency in Usulután

By the mid-1980s, it was clear that, although the FMLN was not able to
defeat the Salvadoran military (by then strongly supported by the United
States), it had developed a sufficient military capacity that it was very unlikely itself to be militarily defeated. In Usulután, the ERP maintained
a base of operations on the eastern face of Mount El Tigre that supported military activity from the Pan American highway to the coast. The
base included a clinic, workshops to build crude weapons, and other established structures. Elsewhere, the FMLN developed a more mobile and
rudimentary infrastructure, such as the field clinic near San Francisco
Javier shown in Figure 5.1. Despite repeated efforts, the military did
not succeed in dislodging the guerrillas from their Usulután strongholds.
The insurgent military capacity reflected the training of some guerrillas in Cuba and of a few top cadres in other countries (particularly
Vietnam), the development of an FMLN communications infrastructure in Nicaragua, safe residence for top political leaders of the FMLN
and family members in Mexico and Nicaragua, medical treatment for

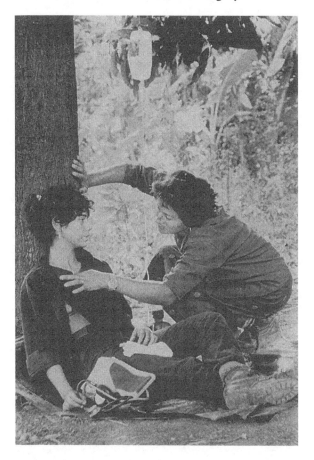

Figure 5.1 FMLN medic and wounded combatant near San Francisco Javier, November 1990. Photograph by Jeremy Bigwood.

wounded combatants in Cuba, and the ongoing flow of arms into the country.[1]

While international support, infrastructure, and arms were important to the FMLN's military capacity, intelligence concerning the movement of government forces, logistical support for the movement of weapons and

---

[1] For analysis of the evolving military balance of the war, see the articles by the Centro Universitario de Documentación e Información of the Central American University in San Salvador, published every month in the journal *Estudios Centroamericanos*, as well as Wickham-Crowley (1992), Byrne (1996), McClintock (1998), and Gibb (2000). On arms flows to the insurgents, see Castañeda (1994: 97–8).

base camps, and the provisioning of guerrilla forces were more important (Wickham-Crowley 1992: 315–16). All such tasks were carried out by *campesinos*, as shown in Figure 5.2. In short, local *political* capacity constituted a significant part of the FMLN's military capacity. An important aspect of insurgent political capacity was the development of various forms of supporting organizations, including the full-time guerrilla army, part-time and local militias, covert networks of civilian supporters, and, later, overt political organizations (described in the next chapter). The ERP commander of southwestern Usulután acknowledged as much in an interview at the end of the war:

Essentially, it was the local people who supplied us. We created various supply networks and also networks of information. Teenagers also participated in local military activity, displaying propaganda and laying contact bombs. There were various levels of militia participation. Some might be mobilized for activities for two, three, or five days – they would participate and then return to their homes. Others would join us for two weeks or a month, depending on whether an operation was planned. (San Francisco Javier, 1992)

After pausing, he added, "On these structures, we, the permanent military force, depended."

In interviews, insurgent *campesinos* emphasized the concrete contributions they made to the insurgency – reporting troop movements, transporting supplies, carrying messages, and joining in local operations – as well as the risks they ran in so doing. One member of the Comunidad La Palma described his role as follows: "Here we had many tasks: taking water to the hidden *compañeros*, providing tortillas. Sometimes we had to pass through the army to do them – if they caught us it was death or castration. Or they would cut off your head. We made a lot of sacrifices passing through the army" (1992). In some areas, the provision of tortillas and water to guerrilla forces was highly organized, as in La Peña, a community east of San Francisco Javier in the late 1980s: "We provided two hundred or so tortillas at a time to the Frente. The houses would take turns. Each house would send twenty-five tortillas, eight houses at a time. In this, *everyone* contributed" (emphasis in original; Comunidad La Peña, 1992). The emphasized "everyone" included the members of the local evangelical church, only one of whom supported the insurgents beyond this mandatory material contribution.

Political capacity during the early years of the war did not take the form of overt political organization in Usulután. Due in large part to its militaristic

124

Figure 5.2 *Campesinos* supplying tortillas to ERP troops near San Francisco Javier, March 1989. The guerrilla receiving the tortillas in the lower photograph died in the November 1989 offensive. Photographs by Jeremy Bigwood.

strategy, the ERP did not initially attempt to build the kind of local organizations that the FPL did in Chalatenango and San Vicente (Pearce 1986: 242–9; Binford 1997: 61–2). In those areas, particularly in Chalatenango, guerrilla leaders encouraged residents to participate in local organizations called *poder popular local* (local popular power). The purpose of these organizations was to provide food and health care to local residents as well as guerrilla forces, typically through cooperative buying of seeds and fertilizer and marketing of surplus as well as the collective cultivation of some land for communal consumption. The FPL also believed that participation in such organizations would politicize residents. In practice, the organizations varied a great deal in their capacity to provide food and services. Their infrastructure was destroyed and participants widely dispersed during the intensifying bombing campaign that began in 1984.

A very old man in the Las Marías area insisted that the principal contribution of the residents of the case-study areas was "silence," the refusal to inform on the guerrillas: "We used to help them by telling the military, 'No, haven't seen anyone' and from there the thing developed until the very end, that is, the peace accords" (1992). According to a ERP leader active in the Tres Calles area in the late 1970s, *campesinos* consistently lied to the security forces concerning the degree of subversive organizing. Even ORDEN members in one *cantón* north of San Marcos Lempa did not report ERP training exercises held during daylight.[2] Silence also protected the leaders of some nongovernmental organizations who were full-time ERP militants assigned to political work in the latter years of the war. This was widely known among insurgent circles, yet they were apparently not denounced as guerrillas to government forces.

I do not mean to suggest that there was no informing on insurgent activity. For example, a high-ranking member of the Resistencia Nacional was an informer whose activities decimated FMLN forces in western El Salvador and San Salvador between 1981 and 1983 (Gibb 2000). In Tenancingo after its repopulation, several residents were threatened and a few killed for supposedly reporting on guerrilla activities. Nonetheless, the FMLN's rural political capacity appears to have been significantly stronger than that of the government. The latter's decisive advantages in numbers, training, and

---

[2] It could be argued that the ORDEN members were coerced into the subterfuge, but given the pervasive repression by the security forces throughout El Salvador based on ORDEN informants, this is unlikely. ERP commander Juan Ramón Medrano reported in his autobiography (Raudales and Medrano 1994: 74–5) that the ERP was occasionally able to secretly recruit ORDEN members, even, on one occasion, an entire patrol.

technology suggests that insurgent political capacity accounts for the ongoing military stalemate. According to U.S. defense analysts, the Salvadoran military proved unable to build popular support in the countryside as a result of past but also ongoing human rights violations against civilians: "With rash and brutal strokes, the armed forces vitiate the careful buildup of government legitimacy as they equate the government's critics with the enemy, repressing trade unionists, campesino leaders, opposition politicians and student protestors with the same or more force than they use on real insurgents" (Schwarz 1991: 25).[3]

Campesino contributions to the FMLN's military capacity also included, of course, the bearing of arms as members of the full-time guerrilla forces. While the initial membership in the five guerilla organizations was largely comprised of students and urban professionals, by the early 1980s the insurgent army was predominantly a *campesino* army (McClintock 1998: 266–70).[4] The top leadership of the FMLN was largely urban, but there was significant mobility within the military ranks for *campesinos*.[5] According to senior FPL guerrilla commander Facundo Guardado, by the end of the war, 95 percent of FMLN combatants were *campesinos*, as were 80 percent of the midlevel commanders (cited in Byrne 1996: 35). Most of the midlevel ERP commanders I interviewed in Usulután were from *campesino* families, as was the FPL commander of the Tenancingo area in the mid-1980s.

For individual insurgent supporters, their particular role in support of the ERP varied over time, as well as between individuals. Some described their role as one of occasionally contributing food and information. Others contributed more continuously. Still others also bore arms on occasion, such as teenage members of a San Francisco Javier militia who transported food, water, and other supplies to ERP troops during the 1989 offensive (see Fig. 5.3). Some began their involvement as armed combatants but left the military structures for less active involvement (e.g., participating in insurgent activities but not bearing arms, or leaving the regular army forces

---

[3] Schwarz, a RAND analyst, wrote his report for the U.S. Department of Defense. According to an assessment of U.S. policy in El Salvador written by four U.S. Army colonels (Bacevich et. al 1988: 40), rural Salvadorans refused to participate in civil defense patrols in large part because they equate such patrols with ORDEN, of which they retain vivid memories.

[4] While statistics from representative surveys of insurgent members do not exist to my knowledge, this claim is also supported by statements by FMLN leaders, the observations of journalists, and my observation of insurgent troops in Usulután and Tenancingo.

[5] According to David Hunt (1974), upward social mobility was also a motive for poor Vietnamese village residents to join the National Liberation Front.

Figure 5.3 Members of ERP militia, San Francisco Javier, 1989. Militias served as auxiliary forces and as a source of new recruits. This militia provided logistical support to ERP troops during the 1989 offensive. Photograph by Jeremy Bigwood.

but joining the local militia). Some did so for personal reasons (often family issues, which for women included pregnancy) or because the organization deemed them more useful in other roles. Others became disillusioned. One Tierra Blanca resident told me how his first political activity was the strike on the Hacienda California for higher wages. He participated in regional and national marches, including the January 1980 march in San Salvador in which nearly two dozen demonstrators were killed. He went into hiding shortly after the march, when the army came looking for him, and then joined the FPL. After two years of procuring supplies for the FPL, he was wounded and returned to civilian life for awhile. Then he joined the ERP for two years. After leaving the ERP's military structure, he returned to Tierra Blanca, where he helped organize the Cooperativa California.

Figure 5.4 Elderly woman delivering supplies to ERP camp, 1989. Supplies were often delivered at night. Photograph by Jeremy Bigwood.

Many *campesina* women actively supported the insurgent forces as civilians, providing tortillas and occasionally other foodstuffs and intelligence to nearby forces. It was often women who took food and water to the guerrillas; they often did so at night, as shown in Figure 5.4. Some were drawn into this role when their husbands or children joined insurgent organizations. Some of those interviewed recounted how they had fled into the countryside from government troops in the early years of the war. A few lived in guerrilla camps or in refugees camps for months or a few years before returning to their homes (or nearby safer areas). Some became supporters after government violence against their family or neighbors. For example, a

129

resident of Tierra Blanca told me that she had been a catechist in the 1970s. After three fellow catechists were killed by security forces, she and three other catechists worked closely with the BPR for a time and then joined the FPL. After several years, she returned in 1984 to the coastal area to work at a "political level" (Tierra Blanca, 1992).[6] Women in the case-study areas faced the threat of sexual abuse and violence at the hands of government forces. Sexual violence by insurgent forces toward civilians appears to have been quite rare and was severely sanctioned by guerrilla commanders.

While some women such as this former catechist became guerrilla fighters, most women who joined the FMLN as full-time members served as cooks, as radio operators, or in other supporting roles.[7] The social mobility enjoyed by some male insurgents did not appear to extend to many women. One measure (albeit crude) of the relative lack of mobility for women within insurgent ranks is to compare the percent of female combatants demobilized at the end of the war, 30 percent, to the number promoted just before the war's end at El Tigre camp, 11 percent.[8] One reason was that the founding ideology of the FMLN paid little attention to feminist issues.[9] Liberation theology generally understood women as essentially mothers whose suffering should be lessened, but not as fully active political subjects. Moreover, leftist ideology subsumed gender struggles under the rubric of class conflict (Vázquez, Ibáñez, and Murguialday 1996: 62–81). Many female combatants suffered the death of partners, sometimes of several, during the years of the war. This wartime instability of relationships led some to more casual sexual practices, others to abstaining from relationships altogether. Some became pregnant and left the guerrilla camps to have the child; some returned after leaving the child with family members or in a refugee camp. In postwar interviews (analyzed in ibid.), some full-time members reported what they

---

[6] The women in the case-study areas did not attempt to mobilize around women's issues, in contrast to the women of northern Morazán, who succeeded after a series of confrontations in winning the passage of foodstuffs through military checkpoints into the FMLN-controlled area.

[7] Of 29 female guerrillas interviewed by Norma Vázquez and her colleagues (Vázquez, Ibáñez, and Murguialday 1996: 114), four served as combatants, 15 as radio operators, six as medics, and the rest in other services.

[8] The fraction of female FMLN combatants comes from Vázquez, Ibáñez, and Murguialday (1996: 21); that for the ERP at El Tigre from an article in the *Diario Latino*, December 2, 1991 (cited in El Rescate Human Rights Chronology).

[9] One instance of social mobility for women is recounted by Karin Lievens (1988: 124–7): In 1984, a school for the cultural, political, and military formation of women combatants was founded in the Tres Calles area. The school appeared to have persuaded some women to become combatants rather than cooks.

had come to see as sexual harassment (advancement or quality of life conditioned on their sexual compliance) by their commanding officers. More common was constant pressure to engage in sexual activity; abstention on the part of the few women in the guerrilla camps was not popular among their male counterparts. Some reported sexual abuse at the hands of other combatants (and a few reported rape), but both appear to have been infrequent.

Changing Military Strategies

By the end of 1983, the FMLN's military capacity was sufficient to control about a fifth of the national territory. In such "controlled zones" the FMLN generally moved at will during the day as well as at night. The guerrilla forces had eliminated fixed government positions, so there was little military presence except during explicit military campaigns into the zones. Some observers in late 1983 judged the FMLN to hold the dominant military position overall (Byrne 1996: 103). While this is open to debate, the government was coming under increasing pressure concerning human rights violations, as organizations such as Americas Watch and Amnesty International issued report after report documenting government atrocities. The reports fueled an emerging social movement in the United States comprised of human rights, solidarity, and church groups that put increasing pressure on the U.S. Congress to curtail funding of the Salvadoran military (Smith 1996).

Yet Salvadoran military officials appeared to doubt that U.S. assistance was in fact conditioned on their human rights record. Indeed, after admitting Christian Democrats into the government, carrying out the 1980 counterinsurgency reforms, and holding contested elections for the Constituent Assembly in 1982, the regime had received increasing amounts of U.S. aid – enough to more than double the size of the army by 1984 – despite ongoing high rates of human rights violations.[10] In late 1983, however, Vice President George H. W. Bush visited El Salvador to convey to the High Command of the Salvadoran military the message that U.S. aid would decrease if the state did not improve its treatment of civilians. In an explicit

[10] Declassified documents show that the United States was well aware of the direct involvement of the military and security forces in ongoing human rights violations. The Reagan administration judged an insurgent victory the greater danger, leaving it little leverage over the military until U.S. officials decided to threaten a cutoff in aid (Scharwz 1991; Byrne 1996; Arnson 2000; Gibb 2000).

quid pro quo, Bush offered other incentives as well, including aircraft and helicopters (Arnson 2000: 103). As is clear from Figure 1.1 (bearing in mind the Truth Commission finding that state forces were responsible for 85 percent of violence against civilians), his message was understood: state violence did decrease dramatically in 1984.

Another factor contributing to the decrease was the Salvadoran military's gradual implementation of the counterinsurgency strategy promoted by the United States. The strategy was twofold (Schwarz 1991; Byrne 1996; Stanley 1996). First, in rebel-held areas, military operations would intensify and would include aerial bombing, the deployment of specialized forces on long-range reconnaissance patrols, and military campaigns of several days' duration, in contrast to the nine-to-five workday of the regular army. Second, counterrevolutionary institutions would be founded, including the writing of a new, more liberal constitution, the holding of contested (but not inclusive) elections, the founding of civil defense patrols, and campaigns to win the hearts and minds of residents. The latter initiatives would be largely focused on contested, not controlled, areas.[11] As one of the military's counterinsurgency campaign documents stated, drawing on Mao's metaphor about civilians being the water in which the guerrillas fish and swim,

taking water from the fish doesn't mean the physical exodus of the population but winning their mind and heart so that they reach an ideological conviction that they can do honest work, conscious that it is better to live in an environment of liberty, justice, and peace than to live under a Marxist dictatorship. (FAES 1996: 21–2)

As part of new emphasis on winning civilian loyalties, the military increasingly carried out campaigns in which military doctors, nurses, dentists, and teachers delivered on-the-spot services. In 1987, I observed such a campaign in Tenancingo (see Fig. 5.5). A few dozen soldiers arrived on foot and spread out across an area southeast of the Villa. Then two helicopters arrived with two dentists, several dental assistants, and a quantity of balloons

---

[11] While in Usulután opposition-allied nongovernmental organizations functioned openly beginning in the mid-1980s (although with a significant degree of harassment, as we see in the next chapter), in FMLN-controlled areas they were targeted much more forcefully. Every one of the thirty-three members of one such organization in northern Morazán, for example, was arrested, and some (one source claims all) were tortured in 1988 (Binford 1999: 36; Thompson 1995: 139). The communities of displaced people living along the Jiquilisco coast were an exception to this pattern: they suffered an extraordinary degree of harassment by government forces (perhaps because of the flow of insurgent arms alleged to occur through the Bay of Jiquilisco).

Figure 5.5 Civic-military action, Tenancingo, 1987. These government soldiers are giving candy and balloons to children. Photograph by Elisabeth Wood.

and other treats for children. Lively music broadcast from speakers drew townspeople to the clinic, which lasted most of the day.

The shift in military strategy began in earnest with the launching in 1983 of the National Plan. After pushing guerrilla forces from the economically important areas of San Vicente and Usulután, military control would be consolidated through the strengthening of local authorities, the restoration of basic services, and the return of cultivation and commerce. In the judgment of U.S. officials (USAID 1987), the initial pilot program in San Vicente did not meet these objectives. Government forces retook the San Vicente volcano, but FPL forces had merely retreated along with some 1,500 civilian supporters (Gibb 2000: 218–21). Residents resisted the attempt to establish civil defense forces, and one-time delivery of services left little changed (Byrne 1996: 148–9). Nor were subsequent efforts in Usulután any more successful. Government troops on various occasions destroyed guerrilla bases in the Tres Calles area, but guerrilla troops and support staff relocated either to the mangrove forests along the coast or to the volcanic highlands (Lievens 1988: 74, 108–13). The guerrillas returned after a few months and rebuilt the destroyed infrastructure. As part of the 1986 United to Reconstruct campaign, government forces first attempted to clear insurgents from the Guazapa volcano (Operation Phoenix) and promoted the repopulation of villages in its outskirts (Edwards and Siebentritt 1991). But when I visited the area in 1987, few families had returned to these villages, and guerrilla forces had reclaimed the volcano slopes.

The ability of the insurgent forces to retreat before government offensives and then quickly rebuild after their departure was a result of a change in guerrilla strategy in response to the new counterinsurgency strategy. The government's growing capacity to locate insurgent forces with spotter aircraft, to deploy government troops rapidly by helicopters, and to bomb controlled zones intensively took increasing toll of FMLN troops and civilian supporters.[12] Once it recognized that the prospects for immediate victory had declined, the FMLN responded with a new strategy of its own. As the air campaign made protection of civilian supporters increasingly difficult (Bourgois 1982, 2001), many civilian supporters were sent out of controlled zones to refugee camps in Honduras or El Salvador. The FMLN broke up its battalion-sized forces into much smaller units and dispersed them throughout the countryside in order to gradually erode government resources through sabotage and to organize local *campesinos*. (For example, the Batallón Rafael Arce Zablah, the pride of the ERP, was broken down into small, mobile units.) The result was a significant increase in FMLN activity in western areas, where guerrilla attacks increased 86 percent between 1985 and 1986, and in San Salvador, where attacks increased 50 percent (U.S. Department of State, cited in Byrne 1996: 150).

As part of the new strategy, the FMLN increasingly emphasized sabotage, the use of mines, and occasional attacks in dense urban areas. In 1986, Joaquín Villalobos, a top military commander and key strategist for the ERP, justified the new tactics as follows: "And hence we can also comprehend why the FMLN resorts to guerrilla actions of attrition. It is not territory that is in dispute, but rather, two things: the incorporation of all people into

[12] Indiscriminate aerial bombing led to 235 deaths during a two-week period in March 1984, according to Americas Watch (1984: 46). On the change in the FMLN's strategy, see Villalobos (1986), Miles and Ostertag (1991), Harnecker (1993: 252–74), and Byrne (1996: 132–6).

the war and the capacity to profoundly weaken the other side" (Villalobos 1986: 178). The fundamental issue was that of sovereignty, whether or not the FMLN was a parallel authority with legitimacy to govern in the eyes of its adherents. Despite Villalobos's emphasis on competition for civilian loyalties rather than territory, control of territory is of course one way such dual sovereignty is asserted by insurgent forces:

In a country as small as El Salvador and with its population density, each square kilometer where the Armed Forces cannot sustain its military power in a stable manner, where they cannot maintain the juridical-political power of the government, and where, in an embryonic or partial manner, another power begins to develop, ends up reflecting an evident duality of political-military power between the FMLN and the army. . . . (ibid.: 177)

As part of this demonstration of the absence of the government's "juridical-political power," the FMLN also forced mayors from contested areas.

The change in strategy, particularly the breaking up of forces into very small units, was not an easy adjustment for the FMLN. According to one ERP political officer, the period following the change of strategy was one of the most difficult. The transition from expected victory to operating in groups of as few as five combatants was deeply demoralizing for many combatants. The ensuing process of "spontaneous purging" (Lievens 1988: 130) drastically reduced the number of full-time guerrilla fighters as many left, too discouraged to continue. According to one estimate, the number dropped from between 10,000 and 12,000 in 1984 to about half that by 1987 (Gibb 2000: 314). Morale reportedly reemerged as the new strategy and tactics proved effective (Lievens 1988: 139). This strategy persisted until the gathering of troops in preparation for the 1989 offensive.

The Repopulation of Tenancingo: Contested Sovereignty

> *La iglesia atravéz de FUNDASAL tomó Tenancingo.* [The Church through FUNDASAL took Tenancingo.]
>
> Departmental commander, 1987

> While I distribute ammunition, the nun distributes Bibles.
>
> Army officer, Cojutepeque, 1987

The competition for civilian loyalties as well as territory made possible the repopulation of Tenancingo, an audacious effort to rebuild the town in the midst of the war based on the right of all residents to return to the area, irrespective of political loyalties. Beginning in 1986, many families returned to Tenancingo under the terms of an unprecedented accord negotiated by the Archdiocese of San Salvador in which the FMLN and the Salvadoran military agreed that the area could be repopulated as a demilitarized or unarmed zone (*"una zona inerme"*). The project took place in the political context of competition over control of the repopulation of abandoned areas, a return to the countryside made possible in large part by the military's emphasis on winning civilian political loyalties and the ensuing *political* competition for those loyalties. In the six months following the Tenancingo repopulation, both the military and organizations allied to the FMLN launched their own repopulation initiatives just north and west of Tenancingo and in other contested regions.[13]

The Tenancingo project was unique among these repopulation initiatives. Not only had both of the parties to the civil war agreed to allow it to go forward and to respect its unarmed nature, but the Archdiocese also insisted that any civilian willing to respect the unarmed nature of the project would be allowed to return. Both were challenges for the armed parties to the war. The first appeared to side-step the claim of each to govern the contested area of Tenancingo. The second called into doubt the claim of each to local political loyalties. Thus the issue of contested sovereignty was at the heart of the politics of the Tenancingo project.

For the military, early drafts of the Tenancingo accord were unacceptable. An agreement between the FMLN and the Armed Forces and the creation of a "neutral" territory would both violate its constitutionally defined responsibilities, according to participants in the negotiations.[14] As a result, each side entered into a separate agreement with the Archdiocese (rather than direct agreements with each other). The most important clause of this unwritten understanding, which I refer to as the Tenancingo accord, was the agreement that members of either army could pass through Tenancingo but neither was to maintain a "permanent presence," a formulation meant to forestall any interpretation of the area as neutral. An additional reason for military opposition was that the project was a public reminder of a recent high-profile intelligence failure. In 1985, the FMLN kidnapped the

---

[13] On the return of FMLN-allied groups from refugee camps in El Salvador and Honduras to contested areas of the countryside, see Argüello Sibrian (1990), Cagan and Cagan (1991), Edwards and Siebentritt (1991), and Thompson (1995).

[14] This section draws on confidential interviews and documents with a wide range of sources familiar with the Tenancingo agreement. For more detail, see Edwards and Siebentritt (1991: 29–46) and Wood (2003).

daughter of President Duarte, her companion, and (in separate operations) almost two dozen mayors. They were freed in Tenancingo in exchange for the safe passage of disabled FMLN combatants out of the country and the release of some political prisoners (Simons 1985). The military agreed to the project on the condition that Tenancingo would not become either a supply or propaganda center for the rebels, that the FMLN would not recruit from the area, and that the Archdiocese, not the Salvadoran development agency implementing the repopulation project, would be the interlocutor between the parties (Interview, San Salvador, 1991).

FMLN representatives initially objected to what they saw as the project's "pacifism" (its focus on conflict resolution rather than political polarization) and its autonomy from their revolutionary project.[15] But the advantages outweighed these disadvantages. In 1985, for the FMLN to enter into an accord, even if technically an accord with the Church, on the same terms as the Armed Forces was a public recognition of dual structures of power. It would be difficult to overestimate the political importance to the FMLN of a dramatic demonstration of the government's lack of control of territory before the domestic and international audiences implicitly promised by the project's unique terms and significant international funding. Nor did it make sense for the FMLN to oppose a project that promised to address the structural injustices against which they claimed to fight the war. And it would be difficult for the FMLN to maintain its public stance of readiness to enter into dialogue with the government if they rejected a concrete initiative by the Archdiocese. The FMLN eventually agreed to the project on condition that the mayor's office not return to the municipality, that no U.S. Agency for International Development funds would be used for the project, that the Archdiocese would be the interlocutor, and that the Armed Forces would not develop an intelligence network among Tenancingo residents or impede the movement of civilians in and out of the project area (Interview, San Salvador, 1991).

As is frequent in agreements, the successful launching of the Tenancingo project partly reflected the willingness of all parties to accept ambiguities inherent in the terms of the accord. For example, what exactly was proscribed by disallowing a "permanent presence"? Did it proscribe an ongoing occupation of the town by one group if it occurred without the construction of a physical "permanent" base? And did the accord proscribe whatever it did

---

[15] In contrast, the FMLN did not allow anyone to join their repopulation initiatives whom they considered a security risk (Thompson 1995).

proscribe within the town (i.e., the Villa), the municipality, or something in between?

According to one source familiar with the details of the negotiations, both sides agreed because each believed it could shape these ambiguities and the project to its political advantage. Certainly, both subsequently attempted to do so. On various occasions the military claimed the project as one of its own repopulation projects, thereby asserting its sovereignty over the contested area. The commander of the Cojutepeque detachment stated on the morning of the return of displaced families to Tenancingo that it was "the first of a military plan . . . called 'United to Reconstruct' . . ." (*El Mundo*, January 29, 1986). A few months later, Armed Forces Chief of Staff General Adolfo Blandón visited Tenancingo accompanied by several colonels and about a hundred troops.[16] The following day a national newspaper carried the story under the headline "Tenancingo Is Protected by the Armed Forces" (*El Diario de Hoy*, May 7, 1986). The story stated that the officials had assured the population that "Tenancingo will no longer be the 'town without law' as it had been called because of the lack of authority in the region." A month later, the commander of the army's Cuscatlán detachment claimed that government forces were working with residents on development projects, and later that residents had asked him to establish a military base (*El Mundo*, June 13, 1986; *La Prensa Gráfica*, June 15, 1986). Blandón stated soon afterward that the army would "reestablish a military presence in the town whenever it is deemed necessary" (*Christian Science Monitor*, September 3–9, 1986). The mayor of Tenancingo repeatedly pressed the government to insist on her right to return her office to the Villa from her temporary office in Cojutepeque; the FMLN adamantly opposed her (Cojutepeque, 1988).

In response to such attempts by the military to claim the project, the development agency carrying out the project, the Fundación Salvadoreña de Desarrollo y Vivienda Mínima (Salvadoran Foundation for Development and Low-Income Housing, or FUNDASAL), issued a press release to assert the project's independence. The release stopped short of reiterating the initial language prohibiting a military presence in the area, however, and

---

[16] Another factor that contributed to the willingness of the Armed Forces to agree to the Tenancingo accord was the fact that Blandón had lived there for several years as a child. Indeed, in a 1987 interview (San Salvador), he told me at length a story of how he had almost been captured by the FMLN in Tenancingo when he had attempted to attend a patron saint's day festival there. As his helicopter descended, he realized that guerrillas were nearby. Fortunately for Blandón, soldiers arrived in the nick of time.

referred only to the prohibition of a "permanent military *base*" (*El Mundo*, June 19, 1986; emphasis added).

Conflicts soon arose in other areas as well. The military objected to FUNDASAL's extension of agricultural credit in *cantones* where civil defense forces were active, fearing that this would lead to an expansion of the project into such areas. The FMLN had recently stepped up its attacks on the patrols. In 1985, for example, it had attacked the civil defense patrols of both Santa Anita and Hacienda Nueva. In the aftermath of the attacks, a representative of Hacienda Nueva went to the military base in Cojutepeque to ask that they be allowed to disband the patrol and turn in their arms, but they were refused (Americas Watch 1986: 81).[17] After the repopulation project began, the military accused FUNDASAL of extending credit to the *cantones* on condition they disband civil defense patrols, an accusation FUNDASAL vigorously denied. A compromise was reached whereby credit was extended to residents and physically disbursed in the *cantones* so that residents were not required to travel to the Villa. The FMLN again attacked the Santa Anita patrol in November 1986. The patrols of both Santa Anita and Hacienda Nueva were allowed to disband in its aftermath, arguably as a result of the project's international profile.

The FMLN also sought to claim the project as its own. A few days after the initial fifty-six families returned to Tenancingo, a celebration marking the event drew dignitaries and diplomats from San Salvador, including the Archbishop, who celebrated Mass. After the service, the FMLN held a press conference in the Villa, an event which reportedly enraged the Armed Forces (Americas Watch 1986: 84). A year later, on the first anniversary of the town's repopulation, the FMLN mounted a dramatic assertion of dual sovereignty. The convoy of vehicles carrying the international visitors – including the Papal Nuncio and ambassadors and representatives from France, West Germany, Spain, England, Italy, Mexico, and Peru – was stopped at a National Police roadblock four kilometers from the Villa, an FMLN roadblock two kilometers later, and a second military roadblock a kilometer later (*El Mundo*, January 29, 1987).

The most important incident took place a few days later, when the government sent nurses to Tenancingo to vaccinate children in the Villa's central square. After two FMLN nurses unexpectedly joined them in the

---

[17] The military also urged Corral Viejo to form a patrol, but a group of residents rallied opposition to the idea. According to interviews in the southern *cantones*, the pressure ceased after *cantón* residents sent letters to the Archdiocese and the Human Rights Commission.

square, the unusual group together vaccinated the children, who passed from the line to one or the other group of nurses by turn. The following day, February 2, 1987, the leftist newspaper *Diario Latino* published two photographs of this joint delivery of services under the headline "*Guerrilleras* and Government Nurses Vaccinate [Residents] Together" (p. 5). One photograph showed the government nurse giving a small child a shot. The other showed two guerrilla nurses doing the same; the government nurse is clearly visible in the background. The caption reads, "In Tenancingo the first real dialog has occurred. Children accomplish more than adults." The FMLN's audacious move implicitly asserted dual sovereignty, and the press coverage depicted a parallel structure of power capable of delivering services equivalent to that of the government.

While the Tenancingo project's high public profile invited such manipulation, it also made possible an unusual degree of political and diplomatic pressure to protect the project. On February 16, 1986, approximately 300 government troops of the Batallón Belloso occupied the Villa in support of Operation Phoenix on the nearby slopes of the Guazapa volcano. They attacked a dozen guerrillas in the main streets of the Villa, after having received an order from the High Command countermanding the terms of the accord, according to the officer in charge of the brigade at the time (Cojutepeque, 1987). The troops shot indiscriminately as they entered, searched the houses, killed one unarmed resident, reportedly raped a woman, and captured two guerrillas (Americas Watch 1986: 85; *Christian Science Monitor*, June 9, 1986). In response, FUNDASAL asked European diplomats to send messages to the government and Armed Forces expressing concern about the incident. Two days later, Blandón responded favorably to a list of concrete actions that he was asked to carry out and reassured project sponsors of his support for the project; the troops left town.

However, there were limits to the ability of sponsors to protect the project. For example, the response of the Armed Forces to the publication of the vaccination photographs was immediate and enduring. Within days of their publication, the commander of the Cojutepeque army detachment once again asked that a military base be established in Tenancingo. His request for a base was denied, but Air Force troops were stationed in the area of the Villa for six months. Troops had been present frequently in the area since November 1986, but they moved close to the Villa after the publication of the photographs, frequently occupying buildings in its outskirts. In an interview, the commander stated explicitly that this move was in response to the vaccination photo and that the military presence was under

140

the control of the High Command and would be permanent (Cojutepeque, 1987). Air Force troops killed three civilians in the *cantón* El Pepeto in the two weeks following the photo's publication in what the human rights agency of the Archdiocese of San Salvador judged indiscriminate attacks on the civilian population; another civilian died in April (cited in the El Rescate Human Rights Chronology). On March 7, Manuel Rafael Gonzalez, a former political prisoner of the military who after his release had apologized to Villa residents for having appeared on television denouncing the local nun, was killed (Americas Watch 1987: 164). Threats and detentions also increased during this period. During my stay in Tenancingo from June to August 1987, groups of two to five heavily armed soldiers were present on the principal street corners, in the central park, and at the main entrance for several hours each day.

The Archdiocese was initially unresponsive to requests by FUNDASAL and Tenancingo residents that the bishops denounce the ongoing presence of the troops.[18] As the town prepared to celebrate its patron saint's day in July, the community council invited Auxiliary Bishop Gregorio Rosa Chavez to Tenancingo to discuss the encroachment. As he arrived on July 24, 1987, Air Force soldiers were searching all vehicles entering the Villa. The bishop soon saw for himself the extent of the troop presence. When he visited a housing project for families from the northern *cantones* at the north side of the Villa, council members showed him six soldiers camping there, as can be seen in Figure 5.6 (top photo). The council and bishop then discussed the possible avenues of protest and appeal (Fig. 5.6, bottom photo). The following Sunday, Archbishop Rivera y Damas referred to Tenancingo in his San Salvador sermon, expressing his worry that "the accord, that neither the military nor the guerrilla stay permanently within the perimeter of the populated areas, is not being fully fulfilled" (*Orientación*, August 2, 1987). (Note that the statement implies an acceptance on the part of the Archdiocese of a quite limited interpretation of the accord area.) With this renewed support of the Church, FUNDASAL sent letters to Generals Blandón and Rafael Bustillo (head of the Air Force), and asked the supporting European agencies and governments to call for the withdrawal of the troops. As a result of this marshaling of political pressure, the troops reduced their

---

[18] One foreign observer who followed the project closely remarked, "The Church moves, but at its own rhythm. Tenancingo is important for the Church, but differently than for FUNDASAL. The Church balances all issues with five others, and Tenancingo is probably the best of all the going issues. So it's not an issue of less attention, but of balance between issues" (San Salvador, 1987).

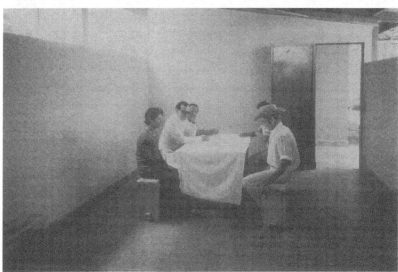

Figure 5.6 Tenancingo Community Council and Bishop Rosa Chavez, Tenancingo, 1987. The council requested that the bishop visit to alert the Archdiocese to the constant presence of government troops with in the town. In the upper photograph, the bishop visits soldiers occupying a Villa house. The lower photograph shows the bishop and council discussing the problem. Photographs by Elisabeth Wood.

presence in the Villa, though they remained in the general area (allowed under this new limited interpretation).

The military forces left the area entirely for a week in January 1988, reportedly to join a massive military operation to the north. FMLN combatants entered the Villa and attempted to reassert their authority. During my month-long stay there, a group of fifty guerrillas kidnapped three residents, an official of the government's Central Electoral Council, a farmer who had claimed that the guerrillas had stolen a cow, and a young man known for talking big when drunk. A few evenings later, guerrillas kidnapped four teenage girls from the Villa because, it became apparent later, they had been flirting with government soldiers and therefore had to be "reoriented." Their absence occasioned worry and fear on the part of their families; they returned unharmed (and not noticeably chastened) the following day. The three adults were also released; the election official was warned to leave town.[19] Soon afterward, government troops returned to the area and the guerrilla presence lessened once again.

The Tenancingo area remained conflicted until the end of the war. Two children were killed and four injured when they set off a land mine in 1988; army helicopters were twice hit by guerrilla fire in the Tenancingo area; combat was reported there occasionally; and on one occasion, a military officer lamented the persistence of guerrillas in the Tenancingo area, compared with other repopulation sites that were under the "relative control" of the army (El Rescate Human Rights Chronology). Despite repeated requests from FUNDASAL and donor agencies, the Armed Forces occasionally held civic-military actions in the Villa, which usually led to a response by the FMLN. In May 1989, the FMLN General Command sent a letter to the town that suggested that residents should prevent any military presence in the town or risk an FMLN attack, and that they oppose any efforts to link its reconstruction efforts with any army or government initiatives (Interview, Tenancingo, 1989). Nonetheless, combat was generally limited to areas beyond the town's periphery. "We've achieved a lot: they don't fight among us; they fight beyond the farming zone," as one resident remarked (Tenancingo, 1989).

Under the umbrella of the Tenancingo accords, FUNDASAL attempted to build new forms of governance and civil society. In contrast to the partisan origins of the agrarian reform cooperatives and the insurgent cooperatives,

[19] These events were also documented by the Universidad Centroamericana's Institute de Derechos Humanos (cited in El Rescate Human Rights Chronology).

the repopulation of Tenancingo took place under a rubric of reconciliation. Yet for the Archdiocese and FUNDASAL, reconstruction did not mean a return to preconflict social relations. In their vision of reconstruction, they emphasized the need for the social and economic transformation of the inequitable structures at the root of the civil conflict. FUNDASAL hoped to achieve a degree of such transformation through the extension of credit and technical assistance to build up *campesinos'* productive and organizational capacity, the creation of alternative sources of employment in the Villa, the participation of the poor in organizations to define and protect their common interests, and the consolidation of those organizations into a set of alternative democratic institutions, particularly a democratically elected and representative local council to govern the Villa (FUNDASAL 1985).

The attempt to create the Community Council of the Villa of Tenancingo to represent and govern a politically heterogeneous population in the midst of the civil war was the most audacious aspect of the project.[20] According to interviews with those familiar with the accord, project sponsors believed that a democratic institution was essential for the peaceful resolution of local conflicts. A self-governing council would ensure that the diversity of political loyalties among residents would be represented and would provide a forum for discussion and clarification of common interests. Moreover, the sponsors hoped the council would eventually represent the residents in negotiations with the Tenancingo elite, as well as with national and international organizations.[21] In short, the council was to become a countervailing structure of power to the traditional one.

Thus FUNDASAL attempted a limited redistribution of income and power in the municipality, yet it did so under formidable constraints. One constraint was the residents' conflicting political loyalties. The project succeeded in bringing back residents of different political loyalties. Families from the northern *cantones* that had spent years living and traveling with guerrillas forces lived next door to Villa families that supported the military and government. A second constraint was the poverty and low rates

---

[20] In Chalatenango and northern Morazán there were somewhat similar experiments in local governance. For example, beginning in 1984, local community councils in Morazán founded schools, set up health committees, and negotiated the terms of commerce and travel with the army. However, these communities did not welcome government-supporting or explicitly neutral residents, and important issues were largely decided by local FMLN officers (Binford 1997).

[21] According to interviews with observers close to FUNDASAL, the development agency was aware of its heavy hand in the initial rebuilding of the town and recognized that if the project was to be judged successful, the council would have to escape its paternalist origins.

of literacy of the families that returned to Tenancingo.[22] A third was their economic heterogeneity. Most male heads of household had been peasant smallholders or sharecroppers before the conflict, but some had been blue-collar or agricultural laborers in the factories or farms of the elite. Few of the women had worked outside their rural households before being displaced from the area. A fourth constraint was the limited means by which reconstruction might occur. In particular, no direct redistribution of assets was possible, as that would have abrogated the necessary acquiescence to the project by the military. A fifth was the lack of employment opportunities. There was little economic activity in the surrounding area as the conflict continued in the municipality and region.

But there were opportunities as well as constraints, most notably the absence of Villa elites, their willingness to lend or rent land and houses to those who did return, the predominance of small holdings in the municipality (which meant that some families had access to their own land), and the profound commitment of those who returned to defend the bottom line of the accord, that neither side establish a permanent military presence.[23] The project also had significant international funding (for the first three years of the project, approximately U.S. $4 million, largely from European governments and nongovernmental organizations). Despite the ongoing conflict over the project in the pages of the domestic and international press, the project proceeded because the accord was respected well enough on the ground that fields were planted, harvests were not lost, and transport of agricultural supplies and products was usually possible.

After rebuilding some of the town's physical infrastructure, FUNDASAL attempted to develop programs and projects that would sustain the town as it gradually turned its attention elsewhere. Among the most successful was its promotion of agricultural cooperatives. In contrast to the reform cooperatives, which held collective title to land, the Tenancingo farmer associations were founded as service cooperatives of smallholders and renters to facilitate access to credit and training. Initially, rates of participation were very high, as were the rates of repayment of loans to rotating credit

---

[22] When the project's emphasis on social change became clear, well-off former residents felt marginalized from the project and stopped attending meetings. While there was no explicit policy to exclude them, they perceived themselves to be excluded by two provisos in the project's credit policies: a ceiling on agricultural loans that they found too low to reestablish a commercial farm and the requirement that recipients live in the municipality.

[23] According to a survey I carried out among a few dozen farmers in Tenancingo, more than half owned land themselves; the rest rented land.

funds. However, participation and repayment rates later declined, and other projects were much less successful. This was particularly true for the extension of small loans for the purchase of animals, repair of houses, or the founding of small commercial concerns such as handicraft shops or corner grocery stores. Loans were not repaid and generally the projects failed. Donors provided a significant amount of funding for a cooperative to sew palm hats in an attempt to provide employment for women, but the cooperative failed to find an adequate market for its hats, which were sometimes poorly made and less attractive to urban consumers than imports.

The Community Council was a partial success. With substantial training and guidance from FUNDASAL staff, the council did to a degree represent the project to political authorities. Initially, it merely met with the many international visitors to the project. In the second and third years of the project, the council negotiated with government ministries for the restoration of services, particularly the reopening of the school. As we saw above, in 1987 the council successfully urged the Archdiocese of San Salvador to denounce the military's presence around the Villa. The council also negotiated with local representatives of the FMLN, occasionally requesting the FMLN to lessen its presence in the Villa. In 1987, the council successfully negotiated the reopening of the *cantón* Jiñuco, but the FMLN refused to allow further expansion of the project to the north.[24] In meetings I observed in 1987 and 1988, council members discussed sensitive issues both among themselves and with various outsiders (as in Fig. 5.6) and resolved a few.

There were limits, of course, to what the council did. Although council members objected in specific instances, the council did not make a systematic effort to end the FMLN's ongoing expulsion of purported government informers from the area. Council members did not participate in meetings of project sponsors with the Armed Forces on either a regional or national level. In meetings I observed, council members relied on FUNDASAL staff for advice on local as well as political matters. The military ignored the existence of the council and communicated its concerns about the project to the Archdiocese or FUNDASAL. The FMLN did not urge residents loyal to the insurgency to actively participate in the council. Nor did local FMLN commanders heed council denunciations of guerrilla abuse of residents, as when the teenage girls were kidnapped.

[24] In early 1991, the FMLN agreed to allow the repopulation of Rosario Périco, but the council played a limited role in the negotiations.

By the end of the civil war, the council was inactive. It no longer met regularly and in interviews individual members appeared thoroughly demoralized. Several factors contributed. Social tensions between families originally from the Villa and those from the northern *cantones*, as well as political tensions between groups with different political loyalties, contributed to a high rate of turnover of council members. While initially such problems were discussed by the council and defused through the reaffirmation of the community's support for the terms of the accords, this role became increasingly difficult. The Air Force's occupation of the Villa in 1987 increased the tension and anxiety of council members. That the military and the FMLN ignored the council also contributed to its decline. When an FMLN-affiliated national organization[25] began organizing in the area in the late 1980s, many townspeople were concerned that their activities would bring a remilitarization of the Villa. And tensions between FUNDASAL and the council deepened when the agency insisted that the council collect utility payments. Residents deeply resented the council's hesitant efforts to do so, arguing that the council should insist that significant funds provided by international donors should be used to pay utility bills. The mayor of Tenancingo resented the rival authority. As traditional political parties reemerged and FUNDASAL lessened its presence in the Villa, relations between the mayor's office and town residents continued to deteriorate.

Civil War in Usulután, 1984–1991

> But I never thought of leaving. My grandchild, trembling, would ask me, "Why don't we leave?" I would reply, "Because one's destiny is what kills; we need not go searching high and low for it. We owe nothing to anyone, neither to the guerrillas nor the military. I belong to the Church."
>
> Elderly *campesina*, Tierra Blanca, 1992

The case-study areas of Usulután remained intensely contested through the end of the war.[26] The FMLN carried out major offensives in Usulután in

---

[25] The Asociación Nacional de Trabajadores Agricolas (National Association of Agricultural Workers).

[26] This section on military conflict in Usulután draws on interviews and reports (compiled in the El Rescate Human Rights Chronology) from newspapers and TV and radio stations, including the ERP's radio station Radio Venceremos, which in the judgment of many observers generally provided accurate reporting of the war.

November and December 1989, March and November 1990, and October 1991. The largest of these was part of the nationwide November 1989 offensive. During the first few days, ERP forces attacked the Sixth Brigade headquarters in the city of Usulután and military posts in Santiago de María and occupied smaller towns throughout the department, including Ozatlán, San Francisco Javier, San Agustín, and Santa Elena. Combat continued in the city of Usulután until December 29. Guerrilla forces shot down two planes near Ozatlán. A major battle on the southern slopes of El Tigre on December 17 and 18 left approximately thirty government soldiers dead. The smaller offensives were much shorter and more narrowly focused. For example, from March 9 to 13, 1990, the ERP attacked government posts in Santiago de María and other major towns in the eastern departments.

The FMLN attacked government outposts (usually National Guard posts but occasionally civil defense posts) in a single town, or in a few neighboring ones, much more frequently. The guerrillas usually attacked during the night or at dawn and quickly retreated as government forces scrambled to respond. For example, the ERP attacked the National Guard post in Chinameca on June 24, 1986, at 5 A.M.; soldiers from various government forces arrived at 7 A.M., to reinforce the guardsmen but found few guerrillas to fight. Occasionally, such attacks would be coordinated across a wider area, as on February 26, 1990, when the FMLN attacked National Guard posts in Jucuapa, Chinameca, and San Sebastian (in the neighboring department of San Vicente) simultaneously. Sometimes in the course of such attacks, ERP forces would insist that all residents convene in the central square for a political meeting. Usually there was an explicit message to be conveyed: that the FMLN would not allow residents to vote in upcoming elections, for example. Such meetings became more frequent in the last months of the war as guerrilla commanders sought to explain the course of peace negotiations to residents. ERP forces also frequently blockaded highways, particularly the coastal highway in Jiquilisco, sometimes for several hours until the approach of government forces. Sometimes guerrillas confiscated consumer goods from cars and distributed them to nearby towns. Occasionally they would hold a political meeting of the stranded drivers and passengers.

ERP guerrillas frequently attacked coffee mills in the Usulután highlands, causing significant damage. The Llach family, the family of the wife of President Alfredo Cristiani (1989–94), were particularly targeted. For example, on December 6 during the 1989 offensive, the Hacienda Santa Petrona south of Santiago de María was sabotaged and coffee distributed to the workers. During the March 1990 offensive, a Llach coffee mill in Santiago was attacked. It was again targeted during the October 1991 offensive.

Government forces made frequent, sometimes sustained, incursions into contested areas of Usulután throughout this period. Typically, a battalion or part of a brigade would deploy in some region to flush guerrillas out of hiding and to destroy guerrilla infrastructure. During the course of such operations, towns and nearby *cantones* would be occupied, the houses searched, and some residents detained for questioning. For example, on January 26, 1988, five *campesinos* were detained by the Arce Battalion in the *cantón* of San Antonio in Chinameca; they were released five days later. Occasionally, young men of the appropriate age would be forcibly conscripted during the course of such operations. Seventy young men were picked up during New Year's celebrations in San Jorge on January 1, 1986.

One consequence of this degree of military conflict was of course the death of civilians in accidents and cross-fire. The government posts attacked by the FMLN were usually located inside town boundaries. Civilian casualties were one result. For example, on August 29, 1989, during an FMLN attack on the Sixth Brigade headquarters in the city of Usulután (only a few blocks northeast of the town square), several houses were destroyed and two adults and four children were killed (*El Mundo*, February 17 and 18, 1988). Land mines, predominantly used by the FMLN, were another source of civilian casualties especially among children. For example, two children (both ten years old) died when a land mine exploded near the Hacienda California on April 19, 1988. With surprising frequency, soldiers on leave had accidents with grenades, leading to the death of family members.

But as in the overall pattern of violence against civilians during the Salvadoran civil war, most injuries and deaths in the case-study areas were not the result of accidents or crossfire but were inflicted intentionally by government troops on *campesinos* thought to be insurgent supporters. Some violence was carried out by rogue civil defense forces, as in Chinameca, where the civil defense commander killed two members of a family and wounded two others during an extortion attempt (he was subsequently arrested by government forces). Press reports and interviews alike confirm testimonies gathered in interviews that during many military operations, civilians were intentionally targeted. For example, in the first two months of 1987, the human rights office of the Archdiocese reported that Marines killed two civilians (one after extended torture) who resided along the Jiquilisco coast and tortured a third; that the Treasury Police detained and tortured a twenty-year-old worker in Chinameca; and that four *campesinos* were detained by the Arce Battalion and tortured in their San Miguel headquarters. Military operations by the Atonal and Lempa Battalions in the Usulután highlands in October 1989 left four bodies in their wake, according to the Archdiocese human rights office. Particularly targeted were members of opposition organizations, such as displaced persons groups and cooperatives, and young men who declined to serve in civil defense units.

Life Under Military Stalemate: Between Two Armies

Nonetheless, in both Cuscatlán and Usulután, state violence against civilians during the military stalemate occurred at a significantly lower level than earlier in the war. Beginning about 1984, conditions for residents of most of the case study areas improved significantly. Some residents who had fled the case-study areas returned, if not to their own homes, to those of family members, or to abandoned houses in nearby safer areas. Throughout the case-study areas, the smallest, most outlying hamlets were not resettled as local residents congregated in the larger *cantones*, a pattern true of other conflicted areas as well (Montes 1987: 315). For these residents, the result of the military stalemate and change in strategies was a new but precarious *local* political equilibrium between the two forces. Violence and deaths continued, but compared with the previous five to ten years of violence and terror, residents reported that they felt both safer and more secure than before and that they preferred rural life under military stalemate to urban misery and dependency. Thus the military stalemate comprised a local political opportunity in many of the case-study areas, even without agreements such as the Tenancingo accord.

In these conditions, cultivation was once again possible in all but the most outlying or particularly contested of the case-study areas. Given their extremely limited resources and the immediate need to feed their families, *campesinos* planted corn and sorghum; only a few managed to plant beans as well. A few families gradually accumulated sufficient capital to buy a pair of oxen, cows, or a pig or two. The renewed cultivation took place under a variety of rubrics. Some rented fields from landlords' agents, as was initially the case on the Hacienda California. Others planted land not their own without the permission of the landlord (or the payment of rent). As one campesino remarked sardonically, "Before the war, we would be lying around for days, with nothing to eat. The war at least allowed us to work" (Montecristo Joya Ventura, 1992). Initially, they did so surreptitiously, because the military when passing through attempted to police property rights. But they soon farmed land with ever increasing boldness, even doing so along roadsides on properties clearly not theirs (as shown in the end-of-the-war maps of Chapter 3). According to a high-ranking ERP political officer, "Two years into the war, *campesinos* began taking land for their basic food needs, sowing basic grains. They began with *minifundias* [microplots] of only half a *manzana*, or perhaps at most one *manzana*" (El Llano, 1992). He continued, emphasizing the guerrillas' role, "Of course, we ourselves were there. Before us there was no space for it. The dynamic reinforced itself: there was the land, there was the necessity to feed oneself – and also a quantity of coffee to sell." Encouraged by the ERP, increasing numbers of *campesinos* found they could stop paying rent on their plots without suffering any ill consequences.

But selling contraband coffee was not a viable option. Though coffee is a perennial and trees continued to produce some beans even without the usual diligent pruning and fertilizing, government forces patrolled major roads and crossroads throughout Usulután, searching both for supplies intended for the guerrillas and for illicitly obtained commodities, principally coffee from the highlands and salt from the flats along the Bay of Jiquilisco. As a result, *campesinos* pulled down coffee groves for firewood and planted cornfields. The guerrillas also destroyed some estates, particularly those of "uncooperative" landlords. One *campesino* leader near San Francisco Javier remarked, "The guerrillas burned the coffee orchards and they encouraged us to raid the estates. Now there is little coffee remaining. We ourselves destroyed it" (El Jobalito, 1992).

The physical bulk of coffee beans meant that coffee was not a "war commodity" like the highly valuable and easily transportable cocaine and diamonds that fuel other civil wars. However, given the significant profits that coffee estates earned in years when the international price was high, the ERP extorted "war taxes" from many landlords in the coffee highlands via threats to destroy the crop or facilities if the taxes were not paid. An ERP commander who collected taxes from landlords in the coffee areas north and east of Santiago de María defended the practice by arguing, "It would not have been just if the war fell only on the *campesinos*: the landlords also had to sustain part of the cost of the war" (Llano Grande, 1992). He stated there were two types of relations with landlords. The first type, he said, occurred with those that had "a degree of conscience." Relations with them were cordial: "We didn't see them as landlords that we had to pressure; we did not define what we asked them for as war taxes but as contributions," and he argued – unconvincingly, of course – that such contributions were freely given. In contrast, other landlords were "totally contrary – even though we tried to approach them, we had no success. We *imposed* war taxes on them." He wrote out for me a formal table of tax rates in which the tax depended on the amount of productive land and the amount of coffee produced. If accurate, the rates were quite moderate, indeed, improbably low; it was not possible to verify the table. He claimed that it was possible for landlords to negotiate lower levels of taxes, but that he imposed higher rates on those "who would have nothing to do with" him and asserted that those who refused would be forced from the area through sabotage and threats, a capacity that the ERP exercised in some areas but not all. The ERP also extorted taxes from some agrarian reform cooperatives in neighboring areas.

In contrast to this area near Santiago de María, landlords abandoned their land in most of the case-study areas. Even in the outskirts of significant towns, residents increasingly cultivated land not their own. The *cantones* near San Francisco Javier were typical. Sixty percent of the farmers worked abandoned land, 32 percent worked crops on rented land, and the remaining 8 percent worked their own land, according to a survey of 822 families in seven communities carried out by an opposition-allied non-governmental organization (INSIDE 1991: 5). Without access to credit, agricultural inputs, and training, however, residents at best managed to produce at a subsistence level despite their access to land. Families grew maize and sorghum, extending their income with small animal husbandry and some cash income from working the coffee harvest near Santiago de María. At the end of the war, only about twenty-five of the original 125 families lived in El Jobalito, a small settlement east of San Francisco Javier (ibid.: 53–8). Only one of the twelve families surveyed worked its own land. Only two families had one or two cows; the others had only chickens and other small animals for family consumption.

While these conditions were significantly better than the chaotic violence of the early 1980s, living and working under these conditions remained difficult and stressful. Perhaps the most difficult challenge was to manage relations with both armies: "In order to survive, you had to give to both sides; even though you belong more to the revolution, you had to give to both. They asked for beans, water, tortillas, sometimes they would pay you" (Interview, Cooperative Los Tres Postes, 1992).

In some parts of the case-study areas, this dilemma recurred constantly; refusing to contribute to one or the other armed force when asked was rarely an option. One resident of the Las Marías area argued that while one's private loyalties might favor the FMLN, supporting the insurgents more actively was dangerous:

It hasn't been easy: there have been massacres, we lived in total poverty. There were two armies: a volunteer army [the FMLN], and one you were forced to join. We were not free to help them [the FMLN]. To give information meant having the house destroyed, and being on the list. (Cooperativa Montecristo, 1992).

Nonetheless, he later founded and became president of an insurgent cooperative.

In contrast, a distinct strategy for survival was to remain neutral. One woman from the Tenancingo *cantón* Corral Viejo told me that "neither the one band nor the other be here; that is what we prefer. The one has as much right to eat as the other; ... both make their purchases and leave" (Tenancingo, 1988). An older man in Tenancingo endorsed this strategy in more sardonic terms:

We live between two armies, the famous *guerrilleros* and the Armed Forces. What we want is demilitarization. We're tired of war after eleven years. We avoid any reason for either side to pick us up; we stay absolutely clean. That is why we oppose a [government] base here, why we refuse credit that requires a political commitment. Either would be to offer your life up. (Interview, Tenancingo, 1991)

In interviews, this neutral strategy sometimes took an extreme form of not attributing violence to either party. A resident of a *cantón* near Ichanqueso in the folds of the Guazapa Volcano to the west of Tenancingo told me about the deaths a few days before of members of the executive council of a local government-sponsored repopulation project as follows:

On July 14 [1987], the president of the *directiva* [the project's executive council] died. We don't know who killed him. We are waiting for things to calm down. We don't know why he was killed. Yesterday, the warehouse keeper was killed. We don't know why; she was a woman, killed by a bullet in the heart at 4 P.M. On July 6, someone else died, not a member of the *directiva*. (Montepeque, 1987)

The third person killed was apparently his cousin. He then briefly recounted the history of the village:

Only twenty families stayed the whole time. We came back in April 1986. Some houses were destroyed. All we could bring back was our frustration and a willingness to work the same as the Mayas had done ... [pause]. We have returned to the time of the Mayas ... [pause]. Recent events have people worried. God only knows who can help.

In the context of a government repopulation project, the repeated reference to the local *directiva* might have been a suggestion that he believed the FMLN had killed at least two of the three. The colonel who at the time was the departmental commander explicitly claimed the FMLN was responsible (Interview, Zacatecoluca, 1987). However, many residents also stated that there had been many government troops in the area at the time, which might have been an implicit suggestion that they were responsible. No one I spoke to made any direct statement as to whom they believed responsible. Perhaps because I visited only once, I could not sort out who had killed the three. In any case, the subsequent references to the time of the Mayas and to God suggests that the resident did not see *any* earthly authority as offering much succor.

Even militant supporters of the insurgency emphasized the difficulty of managing these contrary pressures, blaming the FMLN as well as the military. For example, a leader of an insurgent cooperative in the Las Marías area told me how he survived pressure from both armies through the war:

I passed the entire war here. The FMLN would come and say, "What are you going to contribute?" So you would give a part to them. And those from the Armed Forces would also come; you had to give to them as well. It was the only way to survive. Neither the one army nor the other were able to force us out. Throughout the war, the soldiers would ask, "Why haven't you left?" It got to the point where I would just say to them, "Look, better that you kill me than that I leave here." Neither army could in the end lessen my morale. Never could either the Armed Forces nor the guerrillas force me out of here; here I remained, suffering. This is how we lived the war. (Cooperative Candelaria, un Nuevo Amanecer, 1992)

He continued by reiterating his political loyalty to the insurgency (credibly, judging by several previous interviews with him) and finished with, "I tell you that I have suffered; it has been hard; but now I am happy."

Patterns of Insurgent Support during the Stalemate

Despite these difficult situations, support for the ERP in the case-study areas during the military stalemate were generally a voluntary choice on the part of these *campesinos*, in the following sense. The ERP allowed people to reside in the case-study areas and to plant abandoned land without actively supporting the insurgency and without participating in local organizations *if* they made what I term the *minimum contribution*, which had three aspects.

First, residents had to contribute tortillas and water to the guerrillas (with no or at best little cash compensation). The particular arrangements varied from the highly organized rotation among households in La Peña described above to the simple requirement in most areas that households had to supply food, water, and, frequently, coffee, when asked. The pressure on all households to contribute reflected not only the need for supplies on the part of the ERP, but also the desire to give cover to households supporting the insurgents. According to the leader of an insurgent cooperative, "During the war, we asked the Frente to make everyone collaborate so that the volunteers would not be so notable" (Santa Elena, 1992).

Government forces passing through the case-study areas also coerced material contributions. Households had to supply food, water, and coffee when asked to do so by soldiers. Even late in the war, when insurgent cooperatives openly occupied extensive tracts of land, *campesinos* felt that to refuse such requests would be a provocative signal of commitment to the insurgents that would have grave consequences.

Second, residents could not inform on the insurgents to government forces: suspected informers were interrogated, and if thought guilty or probably guilty, expelled from the area and in some instances killed.[27] For example, in January 1986, two men were taken from their homes in San Agustín by men with black handkerchiefs on their faces. A month later their wives received notes saying that they had been executed for being members of civil defense patrols, according to the Archdiocese human rights office (cited in El Rescate Human Rights Chronology). A year later, in April 1987, four men were taken from the same town by FMLN guerrillas. Nothing more was heard until flyers were found a few weeks later stating that they had been executed by the FMLN. FMLN forces occasionally targeted ARENA party members as well, as when a party activist was taken from his home in Jucuapa and shot (*Diario de Hoy*, April 19, 1989). Executions of suspected informers (and government supporters) were termed *ajustacimientos* ("justice killings"). Human rights reports in the mid-1980s listed five to ten such executions a month in El Salvador. In interviews in both Usulután and Tenancingo I heard of a number of such executions (approximately a dozen in all). Thus as in other civil wars, some of the worst human rights violations by the FMLN took place in the context of the investigation of suspected informers (Kalyvas n.d.). An extreme example occurred on the San Vicente volcano where FPL commander Mayo Sibrian executed

---

[27] For the general pattern of FMLN treatment of suspected informers, see the report of the Truth Commission (1993: 311–12).

hundreds of guerrilla combatants and insurgent *campesinos* in the mid-1980s on suspicion of being informers (Partido Demócrata 1997; Gibb 2000: 291–308).

Third, residents had to treat the FMLN as the local governing authority and comply with its edicts. In Tenancingo, after the schoolhouse doors were stolen, the guerrillas investigated and presented the suspects to the town before expelling them from the area. As we saw above, residents judged by the FPL as too friendly to government forces were sometimes kidnapped. In Usulután, ERP commanders functioned as local authorities to some extent, occasionally settling petty rivalries or disputes and punishing those caught stealing or violating other communal norms. The assertion of local authority also entailed the displacement of governmental authority. The FMLN warned mayors throughout the contested areas to resign, and some 45 percent did (Gruson 1989; Miles and Ostertag 1991: 222). The ERP executed several mayors in eastern El Salvador who refused to leave and kidnapped others in a failed attempt to negotiate the release of two captured commanders (LeMoyne 1985; Truth Commission 1993: 312; Partido Democráta 1997: 333). As a result of this violation of international law, the FMLN was denounced by domestic and international human rights groups (including Americas Watch and Amnesty International) and eventually halted the practice.

Contributions to the insurgency beyond the required minimum were generally voluntary, as suggested by the following observations. First, residents consistently provided a high level of intelligence to the FMLN. Sustained flows of high-quality information are much more difficult to extract coercively than tortillas or water. Second, in dozens of interviews with insurgent *campesinos*, participation was clearly not only voluntary but enthusiastic and reiterated in private settings. Third, after the beginning of the cease-fire, many local *campesinos* attended ceremonies – which became all-night parties – at local ERP bases to celebrate the end of the war. The interactions I observed were generally very informal, with the ease and humor of long-standing relationships. Fourth, several key insurgent informants that I interviewed many times over several years eventually shared confidences they had previously withheld, such as the fact that he or she had at certain times been part of the ERP's military structure and not just a member of civilian supply networks. Although several made increasingly explicit criticisms of the ERP, apparently relishing the role of internal critic, they never gave any indication of coercion but continued to express enduring commitment to the insurgent organizations.

156

There were important exceptions to this pattern of voluntary support, however. For several months beginning in late 1983 to mid-1984 in the context of the widespread demoralization occasioned by the FMLN's breaking up into small mobile groups, teenagers were forcibly recruited by the ERP in Morazán and some of the Usulután case-study areas, and by the FPL in other areas (Americas Watch 1991: 65; Miles and Ostertag 1991: 220). In an article in the *New York Times* (July 4, 1984, p. A3), Commander Ana Guadalupe Martínez of the ERP was quoted as having stated, "There was a lot of sympathy for us but families had not yet sent their sons" – a disingenuous claim that presumed the families would soon do so. The FMLN subsequently suspended the policy, perhaps as a result of the negative publicity but probably also as a result of the negative reaction of civilians in those areas, including the flight of a significant number of families from northern Morazán (Binford 1997: 62).

Based on extended stays in Tenancingo, Tierra Blanca, and San Francisco Javier, my necessarily rough estimate is that approximately a third of residents in the Usulután case-study areas (excepting the towns of Jiquilisco and Santiago de María) actively supported the FMLN, reporting on the movement of government forces, helping move guerrilla encampments, and participating in insurgent organizations. The fraction was somewhat lower in Tenancingo, where approximately a quarter of the residents actively supported the FMLN, an estimate similar to that of a Salvadoran military officer responsible for the Tenancingo area for the eighteen months after the town was repopulated (Interview, Zacatecoluca, 1987). This estimated rate of active participation is very high compared with some classic instances of political mobilization. For example, at the peak of the massive labor mobilization in South Africa in 1987 that hastened the demise of apartheid, 11 percent of nonagricultural workers struck. In the great 1926 general strike in the United Kingdom, 14 to 15 percent of workers participated. And in the largest U.S. strike wave, which occurred at the close of World War II when workers attempted to regain ground lost during the war, 10 percent of workers participated.

The fraction of *campesinos* actively supporting the insurgents of course varied across the case-study areas. One ERP commander claimed that residents in the rural area west of San Agustín were "completely integrated" into various organizations of the FMLN, while in the towns of San Agustín and San Francisco Javier, only 40 to 45 percent were organized supporters (San Francisco Javier, 1992). In my judgment, this exaggerates insurgent support, but probably accurately reflects differences in support between the rural area and the two towns. The insurgent fraction was drastically less in the towns of Santiago de María and Jiquilisco (probably no higher than 10 percent).

Thus the evidence gathered in the case-study areas suggests that about two-thirds of the residents of the Usulután case-study areas (other than the towns Santiago de María and Jiquilisco) did *not* support the insurgency (beyond the coerced minimum), nor did three-quarters of those in Tenancingo. It is difficult to judge, however, whether *campesinos* among this group actively collaborated with the government. Some of those interviewed made explicit statements of loyalty to the government, but none affirmed any proactive role. This does not mean they did not actively collaborate. With the exception of those who lived in the towns of Jiquilisco and Santiago de María, active government supporters would have been well hidden in the case-study areas and unlikely to state this role even in confidential interviews, given the strength of support for insurgents. I return to the experience of those who did not support the insurgency in Chapter 7.

Conclusion

Extensive, voluntary support for the insurgency by *campesinos* in the case-study areas was the political foundation of the FMLN's military capacity. The most crucial form of *campesino* support to the guerrillas involved refraining from providing intelligence to government forces and actively doing so to insurgent forces. *Campesino* support was thereby also crucial to the emergence of dual sovereignty in many of the case-study areas. The form of this sovereignty varied. In the Las Marías area and to a lesser extent the coffee highlands near San Francisco Javier, the ERP was effectively the ruling authority by the mid-1980s. The state exercised authority there only coercively, when government forces engaged in sustained military campaigns. In the towns of Jiquilisco and Santiago de María, the situation was reversed. The state ruled, and the ERP made occasional coercive incursions during its military offensives. In the rest of the Usulután case-study areas, sovereignty was deeply contested. The Tenancingo accord formalized a distinct form of dual sovereignty, one in which both forces agreed to limit their authority.

In contrast to the romantic images among some international solidarity activists, there was no consensus in support of the FMLN in any of the case-study areas. Such consensus is neither typical nor is it necessary for insurgency. "Free-riding" on the benefits of the insurgency (principally, access to land and autonomy from landlords and sometimes from government forces) was possible during the stalemate in the Usulután case-study areas, as long as residents met the minimal contribution. The presence of free-riding confirms the voluntary nature of further contributions to the insurgency. This pattern of voluntary support sharply contrasts with Nora Kriger's emphasis on the importance of coercion in her study of peasant contributions to the Zimbabwean liberation struggle (1992).

While *campesinos* in the contested case-study areas in some sense lived "between two armies" (Stoll 1993), their understanding of those two armies varied. Individuals did not necessarily see both armies in the same light, but weighed their experiences with both and found them distinct. Of course different individuals made distinct judgments about the relative merits of the two armies. The majority of residents complied with demands for food from both armies and otherwise sought to avoid engagement with either party. The insurgent minority – a third or less in all case-study areas – complied with military demands for food but actively collaborated with the FMLN, viewing their participation as the necessary and justified extension of rural mobilization in the 1970s. It was they who forged the changes in social relations described in Chapter 3. How they did so is described in the chapter to which we now turn.

6

The Reemergence of Civil Society

Here in El Salvador there is a new model of agrarian reform:
agrarian reform through armed struggle. The inclusion of land in
the peace agreements is exactly the result of the use of arms.

Insurgent *campesino*, Las Marías, 1992

By the end of the civil war, a vibrant rural civil society of militant *campesino* organizations claimed extensive areas of land in Usulután and other contested areas. Their gradual emergence during the years of the military stalemate reflected the changing terrain of the civil war, as the two armed parties concentrated increasingly on building political loyalties among civilians rather than only on overt military competition. This development posed a profound contrast both to the historical absence of opposition organizations in rural El Salvador (until the mobilization of the 1970s) and to the decimation of overt political organizations in the extreme repression of the early 1980s.

In contrast to the insurgents' success in building a dense network of political organizations, government efforts to quell insurgency through agrarian reform, ongoing repression, and the incorporation of *campesinos* into organizations aligned with the Christian Democratic Party failed. While activists and their organizations in some areas were demobilized by government policies, the reforms did not reach two-thirds of the landless *campesinos*, a subset of whom in contested areas continued to mobilize. And even some beneficiaries of the reforms continued covertly to support the insurgents. *Campesinos* headed most of the organizations that comprised this dense network of associations, an unprecedented representation of the interests of the rural poor.

160

The Reemergence of Civil Society

Civil society comprises the wide variety of groups that lie between the family and the state. Scholars have valued civil society for a range of contributions to human society, including its roles as a safe haven from the state (and in some patriarchal settings, from the family), as an incubator of democratic values under authoritarian regimes, and as a space for personal development. Some have underlined the difficulties of building the organizations that constitute civil society under conditions of political repression (and, worse, civil war); others have stressed the contribution sometimes made by supportive state institutions to the emergence and growth of civil society organizations even under authoritarian regimes (Wade 1988; Fox 1996; Lam 1996; Ostrom 1996; and Skocpol 1996).

But neither the political space provided by inclusive, democratic institutions nor the synergistic assistance of complementary state activities was at work in the emergence of civil society in Usulután. Rather, such organizations emerged in the shadow of civil war through the efforts of insurgent *campesinos*, with the encouragement of their armed FMLN allies. One finds analogies to this surprising development of dense organizational networks under politically repressive conditions in the emergence of trade unions and township organizations in South Africa during the last few decades of apartheid and in the growth of oppositional trade unions in Poland in the late 1970s and early 1980s.

In this chapter I analyze the reemergence of overt opposition organizations during the military stalemate. I first discuss how some reform cooperatives broke with the government to found an opposition organization, then analyze the emergence of insurgent cooperatives in Usulután despite the ongoing targeting of cooperativists by government forces. I then describe the relationships between the various organizations and the ERP, and how during the final year of the war, the prospect of a negotiated resolution to land claims impelled further occupations by a much wider group of *campesinos* in Usulután.

CONFRAS and the Return to Insurgency

The agrarian reform was a political initiative. There was no preparation. At first, we saw some concrete changes but later it was just treason and bad-faith games. Still, the cooperatives have brought changes.

Leader, Cooperative La Maroma, 1992

161

In the wake of the expropriations and violence of the counterinsurgency agrarian reform, the stunned members of the new cooperatives began to work the properties, at first with a degree of advice and credit from the government. Despite the decrease in violence against civilians in the mid-1980s, continued cultivation was an uphill struggle. Conflict continued in many areas and members had little experience with managing large commercial properties. Even in western El Salvador where the impact of the conflict was minimal, many reform cooperatives were soon unable to repay their annual production loans, much less make mortgage payments. Ineligible for further credit, many cultivated only a fraction of their land, working individual family plots of corn and beans and sometimes raising a few cattle (Hernández Romero, Chorro, and Ramirez 1991).

In Usulután, the situation of most cooperatives was much worse. Not only did government forces kill some activists, the FMLN targeted cooperative harvests and pressed individual members to distance themselves from the implementing agency, which the insurgents perceived as a counterinsurgency instrument of the state. For example, the guerrillas twice destroyed the infrastructure of a cooperative south of Santiago de María that grew and processed coffee (interview, San Mauricio, 1992). Government technicians visited the cooperatives less and less frequently, and the general disruption of the "comanagement" of the property by government technicians and the cooperative leadership contributed to the siphoning-off of funds by corrupt managers and officials. By 1984, only two cooperatives in western Jiquilisco received credit. The rest used their few resources to plant corn and beans; the more fortunate households grazed a few head of cattle as indicated in the postwar map of Cooperativa La Normandía (Fig. 1.2). Short of credit and with many members absent, much of the land of some cooperatives was little used. For example, more than 2,000 hectares of arable land of the Cooperativa Nancuchiname, a very large reform cooperative to the west of the Cooperativa California, were not farmed in 1991.

An essential counterinsurgency aspect of the agrarian reform was the founding in 1982 of a new organization of agrarian reform cooperatives, the Federación Salvadoreña de Cooperativas de la Reforma Agraria (Salvadoran Federation of Cooperatives of the Agrarian Reform). *Campesinos* gaining land under the land-to-the-tiller phase were organized into the Unión Comunal Salvadoreña. The incorporation of reform beneficiaries into these organizations was intended to strengthen ties between rural residents and the Christian Democratic Party, thereby undermining insurgent organizations and developing the party's electoral base. These were among the largest organizations with whom the party struck a "social pact" of mutual support under which reform beneficiaries would vote for the Christian Democrat Party, and the party would continue to support the reform sector (Zamora 1991: 185–6; Goitia and Galdámez 1993: 644–50).

The pact soon faltered, however. Inadequate technical and financial support for the reform cooperatives, the frustration of managing large properties with inadequate help, and government violence against cooperative leaders and members in the wake of the expropriations soon had political consequences. The Duarte government's failure in the 1980s to deliver on its stated commitment to a negotiated resolution of the civil war also contributed to a growing disaffection (Lungo Uclés 1995: 158–9). Increasing alienation from the government and the party on the part of some cooperative leaders and members was evident in many interviews in Usulután. One leader of a reform cooperative summarized his analysis of the agrarian reform as follows: "So they didn't finish Phase I; they didn't even begin Phase II; we were unable to repay loans; and soon the majority of cooperatives in the east no longer received any credit" (San Marcos Lempa, 1992). According to another, "There's merely been a change of owner; now we simply work for the bank instead." Many leaders also expressed resentment of the government's refusal to grant full title to some cooperatives, government pressure in the late 1980s to subdivide the cooperatives into smallholdings, and ongoing political manipulation of the cooperative movement by the government. In 1991, I observed a remarkable instance of such manipulation on a trip with government officials to the western part of the country. In a fiery speech to cooperative members receiving titles to small holdings carved out of the former cooperative, the president of the Phase I agency urged those present to vote for the governing party ARENA, the party that would make El Salvador "*un país de propietarios*" (a country of owners). He went on to make the outrageous claim that Roberto d'Aubuisson had been the father of the agrarian reform.

Some cooperative leaders in Usulután interpreted the government's failure to deliver necessary services to the cooperatives as evidence of the agrarian reform's counterinsurgency purposes. For example, a founding member of one of the Jiquilisco cooperatives commented, "The Armed Forces began distributing land to deter the process of *campesino* organization." A member of another cooperative, who became a national opposition leader, argued, "The agrarian reform was not something the government and landlords sought, rather, it was imposed by the social movements of the 1970s, which had reached the point of destabilizing the government. [Reformist President] Molina had promised a land reform and that 'not even a single step backwards' [*ni un paso atrás*] would occur, a phrase that stayed in the memory of many *campesinos*" (La Maroma, 1992). A former colonel who on retirement had joined the Phase I implementing agency as a senior bureaucrat and who clearly opposed agrarian reform, told me the following joke in a 1991 interview: "Molina had sworn that there would not be even a single step backwards from agrarian reform – instead, he took fourteen steps to the right!" – a reference to the mythical fourteen families of the oligarchy.[1] Another cooperative leader noted that the reform was only partially successful in suppressing opposition organization: "In 1980, the *campesinos* were organizing. The Armed Forces began distributing land to deter that process. Those organizations [the Christian Democratic *campesino* organizations] were taken over [by the government], but others soon emerged."

At the national level, the leading symptom of this declining identification with the Christian Democrats and the agrarian reform was the founding in 1984 of new regional federations of reform cooperatives (one in each of the four regions of the country). The new federations formally broke with the Christian Democratic Party in early 1986 to support a new opposition organization, the Unión Nacional de Trabajadores Salvadoreños (National Union of Salvadoran Workers), which led the largest opposition marches since 1980. After a period of fluctuating affiliation, the new federations founded the Confederación Nacional de Federaciones de la Reforma Agraria Salvadoreña (National Confederation of Federations of the Salvadoran Agrarian Reform, or CONFRAS) in 1988 as the national organization of the opposition cooperative movement. By 1992, CONFRAS cooperatives comprised approximately a quarter of the agrarian reform cooperatives, less than that of the Christian Democrat–affiliated federation, which had nearly 40 percent, but nonetheless a significant fraction (Montoya 1992: 55). CONFRAS was as strong (as measured by its fraction of cooperatives and cooperative members) in the much less conflicted western region as in the conflicted eastern region.[2]

---

[1] In the context of discussing the 1979 coup, the former colonel told me another joke: "Why has there never been a coup in the United States? Because there is no U.S. Embassy there!"

[2] Indeed, the CONFRAS-affiliated federation of reform cooperatives in the eastern region, was not particularly strong in Usulután. Its membership comprised only 11 percent of cooperatives and cooperative members in the department. However, the federation controlled more than 25 percent of the *land* in cooperatives as its member cooperatives were often very large (though with few individual members; Montoya 1992).

The Reemergence of Civil Society

The emergence and consolidation of these opposition reform organizations was an important development in the reemergence of a civil society autonomous from the government. Some analysts also emphasize the organization's autonomy from political parties and the FMLN (Hernández Romero et al. 1991: 122; Lungo Uclés 1995). However, the situation was in fact more complicated. Some of CONFRAS's national leaders *were* covertly aligned to the FMLN (in particular, to the ERP). The government's labeling of CONFRAS and other opposition organizations as "facade organizations," while generally false in its implication that such organizations were directly controlled by the FMLN through incorporation of leadership into the insurgent line of command, nonetheless was not entirely incorrect. Opposition organizations often consulted with FMLN factions on critical issues, resulting in a coordinated political strategy. For example, in the 1988 National Debate, a national meeting of civil society organizations initiated by the Archdiocese of San Salvador to develop and articulate support for a negotiated end to the war, CONFRAS and its regional affiliates generally supported the positions of other FMLN-aligned opposition organizations, in contrast to the positions of organizations aligned with Christian Democrats (Debate Nacional 1988). Nonetheless, CONFRAS was significantly more autonomous from FMLN directives than other organizations active in the contested areas of Usulután (as we see below), in large part because its national membership included significant numbers of reform cooperatives far from any FMLN presence or influence.

Political loyalties of reform cooperative members in Usulután evolved along a variety of trajectories. A few members of the cooperatives, including many of those who had been political activists before the reform, continued to work with the ERP, despite the extreme risk of doing so given the ongoing conflict in the area and the proximity of government troops. As overt opposition movements had been eliminated, such participation took the form of covert individual collaboration with guerrilla forces, particularly providing food and information on government troop movements. According to someone who in the early 1980s was an ERP guerrilla, "When the FMLN was nearly wiped out [in early 1981], the reform cooperatives were the only social organizations. Many people within the cooperatives supported the FMLN, sometimes even entire columns of combatants would stop there to rest. But of course there were always informers too" (San Salvador, 1992). By the late 1980s, many leaders of the reform cooperatives in western Jiquilisco publicly advocated opposition political positions

165

endorsed by CONFRAS – but did not, of course, openly advertise their ongoing contact with ERP guerrillas in the area.

Members of other cooperatives in the case-study areas (two in Jiquilisco and four in the coffee highlands) had little involvement with the insurgents but maintained their affiliation with the Christian Democratic federation (and, not incidentally, access to credit as well). One promoter of the Christian Democratic federation who was covertly a member of the FMLN noted that "the agrarian reform did create a long-term base for the Christian Democratic Party. For example, about half of the members of El Limon [a cooperative on an island in the Bay of Jiquilisco] look on the Armed Forces as gods and see the guerrillas as communists" (San Salvador, 1991).

The Emergence of Insurgent Cooperatives

To occupy land for work and to live is not a sin.
Member, Cooperativa Escobares
San Judas, March 1992

Neither phase of the agrarian reform reached the truly landless rural population, those who were neither permanent employees on large properties nor renters of small holdings. Those who worked as occasional day laborers and harvest workers but did not farm land as tenants were not eligible for either program, yet their numbers had rapidly increased in the years before the civil war. In the later years of the war, landless and landpoor *campesinos* founded dozens of insurgent cooperatives throughout the contested areas of Usulután. A few were founded in 1986, many more in 1987 through 1990, and as prospects for peace and land reform as a part of the settlement crystallized in 1991, still more joined the ranks of these organizations.

Reflecting the focus on political work that was the basis of the insurgents' military capacity, these cooperatives were typically founded after a period of reflection and discussion by groups of potential members. The local origins of the insurgent cooperatives – self-selected members who decided whether and when they would declare the cooperative's founding – pose a sharp contrast to the top-down founding of the reform cooperatives in which the military and government technicians initiated the expropriation and decided who would be members. While local initiative was an element in the transfer of small holdings to tenants under the land-to-the-tiller program (the tenant or a group of tenants began the process by filing a claim at the office of the implementing agency), the results were distinct.

The latter group became unorganized smallholders, or, at best, members of service cooperatives, very few of which were effective. In sharp contrast, those who participated in the founding of insurgent cooperatives became members of cohesive organizations with a common interest (defense of land claimed collectively), joined a growing insurgent network, and were introduced to a new political identity and new political practices.

The ERP promoted the founding of such cooperatives as part of the FMLN's new strategy of building political organizations called the *poder de doble cara*, literally "two-faced power." Under the new strategy, the new organizations would present a legal face to the government, insisting on their rights as civilians, and a clandestine, collaborative face to the FMLN (Miles and Ostertag 1991: 224). With no ostensible link to the FMLN, the cooperatives would provide "cover" for clandestine cadres building networks of insurgent supporters and also serve as a recruiting ground for the militias and the guerrilla army (Byrne 1996: 133).

This emphasis on the development of civilian political organizations posed a particular challenge to the ERP, which, unlike the FPL, had historically emphasized military tactics. The ERP judged agricultural cooperatives the best way to build overt organizations of covert supporters in Usulután for two reasons, according to midlevel commanders. A significant rural population lived in and near conflicted areas, in contrast to other contested areas from which the population had been largely pushed. And agricultural production had a potentially high economic value in the department. Cooperatives as one of the few legal forms of rural organization would provide a degree, though small, of legal cover to supporters: cooperatives acquired legal recognition under regulations governing cooperative associations, a status referred to as having a *personería jurídica* (literally, "a legal personality"). They would thus gain some degree of legitimacy in the eyes of some government agencies, or at least in the eyes of international observers, which would raise the cost of harassment of members. Under the leadership of nongovernmental organizations allied to the ERP – whose leaders were in some cases strategically placed ERP political officers – the cooperatives would form a network of overt organizations and expand ERP influence.

Both the ERP and these nongovernmental organizations promoted the founding of insurgent cooperatives in the Usulután case-study areas. The National Association of Agricultural Workers promoted cooperatives in many regions of El Salvador, including Usulután. This group was founded as an unusual effort to resist the development of five parallel organizations in each organizational niche (one for each faction of the FMLN), as was the

167

common pattern (for example, by the end of the war each party had its own women's organization and development agency). In Usulután, however, the association was entirely dominated by the ERP. The most active organization in Usulután was the Federación Nacional de Cooperativas Agrarias (National Federation of Agrarian Cooperatives, or FENACOA), founded in 1984. While its public mission was the promotion of cooperatives among land-to-the-tiller beneficiaries, in fact the organization promoted the founding of insurgent cooperatives and the occupation of abandoned – and sometimes not abandoned – land. The two groups coordinated closely, sharing an office in the city of Usulután until the 1989 offensive. Some cooperatives initially founded by the first later joined FENACOA as it became the more active organization in the Usulután contested areas.

With the active support of local commanders, these organizations began promoting the founding of cooperatives in the Las Marías area in 1985. At first, even militant *campesinos* who had been working covertly with the ERP refused to participate, judging the risks too great. Most residents in the area at the time already had access to land, clandestinely working a small plot of someone else's land and taking firewood from abandoned coffee estates. Many carried out various tasks for the ERP, but joining or forming a cooperative was perceived as an overt challenge to the government, an explicit declaration of opposition that might well bring dire trouble. According to a leader of one cooperative in the Las Marías area,

From 1980 to 1985, even if you were a cooperativist in your heart, even if you believed in it, you would never say so, you would always deny it. Even in 1985 there were only a very few who were willing. Lots of people believed that the cooperatives could be the solution, but also believed that we would be targeted. (San Pedro Los Arenales, 1992)

The Cooperativa Loma Alegre was not founded until September 1991, because residents were too fearful. One leader described how a cooperativist had been horribly tortured and mutilated early in the war and his body left for all to see (Chinameca, 1992). Prospective members also feared that participating in cooperatives might also bring increased pressure from ERP cadres to join opposition political events such as marches in the city of Usulután or San Salvador.

The first insurgent cooperative was the Cooperativa La Luz en el Horizonte, founded in early 1986 in the Las Marías area.[3] The nearby

---

[3] While one FENACOA organizer claimed that another cooperative had notified a landlord in 1984 that his property had been taken over, it was clear from the reactions of the cooperative

Cooperativa La Conciencia followed in April of the same year, as did a few others before the year ended. According to one member of an insurgent cooperative, "Between 1986 and 1989, most of these cooperatives [in the Las Marías area] were founded. Raising up the cooperatives took away the fear." The initial tactic was for militant *campesinos* to take over a service cooperative of land-to-the-tiller beneficiaries, thereby securing the *personería jurídica*, and then occupy land, or formally claim already occupied land. The tactic required the covert cooperation of at least some organizers of the Christian Democratic organization that sponsored these service cooperatives.[4] Both La Luz en el Horizonte and La Conciencia were founded in this way. As a result, not all members of these cooperatives were landless, strictly speaking. Some were land-to-the-tiller beneficiaries who had legal claim to small holdings, but who nonetheless participated or acquiesced in the refounding of their cooperative as an insurgent cooperative. They were not required to support the insurgency in this way (a contribution beyond the coerced minimum), but like reform cooperative members who came to endorse CONFRAS, their hearts and minds had not been won by government counterinsurgency efforts. In interviews, local leaders named government repression of local activists (especially cooperative promoters) as a principal reason for their participation.

However, this tactic was frequently unsuccessful. The Cooperativa Tesoro near San Francisco Javier was similarly refounded as an insurgent cooperative in 1986 but fell apart within a year under the pressure of arrests and harassment of its members. It was once again relaunched in 1988. As the movement spread, FENACOA itself applied for and usually got the *personería jurídica* for new cooperatives.

Government forces responded to the founding of cooperatives with executions, torture, and arrests of their members. As a result, most residents declined to join even toward the end of the decade. In 1987, for example, there were two executions and thirteen arrests (including two allegations of torture) of people attempting to found insurgent cooperatives in

leaders that his claim was not true, all the more evident as he further claimed that FENACOA had occupied nearby properties beginning in 1980, four years before the organization's founding. One cooperative of displaced people claimed their *personería jurídica* had been granted in 1985, apparently through their ties with a displaced persons' organization in the capital.

[4] I could not establish in interviews whether this collaboration between the Christian Democratic organization and the insurgent cooperatives was limited to individual organizers or whether it was more pervasive.

Usulután (El Rescate Human Rights Chronology). In the first six months of 1988, there was one execution (the victim severely tortured) and fifteen arrests of insurgent cooperativists in the department. The Cooperativas La Conciencia and La Luz en el Horizonte endured despite violence directed against their members. On March 5, 1987, two members of La Conciencia were publicly beaten and forced to denounce the insurgents. Two members were arrested in 1988, including the vice-president. On April 11, 1987, four members of Cooperativa Luz en el Horizonte were arrested by the National Guard. They were released three to seven days later. The twelve-year-old son of one member was killed by soldiers of the Sixth Brigade on May 18, 1987. The next day, the vice-president was arrested. He was killed in October.[5] Leaders of other cooperatives described similar incidents that occurred during this period. A cooperative founder was tortured severely during detention; a female member was severely mistreated; and another leader was detained eight times. According to a leader of the Cooperativa Trece de Junio (1992), "You were always afraid; it was not easy to say, 'I am a cooperativist.' The fear never leaves you – half of the community did not want to become organized [join a cooperative], fearing a resurgence of war." Violence subsequently decreased (according to the El Rescate Chronology, there were only six arrests in 1989 and 1990) before increasing again at the end of the war as land claims were increasingly contested (see below).

Surprisingly, the number of insurgent cooperatives continued to grow despite this violence. New cooperatives emerged across the coffee highlands as activists saw earlier ones succeed. The cooperativists' growing confidence was also reflected in the increasing membership of existing cooperatives, as hitherto hesitant residents decided to join. By 1992, La Luz en el Horizonte had approximately 125 members and claimed some 100 hectares. According to a local activist, "Now that some were actually possessing the land, the fear began to subside: we could see that it was really possible" (San Pedro Los Arenales, 1992). He and his neighbors founded a cooperative in 1988, and some members were soon "cooperativists by day, militia members by night." A turning point seemed to have been reached by 1989, as activists became increasingly confident that the military would not renew high levels of violence against them and "began to recognize us as

---

[5] The source (El Rescate Human Rights Chronology) notes that the Armed Forces press office alleged that he had been killed by the FMLN. However, residents in the area attributed the death to government forces, in my judgment the more credible claim.

cooperativists, not just workers. Repression was no longer so bloody but was softer: investigation and blows but no longer death" (ibid.). Not all such efforts succeeded, however. In an area near Santa Elena, where a number of residents had been killed by government forces, a few residents attempted to found a cooperative in the mid-1980s but nearly all others refused (Santa Elena, 1992). When militants tried again in 1989, some 50 percent of the residents still refused to cooperate. Only in 1991 did the Cooperativa Trece de Junio first occupy land.

Selective benefits to motivate participation were present in only a very few cases where ANTA and FENACOA provided fertilizer to help activists persuade hesitant neighbors to join, as in the founding of the Cooperativa San Pedro Los Arenales. But this was the exception. In general, the *campesino* organizations offered their experience, their ability to obtain a *personería jurídica* (which brought legitimacy but no concrete benefits in this period), and the support of the ERP.

Most cooperative members interviewed saw their participation in the founding and development of cooperatives as growing out of their ongoing commitment to the insurgency, once conditions allowed. A member of the Cooperativa Los Tres Postes (1992) explained: "Let me give you a small lesson: We took up this struggle in 1978. From that date we have defended this struggle. That is why we organized ourselves in a cooperative." One cooperative leader argued that it was the FMLN that made possible membership in cooperatives: "Yes, now we are cooperativists! Thanks to the armed struggle of the FMLN" (Santa Elena, 1992).

It was probably no accident that the first two enduring insurgent cooperatives emerged close to the ERP's base in Las Marías, with others gradually emerging in surrounding areas. Proximity to the base in that deeply contested area went hand-in-hand with insurgency: less committed people had fled. And activists throughout the nearby area knew each other well, in part because they crossed paths repeatedly at the base on errands for the ERP. So in the Las Marías area, *campesinos* considering founding a cooperative could follow the progress of La Luz en el Horizonte and La Conciencia closely, marking their success despite ongoing violence. Once it was clear that they had succeeded, others followed suit, founding cooperatives increasingly farther from the base.

The pattern in western Jiquilisco and the area near San Francisco Javier is less tidy than in Las Marías, perhaps because the ERP was weaker there. In Jiquilisco, the first such effort occurred on the Hacienda California in 1987, which took the surprising turn described in the opening pages of this book. The Palomo family's former manager was elected president and residents continued to pay rent to the family until the estate was formally occupied in 1991. The Cooperativa La Merced was founded in 1989. Other cooperatives were soon founded and properties occupied. However, the members of some cooperatives were speedily evicted from some occupied properties. The process was similarly slow in the San Francisco Javier area. Although a few cooperatives were founded in 1986, most were dormant for several years and began formally occupying land only in 1989.

Despite the violence and constraints, by the late 1980s FENACOA had the capacity to mobilize hundreds of Usulután *campesinos* to attend events it sponsored in San Salvador. In July 1987, some 400 *campesinos* in eight buses were briefly detained by members of the Sixth Brigade at brigade headquarters in the city of Usulután while their identifications were noted (El Rescate Human Rights Chronology).

FENACOA's activities did not of course go unnoticed. From its founding, the organization came under sharp scrutiny by the government. Its offices were occasionally searched, its leaders detained, sometimes for several days, and its promoters harassed, sometimes seriously. While apparently seeing FENACOA as allied to the FMLN, the government did not take measures to eliminate the organization, which probably reflected the emphasis on winning civilian loyalties in the contested zone of Usulután as well as the general decline in state violence.[6]

However, government suspicion of and actions against FENACOA deepened in the aftermath of the FMLN's 1989 offensive. Its regional office in the city of Usulután was closed for more than a year. Many opposition organizations in San Salvador had similar problems, as the government claimed that they had assisted the FMLN during the offensive. In the case of FENACOA, the charge was true. Many members of FENACOA cooperatives and some staff members participated in the offensive as members of militias in support of ERP troops in their attack on the city of Usulután, according to those who participated and to ERP commanders. While their efforts had results less dramatic than in San Salvador (one militia member reported that grenades and mortars that had been stored since 1981 refused to launch), the offensive in Usulután and San Miguel kept government forces spread more thinly than if the San Salvador had been the only target.

---

[6] Curiously, FENACOA cooperatives continued to receive *personerías jurídicas*, a fact perhaps also reflecting the assistance of centrist organizations and a degree of covert support for the opposition among relevant bureaucrats.

Indeed, FENACOA was not merely allied to the ERP, according to interviews at various levels of the organization, but at least five of its twelve national leaders (of whom two were well-educated, urban people and the rest *campesinos*) were political cadres of the ERP in the sense that they belonged to specific military lines of command and held particular ranks within the organization.[7] Thus, FENACOA itself well illustrates the *doble cara* strategy. This integration of the organization's leadership into the party organization was a sharp contrast to the vague alliance between the leadership of CONFRAS and the party, which involved merely the coordination of oppositional political strategy.

Most cooperative leaders and many members of FENACOA cooperatives knew that many leaders were party members. They appeared to view FENACOA's close association with the ERP as part of the spectrum of insurgent activities, one that reflected a certain division of labor. One experienced local activist stated, "There were roles for those too old to take up arms. Those who could not join the organization [the FMLN] formed cooperatives" (Leader, Cooperativa El Palmo, 1992). Others downplayed the distinction between the military and political organizations of the opposition; some apparently viewed them as branches of one organization. One of the leaders of insurgent cooperatives in the Las Marías area told me:

Perhaps it should be clarified that the war was fought in two forms: openly in the army [the FMLN] or clandestinely, which was the most dangerous of all. I was taken, they tortured me, they even forced me out of my house – I had a great desire to join the FMLN immediately, but my family said no.

Another characterized the FMLN as the right arm of the political organizations, rather than the reverse, drawing on the image of the peasant as hunter: "That was how we organized ourselves – we even went around with rifles – the right arm that we as *campesinos* have." Guerrilla commanders also spoke of combatants and members of the *campesino* organizations as a single network of support:

Some joined as guerrillas, others collaborated indirectly: guarding the secrecy of the organization, buying materials (food, clothing), transporting heavy weapons and the wounded, helping to hide clandestine hospitals. Those and others also joined organizations, especially cooperatives. (Interview, Las Marías, 1992)

---

[7] In its first few years, FENACOA was apparently a joint effort of the Communist Party and the ERP. The Communist Party pulled out of FENACOA in the late 1980s, taking some ten of twenty-one cooperatives with it.

The ERP contributed to this identification of FENACOA with the armed left by using it as a source of recruits for the military structure of the party, as explicitly stated by the Las Marías commander:

From the beginning and throughout, we acted on the concept that we would grow militarily as we went forward politically. Only with both together would people understand. It was through the political organizations that the taking of conscience accelerated. Political formation took place in the political organizations. Later you might join [the guerrilla army] – but not by forced recruitment, no one could be obliged to participate. (Las Marías, January 1992)

The last statement appears to have been true during much of the war, but the ERP did recruit forcibly for several months in the mid-1980s, as we saw in the previous chapter.

Such identification not only undermined the autonomy of the political organizations but was dangerous for cooperativists, who were frequently seen by the government forces as guerrillas. Some insurgent *campesinos* recognized FENACOA's covert relationship with the ERP as a potential threat to the cooperatives, local communities, and families (hence the initial reluctance to found cooperatives). Many cooperativists, however, courted that identification in interviews during the 1992 cease-fire, frequently and explicitly initiating conversations in interviews about their organization's alliance with the ERP, pointing out the high degree of coordination between local military units and cooperative leaders.

The most militant *campesino* activists in the Las Marías area not only founded insurgent cooperatives but also formed a new organization in the early 1990s (various conflicting dates were given in interviews), the Comité de Defensa de la Tierra (Land Defense Committee), a group of twelve insurgent cooperatives. The committee, which would emerge in the postwar period as one of the most vibrant groups of cooperatives in the case-study areas, met every Wednesday on the grounds of a bombed coffee estate just south of Las Marías. Each of the twelve cooperatives in the area sent one or two representatives to the meeting, and one or two FENACOA organizers usually also attended.[8] During several committee meetings that I attended between 1992 and 1996, participants discussed the evolution of negotiations over land claims, access to credit, and, frequently, the internal politics of opposition organizations, as well as local gossip and news. Members attended regularly and discussion was often lively, occasionally

---

[8] Two of the cooperatives belonged to a Christian Democratic organization but appeared nonetheless to participate fully in the Land Defense Committee.

even boisterous, with much teasing (including, increasingly, of one recurring academic visitor). Committee meetings appeared quite democratic in that members made significant decisions, in sharp contrast to FENACOA and CONFRAS meetings.

The histories of two FENACOA promoters illustrate the role of the organization in the Usulután case-study areas. "Antonio," a FENACOA promoter in the Las Marías region, appeared a remarkably gifted leader despite his relative youth (twenty-five years of age). He exerted significant influence within the Land Defense Committee, not because of FENACOA's relation with the ERP (the Las Marías cooperativists had direct and sustained relations with area commanders), but apparently as a result of his intelligence, persuasion, and character, which earned him the evident respect of the older and more experienced local leaders. Antonio listened closely to cooperativists' needs and grievances, and appeared to value the opinions of committee members despite their lack of schooling. He spent a few weeks in jail at the beginning of the cease-fire for his role in the occupation of the Hacienda Concordia near Jiquilisco; his detention appeared to have little effect on his activism.

In contrast, "Cruz" became an activist in the 1970s through his friendship with a priest in Jiquilisco, who though not himself politically active, encouraged Cruz to attend seminars on cooperatives sponsored by the church. Through such activities, Cruz encountered covert members of the FPL but declined to join. He became a promoter of cooperatives for a Christian Democrat organization and then a promoter for a health organization. He joined FENACOA in the mid-1980s. During the 1989 offensive, Cruz felt very fearful and stayed at home, he said, but rejoined the organization when the regional office reopened. He became a member of the ERP but never served as a guerrilla, in contrast to some of the other staff members. Despite his knowledge of cooperatives and experience in organizing, Cruz was not a particularly gifted organizer. Local people recounted his history of alcoholism and questioned his political judgment, because he sometimes acted like the proverbial bull in the china shop. For example, during the cease-fire (mid-1992) at a meeting of several hundred members of CONFRAS and FENACOA, I stood near Cruz during a speech by Joaquín Villalobos, the top leader of the ERP who had not visited the Usulután coast for several years.[9] As the crowd applauded his speech, Cruz yelled, "We are not facade

---

[9] Villalobos's speech was notable for three things: his rhetorical skill in arguing for the importance of cooperatives and the transfer of land to FMLN sympathizers, his claim that such

organizations, we *are* the Frente! We support you now because we always supported you!" two public admissions that were quite dangerous at that point of the cease-fire and that earned him many cold shoulders.

FENACOA was not the only ERP-affiliated nongovernmental organization active in the Usulután case-study areas. Comunidades Unidas de Usulután (United Communities of Usulután, or COMUS) played a similar role to FENACOA but on a smaller geographical scale. Remarkably, given the history of death squad activity in the area, COMUS was founded in Santiago de María in April 1990 as an organization to provide services to rural people, the bland public statement of its mission. According to one of the founding leaders, COMUS began with the support of the "humanitarian structures" of the Catholic Church, but without public acknowledgment by the diocese of Santiago de María, a relationship characterized by COMUS leaders as a "relation of protection" (San Francisco Javier, 1992). Founders planned the initial meeting quite carefully, intending to test the waters slowly to see whether such an organization would be tolerated in Santiago at that juncture, when peace negotiations were well under way but as yet few concrete agreements had been reached. To test the official reaction, the founders notified the National Police that the organization would soon carry out a literacy campaign. Their prudence was undercut at the organization's inauguration by a priest's introduction of COMUS, as recalled by a founding leader: "COMUS is not a facade organization, but a real concrete organization that works parallel to the Frente," to the consternation of many in the audience.

After its launching, the inexperienced organization soon overextended itself, as it promised far more than it could deliver with its scarce resources. Many of its sixty founding communities had little contact with the organization after its founding. In an effort to reorganize, COMUS moved its office from Santiago de María to San Francisco Javier to be closer to its remaining communities. The organization received steady funding from a European agency, Ayuda en Acción (Help in Action), a charity that appealed to potential contributors to adopt a child and that channeled funds to development projects in the children's communities, rather than to individual children. Although the funds were not large, they enabled COMUS to lend small amounts of credit to some communities and to fund staff member salaries.

---

land transfer would also form the economic base of the FMLN's future political party, and his skill in answering the questions of the gathered *campesinos* for two hours.

The new organization stood in for FENACOA to a certain extent for several months after the 1989 offensive when FENACOA's offices were closed and its personnel were laying low. After the offices reopened, the organizations negotiated a division of labor. COMUS focused on developing local community organizations near San Francisco Javier and persuading the organizations to found cooperatives that would formally occupy land.[10] FENACOA staff members obtained the *personería jurídica* for those communities that formed cooperatives and then worked with the legalized cooperatives.[11] COMUS at the close of the war was far smaller than FENACOA, with only a third as many staff members. While staff members of both organizations in interviews emphasized their coordination, in practice the two organizations appeared also to compete for the affiliation of cooperatives (more affiliations enhanced their appeal to international donors and probably their standing in the ERP).

In contrast to the integration of several FENACOA leaders into the ERP's lines of command, COMUS leaders were not closely linked to the military structures of the party, even though a few had been members of the guerrilla forces some years previously. Nonetheless, COMUS leaders consulted extensively and publicly with local ERP commanders, particularly the political officer of the nearby ERP command post, whose strong influence within COMUS was evident. (His photo is shown in the previous chapter.) In the first few months of the cease-fire, for example, thorny questions were settled by COMUS staff members walking from their office on the main street of San Francisco Javier to the ERP base in the rundown coffee mill a few blocks to the northeast. During the cease-fire and even before his formal demobilization, the political officer became a COMUS staff member.

---

[10] The COMUS network of community organizations and cooperatives was significantly weaker, however, than that built by a sister organization in northern Morazán, a network of community councils founded in 1988 that governed civilian life, including schools and the regulation of timber cutting. Women were particularly active in the civil society of northern Morazán, persuading the army to allow the transit of foodstuffs into the area after a series of confrontations with the military (Thompson 1995; Binford 1997).

[11] While FENACOA sought in its early years to build cooperatives in San Miguel as well, those efforts failed with the exception of a few cooperatives along the Usulután border, especially in Chinameca. However, a handful of agrarian reform cooperatives in western El Salvador were members, a lingering consequence of the fluctuating early alliances between various organizations as civil society emerged from the repression of the early 1980s.

Growing Insurgent Political Capacity: Ongoing Land Conflict at War's End

By the end of the war, these organizations – CONFRAS, FENACOA, COMUS, and the Land Defense Committee – were part of a dense insurgent network of civil society organizations. This network coordinated an extraordinary upsurge in land occupations throughout the contested areas of Usulután as expectations of a negotiated settlement increased. This upsurge began in 1990, accelerated in late 1991, and culminated in 1992. The number of cooperatives (all of which took over land) that were members of FENACOA more than doubled over the period. Not only did insurgent groups increasingly occupy valuable properties along the Jiquilisco coast and in the coffee highlands, they also occupied valuable agricultural infrastructure (such as the California salt flats) as well. While government forces evicted *campesinos* from some properties, the insurgent organizations generally had the political capacity to defend the occupations against eviction.

The situation was particularly difficult in Jiquilisco, where conflict began in January and February 1991 when approximately 200 families with close ties to the ERP returned to El Salvador from refugee camps in Nicaragua, Panama, and Costa Rica.[12] In 1990, the leadership of the Nancuchiname, Mate de Piña, and La Normandía cooperatives (reform cooperatives affiliated with CONFRAS founded on one extremely large estate, the Hacienda Nancuchiname south of San Marcos Lempa) had convinced their membership to formally invite refugees returning from other countries to settle on their land, initiatives that signaled their alignment with the insurgency in general and with the ERP in particular. The Cooperativa La Normandía's initiative failed. Instead of insurgent-allied refugees, the government settled displaced civilians on the designated parcel (as shown in Fig. 1.2). The other resettlements succeeded, however, leading to the founding of Ciudad Romero and Nueva Esperanza on land of the Cooperativas Nancuchiname and Mate de Piña.[13] *Campesinos* in the area sent food and lent tools to support the new arrivals.

---

[12] The chronology of events in Jiquilisco in 1991 and 1992 draws on interviews with participating *campesinos*, ERP commanders, landlords of occupied properties, U.N. observers, and press reports.

[13] The refugees returned to El Salvador from Panama only after a long struggle resisting Salvadoran government efforts to condition their repatriation on their dispersal to various sites in El Salvador chosen by the government. After a series of protest activities, including a 300-kilometer-long march from the refugee camp to Panama City, an occupation of the

The Reemergence of Civil Society

In response, the Sixth Brigade and the Marine Infantry Battalion set up checkpoints along the dirt road from San Marcos Lempa to the new communities and searched and sometimes questioned cooperative members, community residents, and their visitors. In August 1991, these government forces took over part of the Cooperativa Nancuchiname and founded a new resettlement only a few hundred yards from the entrance to Ciudad Romero. The brigade then invited families of soldiers and ex-soldiers to join a new rival community, Nuevo Amanecer (not to be confused with the insurgent cooperative Cooperativa Candelaria un Nuevo Amanecer near Las Marías). According to a government official involved with the resettlement, the initiative was the army's response to the founding of Ciudad Romero: "The real story is Ciudad Romero, and the order came from above the Sixth Brigade. There are 123 cooperatives in the eastern regions on which to settle military families, why choose this one? I'll tell you: Ciudad Romero." Some forty-five families with ties to the military settled in Nuevo Amanecer with logistical and material support from the Sixth Brigade, the Marines, and the Phase I implementing agency. The families of Ciudad Romero and Nueva Esperanza, most of whom had fled the extreme violence of the military in the late 1970s and early 1980s, many after spending months in desperate conditions on the grounds of a parish in San Salvador, viewed this development with great anxiety. When members of the Cooperativa Nancuchiname objected to the usurpation of their land, they were told that they had no grounds to do so: the cooperative had never received legal title and so the Phase I implementing agency was the legal owner.

In a show of support to the cooperative, approximately 400 *campesinos* occupied the coastal highway near the (temporary) bridge over the Rio Lempa on September, 3, 1991. As shown in Figure 6.1, protestors succeeded in blocking traffic along the coastal highway and defied orders to disband (despite the use of tear gas). Organizers had alerted international and domestic journalists as well as human rights organizations, including the recently arrived Observer Mission of the United Nations in El Salvador, of the event. Their presence probably restrained the response of the government forces. The demonstrators eventually agreed to disperse when officials of the implementing agency agreed to meet with them. The agency later reneged, leading to large demonstrations outside their Usulután and San Salvador offices a few weeks later. While the protests did

Salvadoran Embassy, and a hunger strike, the refugees returned to El Salvador and founded Ciudad Romero (*Proceso* 458, January 9, 1991, n.p.)

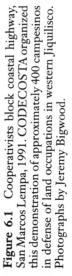

Figure 6.1 Cooperativists block coastal highway, San Marcos Lempa, 1991. CODECOSTA organized this demonstration of approximately 400 campesinos in defense of land occupations in western Jiquilisco. Photographs by Jeremy Bigwood.

not result in the removal of Nuevo Amanecer or end the harassment of the repatriates and cooperative members in the area, no more such settlements were established by outright military occupation of land claimed by insurgent organizations.

This and other protests, such as the defense of the Cooperativa California described in the opening pages of this book, took place under the banner of the Coordinadora para el Desarrollo de la Costa (Coordinator for the Development of the Coast, or CODECOSTA), an organization grouping together twelve CONFRAS and FENACOA cooperatives in western Jiquilisco and the two refuge settlements. In contrast to the organizations described above, CODECOSTA was founded not as an insurgent organization during the civil war but as an organization to promote the development of the area in the postwar period and, in the meantime, to defend occupied properties from the return of landlords or the claims of other parties. While CODECOSTA was nominally constituted by representatives from member cooperatives, in fact the organization was tightly controlled by the ERP. Indeed, the guerrilla organization had encouraged the refugees to settle in the Jiquilisco area, rather than return to their homes in northeastern El Salvador, as part of the party's effort to control the resource-rich coast.

Land occupations accelerated dramatically across the Usulután case-study areas throughout 1991 as part of a national campaign coordinated by the Asociación Democrática de Campesinos (Democratic Association of Campesinos), a national organization comprised of two dozen groups including CONFRAS, FENACOA, and COMUS.[14] One Jiquilisco landlord described the occupation of the properties belong to him and his four siblings as follows:

Last year, a group of about twenty-five people took over one of our lots. They threatened the two farmers to whom we had rented the land. We had to move the renters to other properties, we lost more than half of the deal. They threatened us, too: If you rent it out again, there will be consequences. But the usurpers themselves could not farm the land; they worked only twenty-five *manzanas* [17.5 hectares]. I tried to reach an agreement with them whereby they would farm a particular lot, but they refused. Those who are instigating it all are from FENACOA, it's the same thing as the FMLN. It's the very same people. Then they took over three more lots, which they neither worked themselves nor allowed us to work. We denounced the take-overs to the U.N. mission and in advertisements in newspapers. Our tenants

---

[14] The group included as well the Christian Democratic allied federation of agrarian reform cooperatives, which had joined the ranks of opposition campesinos organizations in 1990, a final defeat of the counterinsurgency efforts of the agrarian reform.

made a formal complaint to the judge in Jiquilisco, who issued an arrest order for some of [the leaders]. Some of them were known to me, four had been *colonos* on our land.... Despite all my efforts, they are still there. (San Salvador, 1992)

He was not able to evict the *campesinos* until the ERP agreed to the absorption of the group onto other properties in 1993.

COMUS intensified its promotion of land occupations in the area surrounding San Francisco Javier. Because there were small holdings as well as larger commercial properties in that area, the issue of which properties to occupy was a delicate one (see Fig. 3.8). Generally, properties were occupied if abandoned or as a punishment for what the cooperativists saw as consistently poor behavior by the owner (e.g., refusal to rent unworked land or speaking badly of cooperative members). Properties belonging to those who had left under accusation of being informers were particularly targeted.

At the war's end, cooperatives in Usulután representing approximately 10,000 people claimed 482 properties comprising approximately 66,500 hectares, about 32 percent of the surface area of Usulután (FMLN 1992).[15] In Jiquilisco alone, 89 insurgent cooperatives claimed properties amounting to 19,000 hectares. Land claims by ERP-affiliated cooperatives were also very high in Jucuapa, San Agustín, and San Francisco Javier. Figure 6.2 presents a conservative estimate of the extent of land claims made by the FMLN and affiliated cooperatives in some of the case-study areas, along with the amounts of land eventually transferred.[16] With the exceptions of Santiago de María, where there was no land claimed, and Santa Elena, where there were few claims, the extent of claims in the contested municipalities is impressive, particularly in Jucuapa, where more than 95 percent was claimed. While many claims were not granted in subsequent negotiations, insurgent cooperatives and the FMLN forced a transfer of approximately 8 percent of the nation's farmland (compared with the 16 percent of the first phase of the agrarian reform and 5 percent of the third; McElhinny 2001:

[15] Not all land occupied by cooperatives was in fact cultivated. For example, of the 413 hectares occupied by the Cooperativa Trece de Junio just south of Las Marías, about 40 percent were not planted or grazed.

[16] This is a conservative estimate of the amount of arable land claimed and transferred relative to the arable land in the municipality, because it is based on total surface area, rather than total arable land. Moreover, the fraction of the total surface area that is arable is undoubtably higher on the claimed and transferred territories than for the municipality as a whole. This is particularly true in the case of Jiquilisco, which includes vast areas of uncultivable marshes. The land claimed is that listed on the June 1992 FMLN inventory (see Table 3.1 and related notes).

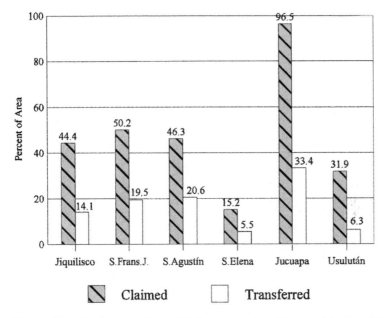

Figure 6.2 Land occupations in Usulután at war's end, by municipality. Calculated from the FMLN's inventory of occupied land (FMLN 1992) and the Programa de Transferencia de Tierra (Government of El Salvador) database (1997).

table 6). Some of the land transferred was among the nation's best farmland. Perhaps ironically, armed insurgency resulted in land not only for FMLN combatants and their supporters but for former government soldiers as well. Figure 6.3 shows an estimate of land occupied at the end of the war as well as the land eventually transferred to the FMLN, its supporters, and ex-soldiers.[17]

Four factors contributed to the accelerating pace of occupations in Usulután at war's end. First, despite the disruption the 1989 offensive brought to the FMLN-allied organizations such as FENACOA, their work was easier in its aftermath. The offensive changed the military balance in the department appreciably, leaving wider regions more easily accessible to cooperative promoters. One ERP commander characterized Mount Taburete as under "political control" since 1984 but "completely free" after

---

[17] The Land Transfer Program in Usulután was carried out as a special project of the European Union, which provided funding and staff for land transfer to ex-combatants of both sides in Usulután (CE-GOES 1996). USAID provided additional funding for transfer of land to civilian supporters of the FMLN.

Figure 6.3 Land occupations and transfers in Usulután. Based on map and data in CE-GOES (1996: Anexo IV). Transfers to ex-combatants and supporters of the FMLN are shown in black, those to ex-combatants of the government in gray.

the offensive (San Francisco Javier, 1992). Another commander (Las Marías, 1993) argued that while the mobilization of political cadres for the offensive meant that they had lost the cover provided by civilian organizations, the damage was not significant, as the chaos and disorder of the offensive itself prevented government forces from taking immediate advantage of their exposure, and they were in any case already identified as guerrilla supporters given their role in the organizations. The presence of surface-to-air missiles, a new development in El Salvador, also contributed to the changed military balance. (A field commander claimed that there were thirty-seven in Usulután alone, probably a significant exaggeration.)

The second factor was the ongoing demonstration that occupations were feasible. Each successful takeover demonstrated a widening, local political opportunity to those considering taking over other land. The presence of U.N. observers of course reinforced this perception. Although eviction efforts were still violent, the presence of observers at many such efforts (alerted by the *campesino* organizations) probably evoked some restraint.

The Reemergence of Civil Society

The third and probably most important factor was the process of negotiations between the FMLN and the government, which by mid-1991 had resulted in a number of crucial interim agreements. By April 1991, militant campesinos throughout the case-study areas understood that those occupying land in the conflicted zones might be entitled to land under the terms of the upcoming peace agreement. According to a COMUS promoter,

> In April 1991, we started occupying properties *manzana* by *manzana*, coordinating things across the area. The war was going to end and further occupations were necessary to defend our achievements and to end up on the list [of occupied properties eligible for legal transfer]. That was the orientation we received [from the ERP]: everyone should occupy what they could. (La Peña, 1992)

This understanding deepened with the signing of the New York Accord in September. The agreement stated that FMLN members and supporters occupying land in contested areas would be able to remain on the land and purchase it on subsidized terms. Although the terms of the postwar land transfer were extremely unclear, the accord led to land occupations throughout Usulután, other contested areas, and even in some government-controlled areas. The pace of attempted evictions also quickened as landlords also realized that defense of their property rights was urgent given the provisos of the accord.

This development of course changed the incentives for *campesinos*. There was now a credible (if far from sure) link between one's occupying land and concrete material benefits of doing so. As a result, the *campesino* organizations were able to mobilize groups and areas that had to date refused to support the insurgents, much less take the public step of land occupation. Increasingly, groups occupied land without obtaining first the *personería jurídica* (a decision that would complicate their status later). FENACOA in particular grew rapidly. By mid-1992, FENACOA had thirty-eight member cooperatives and employed thirty-four people including cooks, promoters, program coordinators, and administrators, in addition to the ten members of the Administrative Council and the five members of the Vigilance Committee.[18] The signing of the peace agreement on January 16, 1992, did not end the occupations, as *campesinos* (both cooperative members and others) made last-ditch efforts to secure land. Some efforts, such as the attempt

---

[18] The source, a report to member cooperatives and donor agencies (FENACOA 1992), might be thought to exaggerate the achievements of the organization. However, my research confirmed the existence and approximate membership size of the cooperatives listed in the case-study areas.

described in the opening chapter to take over the large Hacienda Concordia, failed, but others succeeded, infuriating landlords who had hoped the peace agreement would mean that they could either return to their properties or sell them on acceptable terms.

The fourth factor was the growing political capacity of the ERP-allied organizations that coordinated the occupations. This network extended beyond those directly coordinating occupations such as FENACOA and COMUS to include nongovernmental organizations that conducted research and offered technical assistance to cooperatives in Usulután.[19] It also included international nongovernmental organizations, which offered increased funding to FENACOA and COMUS toward the end of the war, enabling the organizations to pay staff members on a regular basis and to provide some resources to members.[20] For example, late in the war (mid-1990), FENACOA began distributing limited amounts of credit to its member cooperatives. By mid-1992, the organization received significant funding from international donors, including Scandinavian agencies and European solidarity organizations.[21] Thus resource mobilization contributed to collective action, but only late in the war.

As elsewhere in Central America (Macdonald 1997), these nongovernmental organizations rarely met their development goals but contributed significantly to the development of the ties across insurgent organizations. This insurgent network also contributed to the accountability of government forces for actions against civilians, as insurgent activities and violent evictions were publicized by both domestic and international organizations. More diffuse networks, such as networks of Catholic pastoral workers in Usulután, also reinforced this network of ERP organizations by providing

---

[19] Most important were the Instituto de Investigación Social y Desarrollo (Institute for Social Investigation and Development) and the Fundación para la Autogestión y la Solidaridad de los Trabajadores Salvadoreños (Foundation for Self-Development and Solidarity for Salvadoran Workers). Jenny Pearce states that approximately 700 nongovernmental organizations existed in El Salvador by 1989, more than half founded after 1985 (Pearce 1998: 599).

[20] The ERP was much less successful than the FPL in tapping international solidarity for funds. In particular, the FPL controlled much of the funds raised through solidarity networks in the United States. The ERP did slightly better in Europe than it did in the United States but still worse than the FPL. There appear to be three reasons for this: the FPL's closer ties to progressive elements of the Catholic Church, the ERP's militaristic reputation, and the FPL's earlier emphasis on developing international ties.

[21] FENACOA would be extremely unusual among FMLN-allied organizations if all its funding in fact went toward its projects without some "losses" along the way to the party and, to a lesser extent, to individuals.

186

initial contacts with European agencies and confirming reports of human rights violations. Visits by international delegations strengthened the ties between the network and its international allies, sometimes because delegation members were themselves detained by government forces.[22] For example, six young Spaniards were detained during the September 3, 1991, demonstration on the coastal highway (*La Prensa Gráfica*, September 4, 1991). On December 5, 1991, the Treasury Police reported the detention of five "agents of international communism" (two Germans, one Italian, one Spaniard, and one North American) and accused them of instigating the take-over of the Hacienda Las Arañas in Jiquilisco (*El Mundo* and *La Prensa Gráfica*, December 6, 1991).

The insurgent network itself coordinated its activities – most important, land occupations – in several ways. The organizations themselves met regularly. In the dozens of their weekly meetings that I attended in Usulután, an essential part of the agenda was the sharing of information concerning new occupations and eviction attempts. Staff of nongovernmental organizations spread news of the wider pattern of insurgent activity on their visits from San Salvador. Increasingly, militant *campesinos* coordinated their activities by openly visiting ERP base camps to discuss with the commanders and other activists potential land occupations, landlord visits, eviction attempts, and visits of the U.N. observers to their properties. ERP commanders attempted to protect *campesino* organizations from government repression by conditioning the timing of various steps of demobilization on the release of detainees or steps toward the transfer of land. And when in mid-1992 the government circulated a list of ninety-two properties it claimed had been occupied too late to fall under the terms of the peace agreement, the FMLN objected in extremely strong terms. Joaquín Villalobos stated publicly (in the speech I attended in Usulután) that there were three conditions that would prompt the FMLN to break the cease-fire: a coup, renewed repression, and attempts to evict *campesinos* in conflicted areas (although not in isolated cases, he added). For example, Argentina Argueta, the general secretary of FENACOA, was killed at an intersection in the Jiquilisco area by an unknown assailant on February 4, 1992. At a press conference at the Las Marías base camp (which I observed), the ERP commanders of Usulután declared that they would halt their movement to the designated cease-fire areas until the circumstances were clarified and several detained *campesinos*

---

[22] See Foley (1996) for analysis of the contrasting roles of Europe and the United States in the development of civil society organizations.

released. Only after several days did U.N. observers persuade them to continue their withdrawal.

In early March 1992, the ERP coordinated the founding of "public security commissions" across the contested areas of Usulután. CODECOSTA, COMUS, and the Land Defense Committee separately announced to the U.N. observers' regional office that they had formed groups of a dozen of so armed *campesinos* to patrol occupied properties. Of particular concern to the U.N. mission (Usulután, 1992) was the fact that the commissions would be advised by small numbers of ERP guerrillas who would remain near the contested properties, a violation of the peace agreement under which the FMLN was committed to withdraw its forces to designated areas. The commissions then clashed with landlords on a number of occasions. In the Las Marías area, members of the Land Defense Committee took control of a tractor with which a landlord had tried to plow his land. In mid-March, another commission forcibly detained landlord Enrique Novoa and three assistants as they were attempting to bulldoze shacks built by *campesinos* occupying his property, Hacienda Montemar (located south of Ciudad Romero, Nueva Esperanza, and Nuevo Amanecer). After the arrival of U.N. observers, they were released unhurt. A few days later, Novoa returned to the property with nine members of the National Police and four U.N. observers to evict the occupying campesinos. An American priest living in the area, a FENACOA promoter, and the cooperative leader were arrested when they attempted to prevent the evictions; the priest was subsequently deported and the two *campesino* leaders released, one after a few weeks in prison.

A contributing factor to the growing direct involvement of the military structure of the ERP in land occupations was direct self-interest: under the terms of the negotiations, ERP guerrillas would also receive land. As a result, ERP commanders themselves coordinated a few land take-overs to secure valuable properties for their forces. The abandoned Finca Santa Fe just south of San Francisco Javier was formally occupied by the ERP on March 15, 1992. In late 1992, the ERP refused to demobilize the fourth 20 percent of its forces or to begin destroying arms as scheduled until further guarantees were given concerning land. In December 1992, ERP commanders in Las Marías refused to initiate the final demobilization until the government began the transfer of private property (not just state lands, as had been the case until then), including coffee mills.

Confronted with this unprecedented degree of organization, the ongoing stalemate, and the declining returns to agricultural investments throughout

The Reemergence of Civil Society

El Salvador as a result of the varied processes of the civil war, many land-lords of properties in contested areas agreed to sell their properties (Wood 2000).[23] Some Las Marías landlords eager to sell bargained directly with ERP officers in an attempt to force government officials to approve a fast transfer, something officials were reluctant to do, as it would only bolster the FMLN's standing in the first postwar elections. By mid-1992, the stymied negotiations over the transfer of occupied properties to insurgents (both civilian supporters and combatants) threatened the implementation of the peace agreement, as the parties repeatedly failed to reach agreement on the extent and terms of transfer. In October, the United Nations stepped in, offering the parties a take-it-or-leave-it deal that both parties accepted. Its terms were significantly more favorable to the government's negotiating position. The result was a very significant contraction in land transferred to the insurgents from the scale of land occupations at the close of the war, as evident in Figure 6.2.

Conclusion

> The problem of land is that of life. It is not given to anyone; it is a
> right acquired through suffering and struggle.
> CODECOSTA militant, Tierra Blanca, 1996

By war's end, the dominant form of support for the insurgency had shifted from covert support of guerrilla forces to widespread collective action, as some *campesinos* in the case-study areas joined overt opposition organizations, founded cooperatives, and occupied land. Land was still deeply valued by *campesinos*, but residents in the case-study areas already had de facto access to land in the short run. So access to land does not explain participation. Indeed, most apparently felt that the risks of joining an insurgent cooperative and formally occupying the land were too high to merit participation. Nonetheless, land occupations spread outward from guerrilla strongholds as *campesinos*, reluctant at first to take steps that they saw as signaling their support for the insurgency, observed the first successful efforts and their gradual expansion. Thus *campesinos* perceived the widening of local political opportunity for such collective action through this demonstration effect, particularly after the 1989 offensive. The pace of

[23] While civil society had reemerged in San Salvador as well, urban organizations posed much less of a threat to elite interests, as labor organizations did not recover from the repression of the early 1980s (Fitzsimmons and Anner 1999).

this collective action dramatically quickened once the negotiation process signaled that those who occupied land in contested areas might get land as part of the postwar deal. By the early 1990s, insurgent activities took place even in Santiago de María. Opposition organizations held a march in 1990 demanding higher wages for harvest workers, and an ERP-allied nongovernmental organization opened a branch office a mere block from the National Police office.

This widening collective action was coordinated through a network of insurgent organizations that comprised a vibrant civil society in Usulután. Overlapping networks of military and political cadres and militant *campesinos* organized in insurgent as well as reform cooperatives, *campesino* federations, nongovernmental organizations, and the guerrilla's military structure ensured a continual flow of information concerning successful activities. The network also ensured a degree of accountability on the part of government forces in their response. Ties between the leadership of the insurgent organizations in the case-study areas with the ERP varied from the integration of the leadership of FENACOA into its lines of command to the close working relationship between COMUS and local commanders to the occasional consultation by CONFRAS leaders with those of the ERP. Backed by the armed muscle and coordination of the ERP, these organizations succeeded in shaping isolated and covert resistance to government counterinsurgency efforts into much more widespread and overt participation in the insurgency.

The relationship with the ERP also imposed costs on the organizations, an infringement on their autonomy to varying degrees that no doubt undermined their appeal to potential members not willing to take on affiliation with the party. Moreover, a large fractions of funds donated by European and American solidarity groups to nongovernmental organizations (in the case of COMUS and FENACOA, this flow occurred only late in the war) generally went to the FMLN, whatever their intended destination, according to interviews with a range of members of international organizations.

On the other hand, party affiliation made possible the very existence of the organizations. Founders of the insurgent cooperatives were usually already active insurgent supporters who saw their work with the cooperatives as a continuation of their ongoing participation. The cooperatives gradually succeeded in drawing in residents who had not previously supported the insurgents (beyond the coerced minimum), as the survival of the initial cooperatives showed that the costs of doing so were not as high as feared. Domestic and international networks supporting the FMLN raised the cost of repressive state action as moves against insurgent organizations were denounced in San Salvador, Washington, and various European capitals. In dozens of interviews at the close of the war, *campesinos* and landlords alike made clear their understanding that without the support of the FMLN, such cooperatives would soon have been evicted.

This robust civil society emerged in an environment of continuing state hostility and little outside funding. This pattern contrasts with two other forms of rural organization during the civil war are illuminating. On the one hand, state funding for the agrarian reform did not quell insurgency for long. CONFRAS emerged and garnered a quarter of the reform cooperatives as members, and in Usulután many cooperative members collaborated with the FMLN. The pattern documented here suggests that where there is a history of government violence and where land redistribution is not accompanied by adequate services, support for the insurgency may continue or reemerge.

On the other hand, the reconstruction of Tenancingo also contrasts with the experience of insurgent cooperatives. The project demonstrated that given the military stalemate, significant international commitment, and the services of an experienced development agency, a community could be rebuilt such that former residents were welcome irrespective of political allegiances and despite a history of high levels of political violence. However, other project ambitions of fundamental social change were not realized. The project's neutrality meant that aspirations to participation and redistribution that were identified with the insurgency were not tapped and the project remained isolated from opposition forces. The top-down management of the Community Council and other institution-building efforts meant that participants had a lesser sense of achievement and ownership than did participants in the insurgent cooperatives. Other constraints on the project's programs, such as its inability to redistribute assets, reflected the absence of negotiation and reform nationally. In short, the project could not supercede the fact of ongoing war. One close observer of the project assessed its impact this way:

How much effect can FUNDASAL have in Tenancingo? It's a Talmudic risk: How much change of structure can one achieve in two years? It's a matter of making a perturbation, not a fundamental change, yet a perturbation can have power if it is at the core. It was an attempt to try to combine the urgent need for change in social relations with the importance of conflict resolution. In this, they went to the limit of what was possible. Realistically, what is left behind? The people went from being destitute to a reconstituted livelihood at survival levels. And they have the benefit of having participated in addressing issues that trouble them. (San Salvador, 1987)

He concluded, "The experience should not be idealized, but we all learned that even given all the loss, troubles, and fears; it is possible to coexist."

In contrast, with only very minimal funding (until about mid-1990) and very little international presence, insurgents founded cooperatives and built overarching organizations in the contested areas of Usulután. The organizations proved capable of sustained collective action in defense of the interests of its members. The emergence of CONFRAS and the insurgent cooperatives is puzzling, as neither state support nor outside funding accounts for the pattern observed in the case-study areas: the failure of the agrarian reform to quell rural insurgency even among members of reform cooperatives, the demise of the Community Council in Tenancingo, and the emergence of dozens of insurgent cooperatives in Usulután, where access to land was not contingent on participation until the very end of the war.

7

Campesino *Accounts of Insurgent Participation*

What our history has been! We have come to know what a
movement is, we have won a cease-fire. We, as a cooperative,
now we know what it is to be free.

Land Defense Committee, Las Marías, 1992

Why did *campesinos* in Tenancingo and Usulután support the FMLN and
join insurgent organizations, despite the high costs of doing so? The
Salvadoran insurgency was about land. Perhaps access to land, a key material interest of *campesinos*, accounts for why so many *campesinos* participated
in the insurgency, thereby resolving the puzzle of collective action posed in
the opening pages of this book. However, at the time the insurgent cooperatives were formed, residents of the case-study areas had access to land
whether or not they participated, as long as they refrained from informing
on insurgent activities and made occasional material contributions (which
they also had to make to passing government forces). Thus during the middle and later years of the civil war, it was possible for those who did not
support the rebels to reside in the case-study areas as "free riders" on the
benefits of the insurgency. The benefits included improved working conditions in some areas and unprecedented access to land and freedom from
the often capricious authority of landlords and security forces in others.
But none of these benefits required participating in the insurgency beyond
the coerced minimum contribution. In short, the material benefits of the
insurgency took the form of a public good that was available to all residents.
Moreover, many members of agrarian reform cooperatives, who had gained
access to land through government-sponsored reform, also supported the
insurgents.

Perhaps *campesinos* supported the insurgent cooperatives in order to secure legal claim to land in the long run, perhaps believing that participation would lead to the legalization of claims to occupied land. The pattern of participation certainly supports this reasoning in one respect: after peace negotiations signaled the likely end to the war and the possibility of land transfer to FMLN supporters occupying land, participation in land occupations greatly increased. Approximately half of those who took over land did so only toward the end of the war. A survey carried out in 1993 found that the average length of land occupation, as reported by those occupying properties, was three and a half years (Seligson, Thiesenhusen, Childress, and Vidales 1993: 2–16). Even then the risks were significant: violent evictions and attempted evictions of occupied properties were commonplace in late 1991 and in 1992, and were usually accompanied by severe injuries.

On the other hand, half of those occupying land did so *before* peace negotiations began in 1990 and well before April 1991, when the first serious fruits of the peace negotiations were evident. For access to land in the long run to have been the principal motivation for founding or joining an insurgent cooperative, a potential participant would have to have believed (1) that the founding of the cooperative was necessary for long-run access to land, (2) that his participation was necessary to its success, and (3) that he judged that the anticipated benefit – access to land in the long run – outweighed the anticipated costs, including possible retaliation by local landlords or state authorities as well as the everyday costs of attending meetings. Even militant *campesinos* who otherwise supported the FMLN judged the risks too high until 1986 and 1987. Yet from 1987 to approximately 1990, dozens of cooperatives were founded, although the risks were still high (though declining), the selective benefits very few (a bit of credit to a few members of a few cooperatives), and the prospects for the legalization of land claims vanishingly small. It is improbable that potential participants would judge these negligible material benefits worth the risks. Indeed, more than half of the residents of the case-study areas did not join insurgent cooperatives even in 1991 and 1992.

So the puzzle of revolutionary collective action remains. I first explore whether we can garner insight into why some *campesinos* rebelled by systematically examining which type of *campesinos* (tenant, landless Laborer, and so on) participated. Because some insight to the puzzle may be gleaned from the accounts that participants themselves provide, I then analyze the accounts given by *campesinos* who joined the insurgency and those by *campesinos* who did not. I also analyze the maps drawn by insurgent *campesinos*. Drawing on this ethnographic evidence as well as a postwar survey of political attitudes, I conclude that a new insurgent political culture emerged in the case-study areas during the civil war.

Agrarian Class and Mobilization before the Civil War

Inadequate access to land was a key grievance before the civil war, and many insurgent *campesinos* dreamed of owning their own land. Yet the findings reported here suggest that such aspirations per se did not motivate insurgency, as access to land was not a likely outcome contingent on participation. If it had been, we should find that landless and land-poor *campesinos* participated in political mobilization at a significantly higher rate than other poor rural residents.

Ideally, we would test the importance of agrarian class position as a contributor to political participation with data from a representative sample of rural people indicating their levels of political participation and affiliation at various points during the conflict. But even in peacetime, surveys of this sophistication are rare, and one casualty of war is the continuity of the social order that would make the gathering of such data feasible. In the Salvadoran case, the census of 1981 was canceled and no representative surveys were conducted in the contested areas during the war. And war-driven migration from the case-study areas makes impossible a precise quantitative ex post facto reconstruction of the wartime "paths" of a representative prewar population.

However, a very detailed study just prior to the war provides a wealth of valuable information. Based on observations of households in seven *cantones* of central El Salvador from 1974 to 1977, anthropologist Carlos Rafael Cabarrús (1983) analyzed patterns of political affiliation. He classified households into better off (but still poor) middle peasants, land-poor peasants ("proletarian peasants") who earned a substantial part of their income in wages, and landless day laborers. He recorded the political affiliation of each household at the time, whether with the paramilitary ORDEN, the opposition group Federación Cristiana de Campesinos Salvadoreños (Christian Federation of Salvadoran Campesinos, or FECCAS), or two other smaller opposition groups.[1] *Campesino* political affiliations as a percent

---

[1] In addition to FECCAS, there were two small opposition groups, present only in one or two *cantones*. One was affiliated with the Communist Party; the other was not affiliated with any insurgent faction (Cabarrús 1983: 160–2).

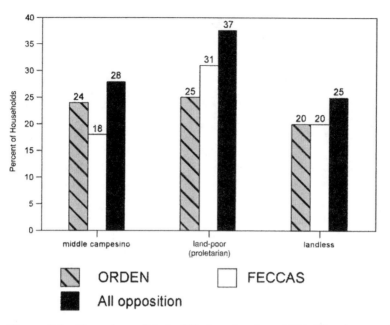

Figure 7.1 *Campesino* political affiliations by class, 1976. The data are from 812 households in seven *cantones* of the municipalities of Aguilares, Suchitoto, and San Martín and refer to the percentage of households in each economic class affiliated, respectively, with the progovernment ORDEN, the opposition group FECCAS, and with all opposition organizations. *Source*: Calculated from Cabarrús (1983: Cuadro 42, p. 173).

of each class are shown in Figure 7.1. In all classes, *campesinos* were more likely to join some opposition group other than ORDEN. However, neither access to land nor its absence appears to explain propensity to mobilize. The order of increasing access to land (landless, land-poor, and middle peasant) is not the order of increasing participation in opposition groups (landless, middle peasant, and land-poor). Nor does the order of decreasing access to land match the order of increasing participation. Although the landless were less likely than the middle *campesinos* or the land-poor to be affiliated with any group, they affiliated equally with both FECCAS and ORDEN (and were more likely to affiliate with some opposition group than with ORDEN, 25 vs. 20 percent).[2] And while the better off middle *campesinos*

[2] "Apolitical" households, those with no affiliation, comprised 47 percent of the middle peasant households, 39 percent of land-poor households, and 54 percent of landless households (calculated from Cabarrús 1983: 173).

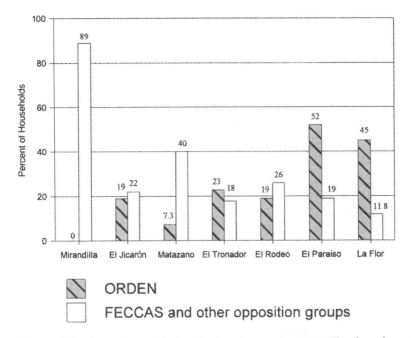

ORDEN
FECCAS and other opposition groups

Figure 7.2 *Campesino* political affiliations by *cantón*, 1976. The data show the percentage of the population of the *cantón* affiliated with the two groupings. There were no households affiliated with ORDEN in Mirandilla. *Source*: Calculated from Cabarrús (1983: Cuadro 42, p. 173).

were more likely to support ORDEN than FECCAS, when the other opposition groups are included, they were more likely to join the opposition than ORDEN. Proletarian *campesinos* were more likely to join FECCAS than ORDEN (31 vs. 25 percent) and were still more likely to join some opposition group than ORDEN (37 vs. 25 percent).

Overall, however, the differences in political affiliation between groups are rather small.[3] *Within* the group I have called *campesinos*, class position appears to provide little insight in differentiating political affiliation before the war (see Fig. 7.2). In El Paraíso, 52 percent of the households joined ORDEN and only 19 percent joined opposition organizations. In

---

[3] Ideally, one should test for the statistical significance of the relationships between the different categories and political affiliation. However, the individual-level data do not appear in Cabarrús's book. Jeffrey Paige interprets this data differently, emphasizing the study's finding that the land-poor were more likely to participate in opposition groups than either middle peasants or the landless (1996: 134–5). Even if the finding were statistically significant, the effect is still quite small.

La Mirandilla, in sharp contrast, 89 percent of the households joined opposition organizations; none joined ORDEN. Yet these two *cantones* were the most similar of all the *cantones*, with roughly a third of households falling in each social category. La Flor and Matazano, the next most similar pair with roughly half of the households land-poor, exhibit a similar contrast.

Cabarrús drew maps of each *cantón* indicating membership of each household in the appropriate extended family. The maps show that political affiliations were often familial: extended families tended to affiliate with either FECCAS or ORDEN. However, many families were sharply divided. In El Jicarón, five of the households of the Meléndez family were affiliated with FECCAS, while four aligned with ORDEN; all three of the multi-household families there had households affiliated with both (ibid.: 207). In El Tronador, the Anzora family was deeply divided, as shown in Figure 7.3.[4] In some of the maps, affiliation sometimes fell along neighborhood lines (as in the map drawn for me by members of the Cooperativa San Pedro Los Arenales, Fig. 2.5), but not in all, as this map shows.

Overall, these data indicate an extraordinarily high level of political involvement in these communities in the mid-1970s. Cabarrús's study also suggests that – setting aside elite households – the political affiliations of rural households before the war were related at best only weakly to their economic position. Locality appears to be at least as strong a predictor of affiliation as economic differences. To my knowledge, there has not been a study of the civil war in these *cantones*, so we do not know how political affiliations there subsequently evolved. However, the weak relationship between political affiliation and economic differences *among campesinos* is echoed in the findings of a survey of political attitudes in the immediate postwar period (reported in detail below), which similarly found remarkably few differences between the political opinions of renters and owners of small parcels of land.

These findings are also consistent with my findings for the case-study areas based on less adequate data gathered during and after the war. Sustained insurgent participation took place in areas that varied greatly in their patterns of residence, labor relations, and class structures. The small-holding *cantones* of northern Tenancingo, the big commercial estates of the coastal plain of Usulután, and the medium coffee estates of the Las Marías

[4] There are slight inconsistencies between the map and a table of affiliations by family (Cabarrús 1983: 218) in the number of affiliated households per family and the name of the families shown; nonetheless, the important point is well illustrated by the map.

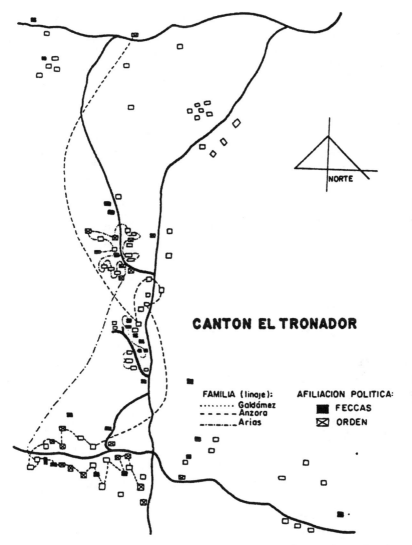

Figure 7.3 Map of *Campesino* political affiliations in El Tronador, 1976. *Source*: From Cabarrús (1983: p. 219). Reprinted with permission.

highlands *all* sustained a decade of revolt. Among the insurgent *campesinos* interviewed were people who before the war had been smallholders, permanent employees resident on the estate, tenants, and landless wage laborers, as well as those engaged in work activities related to agriculture but not directly to farming, such as mechanics and truck drivers. A similar wide range

199

of prewar class positions was present among the *campesinos* interviewed who did not participate in the insurgency.

These observations appear to contrast with other scholarly interpretations of insurgent participation in El Salvador's civil war. Some emphasize that the FMLN strongholds of Chalatenango and northern Morazán were located in areas where smallholding was predominant and peasant communities were less disrupted by the expansion of export agriculture than elsewhere. But other reasons may also account for the FMLN's strength there. The terrain was more suitable for guerrilla warfare (though still far from ideal); there was little of economic value and thus government forces focused defense on other areas; and their remoteness led to the concentration of guerrilla forces there after the failure of the FMLN's offensive in 1981 (Goodwin 1994a: 744). And before the war, agrarian class structure was more complex than this image of smallholding communities conveys. While many *campesino* households had access to some land, for most the size of the parcel was too small to produce the family's livelihood. As a result, these areas were also the homes of migrant laborers who left to harvest export crops every year (Harnecker 1993; Binford 1997: 57).

Certainly, grievances concerning the distribution of resources, particularly of land, played a role in the Salvadoran insurgency, as did emergent insurgent networks, political opportunity, and revolutionary leadership. But as we saw in the opening chapter, if each was necessary to the emergence and continuing strength of the insurgency, neither any single element nor the elements as a group appears sufficient to explain both. What accounts for the willingness of poor *campesinos* to mobilize despite the punishment inflicted by security forces and landlords? What accounts for the deepening of insurgency when the risk of rebellion was at its highest? What accounts for the widening of insurgency in the form of cooperative formation and land occupation when there were no apparent benefits to doing so? The accounts of *campesinos* themselves as to why they supported the insurgency – or did not – may help illuminate these questions. I first analyze the accounts of insurgent *campesinos* before turning to those of nonparticipants.

Campesinos' *Accounts of Insurgency*

Aspiration for land and resentment at its unjust distribution were frequent themes in interviews with insurgent *campesinos*. Participants interviewed in Usulután and Tenancingo recalled with evident emotion – ranging from sadness to indignation to rage – the miserable poverty (*la miseria*) that circumscribed their lives and the lives of their families. Those interviewed perceived two causes of their poverty: low wages and inadequate access to land. The cooperative leader who made the statement with which the chapter begins continued, "From such poverty emerged this mobilization: the great need for land in order to have, year by year, our daily bread." When asked to describe local conditions before the war, interviewees typically responded with detailed statements describing wages and working conditions as well as their resentment toward those conditions. One FENACOA activist stated:

How did I become a militant of the popular movement? It was born out of social resentment, that's how to understand it. I am an unskilled farm worker, my father never gave me anything. I worked for the rich, it was heavy labor. I felt rage, resentment. It was a hard life, sometimes I would cry with resentment when I couldn't finish the assigned task. (Interview, Tierra Blanca, 1992)

Older *campesinos* occasionally listed the wages paid their entire working lives from when they began working as children to the eve of the civil war. What was striking was how short a recitation it was: nominal wages rarely increased.

Many of those interviewed, before describing the repression, violence, and fear of the early years of the war, reiterated their belief that the war arose from a situation of injustice. A member of an insurgent cooperative stated: "Here, we lived in great poverty, with miserable wages. We had to live in conditions of such scarcity, we had no access to land. It was from that lack that the activities of the war developed, the living of such injustices" (Cooperativa Loma Alegre, 1992). Some characterized their situation before the war as one of slavery, a frequently recurring theme: "We legalized the cooperative as a way toward a better future for our children, that they have the possibility of no longer living in slavery." As recalled by those interviewed, the difficulties of prewar social conditions included ongoing social deprecation as well as poverty:

Before the war, we were despised by the rich. We were seen as animals, working all day and still without even enough to put the kids in school. This is the origin of the war: There was no alternative. The only alternative was the madness of desperation. (Cooperative Los Ensayos, March 1992)

Many expressed particular resentment toward their inability to cultivate corn, a resentment that symbolized their lack of autonomy, their dependence on sporadic wage labor, and their subordination.

Being exposed to disrespectful treatment and constant humiliation still rankled older *campesinos* despite the years that had passed since most had worked consistently as laborers on commercial farms. Particularly resented was the arbitrariness with which authority was exercised before the war, as stated by an insurgent cooperative leader:

We *colonos* had to behave with such obedience – we couldn't even disagree with what the authorities said. The only refuge when they kicked you out was to go live alongside the national roadways. The human person was just one more farming implement. (Cooperativa El Carrizal, 1992)

Another emphasized the coercion that informed rural labor relations: "We didn't even know about rights, it was a matter of the rifle enforcing their orders – that was how it was when it began" (Cooperativa Trece de Junio, 1992). Some of those interviewed identified the close local collaboration between landlords and state authorities as central to the problems that led to the war, as in this graphic interview:

Before 1980, we didn't know anything about anything, it was prohibited. We weren't allowed to meet, and anyone who spoke out suffered great harm, sometimes death or torture and would be forced to write out the names of others using his own blood. They wanted to derail the social forces. The authorities were at the disposition of the rich – they had all the guarantees as the National Guard acted as their personal bodyguard. (Cooperativa Trece de Junio, 1992)

One *campesino*, when asked what it had been like before the war and how it was different now, performed an elaborate pantomime of exaggerated deference to the landlord (hands together, head humbly bent, chest and head bowing without eye contact), a sharp contrast to his subsequent pantomime of the wartime attitude (shoulders back, head pridefully up, fist beating the air). This could of course be mere bravado, but the successful defeat of landlord efforts to repossess several properties in his area testifies instead to a significant transformation of local political capacity and attitudes toward erstwhile patrons.

As repression intensified, participants faced difficult choices. One *campesina*, a member of a cooperative near San Francisco Javier, told me:

I had never seen a guerrilla when a man visited me. He only had a pistol; he was a member of ERP. He asked if I wanted to join. I had my husband, son, daughter. I said no; I was fearful and very young. I did not know what it was for. Then three came, asking for food. They clarified the issue: They were forming a group and wanted me to act as a messenger. I was tempted, but scared, and said no. Then seven people came, I felt more confident, I served coffee. But someone fingered [denounced] me to the authorities. I was surrounded by soldiers and they accused me. They told me they were going to take me, that they considered me a guerrilla. (San Francisco Javier, 1992)

The *campesina* declined to elaborate on what followed; some *campesinas* in similar circumstances were raped or otherwise brutalized.

The violent, uncompromising opposition to a more just distribution of land on the part of landlords and security forces recurred in interviews as a justification for insurgent violence. In speaking of repression, *campesinos* often drew on Christian imagery, making parallels between their suffering and that of Jesus Christ, as in this quote from an insurgent cooperativist evoking the image of the Crucifixion:

Quite a few people didn't want to do join the cooperative, they were still terrified – they had experienced it [violence, the war] in their own body. I used to say, look, this struggle and the effort of the FMLN, have cost blood. For us, this bloody body is always present. (Cooperativa Loma Alegre, 1992)

Campesinos drew as well on traditional agrarian practices and symbols: "I was born here, my umbilical cord is buried here. Blood has run, many have died, but the harvest is at hand" (Cooperativa La Maroma, 1992). The burying of a umbilical cord at a particular spot is a powerful ritual in rural culture throughout Mexico and Central America; the "harvest is at hand" is a common biblical allusion to a parable of Jesus.

As these quotes suggest, blood was a recurrent image in the interviews, symbolizing both violence and commitment to land claimed (and implicitly, the insurgency), as in this statement with which a leader of the Cooperativa Nancuchiname began his story: "So many family members have fallen, leaving their blood in the land." The reiteration of images of violence may reflect not only trauma suffered but also the speakers' ongoing reinterpretation of that trauma as martyrdom. According to Anna Peterson, religious Salvadorans who were active participants in the insurgency developed narratives of violence that interpret suffering while working for the reign of God as redemptive sacrifice rather than arbitrary tragedy (1997: 85–6).

Thus insurgent *campesinos* drew on cultural strands rooted in traditional rural culture and new liberationist religion in reconstructing and interpreting their memories of violence. Many articulated their continuing choice to support the insurgency as one so clear on moral grounds that they did not entertain alternatives. Rather, they saw their participation in each stage as a continuation of their insurgent identity, "naturally" arising out of earlier choices and experiences, as we saw in the previous chapter.

The desire for revenge was occasionally expressed in interviews. A typical expression came from an older member of an insurgent cooperative, referring to young men of the community who were combatants with the FMLN. He cited repression as a cause of their joining but traced their motives to vengeance: "When you keep hearing battles all around, in place of being killed yourself, you pick up arms instead. That is why it [the insurgency] grew: to carry out vengeance for the death of a brother" (Cooperativa Trece de Junio, 1992). Most remarkable, however – given the clear motivation for vengeance provided by *campesino* experience in El Salvador – was just how rarely such sentiments were expressed in interviews. This absence may be due to the fact that the FMLN discouraged personal vengeance as a motive, and instead attempted to mold grievances (including desires for vengeance) into more general motivations that could sustain an insurgent army for years to come (Gibb 2000: 169). The key point here is that the dominant tone with which incidents of severe government repression were recounted was one of moral indignation subsumed into a general belief in the justice of the struggle.

In contrast to the descriptions of poverty and humiliation endured before the war, *campesino* leaders' descriptions of their wartime activities were characterized by reiterated assertions of pride and achievement: "There were so many deaths of cooperative promoters – half a battalion of dead for the simple crime of lending help to the cooperatives. But I would say that this 'crime' has been, simply, my accomplishment" (Cooperativa Candelaria un Nuevo Amanecer, 1992). Older people were particularly apt to stress the achievements of the insurgency, often with great emotion contrasting current conditions with those before the war. One leader was uncharacteristically demonstrative when asked what the insurgency had wrought:

Now we have more joyful lives. I feel happy to be able to meet like this with other *compañeros*. We have won so much! I never thought to be able to meet like this – the changes that have been made! Before we worked for such low wages and ate only hard tortillas. Now we ourselves set our hours. I tell you that I have suffered, it has been hard, and I am happy.

This statement stresses both the autonomy made possible by access to land but also pride in the achievements of the insurgency itself. Similarly, one very old man who occasionally attended meetings of the Land Defense Committee in Las Marías stated very firmly, "[T]he peace agreement was not granted voluntarily but only resulted from the fight of us, the *campesinos.*"

Campesino Accounts of Insurgent Participation

That many *campesinos* compare their lives at the close of the war favorably with their memories of past conditions is particularly remarkable given the decline in rural wages during the course of the war. Agricultural wages declined by 65 percent between 1980 and 1992, according to one analysis.[5] Access to land was all the more highly valued in this context of declining income from other sources.

Many insurgent *campesinos* reported with pride the tenaciousness that had enabled them to remain on their land, whether acquired legally or by occupation, despite frequent military conflict in the area:

Here, there is perhaps no one who has not collaborated. The truth is that it has been a deeply suffered war. We have suffered hunger, sometimes eating only bombs [artillery shells, mortars]. It is God who has made us still be here. Here, the bombs have rained like water. (Comunidad La Peña, 1992)

For some, persisting and enduring was itself an achievement, as for this insurgent cooperativist:

There was no opportunity to work your own land, only to work as a laborer. In 1979, the conflict began, and it began with a wave of violence. We suffered in all aspects, it became very difficult. They killed a brother of mine. *But here we are, living here still.* (Cooperativa San Judas Escobares, 1992, as emphasized by speaker)

An elderly man, one of the most dedicated and outspoken members of the Land Defense Committee of Las Marías, reflected, "To live through this war was something very hard, but also a source of great pride: to have stood up to it all. We have achieved quite a lot even though we lost family members." One of the most experienced *campesino* leaders on the Jiquilisco coast reflected ironically, "What an admirable country, admirable! Here we are in war, but working!"

Essential to these assertions of pride is an undercurrent of political and social equality, in sharp contrast to their bitter memories of landlords' expressed contempt. This emphatic leveling of social status marks a conscious shift in perceived relations, and was sometimes very explicit, as stated by this cooperative member:

My opinion is this: God the Father made the land for everyone. He didn't make the land for the rich – we are all sons of Mother Earth. We are in this struggle so that the land would belong to those who work it. The rich man is also the son of Mother

---

[5] Paus (1996: table 12.4). The table reports average daily real minimum wages, but agricultural workers rarely made more than the minimum wage.

Earth, and he has the right to land – but only to the same size of parcel, we don't want any haciendas. (Member, Comunidad El Palmo, 1992)

This leveling of status draws on both Christian and indigenous cosmologies to justify the struggle for land. Similarly, the following simple affirmation by a cooperative leader resounds with pride and the assertion of equality: "We are capable of managing these properties" (Cooperativa San Judas Escobar, 1992).

This assertion of equality was closely associated with both access to land and pride in the achievements of activists and their organizations. Militants consistently claimed *authorship* of the changes that they identified as their work, as did this leader of one of the earliest insurgent cooperatives: "I woke up during the process of the war and I collaborated in the midst of the war. We have already seen a new dawn – we created it despite the great pressure brought to bear by the army" (Cooperativa La Conciencia, 1992). In many interviews, the litany of achievements on the part of the insurgency was intermingled with a recitation of injustices of prewar social relations to retrospectively justify insurgent participation in the war itself. The language is frequently one of freedom and political equality, and, less frequently, also of rights, set against the context of repression and difficulty: "We work the land to be able to survive. The right to live is one we all share" (Cooperative San Judas Escobares, 1992).

Some leaders and activists made more nuanced assessments of the achievements of the war, while similarly emphasizing the justice of its aims and accomplishments to date, as in the opening quote of this book. A similarly measured reflection on the achievements of the war came from a member of an insurgent cooperative in the Las Marías area:

We passed these years with great suffering, it was difficult for us. In eleven years of war, we were never tranquil. But now, we feel a bit free, and not oppressed. Before we didn't have a single freedom; now we have begun to taste freedom. (Cooperative San Pedro Arenales, 1992)

The benefits realized during the war were sometimes explicitly weighed against the costs, as done by this female cooperativist: "The war has given us land. After this war, well, those of us who haven't died, we're living on a bigger piece" (Cooperativa Loma Alegre, 1992). In an interview with several women residents of La Noria (1992), one *campesina* commented with mingled pride and outrage: "We now work in a cooperative, we grow our food, and the kids are studying in school. We're no longer dominated by the landlord. What a shame that so many had to die to achieve these changes!"

Others emphasized the limits to the insurgency's achievements. One young COMUS organizer, who often struck me as more a sociologist than a militant activist, stated, "We are both the beneficiaries and the victims of the war: a bit of fertilizer and a bit of suffering," echoing ironically the "beneficiary" language of agrarian reform agencies. He continued,

Even after eleven years of war, some still do not have land. In truth, what was fought for – that everyone have land and credit – was not won. A lot is still lacking – this man here [gesturing] has no place to live! What has been achieved is still too little. The armed force [of the FMLN] has done its part, now we the *campesinos* have to act.

This last theme of goals still unmet and therefore the need for *campesinos* to continue to organize was reiterated by many cooperative leaders. One experienced Jiquilisco organizer put it: "It's not everything, we have to keep fighting, although now without arms. We know from where we have come, and where we want to go" (Leader, Cooperativa La Maroma, January 1992). That *campesinos* considered their organizations capable of continuing the struggle for land is a measure of their pride in their achievements to date.

Land was a recurring theme in the interviews. Access to land was fundamental to the insurgent vision of a more just world, and greater access to land was judged an achievement of the insurgency. Land and its closely associated values of family and self-sufficiency were central strands of the insurgent political culture. But it does not follow that individual participation in collective action was directly motivated by the desire for land per se, given ongoing de facto access to abandoned land and the ongoing risks of joining cooperatives.

As these excerpts from my interviews indicate, memories of fear and violence, evident in the reiterated images of blood and bodies as well as in explicit statements, remained troubling to many, even years later in the relative security of the cease-fire. Violence and terror leave behind a legacy of silence, fear, and uncertainty that can be deeply corrosive of self-confidence, trust, and hope (Green 1995). Yet remarkably, given this level of violence, activists in the case-study areas had continued to organize during the war. According to Juan Corradi's analysis of repression in Argentina and other Latin American countries, the clue to overcoming the "culture of fear" lies in breaking the sense of inevitability and inertia experienced during periods of extreme repression (Corradi 1992). The achievements of *campesino* organizations in these contested areas are a direct indication of the *campesinos'* having overcome the demobilizing effects of the repression that swept through their communities.

Accounts of Nonparticipants and Patterns of Nonparticipation

In contrast, the themes of pride and achievement are nearly absent in interviews with *campesinos* who did not support the insurgency. Echoes of these themes are confined to the interviews of the few who tenaciously remained on the land in the face of violence. Those interviewed told similar stories of suffering fear and violence during the war, with the important difference that the FMLN figures more often (though not predominantly) as the purveyors of both. A recurrent theme was the responsibility of both militaries for the violence, and a consequent rejection of political involvement in favor of political neutrality.

It is difficult to analyze patterns of nonparticipation in insurgent activity across the case-study areas during the war for two reasons: contemporary sources on local patterns are extremely scarce, and many residents (particularly, nonparticipants) had left the areas. Nonetheless, some patterns of nonparticipation in the case-study areas emerged in interviews, particularly those carried out in Tenancingo. To supplement these sources and because interviewing nonparticipants was difficult in some of the Usulután case-study areas, I also traveled to places where noninsurgent *campesinos* were likely to be: government repopulation sites in Suchitoto in the outskirts of the Guazapa volcano and reform cooperatives in western El Salvador.

Some individuals and families did not support the insurgents because they were immersed in alternative networks. If close family members living in urban areas could offer shelter, other things being equal, insurgency appeared to be less likely. Some were favored clients of powerful local patrons. Such ties meant access to work, health care, and perhaps schooling for one's family, opportunities unavailable otherwise. Some (including many such clients) were members of paramilitary networks such as ORDEN and were therefore accountable to the local commander of the National Guard. Thus some *campesinos* did not participate in the initial political mobilization because these valued ties would be jeopardized were they to do so.

Agrarian reform beneficiaries in western El Salvador reported little history or interest in the FMLN (a silence in sharp contrast to that of many members of reform cooperatives in Jiquilisco). Their experience of the war typically centered not on violence but on the reform itself. A member of an agrarian reform cooperative in western El Salvador told me: "Before, we worked only for the *patrón*. We had nothing, only a miserable daily wage. But now things are different, now we decide for ourselves" (El Socorro, 1991).[6] The salient networks for these cooperative members were the cooperative and the federation to which it belonged.

Some families were or became members of evangelical sects. Evangelical churches proliferated in the case-study areas (as in all of El Salvador) through the years of the war. With few exceptions, these groups advised members to avoid participation in politics. In the mid-1980s, there were eleven evangelical churches in Tierra Blanca; few activists belonged. According to a perceptive if unschooled local observer (La Peña, 1992), residents of La Peña, a *cantón* southeast of San Francisco Javier, lived during the war under one of three "rubrics." Sixteen families participated in what he termed "the organized community," meaning that they actively supported the ERP. Thirty families were members of a local evangelical church, whose members "didn't get involved in anything, they're independent of everything." Some of the church members had small holdings; others rented land. Only one old man participated in both the church and the organized community. Finally, there were a few families who owned larger small holdings and were therefore a bit better off than the rest of the residents still in the hamlet ("*adineraditos*," roughly, "a little bit moneyed") who participated in neither.

Other *campesinos* did not participate because they did not undergo the formative experiences of those who became insurgent supporters. Perhaps Bible study groups did not form in their neighborhood (as in southern Tenancingo, where the proximity to the militant Suchitoto parish that led to participation in northern Tenancingo was not a factor). Perhaps *campesino* organizations such as the BPR did not organize in their neighborhoods.

Yet these patterns were not uniform. Some clients of powerful patrons did support the insurgents, as did some smallholders and evangelicals. In Bajo Jocote Dulce, a dozen kilometers to the east of La Peña, an entire evangelical church joined the insurgency after a church leader was killed by the National Guard. As we saw in Chapter 4, families sometimes divided, often along generational lines, despite having undergone many of the same experiences.

[6] However, the interviews in western El Salvador were carried out during one-time visits. Local history and patterns of political loyalty might emerge as a great deal more complicated if sustained research were carried out.

A distinct pattern that accounts for some anomalies in these patterns is the particular history of local violence. Where insurgent forces had moved brutally against family members or neighbors, relatives and residents were not likely to support those forces. A resident of the *cantón* Ichanqueso, the most successful of the government repopulation projects in Suchitoto, stated

We suffered deeply before 1980. Everyone fled however they could, taking whatever they could, fleeing the violence. This particular town suffered a lot, so many deaths. The *muchachos* ["boys," a reference to the guerrillas] were the ones who killed people; we didn't have a civil defense here. (1987)

Her statement is typical of many residents of the case-study areas who suffered violence at the hands of the FMLN. One Tenancingo woman reported that the FMLN killed her husband, a member of the civil defense patrol, during the first take-over of the Villa in June 1983. She stated with clear bitterness toward the FMLN that he had been forced by the local military commander to participate in the patrol (Tenancingo, 1987). Another woman said with equal bitterness that a cousin and other relatives had been killed as members of the civil defense patrol, but that they were "volunteers who never imagined what things would come to" (Tenancingo, 1988). She went on to state explicitly (if not very credibly), "If the guerrillas had not killed people, perhaps all of us would have gone over to them." Yet this pattern had its exceptions. A sixteen-year-old member of the Tenancingo civil defense patrol was killed in the FMLN's first attack on the Villa in 1983. During the second attack, his father sheltered members of the National Guard in his house. Nonetheless, by the late 1980s the father was active in the Villa on behalf of the FPL (Tenancingo, 1991).

Even where government-allied forces had killed family members or neighbors, few supported the insurgency if government forces appeared locally too powerful, as in Santiago de María. Residents reported the absolute cessation of political activity in any form in Santiago by the early 1980s, whether Christian Democratic Party organizing, mobilization of coffee mill workers, or Bible study groups. Activists were killed or fled the town. Only at the very end of the war did opposition organizations reemerge there.

In the context of profound violence and civil war, most individuals preferred noninvolvement in politics, whatever their wartime experience, either because they felt the risks too great or because they found no group sufficiently appealing. One older farmer from the northern Tenancingo *canton* of El Pepeto stated:

The story of the war is that of the suffering of places like this. The [insurgent] movement had no merit. The meetings worried us, we saw that things were getting worse. In 1979, some fields were burnt, some deaths occurred. The Armed Forces killed some subversives; some with bullets, some by cutting their heads off. We had never seen this before. My son was killed in 1980 by the Armed Forces, also my son-in-law. So we grew all the more worried. (Tenancingo, 1987)

Although two family members had died at the hands of the government forces, this man did not become an insurgent. A religious and independent man, he returned to the Villa in 1986. He participated actively in reconstruction projects and remained avidly neutral. His attitude was typical of most of those interviewed in the Villa. They had witnessed violence, attributed most of it to government forces, and stated that they supported neither one side nor the other. A skilled worker in Tenancingo criticized both parties and the war itself:

There is no organization that directly helps the people; both sides use the people in their own interest. We're just not interested in the things behind the war. It makes no sense that the blood keep running because of the ideologies of the great ones. I am not a partisan of either side; I prefer to denounce both.

One woman, who was sixteen years old at the time of the bombing of Tenancingo, told her family's history this way:

Before the conflict, my father had a small hat factory employing himself and three others. My grandparents would not let me walk around with those participating in marches and demonstrations. There was significant support for the organizations among the youth; their families all had to leave. The National Guard killed one woman coming into the area with food, accused her of passing it to the guerrillas. Some of my relatives were threatened by the army and had to leave. They were threatened because they were churchgoers. They were people who went to church, but fearfully; they never spoke of anything happening in church. (Tenancingo, 1988)

She continued,

After the bombing, we left it all behind. My uncle was hurt, his ears, fingers and part of his nose were blown off in a trench. He had been a member of the army during the war with Honduras; they had taken him up again. My father came to bury him a week later. He later suffered a nervous collapse and could not work for a long time but finally got better. My mother still refuses to return to Tenancingo; she is too frightened of the army, which earlier had threatened her a lot.

Her experience appears to give her cause for conflicting loyalties. The FMLN killed her uncle and her father was traumatized and disabled by this; yet she notes as well the violence and intimidation of the National

Guard and the army. Another person interviewed, a teenager when the Villa was bombed, succinctly characterized the municipality's history:

Until 1980, things in the Villa were quiet. The population was still here; the streets were full every market day. In 1981 or 1982, the critical events began. In 1980, those of Rosario Périco got involved in doctrines against the government. The reaction: massacres were carried out, and Rosario Périco was abandoned. Some came to the Villa, others went to Cojutepeque, San Miguel, San Salvador. Not a single house was left standing. El Pepeto was also abandoned. Copalchán: another *cantón* that witnessed a great massacre by both sides. (Tenancingo, 1989)

He then summarized his sense of the war: "One provokes, the other reacts."

A few nonparticipants endorsed processes of social change on behalf of the poorest Salvadorans and recognized some benefits of the insurgency, but did not agree that violence was justified. A leader of a reform cooperative in Jiquilisco recounted in detail a series of strikes and marches in the area in the 1970s; it was clear that he had been a participant. But he was not an FMLN supporter at the time of the interview: "We have suffered and we continue suffering. We can't hold either side responsible; it is the system of war that has brought us these loses" (San Marcos Lempa, 1992). Similarly, one of the more educated but not wealthy residents of Tenancingo reflected:

It all began here as "help for the *campesinos.*" They organized young people, turning them against the rich, leading them from the Christian Federation of Salvadoran Campesinos to the BPR to the FPL. That's how it began. War never brings anything good.... But there are social changes, positive social changes for workers and for *campesinos.* Now workers can organize, now unions exist. Even here in Tenancingo: Now the rich are outside and one can work for oneself. (Tenancingo, 1991)

From this thoughtful reflection on the changes wrought by the war, one might not guess that the speaker had suffered a great deal during the war. He lost his small hat factory, had been reduced to filling a small plot of corn and beans to support himself, recalled the 1983 bombing with evident trauma, and suffered from alcoholism and a long-standing separation from his wife.

Those who did not support the insurgency were a heterogenous group, yet some patterns are evident. Membership in a valued alternative network or patron-client relationship appears to make insurgent support less likely. The local path of violence also had an effect. Where the FMLN had killed neighbors early on, support was less likely. And proximity to insurgent forces mattered as well. Where there was massive government presence, supportive activities were highly unlikely (whatever residents' private preferences).

Insurgent Political Culture

> What we hope for is to be equal before the law. We have lost the
> fear we had before the war, we have lost the fear.
>
> Leader, Cooperativa La Maroma, 1992

The most important themes in interviews with *campesinos* who supported the insurgency – resentment at the social conditions before the war, aspirations for a more just social and economic order, moral outrage at the repression that followed mobilization, and pride in the achievements of the insurgency – are muted or absent in the interviews with *campesinos* who did not support the insurgency. This pattern suggests that a new political culture emerged during the civil war among those that supported the insurgents. The testimonies above suggest that their political identities and culture were transformed through the years of the civil war, from a culture in which people frequently submitted to subordination to one in which a new identity as militant activists was openly expressed and supported by opposition organizations (including the FMLN itself).

Supporting evidence for the emergence of this insurgent political culture, particularly its emphasis on pride in the achievements of their collective action, comes from the map-making workshops. It was evident that the insurgent *campesinos* who participated in the workshops took pleasure and pride in the task, which was seen as an invitation to document the achievements of their cooperatives. The workshops often began amidst much mutual teasing among the *campesino* participants, particularly at the beginning of the out-of-the-ordinary task. But the map-making also quite regularly elicited explicit expressions of solidarity with fellow participants and of pride in the redrawing of property boundaries during the course of the war and in the drawing of the maps themselves.

The maps drawn by insurgent *campesinos* are expressions of this insurgent culture. In drawing the maps for this project, the cooperativists had to select what to show and how. In this they are of course no different from other designers of maps. Jeremy Black (1997: 12) argues that for any map,

[t]he choice of what to depict is linked to, and in a dynamic relationship with, issues of scale *and* purpose, and the latter issue is crucial. A map is designed to show certain points and relationships, and in doing so, creates space and spaces in the perception of the map-user and thus illustrates themes of power.

Even maps that appear to recreate in miniature purely physical characteristics, such as satellite images or maps of physical geography, undergo a

process of selection by the designer (ibid.: 11–12, 59–60). (Which wave-
lengths from the source data should be included and in what colors? How
exaggerated should differences in altitude be in the map, given that they are
usually trivial compared with the horizontal extent of the area represented?)

All maps are thus cultural representations and vary with the maker and
his or her purpose. In particular, maps of neighborhoods or regions sketched
by individuals vary. For example, neighborhood maps sketched by Polish
teenagers differed not just in what was depicted but in their coherence
(Lynch and Banerjee 1976). Village teenagers drew consistent, detailed
maps of a crowded social landscape; suburban teenagers drew maps that
exhibited little coherence and significant confusion; central city teenagers
drew elaborate maps of detailed street networks crowded with particular
named buildings, shops, and institutions. We cannot conclude from such
evidence that the teenagers' mental images differed as well as their sketches:
the translation from mental image to map is of coursed shaped by the form
and tools of the particular sketching process, each drawer's familiarity with
the process, and so on. Nonetheless, each map-maker chose what and how
to draw.

The maps reproduced here are combinations of the two very common
forms of maps: maps that assert sovereignty, in this case land claims by
insurgent cooperatives, and maps of localities (Black 1997: 12–13). The scale
chosen encloses the properties claimed by the map-makers' cooperative.
Some are essentially maps of the cooperative properties, while others are
drawn at a scale that includes neighboring cooperatives or a nearby town.[7]
The map-makers knew and took time to show the name of every property
(or the owner), appeared to remember the pattern of land use before the
war, and knew or estimated the size of every property.[8] Most important is
the contrast between the prewar and end-of-war maps, which among other
things traces the assertion of insurgent power. The makers took particular
care to indicate the borders of the properties they were in the process of
claiming. On some maps (e.g., Fig. 3.6), the drawers reiterated the word

---

[7] One qualification is that the maps are not independent of each other: members of each
cooperative that participated in the workshops spent some time looking over the maps being
drawn by members of other cooperatives, which could explain some similarities. However,
the maps drawn in the three different workshops are similar.

[8] Roger Petersen (2001: 17) suggests that the ability of Lithuanian people to draw detailed
neighborhood maps years later is itself evidence of the sort of "strong community" that
supports collective action. This is not the case in El Salvador: in highly unequal agrarian communities, deep familiarity with property rights may well come from working on
properties over the course of many years.

"*propiedad*" (property) repeatedly, claiming them plot by plot. Each one is labeled with the slogan "property of the cooperative"; the captions also reiterate the word and thus the claim.

When checked with topographic maps, the maps appear generally to be quite accurate locally, but the scale on the periphery (e.g., the indicated distance to the nearest village or town) is sometimes very distorted. This is typical of maps sketched by ordinary people, which often exhibit varying scales and orientations across the map while retaining what Kevin Lynch termed "topological invariance" similar to that of an "infinitely flexible rubber sheet: while distances and directions may be distorted, the sequence is usually correct" (Lynch 1960: 87). Some maps have what we might term a naive quality; for example, the perspective varies such that three or even four sides of a house are drawn.

One pair exhibits an extraordinary cartographic projection. Figure 7.4 shows in the foreground the hamlet Loma Pacha, which lies east of San Francisco Javier, and the nearly conical hill, Mount Taburete, planted almost entirely in coffee before the war. The hill was owned by three landlords, including one colonel. The author of the map, assisted by two other cooperative members, seem to have imagined standing on the next hill to the east, looking down at the houses of the workers in the hamlet and up toward the hill, and then unwrapping the hidden backside of the hill onto the paper just beyond the triangle of the cone. The author wrote the following on the map (with the original idiosyncratic spelling): "*Asía el serro del taurete propiedades tomadas por personas campesinas,*" which means, "Toward Mount Taburete, properties taken by *campesino* persons," an unprompted assertion of defiance and achievement. As is clear in the corresponding postwar map, Figure 7.5, nearly all of the coffee trees on the hill were destroyed during the war, as the guerrilla encampment there was frequently attacked. The Cooperativa El Jobalito planted corn in the lower skirts of the hill and claimed nearly the entire hill at the war's end. On this map, the author wrote "*Grasias por un recuedo de mi trabajo,*" which means, "Thank you for a remembrance of my work," thereby reminding me to return the map as I had promised and to claim both the redrawing of boundaries through land occupation and the literal drawing of the map as his work.

Other authors wrote similar affirmations on their maps; for example, the authors of the companion map (not included) to Figure 3.2 wrote, "It is a pleasure to participate together with all the *compañeros*" (Cooperativa Las Conchas). These notations on the maps suggest that cooperative members saw the building of cooperatives in the difficult conditions of the war as

215

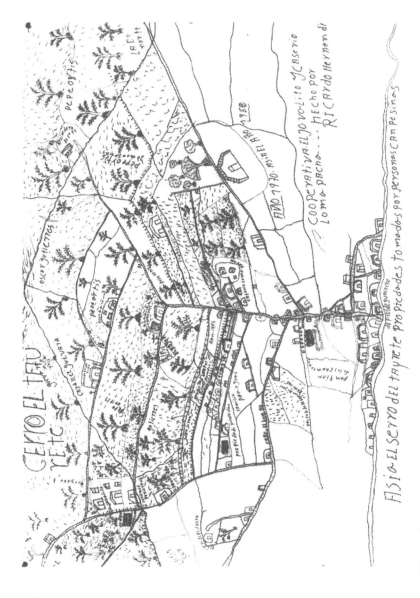

Figure 7.4 Cerro Taburete, 1970–80. Courtesy of the map-makers. A color version of this map can be see online at us.cambridge.org/features/wood.

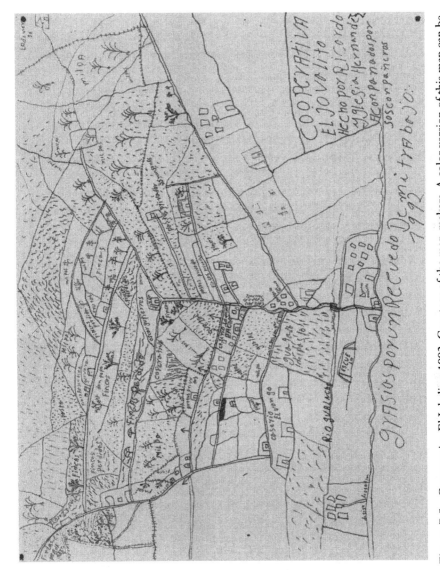

Figure 7.5 Cooperativa El Jobalito, 1992. Courtesy of the map-makers. A color version of this map can be see online at us.cambridge.org/features/wood.

217

a source of pride in the effectiveness of their historical intervention.[9] In general, "the map as plan is the map as product and recorder of human agency" (Black 1997: 165). In this case the maps record the human agency of the drawers themselves.

The naming of participant and cooperative names was also a powerful element of the map-making. The map-makers without exception wrote the full title of their cooperative on each map. Many of the names evoked a sense of achievement: "new dawn," "the guardians," "joyful bluff," "light on the horizon," and "conscience." Others retained the former name of the property but replaced "hacienda" or "finca" with "cooperative." Moreover, I did not ask the map-makers to sign the maps, but most chose to do so. Nearly all identified themselves along with their titles as the leaders of the cooperative, a symbolic assertion of authority and ownership of the properties claimed. The map-makers who inscribed their names did so after a discussion among themselves regarding the purpose of the exercise (which I described as the eventual publication of a history of the war in the case-study areas) and, among some of the groups, of the potential risks given the uncertain conditions of the cease-fire at the time. Judging by these conversations, to sign one's name was an expression of commitment to tell their communal history. The naming of names, particularly for the express purpose of having them published with the maps, thus seemed to be an indication of both a desire to testify to the community's history and to claim authorship of the cooperative's achievements. Thus the maps are ideological constructions, acts of critical remembrance and redemption as well as an assertion of power to claim and hold land.

Maps of course cannot convey all facets of a mental image of a landscape. In particular, some landscapes are laden with religious meaning or are understood as sacred spaces (Downs and Stea 1977: 139; Black 1997: 104). And it is difficult to convey dynamics in maps, particularly the dynamics of guerrilla warfare or modern air campaigns, both of which render front lines of little relevance (Black 1997: 159–61). Yet I suggest that the care with which these maps were drawn conveys an impression of a high degree of meaningfulness of these landscapes to the map-makers, as does of course their willingness to spend two days drawing them. (Recall that on two of

[9] Other scholars who have asked ordinary people to sketch maps of their neighborhood have noted that they often seem proud of their sketch maps, and appear to take pleasure in knowing their neighborhoods well and representing them clearly (Downs and Stea 1977; Brody 1982: 12; Lynch 1985: 250). The drawers of these maps appeared to experience that pleasure as well as their pride in cooperative land claims.

the maps (Figs. 3.4 and 3.7), the makers also marked with crosses the sites of deaths.) And perhaps the depiction of cooperative boundaries and the reiteration of cooperative names – as well as the makers' willingness to draw not one but two maps – are ways not just to convey land claims, but also to assert a sense of agency in the reshaping of that meaningful landscape.

Thus a central and reiterated theme in the maps and interviews with insurgent *campesinos* is that of political efficacy. Participants expressed profound pride in their insurgent activities: they had proved capable of transforming social relations, in acting effectively to realize their interests in land and autonomy. Most analyses of collective action would have difficulty accounting for this claim of *authorship*, a theme that was absent in interviews with nonparticipants. The centrality of this theme for insurgents suggests that acting in the realization of their interests was essential to this transformation of political culture. In the interviews, insurgent supporters acknowledged the difficult choices all residents faced; one source of their pride was having met the challenge despite their fears. And while many of the deeds recounted were local, leaders also stressed their role in building alliances beyond their locale, a broadening of perspective and experience proudly described.

It should be evident that what I mean by *political culture* includes not just "attitudes" toward different institutions (e.g., distinguishing "civic" from other political cultures, a survey-friendly approach often used by political scientists), but also more anthropological and sociological notions of culture. Political culture also includes norms of group solidarity, other collective norms and practices such as rituals and symbols, and beliefs concerning the feasibility of social change and the potential efficacy of the group's collective efforts toward such change. It also includes collective identity, by which I mean "an individual's cognitive, moral and emotional connection with a broader community, category, practice, or institution.... a perception of a shared status or relation, which may be imagined rather than experienced directly ..." (Polletta and Jasper 2001: 285).

Are the values, norms, and beliefs of those insurgent *campesinos* interviewed representative of *campesinos* that participated in the insurgency? As many were leaders of insurgent cooperatives, perhaps those interviewed were significantly more militant than insurgent *campesinos* generally. Ideally, we would compare such testimonies to a group representative of the rural population, or better still, we would have initially chosen candidates for extended interviews in light of the results of a survey of political attitudes of a representative sample of the population (thereby combining the

219

survey approach with the ethnographic approach). But few political opinion surveys of the population of the conflicted areas were carried out during the civil war. Those surveys that were carried out (such as the study of the COMUS communities discussed in the previous chapter) were rarely based on a representative sample of the local population of those areas.[10]

However, soon after the war a survey of political attitudes among people in the conflicted zones was carried out as part of a larger project exploring rural living conditions among five groups of farmers. The five categories were: members of sixty reform cooperatives, beneficiaries of the land-to-the-tiller phase of the agrarian reform ("tillers" in the figure below), owners of land they farmed (the average holding was only 2.1 hectares, so most were smallholders, not commercial-scale landlords), renters of land farmed, and the *tenedores*, that is, *campesinos* occupying land in the formerly conflicted areas (Seligson et al. 1993).[11] More specifically, the *tenedores* occupied land under the aegis of the FMLN (inclusion on the FMLN inventory of occupied properties compiled during the 1992 cease-fire was necessary to be considered a *tenedor*). *Tenedores* were usually, and in Usulután exclusively, organized as insurgent cooperatives. The survey allows comparison between these groups, although the interpretation is complicated by the fact that differences among the five categories may be due to differences in the type of land tenure or whether group members resided in conflicted areas.[12]

---

[10] The Instituto Universitaria de Opinión Público (University Institute of Public Opinion) of the Universidad Centroamericána developed strategies for public opinion polling in the midst of the war, but few of their respondents were residents of the conflicted areas. The U.S. Agency for International Development commissioned a few surveys in contested areas, but the results were not made public (personal communication, William Barnes, June 3, 2001).

[11] None of the *tenedores* interviewed in the survey were from Usulután. However, 75 of the 109 interviewed were from the municipality of Tecoluca in San Vicente (Carr, et al. 1993). The history of the war in Tecoluca is similar to that of southwestern Usulután, except that the dominant FMLN faction was the FPL, not the ERP.

[12] The sample of owners and renters was drawn from fifty nonconflicted municipalities, so differences between these groups and the *tenedores* reflect geographical, historical, and tenure differences. The land-to-the-tiller beneficiaries were drawn from government lists in areas near the other groups of the survey; the report does not say how many were in conflicted areas. The reform cooperative members appear to have been drawn from the subset of reform cooperatives that had completed a government program called "New Options" in which members made decisions concerning the form of tenure the cooperative would have in the future (continued collective title, subdivision into individual small holdings, shareholding in a corporate enterprise, or some combination). Their geographical distribution is not given. See Seligson et al. (1993: 2-4–2-9).

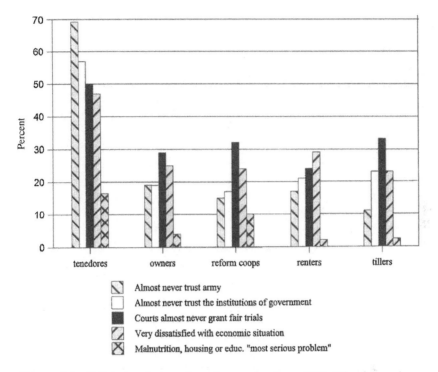

Figure 7.6 Political attitudes of *tenedores* and others, 1993. The figure shows the percentage of each group responding as indicated. The sample properties are described in the text. *Source*: Calculated from Seligson et al. (1993: 2-23–2-25).

Tenedores gave responses to survey questions that indicate a significantly higher degree of what the authors term political "alienation" from the government compared with owners. For example, 69 percent of the *tenedores* stated that they trust the army "almost never," compared with only 19 percent of the owners, 17 percent of the renters, 11 percent of the land-to-the-tiller beneficiaries, and 15 percent of reform cooperative members (Fig. 7.6).

What accounts for this greater alienation? According to the survey, *tenedores* experienced the consequences of civil war to a greater degree than the other groups (as we would expect from this subset of those interviewed, a sample drawn from conflicted areas who occupied land). Three-quarters of the *tenedor* families had lost a family member during the war, compared with only 34 percent of owners (Seligson et al. 1993: 2–27). *Tenedores* had to seek refuge from the war at a much higher rate as well: 74 percent sought refuge elsewhere in El Salvador, compared with 21 percent for owners. For 26 percent of the families of *tenedores*, the war had caused a member to migrate to another country; in just 10 percent of the families of owners had that occurred. Perhaps those who own land are less likely to flee (only one of the 109 *tenedores* interviewed held title to land), but it is unlikely that that alone accounts for the difference: violence in the conflicted zones where the *tenedores* lived was much higher than elsewhere. That the *tenedores* were occupying land under the aegis of the FMLN suggests that their alienation reflected to at least some degree the process of political organizing that occurred in those zones. These findings suggest that the insurgent *campesinos* interviewed for this book were not atypical of *tenedores*.

Might factors other than participation in insurgency explain the differences in political attitudes? The *tenedores* were significantly poorer than the other groups, both in reported household income and in living conditions. The average reported income (combining both farm and other income) for *tenedores* was 22 percent less than that of renters, 28 percent less than owners, and 45 percent less than reform cooperative members.[13] The greater poverty of the *tenedores* is probably the combined effect of several factors. *Tenedores* on average had access to less land (1.1 hectares) than owners (2.1 hectares; ibid.: 2–10). They were probably poorer before the war (the average years of schooling, which for this group of adults in their forties reflects poverty rates much earlier, was only 1.7 for tenedores, compared with 2.2 for owners, 2.4 for reform cooperative members, and 2.6 for land-to-the-tiller beneficiaries; ibid.: 2–29). Their residence in conflicted zones probably depressed their income because employment opportunities were less (even after the end of the war). And their uncertain tenure status probably depressed investment.

But the figure suggests that these differences in political opinion are not accounted for by class (despite the greater poverty of the *tenedores*). The responses of owners, reform cooperative members, renters, and land-to-the-tiller beneficiaries were very similar. In particular, renters are similar to the three categories of owners, a finding one would not expect if agrarian class position were to explain the differences.

To further explore whether the greater poverty of the tenedores and differences in class position from the other groups, rather than insurgent participation per se, might explain these differences in political opinion,

[13] Calculated from Seligson et al. (1993: tables 2.21 and 2.24), where off-parcel income for cooperative members (not given as such) was estimated from the off-parcel income of agrarian cooperatives that participated in the late 1990s "New Options" program (which is given).

we should compare the responses of *tenedores* with those of the landless agricultural population generally. But that group was not polled by this 1993 survey. A 1995 survey did so, however, and found that political attitudes among landless agricultural workers differed little from those of other categories of landholding (Seligson and Córdova Macías 1995). But their attitudes differed significantly from those who had voted for the FMLN candidate in the 1994 elections, a group whose political attitudes are similar to those of *tenedores* in their alienation. In analyzing geographically distributed data, support for "radical political change" was 6 percent or less among all groups except for those resident in zones governed by the FMLN (23.5 percent). The proportion was even higher for those resident in FMLN zones who were also FMLN voters (32.1 percent; ibid.: 39). (In the United States and Great Britain, support for radical political change expressed in similar surveys is only 5 percent; in Nicaragua, Mexico, and Guatemala, 11 to 12 percent; and in South Africa, 25 percent.) Residents of FMLN zones were also more politically tolerant, attended municipal meetings at a much higher rate, and characterized municipal services much more favorably than other groups, a striking result given the absence of services in most of those areas (ibid.: 57, 95–6, 102).

The results of another survey also suggest that it was participation, rather than other factors, that accounts for insurgent political culture. In a postwar survey of over 400 residents of three regions of the department of San Vicente, which borders Usulután on the west, Vincent McElhinny (n.d.: chapter 6) found that respondents in the region where the FMLN had been most active (the municipality of Tecoluca) tended to be more politically active, expressed a stronger sense of personal political efficacy, participated more in development projects, and remained more committed to revolutionary social change and equity than respondents in the other nearby municipalities dominated by government forces during the civil war.[14]

Another kind of evidence of the strength of the new political culture comes from landlords of properties in the case-study areas. In interviews in San Salvador, the town of Jiquilisco, and Cojutepeque, several expressed

[14] These findings were found to hold when the interview sample was increased to a regional level, adding municipalities from La Paz and Usulután. McElhinny's measure of political efficacy may underemphasize the sense of political efficacy in areas of insurgent participation. His survey questions focused on whether respondents agreed or disagreed that people did not vote for various reasons, which probed their opinions about the efficacy of voting rather than their sense of efficacy in building insurgent organizations or in occupying land (McElhinny 1999: 39).

concern that should they return to their properties after the war, they would face assertive and well-organized workers supported by a panoply of new organizations. And they would do so without their traditional command of local security forces. For example, one landlord of coffee estates and a mill in the Las Marías area described how his grandfather and father built the enterprise and continued, "I was born on the property; now it's a museum of weapons for the FMLN. How could I work it again, with [FMLN] ex-combatants at my shoulder?" (San Salvador, 1992). He went on to describe how he organized a group of approximately sixty landlords of occupied properties in the Usulután coffee highlands to work as a group to expedite the sale of their properties under the terms of the peace agreement. Another landlord, the representative of one of the most powerful families owning land along the Jiquilisco coast, described in an interview why he and his siblings had decided to sell the property:

I am absolutely willing to sell. It's been a nightmare, trying to work it or to rent it. We are convinced we have to sell, at market prices or not. It's going to kill us. Why must we sell? First, if we want to work the property, they [the insurgent *campesinos* occupying the property] are not going to let us. Second, we do want to cooperate with the peace process, we're conscious of that. Third, we need to pay the bank. With the losses and the strikes, we lost the working capital. So it's a distress sale. (San Salvador, 1992)

(As his family had extensive investments in urban enterprises, he is here referring narrowly to the finances of the property, not the family.) Despite his family's traditional influence in the area, he found it difficult to visit the property: "I felt they were so closed – I haven't visited for months, nobody talks to me when I go." Thus the unprecedented strength of *campesino* organization and the new insurgent political culture convinced many landlords to sell their properties (Wood 2000: 64–7).

Conclusion

Many *campesinos* ran extraordinary risks to support the insurgency over many years. That they did so despite the absence of benefits contingent on their participation raises doubts about the explanation of participation in collective action provided by standard rational actor models. In El Salvador, either participation was not prompted by consequentialist considerations or the "benefits" realized by participants went beyond the conventional material benefits stressed in most rational actor accounts.

Campesino Accounts of Insurgent Participation

The evidence presented in this chapter suggests that an emergent insurgent political culture was key to generating and sustaining the insurgency despite its high costs. Insurgent *campesinos* came to interpret insurgency as justified by the injustice of existing social relations and state violence, and to interpret its costs, even the highest of them, as meaningful sacrifices. For many, liberation theology had offered a Church-sanctioned condemnation of their poverty, the hope that change was possible as it was God's will, and a framework in which the costs of change could be interpreted. The early guerrilla networks drew on this change in rural political culture, coordinating protest into rebellion and offering an alternative form of collective action for those outraged by governmental repression.

But what beneficial consequences might be powerful enough to motivate risky actions under circumstances unfavorable (particularly initially) to success? What led some people in the *cantones* studied by Cabarrús to identify with the government and others with the opposition? The divisions within families and neighborhoods, as well as the local homogeneity of some *cantones*, would seem to have less to do with the details of economic position than with the *process* by which class resentment sometimes hardens into a commitment to collective action.

We are thus left with a number of unanswered questions. Under the difficult conditions of these rural communities, what processes facilitated the emergence and consolidation of *campesino* collective action? What accounts for the channeling of collective action into various forms? Under what conditions does initial protest become revolt, under what further conditions does revolt become sustained rebellion? How do interests and ideology evolve to support sustained revolutionary collective action?

The interviews with insurgent *campesinos*, the contrast between the accounts and experiences of insurgents and noninsurgents, the *campesino* maps, and the evidence of a new insurgent political culture among participants suggest that an account of participation in insurgency requires a consideration of the moral and emotional dimensions of participation.

8

Explaining Insurgent Collective Action

On my first visit to the Cooperativa Candelaria un Nuevo Amanecer and the Cooperativa Montecristo, two groups of insurgent *campesinos* occupying properties high on the side of a war-ravaged volcano north of San Jorge (recall Figs. 3.5 and 3.6), I arrived a bit late at the meeting place, an isolated peasant home. I had reached there by driving about an hour up a dry river bed (whether it was the *right* river bed or not was not clear until the very end), a definite challenge for my small pickup truck. As arranged at a regional meeting of the Las Marías Land Defense Committee the previous week, I expected to meet with cooperative leaders to discuss the history of the difficult emergence of the cooperatives in the midst of the civil war. Rather than three or four people, I found over fifteen people gathered in the farmyard. Another seven soon arrived. The interview took four hours, as almost everyone, men and women alike, wanted to speak, to tell what had happened to a brother or sister, or to tell a story of the time they occupied some property.

At the end of the interview, I asked for the names of a few people for whom I could inquire when I returned to visit again, as I feared that I would not again succeed in finding the place. I reiterated the strict confidence with which I would treat the names, for the political situation was far from settled and violence against those occupying land continued. The meeting broke up, and with their permission I recorded the names of the leaders of the cooperatives in a notebook I kept separate from my notes of the meeting.[1] A few more asked whether their names could also be written down. Then

---

[1] I returned to San Salvador immediately after the interview and did not take either notebook with me again into the case-study areas.

one by one, every person attending the meeting came to recite his or her name and solemnly to watch it be recorded.[2]

As I found my way down the riverbed to the road I reflected on how this apparently simple act of naming and being named becomes an extraordinary testament when set in the context of a war in which tens of thousands of civilians were killed, including loved ones of those present that day, often for nothing more than having participated in just such a cooperative meeting.

Why are people sometimes "brave to the point of foolishness," bearing risks not explicable on the basis of expected outcomes (Calhoun 1991: 51)? Why did people so similarly situated in terms of their economic circumstances before the war act so differently from one another? Why, as we have seen across the distinct agricultural regions of Usulután, did *campesinos* with such different holdings of land and relationships to landlords sometimes act so similarly? Why in the face of mounting repression did protest deepen to armed insurgency? And if repression played a role in the emergence of insurgency, moving a small core of committed activists from nonviolent protest to support for the armed guerrillas, why did participation in insurgent activities continue to grow after repression subsided significantly?

Conventional explanations for collective action based on strong communities, political opportunity, class position, and selective incentives, while illuminating some aspects of the Salvadoran insurgency, do not take us far in explaining insurgent collective action in circumstances of such high risk, as we have seen in previous chapters. Preexisting communities and social networks were too weak to provide the social sanctions and ongoing social bonds sufficient to overcome the collective action problem. Networks played important roles, to be sure, but they emerged during mobilization and in part as its consequence. Liberationist networks developed in the mid-1970s, as did covert guerrilla networks. Protest deepened to insurgency as political opportunity *narrowed* in the late 1970s. After the suppression of those networks during the period of extreme state violence, insurgent networks gradually reemerged as the FMLN forced authorities from some of the case-study areas, and then spread as collective action proved feasible. Aside from the obvious absence of medium and large landlords in insurgent ranks, support for the insurgency once war began was related only weakly

---

[2] It might be argued that those present gave me their names in the belief that some material benefit would result. However, I had on several occasions made clear to members of the commission that I had no relation to any nongovernmental organization and that my interest was solely in writing a history of the civil war, a purpose I reiterated (as always) at the beginning and end of the interview.

227

to prewar class position. Broadly speaking, the Salvadoran civil war pitted an insurgency championing the demands of the socially and economically excluded against the traditional alliance of the economic elite and the military, only a very few of whom took the risk entailed by supporting the insurgency. But among the excluded, as we have seen, economic class position did not map local residents neatly into the categories of insurgent and government supporters.

Nor do material selective benefits explain participation. During the period of extreme state violence, some residents retreated with the FMLN and thereby gained some short-run protection from government forces (sometimes a safer course than attempting to remain or to move toward government-held areas), but they did not subsequently support the FMLN. Moreover, the FMLN did not attempt to protect particular households or communities in the case-study areas. During the military stalemate, those who did not support the insurgency had access to the meager material benefits of the insurgency – land – without paying any contribution beyond the coerced minimum whenever supporters did. In this sense, the insurgents provided public goods and most residents were free riders.[3] In most of the Usulután case-study areas, *all* households had access to land for subsistence cultivation as a result of the FMLN's having expelled government forces and landlords from the area. It was the armed presence of the FMLN, not membership in a cooperative, that assured access to land from year to year. So neither protection nor access to land explains participation in insurgent cooperatives. Even more striking, some of those who gained land as a result of the government's agrarian reform also supported the FMLN.

I first summarize the empirical findings from the case-study areas, in light of which I give my interpretation of insurgent collective action in rural El Salvador. (A formal model of this account is in the Appendix.) Because

---

[3] Access to land is not normally understood as a public good. Public goods have two properties: They are nonrival (my use does not lessen your use) and nonexcludable (it is difficult to exclude users). Whether something is a public or a private good is not determined solely by the physical characteristics of the good but by whatever affects rivalness and excludability. Land is of course generally a rival good. However, *access* to land (in general, not to any particular plot) in these circumstances was a public good. Because land was abundant relative to the population in the contested areas, access to land was effectively nonrival. And the FMLN did not attempt to exclude from abandoned land anyone who met the coerced minimum contribution. At the war's end, membership in an insurgent cooperative credibly promised a selective benefit, namely, legal title to occupied land. During the land grab that followed, a land occupation project became a common pool activity (rather than a public goods one), as benefits were at least weakly contingent on participation and access became rival.

the empirical evidence is inevitably open to a variety of interpretations, I consider two caveats and then offer two additional considerations supporting the plausibility of my account. The first is the accumulating evidence from social science experiments that reasons similar to those I emphasize help explain the responses of subjects in social science experiments exploring the propensity to cooperate in various well-controlled situations. The second is my account's consistency with other cases of collective action on the part of long-subordinate social actors. In conclusion I address the implications of the argument of this book for more general issues in the literature on collective action, social movements, and peasant rebellion.

Patterns of Insurgent Collective Action

An explanation of the puzzle of insurgent collective action in the high-risk circumstances of the Salvadoran civil war should account for the observed patterns of participation – and nonparticipation – across time and space in the case-study areas, briefly summarized as follows.

Approximately a third of the residents of the case-study areas voluntarily participated in the insurgency, some for more than a decade, despite their keen awareness of the risks they thereby ran. Participation took various forms on the part of different people and at different periods of time. In most of the case-study areas, many landless laborers and land-poor peasants, some smallholders, some beneficiaries of the counterinsurgency agrarian reform, and some self-employed skilled laborers supported the insurgents with food, water, and military intelligence. Some of them also served as militia members and leaders of insurgent cooperatives. A very few had also at some time served as full-time members of the guerrilla forces. Some participated in the mobilization of the 1970s and again in the founding of insurgent cooperatives but lay low during the intervening years of extreme violence. Most residents did not participate in the insurgency.

Some communities that appeared very similar before the civil war had very different trajectories through the war. The northern and southern *cantones* of Tenancingo, for example, were indistinguishable in terms of social structure before the war, yet the northern ones generally supported the insurgents, while the others supported the government. And along the coastal plain, eastern and western Jiquilisco are indistinguishable, yet support for the insurgency emerged in the western part but not the east.

There were some patterns among insurgent supporters. An important correlate of whether a *campesino* supported the FMLN or not was the history of violence against family members and neighbors. In neighborhoods or among families where government forces and their allies had carried out significant violence, as in northern Tenancingo and western Jiquilisco, support for the FMLN was more likely (*if* the area was not entirely dominated by government forces, as was Santiago de María). Where the FMLN had carried out significant initial violence, as in southern Tenancingo, support for the FMLN was much less likely (and some residents participated in civil defense patrols).

The form of insurgent collective action varied over time; new forms emerged from previous ones. In the first period of the insurgency, before the civil war, many *campesinos* participated in strikes, marches, and demonstrations, some of them as an outgrowth of their involvement in Bible study groups informed by liberation theology. (Some also covertly supported the then tiny covert guerrilla networks also active during this period; a very few, often the teenage younger sons of smallholding families, joined the organizations as full-time recruits.) The subsequent repression together with the 1980 agrarian reform comprised a second period (1979–83) of extreme violence and chaos in the case-study areas, and normal forms of political mobilization disappeared entirely. Those few *campesinos* who supported the FMLN during this period did so individually and covertly. During the third period of military stalemate (1984–91), some reform cooperatives in Usulután joined new overt opposition organizations, and some of their members covertly supported the insurgents. Insurgent collective action increasingly took the form of participation in insurgent cooperatives that occupied land. The first were founded near guerrilla strongholds; they then spread across most of the case-study areas. The military stalemate also made possible the repopulating of the Villa of Tenancingo and its subsequent defense against attempts by both sides to use the project to their advantage. At the end of the war (after peace negotiations began and through the first months of the cease-fire, 1991–2), the number of insurgent cooperatives and cooperative members rapidly increased. Joining an insurgent cooperative in this last period poses no puzzle, as definite material benefits were credibly contingent – for the first time – on cooperative membership.

There is additional evidence that may help resolve the puzzle, namely, insurgent *campesinos'* accounts of their participation, nonparticipants' accounts of their experiences, and the emergence of an insurgent political culture among FMLN supporters by the end of the civil war. When asked about the history of the war in their community, insurgent *campesinos* returned time and again to several themes: the injustice of prewar land distribution and labor relations, their desire for land, the contempt with which they were treated by landlords, the brutality with which government forces responded to nonviolent strikes and demonstrations, the fear with which they lived during the war, and the suffering of their families. The assertion of political and social equality, in sharp contrast to their experiences before the war, also runs through the interviews. Significantly, they also repeatedly asserted their pride in their wartime activities and consistently claimed *authorship* of the changes that they identified as their work, a claim difficult to account for in most explanations of collective action. In contrast, those who did not support the insurgency emphasized the exercise of violence by both armies, and some particularly emphasized that of the FMLN. While a few noninsurgents claimed their staying on the land as an achievement, there were few expressions of collective pride or defiance or assertions of equality on their part.

An Interpretation of High-Risk Collective Action

My interviews with *campesinos* as well as the patterns of mobilization convince me that there were three reasons that participants supported the mobilization and insurgency, which I will term *participation, defiance,* and *pleasure in agency.* In addition, two contingent, path-dependent aspects of the civil war – *local past patterns of violence* and *proximity to insurgent forces* – also shaped participation in the insurgency. All concern local *processes* of the civil war, and all emerged during the course of the civil war and its antecedent mobilization. My account of *campesino* insurgency also concerns *campesinos'* evolving beliefs about local constraints and opportunities, including likely outcomes, and cultural practices.

By *reasons for acting,* I mean values, norms, commitments, emotions, material interests, and aversions.[4] By *beliefs,* I mean understandings of the probable consequences of various courses of action. By *practices,* I mean culturally meaningful activities such as rituals.[5] By *path-dependent outcomes,* I

---

[4] I use *reasons* rather than preferences, as people appear to act for a wide variety of reasons, not all of which are well captured by a well-ordered, transitive, complete, and relatively stable preference structure. People act not just on preferences but out of weakness of will, short-sightedness, or on aversions not chosen by themselves (Bowles 2003: chapter 3). Moreover, they often do not calculate risks or trade-offs over time as assumed by conventional economic theory.

[5] In the formal model I interpret the general prewar pattern of *campesino* acquiescence as a "convention" in which acquiescence was the best course to pursue, as almost everyone else

mean persistent outcomes that might have been different if initial events had been different (in the language of economists, there are multiple equilibria); path-dependent processes shape such outcomes.

Participation

Many participants appear to have taken part during the 1970s because they had come to value *participation* per se: to struggle for the realization of the reign of God was to live a life valuable to oneself and in the eyes of God despite its poverty, humiliations, and suffering. Resentment of those life conditions was not enough to motivate participation; nearly all *campesinos* interviewed resented the poverty and humiliation they endured before the war. Resentment of the subordinate position of one's ethnic group in an ethnic status hierarchy has been a frequent motivation for ethnic political violence in Eastern Europe, typically triggered by sudden reversals in group position due to war or the collapse of a multiethnic state (Petersen 2002). In contrast, in El Salvador, it was new beliefs, not a sudden status reversal, that linked resentment to collective action. Under the influence of liberation theology, some *campesinos* came to believe that social justice is the will of God. An immediate implication was the righteousness of participating in the struggle against injustice. The result was a new sense of hope and dignity and a new belief in the possibility of effective political participation. Together these new values and beliefs sustained participation by many, despite the movement's few victories.

By *participation*, I do not mean participation in any activity but participation in activities that reflect moral commitments. I might value participation in some sporting event, but that would not motivate me to participate if the risks were high. But merely holding a moral commitment is not enough to sustain insurgent collective action. Either I must also value participation in realizing the commitment or I must believe that my contribution is somehow essential to the realization of the commitment. It is unlikely that Salvadoran *campesinos* or other insurgent participants believed the latter. Rather, they acted on their moral commitments because they valued participation in its realization as well.

was also acquiescing. I analyze how the convention of acquiescence could be disrupted and replaced with a new convention of insurgent participation through a cascading demonstration of the decreasing risks and increasing benefits of insurgency. The emotional and moral benefits were increasingly valued as the new participatory political culture grew in strength.

Explaining Insurgent Collective Action

That participation is valued is not unusual for protest movements. James M. Jasper (1997) observes that "the pleasures of protest" include not only companionship, a sense of community and identity, the euphoria of crowds (what Emile Durkheim called "collective effervescence"), all of which are also available at soccer matches, but also the pleasure of working toward a moral vision and striving for a meaningful life. Sometimes, as in El Salvador, it is religion that provides that vision. Drawing on his comparison of organizing among low-income residents of U.S. cities, Richard L. Wood (2002: 261) shows that "certain forms of religious culture – like certain forms of any culture – enable such participation, while others constrain it."

Defiance

Some activists who suffered at the hands of the authorities or saw the suffering of their families or neighbors supported or joined the insurgents because of feelings of moral outrage at the government's response to what they perceived as their just activities. The second reason is thus *defiance*: supporting the insurgency despite the violence of the government, a refusal to acquiesce. Continued activism expressed defiance and asserted a claim to dignity and personhood. Its value was not contingent on success or even on one's contributing to the likelihood of success. (The defiant were not, however, suicidal; they did not carry out activities without some regard for their safety.)[6] In that way, defiance is similar to participation, but their affects are quite different. Defiance is negative, someone one does because one must, while participation is pleasurable. Derrick Bell (1992: xvi) noted a similarly high valuation of defiance on the part of some participants in the U.S. civil rights movement, including one elderly woman who, far from believing the movement would win, "recognized that – powerless as she was – she had and intended to use courage and determination as a weapon to, in her words, 'harass white folks.' ... Her goal was defiance, and its harassing effect was likely more potent precisely because she did what she did without expecting to topple her oppressors."

There appear to be two reasons for the salience of defiance in El Salvador. First, liberation theology provided a consistent and meaningful

[6] Dennis Chong (2001: 227) suggests that moral commitments and other intrinsic motives are rarely acted on unconditionally; strategic considerations shape most collective action when such motives are valued.

interpretation of violence and death. Suffering and even martyrdom were to be expected in the course of realizing God's reign in an unjust world (Peterson 1997). Second, if family members and fellow activists were not to have died in vain, those remaining must not forsake the struggle for justice, but continue it. Defiance, like participation, depends on a moral commitment that is highly valued: few people would run high risks to stand up to an unjust soccer referee. Thus witnessing state violence may strengthen, not weaken, insurgent support.

Jeff Goodwin (2001) recognizes two ways in which some states "construct" revolutionary mobilization. First, indiscriminate state violence, he states, may have the unintended consequence that some see supporting the insurgents "as the only alternative (other than flight) to violent death" (ibid.: 162). Perhaps a few Salvadorans joined the insurgency seeking protection, a factor David Stoll (1993) emphasizes in his analysis of the Guatemalan insurgency. But flight was almost always a possible choice in the Salvadoran case. Many, perhaps most, *campesinos* fled the most repressive areas, perhaps after initially retreating from a government advance with guerrilla forces. So this first interpretation does not explain Salvadoran insurgency; there *were* other ways out.[7] Second, state terror reinforces the cognitive plausibility and moral justifiability of a radical political orientation (Goodwin 2001: 39–40, 47). The evidence from the contested areas suggests that the second process had significantly greater weight in the Salvadoran case.

Pleasure in Agency

Other *campesinos* participated for a third reason. In interviews, insurgent *campesinos claimed authorship* of the successes of their collective actions,

[7] Stoll's (1993) analysis of survival strategies among the Ixil Maya in the wake of the extreme violence, particularly their construction of ways to rebuild a degree of autonomy despite army occupation, is an enduring contribution. However, he argues beyond his evidence in attributing Ixil support for the guerrillas before 1982 solely to coercion, that is, a forced choice for a civilian population caught between two armies. His interviews took place in a town under control of the military where continued support or sympathy for the insurgents would necessarily be muted. After 1983, the army had an explicit strategy of dividing the populace from the guerrillas; explicit neutrality was not an option (Schirmir 1998: 82–7). And his interviews suffer from selection bias: approximately a third of the Ixil population was absent from the area at the time of the interviews, the 12,000 hiding from the army in the mountains and the 15,000 killed. Thus those most likely voluntarily to support the rebels were absent, and many were dead.

expressing great pride and joy not simply in their participation but in their effectiveness. This suggests that in carrying out insurgent activities, participants experienced a pleasure in agency: they had redrawn the contours of their world. Time and again I saw this pleasure relived as groups of *campesinos* gathered to tell me the story of their cooperative and its claiming of land or to draw for me the "before" and "after" maps of their locality.

By *pleasure in agency*, I mean the positive affect associated with self-determination, autonomy, self-esteem, efficacy, and pride that come from the successful assertion of intention.[8] But I mean something more specific in two ways. First, by using the abstract term *agency* rather than the plainer "effectiveness" or the more common "efficacy," I mean to stress that this increased self-esteem and pride in self-determination and efficacy occur not just in *any* intentional activity but in the course of making history, and not just any history but a history they perceived as more *just*.[9] For some socially subordinate people of El Salvador, the drawing of what they judged as more just boundaries of class and citizenship through their own agency was profoundly meaningful, a source of pride and pleasure. (Scaling a high mountain or playing soccer well is also a source of pride and pleasure but is not the same thing.) Second, the pleasure in agency is a collective experience, as this redrawing of boundaries and reshaping of history by subordinate people is a collective enterprise.

Thus pleasure in agency is the pleasure in together changing unjust social structures through intentional action. Pleasure in agency differs from participation because the former depends on expectations of success, in achieving valued social change, not simply on participating in a movement claiming to seek social change. Thus pleasure in agency (but not participation or defiance) is a frequency-dependent motivation: it depends on the

---

[8] To refer to the "pleasure" of rebellion may evoke Banfield's "Rioting Mainly for Fun and Profit," in which he famously argued that the inner-city riots of the mid-1960s were not caused by racial oppression and could not be prevented by addressing the mistreatment of African Americans (Banfield 1968). My argument differs from his in my emphasis on the pleasure subordinate people may take in exercising agency, a human capacity from which they had long been excluded. This is distinct from Banfield's emphasis on the thrills of pillage due to the temporary suspension of law enforcement.

[9] Jon Elster (1996: 1396) states that "certain emotional satisfactions can arise only as by-products of activities that are undertaken for other ends.... I may feel proud of my achievements, but I will not achieve much if I am moved only by the desire to feel pride." He might have made a stronger argument. Without valuing some action, he would have *no reason* to feel pride (or the pleasure in agency) in the action.

likelihood of success, which in turn increases with the numbers participating (Schelling 1978; Hardin 1982). Yet the pleasure in agency is undiminished by the fact that one's own contribution to the likelihood of victory is vanishingly small.

For insurgent *campesinos*, the pleasure in agency was a strong motivation to participate partly because of the contrast it posed to the fatalism and subordination that dominated the *campesino* world view and life experience until the 1970s. These long socially subordinate people who renewed their activism after the second period of widespread violence took profound pride in doing so. To make a public claim in pursuit of one's own material interests, to occupy *land* with all its cultural and symbolic meaning in El Salvador, to refute elite perceptions of one's incapacities, and, perhaps, thereby to undercut lingering feelings of one's inferiority together created a deeply felt sense of pleasure experienced together by participants, a public assertion of dignity, self-worth, and insurgent collective identity. This public claim appears to have been in part a claim for *recognition* as persons of full worth, indeed, a claim for recognition as persons capable of agency, as essential aspect of a human being's sense of self (Taylor 1985). The frequency with which insurgent *campesinos* stressed the nonhuman treatment they endured before the war and the prideful assertion of authorship of changed boundaries reflects the salience of *personhood* in this new identity. John Hammond (1998) studied insurgent *campesinos* who participated in popular education workshops in Morazán: for them, learning to read against the odds of poverty and social denigration was the source of a newly felt power to act.

Thus despite my emphasis on emotional and moral reasons for acting, aspirations for land did play an important role. In particular, pleasure in agency is a powerful motive only when it generates a strong sense of collective efficacy in realizing a highly valued goal. Participants' pleasure in agency was not in some arbitrary achievement but in their effectively acting to assert their claim to land, although not in a productive or legal sense, as they already farmed as much abandoned land as they could manage without credit and training. So access to land would not by itself motivate participation in the insurgent cooperatives given the high risks. Access to land was a central part of *campesinos'* vision of a more just world. Land occupation was a moral and political claim, not a legal one (until the end of the war). Access to abandoned land also gave insurgent *campesinos* the autonomy to continue their insurgent activities as they no longer had to depend on landlords or local authorities for their (meager) livelihoods.

Explaining Insurgent Collective Action

These reasons for acting were often mixed together, as the interviews suggest.[10] Pleasure in agency is of course related to defiance, which is in part pride in exercising agency in defiance of unjust authority (but defiance does not depend on expectations of success). An insurgent might act out of pride in acting as an insurgent, thereby expressing his insurgent identity and membership in the insurgent community. He might act on moral principles, to build a more just world or to express outrage, but also to experience pride in having the courage to have done so. He might act to assert his political efficacy, even his capacity to make history, capacities long denied by landlords and state authorities. And for some participants, as we have seen, revenge for violence against loved ones was mixed in as well, to some extent reinterpreted as part of realizing justice.

Path-Dependent Processes

Whether these three reasons led to insurgent mobilization in a locality depended critically on the details of local history. Mobilization in the 1970s was strongest where liberationist or guerrilla networks were present. Defiance was more powerful where *campesinos* themselves experienced or saw state violence. And a substantial fraction of *campesinos*, those motivated by pleasure in agency, were moved by the prospect of success in insurgent activity, rather than participation or defiance per se, and this depended on their beliefs about what others would do.

Insurgent collective action was *path-dependent*: where it emerged depended on the paths of both violence and activism in the local area. After state violence subsided somewhat, in areas where there were enough defiant *campesinos*, support for the insurgents, if some were nearby, emerged, and in some areas began to take more collective forms. Whatever their feeling of moral outrage and willingness to act on defiance, *campesinos* with no proximity to insurgent forces rarely acted in support; even the defiant were not suicidal in the Salvadoran context. Thus there were two contingent factors that further shaped who acted: *past patterns of local state violence* and *proximity to insurgent forces*. The latter was often a matter of timing: many areas of Usulután that had little insurgent presence in 1980 or 1981 had a

---

[10] Jane Mansbridge (2001) argues that other-regarding motives of love and duty are usually combined with "self-enhancing" motives of self-esteem, honor, and reputation in oppositional social movements.

significant insurgent presence by 1983.[11] Thus we should not conclude that only the visibly active *campesinos* were morally outraged at state violence and valued defiance of unjust authority; rather, only for this group were insurgent values combined with sufficient insurgent opportunity. The defiant helped build the military capacity for the FMLN to force the retreat of landlords and local authorities from most of the case-study areas and rendered the state's coercive forces only intermittently present.

Where such successful collective actions took place, pleasure in agency motivated further collective action through a recursive process. Those who participated experienced the pleasure in agency. Their success *reinforced* insurgent values and norms (rebellion, constructing the FMLN as a political authority, solidarity among insurgents, political efficacy), beliefs (that local political opportunities are sufficiently wide, that the insurgent strategy is a good one), and practices (how the action was carried out). Part of the new political culture was a new collective identity as a member of a new community that together carried out challenging deeds and celebrated together their success. As yet inactive neighbors who valued insurgent goals witnessed their success and reevaluated the likely costs and benefits (including the pleasure in agency) of joining in. For some, the reevaluation met their threshold for likely success (perhaps they estimated that a sufficient member of other neighbors would also now join in), and they joined the next round of insurgent activity. Once begun, the process reinforced insurgent political culture, insurgent social networks, and thus collective action as the cycle of action, success, pleasure in agency, and reinforcement of insurgent culture recurred. Not all *campesinos* chose to run those risks, of course. Some had higher thresholds for likely success and waited to see the results of subsequent rounds. Others did not value what the insurgent *campesinos* valued and so would take no pleasure in successfully carrying out an insurgent activity.

But what sets in motion this recursive process? Why initial participants act is a puzzle in all frequency-dependent processes. Both path-dependent processes – past state violence and insurgent forces in sufficient proximity – were necessary to set this process in motion. If they were not significantly harmed in the process, some neighbors may have joined. If enough do so, they will succeed in successfully carrying out an insurgent action and

---

[11] Stathis Kalyvas (n.d.) analysis the logic of violence in civil wars to show how violence is generally jointly produced by insurgent and state forces, with the policing of informants playing a pivotal role. See the following note.

experience the pleasure in agency, setting in motion the process of more cautious neighbors joining in.

The founding of insurgent cooperatives and the occupation of land in Usulután followed such a logic. Their founding cascaded outward from guerrilla strongholds as successful activities in one area signaled lowered expected costs of collective action and higher expected benefits (including the pleasure in agency) to neighboring areas. A similar process occurred in the countryside during the French revolution, according to John Markoff (1996: 273). Insurgent peasants acted on an evolving sense of likely costs and benefits, and changed their assessment of risk as information emerged:

... peasant communities, more or less hungry, more or less under the thumb of the state, more or less literate, more or less in the market, are looking at one another, at what happened last month, at the local National Guards, at the political situation in nearby towns and distant capitals, and are making judgments of danger and opportunity.

This recursive process was much weaker in Tenancingo, where the community council was from its founding directed "from above." Council members participated in unprecedented activities but did so under the direct guidance and protection of the development agency and the Archdiocese of San Salvador. In contrast, insurgent *campesinos* in Usulután chose when to found cooperatives, which properties to occupy, and when to act, and they claimed land increasingly far from the protection of anyone.

This path-dependent aspect of rebellion also explains other, perhaps unexpected patterns of the insurgency.[12] For example, after extensive and arbitrary government violence subsided in the case-study areas, rather than ending insurgency as might be expected if *arbitrary* state violence fuels

---

[12] Approaches that emphasize the structural or ideological preconditions for rebellion overlook such dynamic and spatial aspects of insurgency. For example, Kalyvas (n.d.) shows that violence during the Greek civil war followed a particular pattern. Homicides did not generally occur in areas where one side was in control or where there was a balance of power between the two sides. Rather, homicides occurred where one side was more powerful but where the other party had some, perhaps intermittent, presence, as well. The reason is that the victims were accused of serving as informers for the weaker party. In such areas, these accusations were credible because potential informers had a degree of access to the party to which they supposedly bore loyalty. And accusers would not fear immediate retribution given the weakness of that party. Initial processes of rebellion may create conditions that support further insurgency. In El Salvador, the experience of state terror led to a commitment to armed rebellion. And after insurgent forces expelled authorities, the resulting psychological, material, and political autonomy made possible by access to land enabled new patterns of participation not predicted by prewar class position.

participation (because in that case nonactivists are as likely targets as activists; Mason and Krane 1989), the opposite occurred. Given the history of state terror, defiant *campesinos* saw the opening as a political opportunity for renewed activism.

The three reasons for participating in insurgency and the path-dependent processes by which they became effective in rural El Salvador share little with Olson's conventional formulation of the collective action problem. They have a particular common form: they are *intrinsic* to the process of participation itself, or *process-regarding*; they are *other-regarding*; and they are *endogenous* to the course of the war.

I discuss each in turn. In contrast to the material benefits of the insurgency that participants and nonparticipants alike could share, these reasons were contingent on participation and thus have the formal structure of selective or process-regarding benefits. The reason of course is that the experience depends on the process and not on the consequences of the action. These *intrinsic*, or *process-regarding*, reasons are thus akin to expressive motivations; indeed, participation in itself and defiance are well understood as expressive motivations. (But pleasure in agency is only partly intrinsic, as it also depends on the expected consequences of one's action.)

These reasons for participating are *other-regarding* in that they have meaning (and are thus motives) only in reference to a wider community of those with whom one acts to make history and those whose suffering is given meaning through continued activism. Moral commitments were embedded in the new forms of community that had emerged during the course of the war. And deaths by unjust authorities legitimized insurgent agency by those left behind.

But if an interpretation based on process-regarding and other-regarding motivations is to be persuasive, the emergence of insurgency-supporting values and beliefs should be accounted for (Taylor 1988: 86–9). In El Salvador, participation, defiance, and the pleasure in agency were *endogenous* to the processes of the civil war: they emerged as a result of those processes. Participation in liberationist networks enabled the imagining of different futures and the positive judgment that change was possible as the result of one's own action.[13] State terror forged defiance on the part of some of those who had participated (and even some who had not). And

---

[13] Such processes of imagining different futures and judging whether action toward a valued different future is practical in present circumstances are central to the exercise of agency (Emirbayer and Mische 1998; see also Sewell 1992 and Emirbayer and Goodwin 1994).

the pleasure in agency deepened as defiant *campesinos* (and gradually other *campesinos* as well) strengthened insurgent military and political capacity.

Caveats Considered

The reader may worry that participation per se, defiance, and pleasure in agency are ex post facto reconstructions reflecting the outcome of insurgent collective action, rather than reasons for acting at the time of the events recounted. Perhaps insurgent political culture changed rapidly at the end of the war, not through the gradual recursive process described above. This concern draws on the fact that the clearest evidence for these reasons as motives comes from material gathered at the end of the war, the subset of interviews carried out during the cease-fire and the maps drawn for me during the cease-fire by cooperative leaders.[14] While this objection cannot be laid definitively to rest without having actually observed insurgent activity such as land occupations earlier in the war (even at war's end, I was not privy to such sensitive details beforehand), there are a number of reasons to think it unpersuasive.

First, I inferred these reasons for action from my interviews and my observations of meetings and informal interactions, not from responses to a bald query about motivations, which indeed might well have elicited an ex post rationalization. Moreover, there was striking consistency between public testimonies and what I was told privately by people, many of whom I came to know quite well over a period of years. Second, there is some direct evidence that pleasure in agency may have been a reason for participation early on and is thus not merely a postwar value. Some of those interviewed recalled early strikes and marches with pride and in extraordinary detail. There are also some suggestions in the literature along these lines. According to Cabarrús (1983: 135), after workers in Aguilares carried out a successful strike before the war, "the workers could not forget the triumph that had emerged from this first solidarity." And Lungo Uclés (1995: 155) notes that a series of land occupations by *campesino* organizations in the late 1970s broke participants' fear and passivity: "As a result of the land takeovers, the Salvadoran countryside was changed forever." Third, the transformation of

---

[14] The reader may have noted that pleasure in agency was more prevalent in interviews with insurgent campesinos in Usulután than in Tenancingo. That does not imply support for the ex post alternative interpretation, however, as residents of Tenancingo did not experience the recursive process of insurgent activity as strongly.

political culture evident in insurgent interviews and maps is profound. It is unlikely that such a profound change in political culture occurred during a brief time at the end of the war. Fourth, insurgent political culture placed great emphasis on political efficacy, an emphasis difficult to explain without its having played an important role *throughout* the process: the achievements which insurgents valued were built up over years, not in a single grandly efficacious act at the end of the war. Fifth, while the processes of social construction of memory make problematic any ex post facto interpretation of motivations, social memories may be incorrect but they are not arbitrary: Their evolution occurs for particular cultural reasons, as shown in the work of Alessandro Portelli (1991, 1997). Sixth, those bearing the insurgent political culture are largely those who supported the insurgency, as we saw in the previous chapter, which supports the recursive interpretation emphasizing repeated experience, as it was those who had participated in the insurgency who also expressed insurgent values at war's end.

For these reasons, it seems reasonably parsimonious to assume that the transformation occurred gradually in the iterated way described above, and, moreover, that it reflected the experience of participation, and thus that those reasons motivated earlier insurgent activity.

A second concern the reader may have is that it might have been merely participants' beliefs about the feasibility of collective action that evolved, not their values and culture. Perhaps before the 1970s mobilization there existed what James Scott (1990) terms a "hidden transcript" of resistance within *campesino* political culture that valued participation, defiance, and agency that could not be expressed before the war (except through the "weapons of the weak," such as stealing small amounts of coffee or firewood; Scott 1985) but that was increasingly expressed as overt rebellion once circumstances allowed. Because I had fewer interviews with those who chose not to participate (and none that took place before the onset of the war in 1980), one may worry that the values and beliefs expressed by the participants were either common to participants and nonparticipants alike or had been held for decades by those who did eventually join in and thus cannot explain the insurgency.

There is no practical way to lay these concerns definitively to rest given the thin ethnographic record of prewar El Salvador. But none of my informants gave any hint that defiance and pride in agency were widespread values *before* the mobilizations of the 1970s. As we saw in the previous chapter, surveys carried out at the end of the war document considerable heterogeneity of political attitudes among rural Salvadorans, as well as one overall pattern: participation in the insurgency was associated with those attitudes consistent with insurgent political culture. Of course a process of self-selection of those who held such values before the year could account for that outcome, but given the profound transformation of expressed political culture, I am inclined to believe that values as well as practices and beliefs concerning the feasibility of collective action evolved during the course of the war.

If participation, defiance, and pleasure in agency can be interpreted as reasons for participation as well as expressions of the new political culture, then my interpretation accounts for high-risk collective action during the Salvadoran civil war where alternative theories appear not to. In particular, my interpretation accounts for the evolving patterns of *campesino* collective action over time and across space and for the emergence of the insurgent political culture, with its emphasis on making a more just history, authorship, and achievement. It is of course difficult to offer persuasive evidence of motivation for collective action in the high-risk circumstances of civil war. The persuasiveness of my interpretation must rest on the overall plausibility of my account in light of the failure of alternative explanations.

Lessons from Social Science Experiments

An additional reason I find my interpretation plausible comes from recent experiments on human motivations in social psychology, economics, and sociology. Many social scientists base their analysis of collective action on material, self-regarding, and fixed reasons for acting (i.e., preferences) defined over action outcomes. I have departed from this tradition to emphasize process-regarding, other-regarding, endogenous, moral, and emotional reasons for acting. Recent experiments have found such alternative types of motivations, sometimes called *social preferences*, to be powerful and ubiquitous reasons for cooperation in producing a collective good. In particular, these studies suggest that other-regarding motives such as envy, altruism, spite, reciprocity, and revenge are common.[15]

The first finding of relevance is that subjects who play public goods, ultimatum, and other kinds of games with one another in experimental settings frequently fail to behave like narrowly self-interested individuals whose actions are explained by maximizing their own material benefits. In short,

---

[15] Ostrom (1998), Bowles (2003), Camerer (2003), and Camerer and Fehr (2003) survey recent findings of these behavioral experiments.

they fail to free-ride. In public goods games, for example, subjects often initially contribute much more than a narrowly self-interested calculation of the benefits accruing under the various alternative strategies would predict. Whether or not in subsequent rounds their behavior tends toward that predicted by self-regarding preferences over material goods (contributing nothing) depends on precisely how the game is structured, such as whether participants are allowed to communicate about who has contributed what. High levels of voluntary contributions occur when participants are allowed at a cost to themselves to punish those who in previous rounds contributed little (Fehr and Gächter 2002; Camerer and Fehr 2003). Of course, punishment of low contributors is itself a public good, so free-riding participants in the game would be expected to neither contribute nor punish. The fact that this public-spirited behavior occurs even during last round of the game among strangers, when it cannot possibly enhance the future material payoff of the punisher, suggests that nonselfish (other-regarding) motives are at work.

The second finding is that participants in ultimatum games are willing to forgo large benefits in order to punish other players whom they perceive as having treated them or someone else unfairly. In such games, one player of two is provisionally given some sum of money and both are told that if he makes an offer of a share of the money to another player, and if that player accepts the offer, the money is given to them, split between them according to the offer. If the offer is rejected, they both get nothing. So if the first player receives $10, it is narrowly self-interested to make the other player the lowest possible offer, namely, $1, as it is for the other player to accept – after all, the responder is better off in dollar terms accepting than if the players fail to agree on an offer. But in experiments, participants typically reject the offer if it is less than about $3, and when asked why, they often say that the offer was unfair. The participants prefer, then, to assume costs (forgoing what they could have had) in order to punish those making unfair offers. Lest it appear that participants are responding to the pettiness of the incentives usually offered in such settings, similar patterns occurred virtually uniformly when the experiments were repeated in over a hundred experiments across a range of world settings, including some where the stakes were as high as a third of the subjects' average annual expenditures (Fehr and Gächter 2000; Fehr and Fischbacher 2001).

Experiments also suggest that individuals care not only about what they get, but also about *how* what they get is determined, that is, their preferences are *process-based* (Bowles 2003: chapter 3). For example, when ultimatum game offers are generated by a computer or a third party, rather than by the proposer who stands to benefit from a low offer, the respondent is much less likely to refuse the offer. Similarly, when proposers are not selected randomly but are assigned on the basis of success on an exam, even one that is transparently trivial, respondents are much less likely to reject low offers.

The third finding of relevance is that the participants are heterogeneous. An analysis of data from many experiments found that 40 to 66 percent of the experimental subjects make choices indicating social preferences, while 20 to 30 percent make selfish choices that maximize their personal earnings (Fehr and Gächter 2000). Individuals were also versatile, sometimes making choices indicating social preferences and at other times making selfish ones (Bowles 2003: chapter 3). Among the relevant experimental evidence (some of it surveyed in Bowles 1998 and 2003) is the fact that merely labeling a game "The Wall Street Game" or "The Exchange Game" leads to significantly more self-regarding behavior than when it is labeled "The Community Game," despite the fact that the games were otherwise exactly alike. So it appears that people's behavior is affected by cues about the situation in which they find themselves.

Finally, the proposition that preferences are *endogenous* – that they evolve under the influence of changing circumstances rather than remaining fixed – has gained empirical support in recent years (Bowles 1998, 2003). Melvin Kohn and his colleagues found that occupation affects personality (Kohn, Naoi, Schoenbach, Schooler, and Slomczynski 1990). Occupation also affects how parents raise children. Those who follow orders in the workplace raise their children to respect authority; those whose work involves more autonomy raise their children to be creative (Kohn 1969). Scholars have recently carried out ultimatum and public goods games experiments in hunter-gatherer and other nonindustrial societies (Henrich, Bowles, Boyd, Camerer, Fehr, Gintis, and McElreath 2001). They have found sharp distinctions in how individuals in different societies play such games; the differences appear to correspond to how production in organized in each society. The notion that preferences may be endogenous in some circumstances, which was once anathema in economics where the *de gustibus non est disputandum* (there is no accounting for tastes) dictum once held sway, is now given serious consideration. (Indeed, one of the authors most responsible for the popularity of the above dictum, Gary Becker, titled his 1996 book *Accounting for Tastes*.)

There is also evidence from this literature about the salience of intrinsic motives. Edward Deci (1975: 23), a leading contributor to the literature on this subject, defines intrinsically motivated activities as ones "for which there is no apparent reward except the activity itself.... The activities are ends in themselves, rather than means to an end." The salience of intrinsic motives and the manner in which they may be evoked or extinguished by particular situations have been documented in literally hundreds of empirical studies (Deci and Ryan 1985; Lepper and Greene 1978; Ross and Nisbett 1991). Moreover, the psychological mechanisms that appear to underpin intrinsic motivations suggest the importance of the pleasure in agency as well. Deci (1975) concludes that intrinsic motivations reflect a fundamental desire for feelings of competence and self-determination. The reference to competence of course suggests an element of successful assertion of these motives. I have defined participation, defiance, and pleasure in agency with reference to highly valued ends, which render intrinsic motives (the pleasure in realizing those ends) all the more powerful.

I do not wish to exaggerate the relevance of laboratory experiments for the understanding of *campesino* collective action – or for that matter for any behaviors in nonlaboratory settings. However, it is worth noting that, though in dramatically different settings, the experimental subjects' explanations of their choices echo many of the themes expressed by *campesinos*: an affirmation of norms of fairness and justice, a willingness to act on the behalf of those norms, and a positive valuing of nonconventional preferences.

Comparable Cases

There is another quite different reason that I have confidence in my account. The reasons for insurgent collective actions stressed here – participation, defiance, and pleasure in agency, as well as closely related reasons, such as self-respect, honor, dignity, recognition, and reputation – appear to have played powerful roles in other, quite diverse, cases of collective action by long subordinate social actors.

Where social subordination is accompanied by expressions of contempt, we should expect to find that these reasons may motivate insurgent collective action. In particular, pleasure in agency is more meaningful, and thus more motivating, in contexts where participants have little experience of political efficacy. Middle-class participants in environmental movements may experience and be motivated by the expression of moral outrage and the various pleasures of protest such as marching, chanting, and singing together, but they are likely to take their agency for granted.

Explaining Insurgent Collective Action

The U.S. civil rights movement is a case where we should find participation and pleasure in agency as reasons for collective action. Doug McAdam (1982) emphasized the importance of feelings of political efficacy among participants in the U.S. civil rights movement as a key element of the "cognitive liberation" that was essential to black insurgency in that movement. And as we saw above, defiance motivated some participants as well. In a later work, McAdam (1988) explores why some young activists in the northern part of the United States were willing to participate in voter registration and education campaigns in Mississippi during Freedom Summer, the summer of 1964. According to him, the activists acted on normative commitments to the goals of the campaign because their earlier participation in civil rights actions had led to a deeper sense of identification with the movement and its goals. Compared with applicants who applied but did not go to Mississippi, participants were more involved in civil rights and other organizations and had more friendships with others applying. Participation in Freedom Summer changed the life course of many who went south that summer: "What many of the volunteers glimpsed in Mississippi was a way of life, a form of community, and a vision of themselves far more exhilarating and engaging than any they had known before. Here was high moral purpose, adventure, and rich community all rolled into one" (McAdam 1988: 137). For those who participated, "politics" became so salient that they made choices concerning careers and partners different from those with similar initial values who had applied to go but did not. Thus the process appears similarly recursive and endogenous: participants' values changed as activists became more involved in the movement. As in El Salvador, collective identity was an *outcome* of collective action (Calhoun 1991).

The transformative power of participation is also seen in another case of high-risk collective action. In his analysis of the stories told by Lithuanians of political violence in their rural communities in the 1940s during occupation by the Soviets and the Germans, Roger Petersen (n.d.) identified three distinct types of narratives: personal narratives characterized by grief and vivid recollections, well-rehearsed collective narratives that focused on angrily identifying and blaming those responsible for violence, and proud collective narratives told by those who participated in resistance and rebellion.

An interesting contrast to the Salvadoran case is provided by the extensive land occupations during the Portuguese revolution. According to a survey carried out by Nancy Bermeo (1986: 98), direct selective incentives played a role. Approximately half (46 percent) of those who participated were landless and unemployed workers who seized land as a way to acquire a job. Moreover, the risks of occupying land were much lower in Portugal at that time than in El Salvador. In other aspects, however, rural political mobilization was similar. Successful occupation led to further occupations in adjacent areas, and the pace of occupation accelerated as a regime transition neared (ibid.: 56, 75). And those who participated in the occupations came to hold distinct, more radical, and participatory political attitudes, participating more frequently in demonstrations and asserting a higher sense of political efficacy (ibid.: 136–42).

When Barrington Moore (1978: xiii) began what was to become his historical study of "why people so often put up with being the victims of their societies and why at other times they become very angry and try with passion and forcefulness to do something about their situation," he initially intended to title the resulting work "a study of moral outrage."[16] In analyzing the pattern of collective action by German industrial workers from 1848 to 1933, Moore suggests that collective action generally occurred when norms of fairness were violated, and took more revolutionary forms when revolutionary parties were present, findings that are generally similar to the interpretation presented here.

In the Huk Rebellion in the Philippines, defiance was an essential element of the meaning of the movement for participants, according to Benedict J. Kerkvliet. One elderly man reflected, " 'We showed them [the landlords and government] we weren't slaves. . . . We didn't lie down like whimpering dogs when they started to whip us. We stood up to them and fought for what was rightfully ours' " (Kerkvliet 1977: 269). However, the extent to which defiance motivated insurgency is not clear from Kerkvliet's account. The overall trajectory of insurgent collective action in central Luzon was similar to that in El Salvador. In particular, state repression led many to embrace armed rebellion, which suggests that defiance might have played a similarly key role.

Pride, respect, and dignity appeared to play a role in the Vietnamese Revolution, according to David Hunt. Drawing on transcripts of interrogations with defectors from the National Liberation Front in Vietnam, Hunt (1974) explores why other cadres did not defect during the intense aerial bombing of areas controlled by the front that began in 1965. Those

---

[16] Moore changed the title from *A Study of Moral Outrage* to *Injustice: The Social Bases of Obedience and Revolt*, as he decided that "injustice" better captured the tone of popular anger than "moral" (Moore 1978: xiii–xiv).

who did not defect were generally from the poorest strata of the village. Front ideology put the poorest into the local vanguard role as a way to undermine the long-standing ideological justification of their poverty. According to Hunt, this inversion of social position led to feelings of pride and assertions of dignity and respect on the part of these very poor farmers. They stayed with the insurgency even as conditions worsened dramatically, thereby contributing to the eventual overthrow of the regime.

Motivations similar to defiance and the pleasure in agency appeared to have played a role in the emergence and rapid spread of *rondas campesinas* (nightwatch patrols) in the highlands of northern Peru beginning in the late 1970s. According to Orin Starn, participants were acting in defense of their own interests to protect their animals from theft, but their motivation also involved a search for recognition and respect and pride in the achievement of dignity and order (1999: 28–33). A similar process took place in urban areas. Susan Stokes (1995) reports that popular culture in the shanty towns of Lima bifurcated into distinct forms. One subculture, the radical branch, developed an "ideology of participation" in which the claim of poor citizens to rights before the state was central, in contrast to the clientelist subculture, in which self-help was the dominant ideology (Stokes 1995: 70–6). What distinguished those who embraced the first from those who advocated the second, according to Stokes, was political experience, ranging from participation in Velasco-era corporatist experiments to experience in later organizations based on liberation theology or leftist political ideology. Stokes does not suggest that pleasure in agency became a motivation for collective action, only that participation was seen as valuable in itself.

The closely related claim to dignity or recognition as moral equals appears to be among the reasons for participating in some other insurgent movements. In his analysis of the trajectory of peasant collective action during the French Revolution, John Markoff (1996) argues that an assertion of dignity and the contestation of traditional authority are essential to explain that trajectory. Insurgent violence, almost all of which was directed against property, not people, was, he argues, an assertion about whose definition of value was to matter, thereby an assertion of dignity based on an emerging concept of citizenship and equal moral worth (1996: 108, 225–7). According to Ranajit Guha (1983a: 59, 143–6), the "urge to self-respect" and "prestige" were more important in peasant insurgency in colonial India than were economic demands. A similar assertion of moral dignity underlay the struggle for indigenous rights in the Zapatista uprising, according to Neil Harvey (1998). And of course a claim for citizenship on equal terms was a motive for insurgency in South Africa as well as in the United States (Seidman 1994). However, movements that organize around appeals for recognition of moral dignity and equal citizenship may combine those appeals with older political practices, as in the *navista* movement of San Luis Potosí, Mexico, a civic opposition movement that though more autonomous than its predecessor movements was still dominated by a single powerful figure (Pansters 1996).

Dennis Chong (1991) in his analysis of the U.S. civil rights movement stresses the social and psychological benefits accruing to participants. He argues that unconditional cooperators (akin to the defiant *campesinos*) built the movement by winning sufficient interim victories demonstrating the possibilities of success, so that conditional cooperation became a rational response. In contrast to the argument here, Chong emphasizes social sanctions and concerns for reputation rather than defiance or the pleasure in agency per se. However, as James Jasper (1997: 27–8) points out in his critique of Chong's argument, Chong acknowledges that one of the best ways to sustain a reputation for altruism and service is to develop a *genuine* interest for others. While Chong's interpretation is consistent, there is little evidence presented that supports his emphasis on acting for a reputation for some value over acting for that value itself.

Honor may appear to be closely related to reputation. Craig Calhoun argues that defending their honor was a principal motivation for Chinese students at Tiananmen Square. However, he shows that for participants, honor was not just a matter of reputation but a particular way of evaluating *oneself* against culturally valued models. During the weeks leading up to the final confrontation, students suffered a recurrent sense of insult to their honor by government officials, leading to feelings of outrage and anger (Calhoun 1991: 65). As a result of their immersion in intense social networks and the importance of honor, the students ran high risks: "[P]articipation in a course of action over time committed one to an identity that would be irretrievably violated by pulling back from the risk" (ibid.: 51). Such collective action is not self-serving but "self-saving" (ibid.: 69). Thus the cultural processes of the movement sustained collective action to its tragic end.

A similarly powerful collective identity contributed to a lack of caution on the part of urban trade unionists in the extremely dangerous context of Guatemala in 1980, according to Deborah Levenson-Estrada. She traces the emergence of a particular political culture and identity among urban unionists to its roots in Young Catholic Worker circles of the 1950s. The movement emphasized the power of people to transform life, the importance of moral self-empowerment, and the rights of workers as human beings and as workers (1994: 85–6). These were key elements of the movement's social identity: "Activism required that workers perceive themselves, subjectively, in ways that made action possible in the specific situation that was theirs. An important part of this self-identity was the notion that trade unionists should make history" (ibid.: 232). The outcome was a trade union movement strong enough to attempt to organize workplaces in a context of severe repression. But another result of this voluntarist strategy, according to Levenson-Estrada (ibid.: 232–3), was a "disastrous triumphalism" that blinded the movement to the repressive capacity and will of the state that decimated the movement in 1980.

Thus in these various settings, reasons for acting that seem related to participation, defiance, and pleasure in agency appear to have played a role in the mobilization of long subordinate people, sometimes in circumstances of high risk and sometimes to tragic ends. Further research is needed to trace more precisely the role of such reasons for actions and how they emerged in particular social and cultural contexts. If the argument presented here holds more generally, as I believe it may, such tracing would find that participation in insurgent activities has cultural as well as political consequences that may, in some circumstances, reinforce insurgent values and beliefs such that insurgency continues despite high risks.

Implications

The argument presented here thus emphasizes the salience to insurgent participants of reasons for acting that concern others as well as themselves, the process of mobilization itself, the intentions of other actors, the outcome of actions for both themselves and other actors, and the endogeneity of values, beliefs, political culture, political identity, and political opportunity. And key reasons for acting were moral and emotional, not material interests. I hope this argument has not merely traced the existence of the "black boxes" of political mobilization (social networks, political opportunity, organization, insurgent culture, etc.) but analyzed their internal relations and the causal processes that link and constitute them (McAdam et al. 2001).

My account suggests that those who supported the insurgency were often brave and generous. It does not suggest that they were irrational. Like conventional explanations for collective action, my interpretation emphasizes intentional action taken with the purpose of realizing one's interests or values as the key element of the microfoundations of collective action. Despite the risks involved, insurgent *campesinos* had cogent and enduring reasons for participating, which they articulated to me at length and with remarkable consistency. Acting for these reasons was not irrational either in the substantive sense of "unreasonable" or in the formal sense of "inconsistent or incomplete." These reasons for action thus pose no challenge to the intentional emphasis of rational choice approaches. I do not know whether my respondents acted wisely; some certainly acted heroically and others venally. But I am quite sure that they acted intentionally in the pursuit of their ends, often carefully weighing the benefits and costs.

My interpretation of *campesino* insurgency thus does not differ from rational choice accounts in its presumption of intention. However, it does differ from most such accounts in three ways.

First, my interpretation suggests the importance of reasons for acting absent from such accounts, namely, emotions. Emotions are often complementary to rationality. They have cognitive antecedents; they are occasioned by beliefs (Elster 1998). They trigger action by changing the relative salience of desires (Petersen 2002). Some are of short duration, triggering an "action tendency" toward an immediate response, such as the impulse to flee on being frightened. Others, more relevant for collective action, are long-standing, such as love or revenge. For example, moments of collective effervescence or euphoria are short-lived emotions that bear a resemblance to pleasure in agency, but pleasure in agency in the Salvadoran setting was profound and long-enduring, as evident in the pride in authorship of long-past actions of defiance.

Some scholars of collective action acknowledge moral and emotional reasons for collective action. Tibor Scitovsky (1976) argued that contributing to a public good may be a "pleasure," not a cost. Albert Hirschman (1982: 89) emphasized that acting "to change society for the better" and joining together to do so was "pleasurable, in fact, intoxicating, in itself."[17] Still others have argued that the meaningfulness of participating in the making of history may motivate collective action (Hardin 1982). In contrast to much of the literature on collective action, which when it recognizes such motivations at all does so as a theoretical possibility or based on a brief anecdote, I have shown empirically how pleasure of agency emerged as a powerful motivation over the course of the insurgency.

---

[17] However, Hirschman argued that the impetus to participation was disappointment in private pleasures, a motive unlikely to motivate participation in these high-risk circumstances by socially subordinate people.

Explaining Insurgent Collective Action

Recent scholarship on social movements concurs with the centrality of moral and emotional reasons for collective action. Not only do social networks provide channels for information and the possibility of sanctioning nonparticipants, but the affective bonds between members motivate participation even if the calculation of tangible costs and benefits does not (Jasper 1997; Jasper 1998; Goodwin, Jasper, and Polletta 2001; Mansbridge 2001). In high-risk settings, part of the cultural work of the movement is to mitigate the fear of reprisals or violence that participants feel through rituals. In the U.S. civil rights movement and in the East Germany democracy movements, rituals such as songs, chants, and welcoming ceremonies generated collective effervescence in mass meetings, thereby evoking emotions that reknit commitment to the movement (Goodwin and Pfaff 2001). And the causal force of widening political opportunity at the national level has emotional consequences as a symbol of hope that may override the immediate local experience of increased repression, as did the decision in *Brown v. the Board of Education* (1954), which signaled the possibility of change despite the dramatic increase in repression in the U.S. South that followed on its heels (Goodwin et al. 2001: 7–8).

What my interpretation may contribute to this literature is an emphasis on the importance that long-subordinate social actors grant to the exercise of agency per se. To act in defiance of unjust authority, to claim recognition as equal subjects whose personhood needs be respected, to act effectively for the realization of essential interests, and to publicly assert the power of collective efficacy may be important reasons for the emergence of insurgent collective action elsewhere as well as in El Salvador, as we saw in the previous section. Karl Marx observed in *The Eighteenth Brumaire of Louis Bonaparte* that "[m]en make their own history, but they do not make it just as they please." The argument presented here suggests that in circumstances of high risk, participants may do so in part because of the value they place on making a more just history.

Second, while the other-regarding aspect of the reasons for action emphasized here are consistent with rational choice approaches, the intrinsic, or process-regarding, aspect is not. Reasons that refer irreducibly to the process itself or to a noninstrumental value and not to the outcomes of action are problematic because they challenge the consequentialist framework of rational choice (Sen 1977; Taylor 1988: 85–90; Chong 2001). In particular, acting out of moral commitment is not well understood in consequentialist terms, unless one infers that what matters is not the commitment but having the reputation for having the commitment, as Dennis Chong (1991) suggests in his analysis of the U.S. civil rights movement. An alternate way to reconcile normative commitments with the consequentialist framework is to interpret that commitment as a preference for being the kind of person who has that commitment. For example, I may keep a promise to my dead grandmother that no one else knows about or would care about if they knew because I want to be a promise-keeping kind of person.

Both these attempts to reconcile moral commitments with consequentialist approaches understand observed human behavior by imputing a preference to the actor that is not recognized by the actor herself. The first and, perhaps, also the second attempt do not square with our introspective experience of what it is to have a moral norm or a value. Yet as the behavioral experiments reviewed above show, social preferences are ubiquitous. Taking them seriously should be a more promising line of research on collective action than imputing unrecognized motives.

Third, the values, norms, practices, and beliefs relevant for collective action were not fixed over the course of the civil war but evolved endogenously. Process-regarding and other-regarding motives, whose salience varied among potential participants for reasons of character and history, fueled participation through a spiral (virtuous or vicious, according to one's lights) of participation reinforcing an emergent insurgent political culture, whose bearers had the confidence to perceive and grasp new political opportunities and whose values of solidarity and participation led to further collective action, which forged new opportunities and again reinforced insurgent values, perceptions, and identities. This suggests that the common practice in applications of rational choice theory of assuming universalistic and fixed preferences is unwarranted and obscures dynamics essential to understanding collective action. If social scientists are to succeed in the construction of "analytic narratives" (Bates, Greif, Weingast, and Rosenthal 1998) that compellingly recreate the structures of choice and dynamics of historical political processes, the endogeneity of reasons for acting should be explored.

Of course this spiral does not necessarily occur. As Jeff Goodwin (1997) argues in his study of the Huk Rebellion, emotional ties may dampen participation if insurgents find themselves too torn between the claims of family and the organization, or if the guerrilla organization cannot successfully manage tensions among its members, including conflict over sexual and emotional relations. The study of intrinsic, other-regarding, process-based, and endogenous preferences may be as important to explaining quiescence as it apparently is in explaining insurgent collective action.

Explaining Insurgent Collective Action

The interpretation advanced here may help clarify *how and when* re-pression fosters mobilization rather than quiescence. The rising spiral of insurgent collective action described above is contingent on the evolving balance of military force. It may turn downward if the costs prove so high that defiance costs too much. In the Guatemalan highlands, after guer-rilla forces proved too weak to protect participants from the genocidally brutal response of government forces in the wake of the insurgents' dis-astrous insurrectionary strategy, most Ixil Maya chose to live under army protection (Stoll 1993). They did so despite the military's responsibility, ac-cording to the Guatemalan truth commission, for more than 90 percent of the violence. But in other circumstances, repression may result in levels of defiance that may help sustain insurgency. It appears that the consequences of government repression depend on whether initial insurgent capacity is sufficiently strong relative to initial government reaction, perhaps because the government's repressive capacity is constrained for some reason. If so, *campesinos* may actively choose insurgency as an expression of sustained dis-sent, not merely as way of securing protection, a finding at odds with Stoll's position.

The pattern of insurgent collective action during the Salvadoran civil war shows how political opportunity is produced along the trajectory of protest and how local and national structures of political opportunity in-teract. Insurgents created their own political opportunities, expelling au-thorities from areas and initiating the case of insurgent cooperative land claims. Local political opportunity also depended in part on national op-position organizations. National organizations strengthened ties between cooperatives and forged contacts with journalists in San Salvador, which made possible an unprecedented degree of accountability for actions by government forces. The military threat posed by insurgent military forces forced hard-line military groups to tolerate counterinsurgency reforms (lest U.S. assistance be jeopardized), which made possible the reemergence of overt opposition organizations. At the national level, the continuation of the insurgency eventually forced the government and elite to agree to ne-gotiations, which in the newly democratic rules of the game eventually institutionalized a different structure of political opportunity, particularly the holding for the first time of inclusive elections.

Perhaps, in light of these implications, this analysis of a particular case of insurgent collective action will contribute to our understanding of high-risk collective action. I hope so. But if I have merely succeeded in telling well the history of the civil war in the case-study areas, I will be pleased. I close where

I began, on the Cooperative California. One member of the cooperative told me in my last interview with him: "It has been a long twelve years. This Hacienda California, for me it is the whole story in miniature. Here fell my first drop of blood; this land is bathed in blood. For twelve years it has been a laboratory [for change], but twelve years is enough" (Tierra Blanca, 1992).

Epilogue: Legacies of an Agrarian Insurgency

> We shed blood all these years in order to buy land at market prices?
>
> *Campesino* activist, Tierra Blanca, 1992

In the course of El Salvador's civil war, insurgent *campesinos* redrew boundaries of class, culture, and citizenship. By the end of the war, insurgent cooperatives occupied about a third of Usulután's farmland. While desperately poor, insurgent *campesinos* in most of the case-study areas enjoyed an unprecedented autonomy from landlords and traditional authorities. They participated in a dense network of insurgent organizations that defended land occupations against the return of the landlords. The settlement that ended the civil war between the two parties was a democratic political bargain: in exchange for laying down their arms and abandoning their socialist objectives, the insurgent organization joined the polity, which was to be reformed along liberal democratic lines. Over the next several years, the provisions of the agreement were generally carried out, despite resistance on the part of the government to the implementation of some aspects of the agreement. That positive outcome required an extended process of negotiation and ongoing pressure on government officials (and to a lesser extent on the FMLN) by the United Nations in its role as observer and verifier of the peace agreement and by donor countries in their capacity as funders of reforms.[1] Since 1994, elections have been held regularly and the FMLN has garnered an increasing share of political power, becoming the leading party in the national legislature in the 2000 elections. The required reforms to military, police, judicial, and electoral institutions have been

---

[1] On the implementation of the peace agreement, see Montgomery (1995), Popkin (2000), Wood (1996, n.d.), and the various reports by *Hemisphere Initiatives*.

carried out to a significant degree. And in some areas of the countryside, an unprecedented civil society continues actively to pursue *campesino* interests.

In this brief epilogue, I discuss the aftermath of the war for the rural poor of El Salvador, with particular attention to the case-study areas. What were the legacies of the wartime process of mobilization and organization for the postwar period? Is there evidence that the new patterns of participation and citizenship endured in postwar El Salvador?

One of the provisions of the peace agreement was that ex-combatants of both sides and civilian supporters of the FMLN occupying properties in the contested areas, that is, the *tenedores*, would be entitled to land, which they would purchase over a long period at subsidized interest rates from a government agency. Because the peace agreement was vague on key points, a long process of negotiation mediated by the United Nations between government and FMLN representations eventually defined the scope and terms of the land transfer.[2] While negotiations were made significantly more feasible by the willingness of international organizations to provide funding to buy out the landlords, the process ran aground repeatedly. One reason was the linkage between land transfer and the implementation of other terms of the peace agreement, such as the dissolution of particular security forces in the peace process's complicated chronology of staggered demobilization. The inadequacies of the Salvadoran land registry and the postwar mobility of potential beneficiaries also complicated the transfer. Government officials with close ties to the governing party who feared that a rapid transfer would bolster the FMLN's standing in postwar elections delayed the process. Delays and problems also arose as the inadequacies of the demobilization benefits (various packages of training and credit) became evident.

Thus the process was difficult, occasioning several suspensions of the FMLN's demobilization of its forces and precipitating the intervention of the U.N. Secretary-General to settle the outstanding issues. The outcome did not favor *campesinos* occupying land, as the parties agreed that the transfer of land per beneficiary would be quite low. The result was the significant difference between land occupied and transferred that we saw in Figure 6.2.

However, postwar political mobilization eased the terms of transfer for both civilians and ex-combatants alike. Sustained pressure on the

[2] See Wood (1995, 1996), del Castillo (1997), and Flores (1998) for analysis of the land transfer negotiations.

Epilogue

government by peasant organizations eventually led to a substantial easing of the debt carried by most cooperatives (Foley, Vickers, and Thale 1997; Kowalchuk 2000). For insurgent *campesinos*, this was a major victory. One cooperative leader with long-standing experience in mobilization and insurgency remarked to me, "We have forced the transfer of land, entirely against the government" (Tierra Blanca, 1996).

Although the scale of postwar land transfer was much less than insurgents had hoped, the war left changes in the agrarian structure in El Salvador as a result of the 1980 agrarian reform, the postwar transfer, and war-driven urbanization and migration processes. At the national level, according to the best estimate – Vincent J. McElhinny's analysis of the 1998 Multipurpose Household Survey – landholdings over 100 hectares declined from 38.7 percent of farmland in 1971 to 23.1 percent in 1998 (2001: table 7).[3] Medium-sized farms (20–100 hectares) rose from 25.5 to 31.1 percent, and small farms (0–20 hectares) from 35.9 to 45.7 percent of farmland. The composition of the economically active agricultural adult population changed as well. Landowners in 1998 comprised 23.3 percent, compared with 14.4 percent in 1971 (ibid.: table 5). Similar declines occurred in the fraction of the land-poor (from 22.0 percent to 16.2 percent) and in the fraction of temporary day workers (from 38.1 percent to 27.4 percent).

However, the fraction with access to land (the landed and the land-poor together) has changed little, from 39.5 percent to 36.4 percent. And the decline in temporary day workers is mostly accounted for by the increase in those working on family plots, from 8.4 percent to 14.9 percent. Thus rural landlessness remained very high after the war, despite the distribution of about 30 percent of farmland through the 1980 agrarian reform and the peace agreement (Seligson 1995; McElhinny 2001: table 6).

The land transfer process in Usulután benefited from a European Community initiative that targeted ex-combatants of both sides in the department and made available more training and credit than was available in most other areas. (USAID funded the transfer to civilians in Usulután in a parallel but not as well-funded program.) In Jiquilisco, Jucuapa, San Agustín, and San Francisco Javier the amount transferred amounted to more than 14 percent of the surface area (see Fig. 6.2). In the department as a whole, about 6 percent of surface area was transferred. According to McElhinny's estimate (2001: table A1), the Gini coefficient for land

[3] However, McElhinny (2001) notes that there are problems with these figures due to the underreporting of large farms.

inequality (inequality in farms, not family holdings) in Usulután fell from 0.832 in 1971 to 0.795 in 1998, still quite high. However, the number of beneficiaries settled on the plots transferred made it unlikely that any substantial fraction of them could make anything but an extremely marginal living farming the land. For example, the Cooperativa California was divided among six cooperatives, the Tierra Blanca group itself, a group of demobilizing ERP combatants, and four cooperatives that had occupied land nearby. The beneficiaries received only two hectares each. (The average parcel transferred was 2.9 hectares; ibid.: table 6.)

Although rural poverty rates fell after the war, from 65.0 percent in 1992 to 58.6 percent in 1998 for total poverty (household income less than twice the cost of a basic food basket), and from 34.0 to 25.6 for extreme poverty (household income less than the cost of a basket), they remained quite high (Conning, Olinto and Trigueros, Arguello 2001: table 2). Adult literacy and life expectancy rates remain much worse in the countryside than in urban areas. Declining rural wages – the real minimum wage for coffee and sugar harvests fell 12.1 percent and 11.0 percent, respectively, between 1993 and 1998 – and worsening terms of trade for agricultural goods contributed to enduring rural poverty (ibid.: 7).

Thus after the civil war, life remained very difficult for the rural poor of El Salvador. The postwar crime boom also brought suffering. Crime rates in postwar El Salvador were extraordinarily high, particularly the homicide rate, which was 138 per 100,000 inhabitants in 1994 and 1995, compared with prewar rates of 33 and *exceeding* the rate at the height of the war violence of 55.3 (including war deaths) in 1982 (Cruz and González 1997; see also Call 1999). This homicide rate was (along with Colombia and South Africa) among the world's very highest, sixteen times the U.S. rate (Spence, Lanchin, and Thale 2001: 17).

In early 2001, two earthquakes devastated significant areas of El Salvador. The first quake alone left 681 people dead, and more than 20,000 homes destroyed (CIDAI 2001a: 16).[4] In February 2001, the government estimated accumulated damages at about $3 billion, or about 22 percent of national income (CIDAI 2001b: 6). A later and more conservative estimate puts the accumulated damage at 12 percent of GDP (Spence et al. 2001: 1). Undoubtably, postquake poverty figures are significantly higher than those given above due to the damage to infrastructure and the displacement of families from their work and homes. Southwestern Usulután was

[4] See CIDAI (2001c: Cuadro 1) for a detailed estimate of the costs of the first earthquake.

hit particularly hard by the quakes, as it had been by flooding in previous years.

The principal achievement of the peace process, in addition to the fact that El Salvador, unlike many countries, did not return to war, is a significant democratization of political power (Wood n.d.). Electoral competition increased at both the legislative and the municipal levels. In coalition with other parties, the FMLN made a respectable showing in the 1994 presidential elections, forcing the presidential election into a runoff round (which it lost to ARENA by a wide margin). The FMLN (without a coalition) won twenty-one of the eighty-four seats in the unicameral legislature in 1994.

However, the FMLN split soon after the elections, when the leadership of the ERP together with some leaders of the Resistencia Nacional, another of the five guerrilla organizations, dramatically broke with the FMLN in the inaugural session of the new legislature. The group subsequently founded a new party, the Partido Demócrata. The FMLN lost seven of its twenty-one seats in the split. However, this move to found a separate party proved a severe miscalculation, as most supporters remained with the FMLN or switched back to the FMLN after the new party's leadership entered into a pact with ARENA to support an increase in the value added tax. The Partido Demócrata's share of valid votes in 1997 was an abysmal 1.2 percent for the legislature and 1.0 percent for mayoral elections (Acevedo 1998: 217); in coalition with the Christian Democrats, it won only three seats in the legislature and four municipalities. Nor did its record improve in the subsequent election. In 2000, in coalition with another small party, the Partido Demócrata again won only three seats and four municipalities. The party did not even retain its traditional stronghold of the northern Morazán. Of the twenty-one ex-conflicted municipalities in the department, the coalition won only two in the 2000 elections, while the FMLN won four (and one nonconflicted municipality).

The split within the FMLN deeply troubled many insurgent *campesinos* in Usulután, as they believed that divisions would only undermine their struggle for land, credit, higher wages, and political power. One longtime Tierra Blanca leader remarked bitterly, "It's all up in the air. The gravest consequence would be if the government failed to legalize our [property] titles as a result of these political divisions" (Tierra Blanca, 1995). Many longtime supporters of the ERP became deeply demoralized when the ERP leadership left the FMLN, viewing it as a betrayal of the struggle. Most midlevel commanders did not follow their leaders into the new party but formed a new group, the Tendencia Democrática (Democratic Tendency) within the FMLN. One commander explained:

The split reflected ongoing disagreements between us and the leadership. We agree it's no longer an issue of revolution. But we disagreed that leaving the FMLN was a way to gain people's support. . . . And the internal dynamic was not very democratic. I think it's a problem that stems from the war: the Frente was a political-military organization. It was our responsibility to issue orders. (Tierra Blanca, 1996)

The split left the leaders of the Democratic Tendency weaker within the FMLN.

Despite the split, the FMLN has made a surprisingly effective transition from a guerrilla army to a political party, increasing its share of legislative seats, municipalities, and votes (but not in presidential races), from election to election. In 1997, the FMLN won 27 seats in the legislature, only one fewer than ARENA's 28 seats. The party performed poorly in the 1999 presidential election, failing to even force a second round, perhaps because of the well-publicized divisions between party factions in choosing a candidate (Spence et al. 2001). After the March 2000 elections, however, it was the leading party in the national legislature, holding 31 seats to ARENA's 29. However, this lead position did not translate proportionally into power over policy, as the recovering Partido de Conciliación Nacional (the party that ruled before the war) voted with ARENA, as did the still-declining Christian Democrat Party.

Particularly striking was the FMLN's increasing ability to compete in municipal elections. (El Salvador's 265 municipalities encompass the entire country and constitute the sole form of local government.) As indicated in Figure E.1, the fraction of municipalities the party governs (either solely or in coalition) has increased nationally from just over 6 percent in 1994 to 21 percent in 1997 and 28 percent in 2000. In Usulután the increase has been even more spectacular, rising from 0 percent in 1994 to 13 percent in 1997 and almost 35 percent in 2000. In the case-study areas, the party continues to increase its vote share in every municipality (Fig. E.2). While the FMLN did not win in any of the case-study municipalities in 1994, in 1997 it won control of Jiquilisco, San Agustín, Tenancingo, and – perhaps remarkably so, given the relative absence of overt FMLN organizing in the town – in Santiago de María. In 2000, of these the FMLN lost only San Agustín but gained Tecapán and Santa Elena.

There appear to be two underlying patterns to the FMLN's growth at the municipal level. The party has broad appeal in urban areas (Zamora

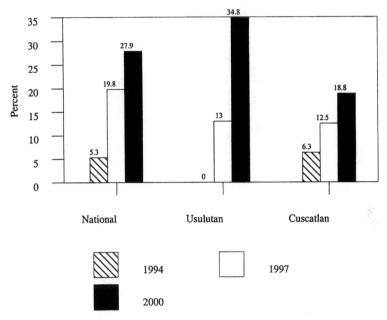

Figure E.1 Percentage of municipal elections won by the FMLN, 1994, 1997, and 2000. The FMLN won no municipal elections in Usulután in 1994. The percentage includes elections won in coalition with other parties. *Source:* Calculated from Supreme Electoral Tribunal (Government of El Salvador) databases.

1998: 265–7). For example, in coalition with other parties, it has governed San Salvador since 1997. The party won the 2000 municipal elections in 13 of the 15 largest municipalities, while ARENA did not win in *any* (Spence et al. 2001: 5). And the party has increasing appeal in some former conflictive zones. Of the 115 municipalities that were conflicted during the war, the FMLN (by itself or in coalition) won 14 in 1994, 30 in 1997, and 37 in 2000.[5]

However, the importance and strength of the legacy of political mobilization varied significantly even across areas whose wartime history was similar. For example, in Las Marías the Land Defense Committee has proven an effective grass-roots organization, bargaining with various government agencies and nongovernmental organizations over the terms of development assistance. In contrast, insurgent *campesinos* in Jiquilisco

---

[5] Calculated from Government of El Salvador electoral data using coding of municipalities as conflicted zones from Checchi and Company Consulting, Inc., and Daniel Carr and Associates (1994).

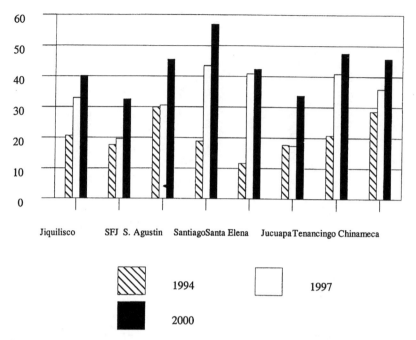

Figure E.2 FMLN's vote share in Tenancingo and selected Usulután munici-palities. Indicated are the fraction of valid votes cast for the FMLN in municipal elections. The FMLN won in none of these municipalities in 1994; in Jiquilisco, San Agustín, Santiago de María, and Tenancingo in 1997; and in Jiquilisco, Santiago de María, Tenancingo, Santa Elena, and Chinameca in 2000. *Source:* Calculated from Supreme Electoral Tribunal (Government of El Salvador) databases.

became deeply disillusioned within a few years of the peace agreement as a result of the extensive manipulation of local organizations by the ERP and the Partido Demócrata. Only in the wake of the flooding in 1996 did a significant local organization – the Coordinadora del Bajo Lempa (Coordinator of Lower Lempa, the area south of the coastal highway) – reemerge there.

However, the transition from a guerrilla army to a political party was particularly difficult for several of the Usulután commanders interviewed for this book. The departmental commander, who during the cease-fire was responsible for negotiating the land transfers for the ERP, was killed in a dispute with a landlord following a car accident along the coastal highway. The commander of southwestern Usulután, whose reentry was said to be particularly rocky, was killed in a bar fight. "Eric," the ERP political officer based near San Francisco Javier who joined the staff of COMUS at war's end, died in an automobile accident. Others, however, settled into postwar life, some as staff members of erstwhile insurgent organizations.

The principal legacy of the agrarian insurgency was not, then, a fundamental redistribution of wealth despite the transfer of some land to insurgent combatants and their supporters, but rather the constitutional reforms that FMLN supporters hoped would eventually enable a fundamental redistribution of political power. At the turn of the twenty-first century the FMLN governed the nation's capital and more than a quarter of its municipalities, a suggestion that the redrawn boundaries of citizenship and culture of endured.[6] For all its socialist rhetoric, the Salvadoran insurgents forged something closer to a French revolution than a Bolshevik one.

The struggle for land continues in El Salvador. In 1995, campesinos invaded properties throughout El Salvador. Drawing on the network of *campesino* organizations that emerged during the civil war, campaign organizers attempted to force the government to investigate enduring violations of the constitutional ceiling on landholding. In contrast to the successful mobilization for the reduction of agrarian debt, the campaign achieved little, in part because organizers failed to maintain the movement's initial alliance with the FMLN as tensions increased over the movement's tactics and timing, reflecting deeper tensions over the movement's autonomy from the party (Kowalchuk 2000: 330–3). Whether or not the *campesinos* of Usulután and Tenancingo, having achieved representation, will one day also gain the property to fulfill the *campesino*'s ideal of personal autonomy based on an independent livelihood on the land, remains to be seen.

---

[6] Further evidence of the persistence of an insurgent political culture is evident in a recent public opinion survey (Seligson, Cruz, and Córdova Macías 2000: 68–9).

Appendix: A Model of High-Risk Collective Action by Subordinate Social Actors

The model presented here will clarify two puzzling aspects of the Salvadoran rural insurgency. First, I show how the reasons for action central to my interpretation account for insurgent collective action, even when the primary material benefits sought by these organizations (access to land) were not contingent on participation. Second, I also want to illuminate how radical forms of *campesino* collective action, which owed their emergence to extraordinary circumstances – the terror of the late '70s and early '80s and the military stalemate of the mid-'80s – could have persisted after those circumstances had passed.

The formal model presented here draws on the rational actor approach in that individuals decide whether to participate or not based on anticipated costs and benefits, which in this case depend on how many others participate. I draw on Thomas Schelling's (1978) representation of collective action as an n-person coordination game among individuals facing a binary choice to participate or not. It differs from most such models, however, in that the likely outcomes of participation are not evaluated in terms of conventional self-regarding and outcome-oriented preferences. Rather, some individuals value defiance, an intrinsic motivation, and/or pleasure in agency, one contingent on both participating oneself and the action's success.[1]

Moreover, Schelling's tipping model leaves unresolved how a group of individuals move from general nonparticipation to general participation. To model that process, I draw on the work of David Lewis (1969)

---

[1] I here ignore those who value participation in itself, as it does not add anything: everywhere below replace "the defiant" with "the defiant and those who value participation in itself" and everything follows.

and of Peyton Young (1996, 1998) on conventions. A *convention* is one of several possible outcomes in which almost everyone adheres to a given strategy as long as he or she believes the others will do so as well. The puzzle then is to explain how a situation in which few participate in collective action evolves to one in which many participate. Young's influential account induces the shift from one convention to another through the effects of what he calls idiosyncratic play, that is, behaviors deviating from the status quo convention that are not explained by the model. In contrast to Young, for whom these deviations are random shocks ("trembles" to a game theorist, mutations to a biologist), my account stresses the intentional and collective nature of individual's departures from the convention of acquiescence.

Consider a large population of subordinate people as described in the text, living in local groups. Each group is large enough so that no member believes his or her own decision to participate in an insurgent collective action would significantly affect the likelihood of success of the action. The individuals are alike in their material circumstances but differ in what they value. Some value defiance and the pleasures of agency as reasons for action. I set aside the value of participation per se, the third reason discussed in Chapter 8, because it would clutter the model without adding much insight. Others, whom I call "the instrumentalists," do not value defiance or the pleasure in agency and will participate only if some conventional benefit is contingent on their participation.

Suppose each individual's strategy set is simply {participate (P), do not participate (N)}. Access to land was not contingent on supporting the insurgency in the midst of the Salvadoran civil war (Chapter 5), so the instrumentalists always choose N. After each actor has simultaneously chosen an action, an outcome is probabilistically determined {success (S), defeat (D)} with the likelihood of success increasing in the fraction f of the local group choosing P.

An individual who values to some degree both defiance and agency in considering whether to participate takes account of three aspects of possible payoffs. Defiance benefits (δ) accrue by dint of participation, irrespective of the outcome, while the pleasure of agency (α) and the cost of losing (λ) accrue respectively in the event of a success or a failure. The payoffs to nonparticipation are independent of the success or failure of the action and are normalized to zero. We assume that the individual will choose the action that maximizes his or her expected payoff, π, that is, the payoffs in case of success and failure weighted by the likelihood of

Appendix

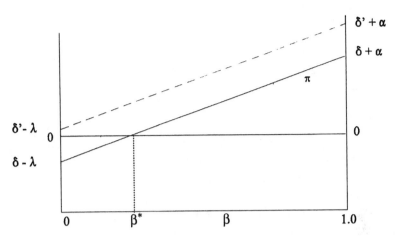

Figure A.1 Defiance and agency in a frequency-dependent model. β is the estimated likelihood that the collective action will be successful. The horizontal line depicts expected benefits of not participating; the other two depict expected benefits of participation for a high- (dashed) and low-defiance person.

these events (β and 1 − β, respectively) in the mind of the actor.[2] We can express π as

$$\pi = \beta(\delta + \alpha) + (1 - \beta)(\delta - \lambda)$$

The expected payoff to participating is thus linear in β and can be represented graphically as in Figure A.1. The expected payoff to not participating is the straight horizontal line. (For the time being, ignore the dashed line.)

Individuals do not know how many will participate in a given action, but they form beliefs about this on the basis of the recent history of their community and adjacent communities. The likelihood of success of an action is based on these beliefs along with other recent events (e.g., the presence of government forces in the area).

Consider first the person (whose payoffs are represented by the solid upward sloping line in Fig. A.1) for whom δ − λ < 0. This is someone who will not participate unilaterally. However, if he or she believed that the probability of success was at least β*, the value of β for which the expected values of participating and nonparticipating are equal, then participation would be his or her expected payoff-maximizing action.

---

[2] The payoffs are in Von Neumann-Morgenstern utilities, that is, they are unique up to a linear transformation, allowing cardinal comparisons of the difference in utility associated with different outcomes for a given individual, but not entailing utility comparisons across individuals.

But how might $\beta > \beta^*$ come about? Define strongly defiant members as those will participate even if $\beta = 0$. Perhaps as a result of the loss of a loved one to the armed forces or a death squad, there might be a number of "strongly defiant" individuals in the community with $\delta' - \lambda > 0$ (as indicated by the dashed line in the Fig. A.1). There are two reasons why such clusters of defiant individuals were likely to emerge in the Salvadoran countryside. First, deaths as a result of state violence tended to be clustered both spatially and temporally. The majority of deaths occurred in the early years of the war, which gives a temporal clustering. And deaths in the countryside tended to occur in groups as government forces swept into insurgent areas or targeted entire families of suspected insurgents. Second, because many of the localized groups we are considering are quite small – a few dozen family units, for example – there was a relatively high probability that the critical mass of defiant individuals would emerge. The reason is similar to the increased probability of sampling error for small groups in statistics. Combinatorial analysis shows that a random draw is more likely to introduce a large deviation from an expected value error for small populations than for large. If the likelihood that any individual member becomes defiant is less than the critical value f^*, then in very large groups the likelihood that the fraction of defiant individuals will exceed f^* is very small. In small groups, this likelihood is considerable. (This defiant critical mass would act only if the costs of failure, λ, were not too high. If $\delta' - \lambda < 0$ because, for example, government troops were stationed nearby, no collective action would occur.)

To better capture the frequency dependence of the expected payoffs, define the fraction participating in period t as f_t. (I ignore the fact that for small groups this fraction takes on only as many values as there are members of the community, but instead treat it as a continuous variable). Then the likelihood of success is

$$\beta = \beta(f_{t-1}, z)$$

where the function β is increasing in f_{t-1}, and z is a vector of other influences on the individual's belief in the likely success of the action.

Define a critical mass of recent past participants, f^*_{t-1}, as the smallest value of f_{t-1} such that $\beta(f^*_{t-1}) > \beta^*$. Then if $f_{t-1} > f^*_{t-1}$, the others (those not "strongly defiant," indicated by the solid line in Fig. A.1) would also participate, and the convention would "tip" to participation. It is easy to see that in the subsequent period participation would remain high, in the

Appendix

absence of an adverse shift in the belief function (perhaps due to the failure of the action or unfavorable military reports).

Then f_{t-1}^* and β^* define a kind of "insurgency threshold" that gives the number of defiants (as a fraction of the population) necessary for insurgent collective action, given a particular belief function. Setting $\pi = 0$ to find β^*, the fraction for which the expected payoffs to participating and not participating are equal, and solving for β^*, we have

$$\beta^* = (\lambda - \delta)/(\lambda + \alpha)$$

This expression appears to illustrate some intuitions, as we can see by differentiating this expression with respect to parameters reflecting the costs of failure, the pleasure of efficacy, and the value of defiance. First, we have

$$d\beta^*/d\delta < 0,$$

which is readily understood as the larger the value given to defiance, the less high is the insurgency threshold, and

$$d\beta^*/d\alpha < 0,$$

understood as the larger the value placed on the pleasure of agency, the less difficult to surmount is the insurgency threshold. Finally,

$$d\beta^*/d\lambda = (\alpha + \delta)/(\lambda + \alpha)^2 > 0,$$

understood as the greater the cost of failed participation, the more demanding are the requirements for self-sustaining collective action.

Figure A.2 depicts a plausible relationship between the recent fraction of participation and the individual's beliefs. The solid line shows that for low recent past participation rates, success is believed to be very unlikely, but that the likelihood of success is believed to be steeply rising in recent participation at some critical point. The dashed line indicates an exogenous shift in beliefs favoring the success of the action, and might be occasioned, for example, by news that a significant FMLN military force was in the area.

Insurgent organizations actively work on these relationships. They attempt to shift perceived values of the parameters through discussion and persuasion so as to shift the insurgency threshold downward.[3] Fostering

---

[3] In contrast to Young, who relies on uncorrelated stochastic events to tip the convention from one basin to another, intentional collective will result in the bunching of deviations from the convention that may accelerate the tipping process. For an extended discussion, see Bowles (2003: chapter 12).

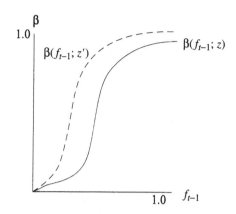

Figure A.2 Belief in the likelihood of success: past patterns and new information. The solid curve shows how the likelihood of success, β, of some insurgent action depends on the fraction who participated in the past period f_{t-1}. The dashed curve shows the effect of new information that favors the success of the action.

defiance by spreading news of government atrocities might increase the value potential participants put on defiance, thereby lowering the threshold and making participation more likely. Organizers try to ensure the high spirits of a group carrying out an activity; increasing the pleasure of agency also lowers the threshold. Successful activities are given extensive word of mouth publicity to increase potential participants' sense of the pleasure they too could experience. And organizers attempt to persuade potential participants that the costs, should an attempted activity fail, are less than thought (λ lower), thereby also lowering the threshold. One way the latter effect occurs is through a failure by some group that is *not* followed by severe costs (which would have tipped the dynamic in the other direction). And organizers may attempt to convince potential participants that the probability of success is not dependent on the numbers participating (contrary to the model), but that a few participants could carry it off, which would be increasingly credible if potential participants see neighbors in fact succeeding. One of the main contributions of insurgent political organization and leadership during the mid-1980s was to convince *campesinos* that what happened yesterday, or in a nearby locality, is a better guide to what will happen today than is the long history of violent retribution for not acquiescing.[4]

---

[4] In other words, they attempt to substitute a learning process for which γ approaches unity for the traditional, highly inertial one.

Appendix

This bandwagon effect might happen for a different reason than above. Rather than all nondefiant individuals having the same threshold, in a more realistic version, the thresholds are distributed among the population. (This is more consistent with the observed pattern in the case-study areas, as not all residents of a particular area joined at once.) For example, a second individual might not value defiance as much as the first, and for her the intersection f_{t-1}^* would be farther to the right. If she valued defiance only a little less than the first, the first's joining would be enough for her threshold to be met and she would join. If the third person valued defiance only a little less than the second, then he would join, and so on.

It should be obvious that whether or not this "bandwagon" or "cascade" effect takes place depends on the distribution of thresholds for participation. (Perhaps the second person values defiance so little that her threshold lies far to the right, and the first person's joining is not sufficient for her to join as well.) But what accounts for the such differences in threshold? Did they precede political mobilization or reflect the processes of the civil war? According to Timur Kuran (1995), such "private preferences" are not detectable ex ante in conditions of repression and violence; all we can observe is, ex post, whether the distribution of thresholds was sufficient to sustain collective action. Roger Petersen (2001) disagrees, arguing that the social structure of communities in Lithuania determined the relative thresholds for community members falling in different groups. Whether or not that was the case in El Salvador is difficult to reconstruct, as those effects were confounded by extreme violence. In any case, the calculations as to how many were likely to join were undoubtedly shaped by prior, local processes of mobilization, including the presence of liberationist priests and insurgent forces, the path of violence through the area, and so on.

A more dynamic extension of the above model would illuminate patterns of insurgency still more by considering how the parameters evolved over the course of the war. The costs of participation, λ, decreased as the war continued, because the insurgent armed forces drove government troops from the area and community members no longer relied on the good will of landlords for income but had direct access to subsistence. As insurgent networks strengthened, the pleasures of agency may have increased as insurgent culture became more rich in rituals and ways of celebrating victories.

Where the underlying conditions are captured by a model such as this, the Olsonian representation of the problem of insurgency as an intractable n-person prisoner's dilemma fails to capture the logic of rebellion for two reasons. First, there were some, the strongly defiant, for whom participation

273

was a dominant strategy. (Olsen's account of "privileged groups" or individuals in whose interest it was to provide the public good unilaterally recognizes this possibility.) Second, for some, the evaluation of the benefits and costs depended on the numbers of others who were expected to participate. As more collaborated so that action was collective and efficacious (and therefore both pleasurable and less risky), *campesinos* faced a coordination (assurance) game because the benefits clearly justified ongoing mobilization as long as sufficiently many others did the same (but not otherwise).

Chronology of El Salvador's Civil War

1932	La Matanza: Tens of thousands of mostly indigenous people killed in aftermath of uprising.
1960s	ORDEN set up in countryside.
1970	FPL is founded.
1970s	Liberation theology practiced in some areas of the countryside.
1972	Christian Democrat José Napoleón Duarte wins presidential election, military intervenes, claims victory, and exiles Duarte. ERP is founded.
1975	A student march protesting the Miss Universe pageant is machine-gunned by security forces; at least 15 killed. Founding of the BPR.
1976	President Molina announces agrarian reform; subsequently defeated.
1979	May: Security forces kill 23 on steps of San Salvador cathedral. October: Coup by junior officers.
1980	January: Civilian members leave government as state violence against civilians continues; Christian Democratic Party and military join forces to form new government. January 22: 20 killed and 200 wounded in largest demonstration in Salvadoran history. March: Agrarian reform (Phase I) carried out. March 24: Archbishop Oscar Arnulfo Romero assassinated. March 30: Government forces fire on Romero's funeral march, 35 killed. May: At least 300 *campesino* refugees fleeing the Salvadoran army are killed by the Salvadoran and Honduran armies at the Sumpol River.

November: Founding of FMLN. Six civilian opposition leaders killed by rightist forces.

December: Four U.S. churchwomen killed by members of the National Guard.

1981   January 3: Two Americans and one Salvadoran associated with agrarian reform assassinated, military officers implicated.

January: FMLN launch "final offensive," quickly defeated.

December: Atlacatl Battalion kills 1,000 people at El Mozote, Morazán.

1982   March: Constituent Assembly elections, Roberto d'Aubuisson, founding member of the National Republican Alliance (ARENA), becomes President of the Assembly, and right-wing parties gain control of agrarian reform institutions.

1984   March: Presidential elections are held; José Napoleón Duarte takes office; U.S. Congress approves an escalation of military aid to El Salvador.

1985   March: Christian Democrats victorious in legislature and municipal elections.

July: Archdiocese of San Salvador announces Tenancingo initiative.

late 1985: Salvadoran military and U.S. administration launch United to Reconstruct, the most comprehensive counterinsurgency program since the outset of the civil war.

1986   January 28: Fifty families return to Tenancingo.

1987   August: Central American governments sign Arias peace plan. Political opening in El Salvador results in the return of some opposition leaders from exile.

1988   March: ARENA wins Legislative Assembly elections.

1989   January: FMLN peace initiative.

March: ARENA candidate Alfredo Cristiani wins the presidency.

October 31: Offices of two opposition organizations are bombed in San Salvador.

November 11: FMLN launches offensive in San Salvador and elsewhere.

November 16: Atlacatl Battalion executes six Jesuit priests in San Salvador.

November 21: FMLN offensive spreads to wealthy neighborhoods of San Benito and Escalón.

December: FMLN and government (separately) ask United Nations to mediate negotiations.

1990   San Jose Accords (July 26): Agreement that a U.N. mission will observe human rights violations.

1991   The Mexico Accords (April 27): Constitutional amendments, including military, electoral, and judicial reforms; establishes Truth Commission for the investigation of human rights abuses.

July: U.N. Observer Mission begins work in El Salvador.

September 25: The New York Accords whereby an Ad Hoc Commission will review officer corps human rights records, a new civilian police force will be founded; ex-combatants from both sides and *campesinos* occupying land will gain title to land.

1992   January 16: Final peace agreement is signed at Chapultepec Castle, Mexico City.

End of January: Arrests of *campesinos* occupying land in Jiquilisco and elsewhere.

February 1: Formal cease-fire begins.

June 28: National Guard and Treasury Police are abolished.

July 1: First 20 percent of FMLN forces demobilized.

September: Ad Hoc Commission presents list of names of military officers to be purged.

September 24: Second 20 percent of the FMLN forces demobilized.

Mid-October: After U.N. intervention in negotiations over terms of land transfer, agreement reached concerning its scope and terms.

October 31: Third 20 percent of FMLN forces demobilized.

December 1: Fourth 20 percent of FMLN forces demobilized.

December 15: Final 20 percent of FMLN forces demobilized; Day of National Reconciliation marks end of armed conflict in El Salvador.

1993   March 15: Truth Commission releases its report; ARENA legislators push through general amnesty.

July 1: Minister of Defense and military High Command resign.

1994   March 20: First inclusive elections in El Salvador; FMLN competes as part of leftist coalition.

References

Acevedo, Carlos. 1998. Las limitaciones del sistema de partidos para enfrontar los problemas fundamentales del país. In *Las elecciones de 1997: Un paseo mas en la transición democrática?*, edited by Héctor Dada Hirezi. San Salvador, El Salvador: FLACSO.

Adler, Glenn. 1992. The Politics of Research During a Liberation Struggle: Interviewing Black Workers in South Africa. In *International Annual of Oral History, 1990. Subjectivity and Multiculturalism in Oral History*, edited by Ronald J. Grele. New York: Greenwood Press.

Americas Watch. 1984. *Free Fire: A Report on Human Rights in El Salvador.* New York: Americas Watch and Lawyers Committee for International Human Rights.

Americas Watch. 1986. *Settling into Routine: Human Rights Abuses in Duarte's Second Year.* New York: Americas Watch.

Americas Watch. 1987. *The Civilian Toll, 1986–1987. Ninth Supplement to the Report on Human Rights in El Salvador.* New York: Americas Watch.

Americas Watch. 1991. *El Salvador's Decade of Terror: Human Rights Since the Assassination of Archbishop Romero.* New Haven: Yale University Press.

Americas Watch and the American Civil Liberties Union (ACLU). 1982. *Report on Human Rights in El Salvador.* New York: Vintage Press.

Amnesty International. 1977. Background to Rural Prisoners in El Salvador: Translation of Protest Document Issued by Peasant Federations Concerning Unacknowledged Prisoners, April 26, 1977. Amnesty International Dossiers, 1975- . North and Latin America. Vol. Dominican Republic E3 – El Salvador E7, no. 14. Document E4: El Salvador, External for Information, AI Index no. AMR 29/13/77. Microfilm.

Anderson, Thomas P. 1971. *Matanza; El Salvador's Communist Revolt of 1932.* Lincoln: University of Nebraska Press.

Argüello Sibrian, Petrona Josefina. 1990. El desarrollo del pensamiento político/ideológico de los campesinos desplazados por el conflicto armado en El Salvador. Master's thesis, University of San Salvador.

Arnson, Cynthia. 2000. Window on the Past: A Declassified History of Death Squads in El Salvador. In *Death Squads in Global Perspective: Murder with*

Deniability, edited by Bruce B. Campbell and Arthur D. Breener. New York: St. Martin's Press.

Auyero, Javier. 1999. Re-Membering Peronism: An Ethnographic Account of the Relational Character of Political Memory. *Qualitative Sociology* 22: 331–51.

Bacevich, A. J., J. D. Hallums, R. H. White, and T. F. Young. 1988. American Military Policy in Small Wars: The Case of El Salvador. Paper presented at John F. Kennedy School of Government, Harvard University.

Banfield, Edward C. 1968. Rioting Mainly for Fun and Profit. In *The Unheavenly City*. Boston: Little, Brown.

Bates, Robert H., Avner Greif, Barry R. Weingast, and Jean-Laurent Rosenthal. 1998. *Analytic Narratives*. Princeton, N.J.: Princeton University Press.

Becker, Gary. 1996. *Accounting for Tastes*. Cambridge: Harvard University Press.

Bell, Derrick A., Jr. 1992. *Faces at the Bottom of the Well: The Permanence of Racism*. New York: Basic Books.

Bermeo, Nancy Gina. 1986. *The Revolution Within the Revolution: Workers' Control in Rural Portugal*. Princeton, N.J.: Princeton University Press.

Biggs, Michael. 1999. Putting the State on the Map: Cartography, Territory, and European State Formation. *Comparative Studies in Society and History* 41(2): 374–405.

Binford, Leigh. 1996. *The El Mozote Massacre: Anthropology and Human Rights*. Tucson: University of Arizona Press.

Binford, Leigh. 1997. Grassroots Development in Conflict Zones of Northeastern El Salvador. *Latin American Perspectives* 93(2): 56–79.

Binford, Leigh. 1999. Hegemony in the Interior of the Salvadoran Revolution: The ERP in Northern Morazán. *Journal of Latin American Anthropology* 4(1): 2–45.

Binford, Leigh. 2002. Violence in El Salvador: A Rejoinder to Philippe Bourgois's "The power of Violence in War and Peace." *Ethnography* 3(2): 201–20.

Binford, Leigh. 2003. Priests, Catechists, and Revolutionaries: Organic Intellectuals in the Salvadoran Revolution. In *Community, Politics, and the Nation-State in Twentieth-Century El Salvador*, edited by Leigh Binford and Aldo Lauria-Santiago. Pittsburgh, Pa.: University of Pittsburgh Press.

Black, Jeremy. 1997. *Maps and Politics*. Chicago: University of Chicago Press.

Boland, Roy C. 2000. *Culture and Customs of El Salvador*. Westport, Conn.: Greenwood Press.

Bonner, Raymond. 1984. *Weakness and Deceit: U.S. Policy and El Salvador*. New York: Times Books.

Bornstein, Brian H., Lesley M. Liebel, and Nikki C. Scarberry. 1998. Repeated Testing in Eyewitness Memory: A Means to Improve Recall of a Negative Emotional Event. *Applied Cognitive Psychology* 12: 119–31.

Bourgois, Philippe. 1982. What U.S. Foreign Policy Faces in Rural El Salvador: An Eyewitness Account. *Monthly Review* 34(1): 14–30.

Bourgois, Philippe. 2001. The Power of Violence in War and Peace: Post–Cold War Lessons from El Salvador. *Ethnography* 2(1): 5–34.

References

Bowles, Samuel. 1998. Endogenous Preferences: The Cultural Consequences of Markets and Other Economic Institutions. *Journal of Economic Literature* 36(1): 75–111.

Bowles, Samuel. 2003. *Economic Behavior and Organization*. Princeton, N.J.: Princeton University Press.

Bradley, Margaret M. 1994. Emotional Memory: A Dimensional Analysis. In *Emotions: Essays on Emotion Theory*, edited by Stephanie H.M. van Goozen, Nanne E. Van de Poll, and Joseph A. Sergeant. Hillsdale, N.J.: Lawrence Erlbaum Associates.

Brockett, Charles D. 1990. *Land, Power, and Poverty: Agrarian Transformation and Political Conflict in Central America*. Boston: Unwin Hyman.

Brockett, Charles D. 1992. Measuring Political Violence and Land Inequality in Central America. *American Political Science Review* 86(1): 169–76.

Brody, Hugh. 1982. *Maps and Dreams*. New York: Pantheon.

Browning, David. 1971. *El Salvador: Landscape and Society*. Oxford: Oxford University Press.

Byrne, Hugh. 1996. *El Salvador's Civil War: A Study of Revolution*. Boulder, Colo.: Lynne Rienner.

Cabarrús, Carlos Rafael. 1983. *Génesis de una revolución*. Mexico: Ediciones de la casa, Centro de Investigaciones y Estudios Superiores en Antropología Social.

Cabarrús, Carlos Rafael. 1985. El Salvador: De movimiento campesino a revolución popular. In *Historia Política de los Campesinos Latinoamericanos*, edited by Pablo González Casanova. Mexico: Siglo Veintiuno Editores.

Cagan, B., and S. Cagan. 1991. *This Promised Land El Salvador: The Refugee Community of Colomoncagua and their Return to Morazán*. New Brunswick, N.J.: Rutgers University Press.

Calhoun, Craig. 1991. The Problem of Identity in Collective Action. In *Macro-Micro Linkages in Sociology*, edited by Joan Huber. Newbury Park, Calif.: Sage Publications.

Call, Charles T. 1999. Crime and Peace: Why Successful Peace Processes Produce the World's Most Violent Countries. Paper presented at the Annual Conference of the International Studies Association, Washington, D.C., February.

Camerer, Colin. 2003. *Behavioral Game Theory: Experimental Studies of Strategic Interaction*. Princeton, N.J.: Princeton University Press.

Camerer, Colin F., and Ernst Fehr. 2003. Measuring Social Norms and Preferences Using Experimental Games: A Guide for Social Scientists. In *Foundations of Human Sociality*, edited by Joe Henrich, Samuel Bowles, Robert Boyd, Colin F. Camerer, Ernst Fehr, Herbert Gintis, and Richard McElreath. Oxford: Oxford University Press.

Cardenal, Rodolfo. 1985. *Historia de una esperanza: Vida de Rutilio Grande*. San Salvador, El Salvador: UCA Editores.

Carr, Daniel, et al. 1993. *ABT Survey of Rural El Salvador*. San Salvador, El Salvador: ABT Associates.

Castañeda, Jorge G. 1994. *Utopia Unarmed: The Latin American Left After the Cold War*. New York: Vintage Books.

CE-GOES (Comisión de la Unión Europea y República de El Salvador). 1996. *Informe Final*. Programa de Emergencia para la Reinserción Productiva de los Desmovilizados en la Agricultura. Proyecto CE-GOES ALA 92/18 (project of the European Community and the Government of El Salvador). Hamburg: Gesellschaft füürAgarprojekte MBH.

CELAM (Consejo Episcopal Latinoamericano). 1978. *Los obispos latinoamericanos entre Medellín y Puebla: documentos episcopales 1968–1978*. San Salvador, El Salvador: UCA Editores.

Checchi and Company. 1981. Agrarian Reform in El Salvador. Report presented to the Agency for International Development, San Salvador, El Salvador.

Checchi and Company Consulting, Inc., and Daniel Carr and Associates. 1994. Final Report: Evaluation of the Social Stabilization and Municipal Development Strengthening Project. San Salvador, February 1994. Reprinted as Anexo No. 2 in *De la guerra a la paz: Una cultura política en transición*, by Mitchell Seligson and Ricardo Córdova Macías 1995. El Salvador, El Salvador: IDELA/University of Pittsburgh/ Fundación Ungo.

Chong, Dennis. 1991. *Collective Action and the Civil Rights Movement*. Chicago: University of Chicago Press.

Chong, Dennis. 2001. *Rational Lives. Norms and Values in Politics and Society*. Princeton, N.J.: Princeton University Press.

CIDAI (Centro de Información, Documentación y Apoyo a la Investigación). 2001a. Terremoto del 13 de enero en El Salvador. Resumen de información. *El Salvador Proceso* 935: 14–16.

CIDAI (Centro de Información, Documentación y Apoyo a la Investigación). 2001b. Los terromotos de enero y febrero: Implicaciones económicos. *El Salvador Proceso* 940: 6–7.

CIDAI (Centro de Información, Documentación y Apoyo a la Investigación). 2001c. Consideraciones económicas, sociales y políticas del terremoto del 13 de enero. *Estudios Centroamericanos* 627–8: 29–58.

Colindres, Eduardo. 1976. La tenencia de la tierra en El Salvador. *Estudios Centroamericanos* 31(335–6): 463–72.

Colindres, Eduardo. 1977. *Fundamentos Económicos de la Burguesia Salvadoreña*. San Salvador, El Salvador: UCA Editores.

Comisión Interamericana de Derechos Humanos. 1982. *Informe Anual de la Comisión Interamericana de Derechos Humanos, 1981–1982*. Reproduced in *Estudios Centroamericanos* 410 (December): 1151.

Conning, Jonathan, Pedro Olinto, and Alvaro Trigueros Arguello. 2001. Managing Economic Insecurity in Rural El Salvador: The Role of Asset Ownership and Labor Market Adjustments. Mimeograph.

Corradi, Juan. 1992. Toward Societies Without Fear. In *Fear at the Edge: State Terror and Resistance in Latin America*, edited by Juan E. Corradi, Patricia Weiss Fagen, and Manuel Antonio Garretón. Berkeley and Los Angeles: University of California Press.

Cruz, José Miguel, and Luis Armando González. 1997. Magnitud de la violencia en El Salvador. *Estudios Centroamericanos* 588.

References

CUDI (Centro Universitario de Documentación e Información). 1982. Informe sobre la guerra civil: Elementos para su Analysis Durante el période julio-septiembre de 1982. *Estudios Centroamericanos* 407–8: 911–20.

CUDI (Centro Universitario de Documentación e Información). 1983. Informe Especial. La guerra civil: Elementos para su analysis Octubre-diciembre de 1982. *Estudios Centroamericanos* 411: 37–49.

Das, Veena. 1990. Our Work to Cry: Your Work to Listen. In *Mirrors of Violence: Communities, Riots and Survivors in South Asia*, edited by Veena Das. Delhi and New York: Oxford University Press.

Debate Nacional. 1988. Documento Final. *Estudios Centroamericanos* 478–9: 731–66.

Deci, Edward L. 1975. *Intrinsic Motivation.* New York and London: Plenum Press.

Deci, Edward L., and Richard M. Ryan. 1985. *Intrinsic Motivation and Self-Determination in Human Behavior.* New York and London: Plenum Press.

del Castillo, Graciana. 1997. The Arms-for-Land Deal in El Salvador. In *Keeping the Peace: Multi-Dimensional UN Operations in Cambodia and El Salvador*, edited by Michael W. Doyle, Ian Johnstone, and Robert C. Orr. Cambridge: Cambridge University Press.

DGEC (Dirección General de Estadística y Censos). 1974. *Tercer censo nacional agropecuario 1971*, vol 1: *Características a nivel nacional, departamental y municipal.* San Salvador, El Salvador: DGEC.

DGEC (Dirección General de Estadística y Censos). 1975. *Tercer censo nacional Agropecuario 1971*, vol 2: *Características a nivel nacional, departamental y tamaño de la explotación.* San Salvador, El Salvador: DGEC.

DGEC (Dirección General de Estadística y Censos). 1977. *Cuarto censo nacional de población 1971*, vol 1. San Salvador, El Salvador: DGEC.

Downs, Roger M., and David Stea. 1977. *Maps in Minds: Reflections on Cognitive Mapping.* New York: Harper and Row.

Durham, William. 1979. *Scarcity and Survival in Central America: The Ecological Origins of the Soccer War.* Stanford, Calif.: Stanford Univeristy Press.

Economic Commission for Latin America. 1984. The Crisis in Central America: Its Origins, Scope and Consequences. *CEPAL Review* 22 (April): 53–80.

Edwards, Beatrice, and Gretta Tovar Siebentritt. 1991. *Places of Origin: The Repopulation of Rural El Salvador.* Boulder, Colo.: Lynne Rienner.

Ellacuría, Ignacio, and Jon Sobrino, eds. 1991. *Mysterium liberationis: Conceptos fundamentales de la teología de la liberación.* San Salvador, El Salvador: UCA Editores.

Elster, Jon. 1996. Rationality and the Emotions. *The Economic Journal* 106: 1386–97.

Elster, Jon. 1998. Emotions and Economic Theory. *Journal of Economic Literature* 36: 47–74.

Emirbayer, Mustafa, and Jeff Goodwin. 1994. Network Analysis, Culture, and the Problem of Agency. *American Journal of Sociology* 99(6): 1411–54.

Emirbayer, Mustafa, and Ann Mische. 1998. What Is Agency? *American Journal of Sociology* 103(4): 962–1023.

FAES (Fuerzas Armadas de El Salvador). 1996. *Campaña de contrainsurgencia "Unidos para Reconstruir."* San Salvador, El Salvador: FAES.

Farah, Doug. 1988a. Death Squad Began as Scout Troop. *Washington Post,* 28 August, p. A1.

Farah, Doug. 1988b. Salvadoran Death Squads Threaten Resurgence. *Washington Post,* 28 August, p. A20.

Fehr, Ernst, and Urs Fischbacher. 2001. Why Social Preferences Matter. Paper prepared for the Nobel Symposium on Behavioral and Experimental Economics, December 4–6, Stockholm.

Fehr, Ernst, and Simon Gächter. 2000. Fairness and Retaliation: The Economics of Reciprocity. *Journal of Economic Perspective* 14(3): 159–81.

Fehr, Ernst, and Simon Gächter. 2002. Altruistic Punishment in Humans. *Nature* 415: 137–40.

FENACOA (Federación Nacional de Asociaciones Cooperativas Agropecuarias). 1992. *Décima segunda Asamblea Federal. Memoria de labores 1991–1992: Unidad, solidaridad y justicia social.* San Salvador, El Salvador: FENACOA.

Fitzsimmons, Tracy, and Mark Anner. 1999. Civil Society in a Postwar Period: Labor in the Salvadoran Democratic Transition. *Latin American Research Review* 34: 103–28.

Flores, Margarita. 1998. El Salvador: Trayectoria de la Reforma Agraria, 1980–1998. *Revista Mexicana de Sociología* 60: 125–51.

FMLN (Frente Farabundo Martí para la Liberación Nacional). 1992. *Inventario de Tierras en Zonas Conflictivas.* San Salvador, El Salvador: FMLN.

Foley, Michael W. 1996. Laying the Groundwork: The Struggle for Civil Society in El Salvador. *Journal of Interamerican Studies and World Affairs* 38: 67–104.

Foley, Michael W., George R. Vickers, and Geoff Thale. 1997. *Land, Peace, and Participation: The Development of Post-War Agricultural Policy in El Salvador and the Role of the World Bank.* Washington, D.C.: Washington Office on Latin America.

Foran, John. 1993. A Theory of Third World Social Revolutions: Iran, Nicaragua, and El Salvador Compared. *Critical Sociology* 19(2): 3–28.

Fox, Jonathan. 1996. How Does Civil Society Thicken? The Political Construction of Social Capital in Rural Mexico. *World Development* 24: 1089–103.

FUNDASAL (Fundación Salvadoreña de Desarrollo y Vivienda Mínima). 1985. *Proyecto de repoblamiento y reconstrucción de Tenancingo.* San Salvador, El Salvador: FUNDASAL.

Funkhauser, Edward. 1992. Mass Emigration, Remittances, and Economic Adjustment: The Case of El Salvador in the 1980s. In *Immigration in the Work Force: Economic Consequences for the United States and Source Areas,* edited by G. J. Borjas and R. B. Freeman. Chicago: University of Chicago Press.

Gibb, Tom. 2000. *Salvador: Under the Shadow of Dreams.* Unpublished book manuscript.

Gibb, Tom, and Douglas Farah. 1989. Magazine Story on Death Squads in El Salvador. Typescript.

Goitia, Alfonso, and Ernesto Galdámez. 1993. El Movimiento Campesino el El Salvador: Evolución y Lucha. *Realidad Económico-Social* 36: 637–67.

Goodwin, Jeff. 1994a. Old Regimes and Revolutions in the Second and Third Worlds. *Social Science History* 18(4): 575–606.

References

Goodwin, Jeff. 1994b. Toward a New Sociology of Revolutions. *Theory and Society.* 23: 731–66.

Goodwin, Jeff. 1997. The Libidinal Constitution of a High-Risk Social Movement: Affectual Ties and Solidarity in the Huk Rebellion, 1946–1954. *American Sociological Review* 62: 53–69.

Goodwin, Jeff. 2001. *No Other Way Out: States and Revolutionary Movements, 1945–1991.* Cambridge: Cambridge University Press.

Goodwin, Jeff, and James M. Jasper. 1999. Caught in a Winding, Snarling Vine: The Structural Bias of Political Process Theory. *Sociological Forum* 14(1): 27–54.

Goodwin, Jeff, and Steven Pfaff. 2001. Emotion Work in High-Risk Social Movements: Managing Fear in the U.S. and East German Civil Rights Movements. In *Passionate Politics: Emotions and Social Movements*, edited by Jeff Goodwin, Francesca Polletta, and James M. Jasper. Chicago: Chicago University Press.

Goodwin, Jeff, and Theda Skocpol. 1989. Explaining Revolutions in the Third World. *Politics and Society* 17(4): 489–509.

Goodwin, Jeff, Francesca Polletta, and James M. Jasper. 2001. Introduction: Why Emotions Matter. In *Passionate Politics: Emotions and Social Movements*, edited by Jeff Goodwin, Francesca Polletta, and James M. Jasper. Chicago: Chicago University Press.

Gordon Rapoport, Sara. 1989. *Crisis política y guerra en El Salvador.* Mexico: Siglo Veintiuno Editores.

Green, Linda. 1995. Living in a State of Fear. In *Fieldwork Under Fire: Contemporary Studies of Violence and Survival*, edited by Carolyn Nordstrom and Antonius C. G. M. Robben. Berkeley and Los Angeles: University of California Press.

Green, Linda. 1999. *Fear as a Way of Life: Mayan Widows in Rural Guatemala.* New York: Columbia University Press.

Gruson, Lindsey. 1988. Rebel Attacks on the Rise in Salvador. *New York Times*, 20 October, p. A3.

Gruson, Lindsey. 1989. Salvador Rebels' Drive on Mayors Is Bringing Chaos to Rural Areas. *New York Times*, 9 January, p. A1.

Guha, Ranajit, 1983a. *Elementary Aspects of Peasant Insurgency in Colonial India.* Delhi: Oxford University Press.

Guha, Ranajit. 1983b. The Prose of Counter-Insurgency. In *Subaltern Studies II.* Oxford and New York: Oxford University Press.

Gutiérrez, Gustavo. 1973. *A Theology of Liberation: History, Politics, and Salvation*, translated and edited by Sister Caridad Inda and John Eagleson. Maryknoll, N.Y.: Orbis Books.

Halbwachs, Maurice. 1992. *On Collective Memory*, translated and edited by Lewis A. Coser. Chicago: University of Chicago Press.

Hammond, John L. 1998. *Fighting to Learn: Popular Education and Guerrilla War in El Salvador.* New Brunswick, N.J.: Rutgers University Press.

Hardin, Russell. 1982. *Collective Action.* Baltimore, Md.: Johns Hopkins University Press.

Harley, J. Brian. 1988. Maps, Knowledge and Power. In *The Iconography of Landscape: Essays on the Symbolic Representation, Design and Use of Past Environments*, edited by Denis Cosgrove and Stephen Daniels. Cambridge: Cambridge University Press.

Harley, J. Brian. 1992. Rereading the Maps of the Columbian Encounter. *Annals of the Association of American Geographers* 82(3): 522–42.

Harnecker, Marta. 1993. *Con La Mirada en Alto: Historia de las FPL Farabundo Martí a través de sus Dirigentes*. San Salvador, El Salvador: UCA Editores.

Harvey, Neil. 1998. *The Chiapas Rebellion: The Struggle for Land and Democracy*. Durham, N.C.: Duke University Press.

Hatfield, Mark O., Jim Leach, and George Miller. 1987. *Bankrolling Failure: United States Policy in El Salvador and the Urgent Need for Reform*. U.S. Congress: Arms Control and Foreign Policy Caucus.

Hayden, Dolores. 1995. *The Power of Place: Urban Landscapes as Public History*. Cambridge, Mass.: MIT Press.

Henrich, Joe, Samuel Bowles, Robert Boyd, Colin F. Camerer, Ernst Fehr, Herbert Gintis, and Richard McElreath. 2001. In Search of *Homo economicus*: Behavioral Experiments in 15 Small-Scale Societies. *American Economic Review* 91: 73–8.

Hernández Romero, Pedro Juan, Miguel Antonio Chorro, and Aracel Del Carmen Ramirez. 1991. *La situación actual del cooperativismo en El Salvador*. San Salvador, El Salvador: CSUCA/INVE-UES/COACES.

Heston, Alan, Robert Summers, Daniel A. Nuxoll, and Bettina Aten. 1995. *The Penn World Tables*. Version 5.6 (http://pwt.econ.upenn.edu).

Hirschman, Albert O. 1982. *Shifting Involvements: Private Interest and Public Action*. Princeton, N.J.: Princeton University Press.

Hunt, David. 1974. Villagers at War: The National Liberation Front in My Tho Province, 1965–1967. *Radical America* 8: 1–184.

INSIDE (Instituto de Investigación Social y Desarrollo). 1991. *Diagnóstico de las Comunidades Atendidas por COMUS*. San Salvador, El Salvador: INSIDE. Typescript.

ISTA (Instituto Salvadoreño de Transformación Agraria). 1991. *Memoria de Labores: Ciclo Agrícola 90/91*. San Miguel: Region Oriental Agraria.

Jasper, James M. 1997. *The Art of Moral Protest: Culture, Biography and Creativity in Social Movements*. Chicago: University of Chicago Press.

Jasper, James M. 1998. The Emotions of Protest: Affective and Reactive Emotions in and Around Social Movements. *Sociological Forum* 13(3): 397–423.

Jelin, Elizabeth. 1996. Citizenship Revisited: Solidarity, Responsibility, and Rights. In *Constructing Democracy: Human Rights, Citizenship, and Society in Latin America*, edited by Elizabeth Jelin and Eric Hershberg. Boulder, Colo.: Westview Press.

Jing, Jun. 1996. *The Temple of Memories: History, Power, and Morality in a Chinese Village*. Stanford: Stanford University Press.

Johnson, Kenneth. 1993. Between Revolution and Democracy: Business Elites and the State in El Salvador During the 1980s. Ph.D. thesis, Tulane University.

Joint Group. 1994. Report of the Joint Group for the Investigation of Illegal Armed Groups with Political Motivation in El Salvador. San Salvador, El Salvador, 28 July. Mimeograph.

References

Kain, Roger J. P., and Elizabeth Baigent. 1992. *The Cadastral Map in the Service of the State: A History of Property Mapping.* Chicago and London: University of Chicago Press.

Kalyvas, Stathis. n.d. *The Logic of Violence in Civil War.* Unpublished book manuscript.

Kelly Rivera, Ana, Edy Arelí Ortiz Cañas, Liza Domínguez Magaña, and María Candelaria Navas. 1995. *Valió la Pena?! Testimonios de salvadoreñas que vivieron la guerra.* San Salvador, El Salvador: Editorial. Sombrero Azul.

Kerkvliet, Benedict J. 1977. *The Huk Rebellion: A Study of Peasant Revolt in the Philippines.* Berkeley: University of California Press.

Kincaid, A. Douglas. 1987. Peasants into Rebels: Community and Class in Rural El Salvador. *Comparative Studies in Society and History* 29(3): 466–94.

Kitschelt, Herbert P. 1986. Political Opportunity Structures and Political Protest: Anti-Nuclear Movements in Four Democracies. *British Journal of Political Science* 16: 57–85.

Kohn, Melvin. 1969. *Class and Conformity.* Homewood, Ill.: Dorsey Press.

Kohn, Melvin, Atsushi Naoi, Carrie Schoenbach, Carmi Schooler, and Kazimierz Slomczynski. 1990. Position in the Class Structure and Psychological Functioning in the U.S., Japan, and Poland. *American Journal of Sociology* 954: 964–1008.

Kowalchuk, Lisa. 2000. In the Eye of the Beholder: Politics and Perception in the Salvadoran Peasant Movement. Ph.D thesis, York University.

Kriger, Nora. 1992. *Zimbabwe's Guerrilla War: Peasant Voices.* Cambridge: Cambridge University Press.

Kuran, Timur. 1995. *Private Truths, Public Lies: The Social Consequences of Preference Falsification.* Cambridge: Harvard University Press.

Lam, W. F. 1996. Institutional Design of Public Agencies and Coproduction: A Study of Irrigation Associations in Taiwan. *World Development* 24: 1039–54.

Lauria-Santiago, Aldo A. 1999. *An Agrarian Republic: Commercial Agriculture and the Politics of Peasant Communities in El Salvador, 1823–1914.* Pittsburgh, Pa.: University of Pittsburgh Press.

LeMoyne, James 1985. Salvadoran Rebels, in New Tactic, Are Kidnapping or Killing Mayors. *New York Times,* 12 May, pp. A-1, 4.

Lepper, Mark R., and David Greene. 1978. *The Hidden Costs of Reward: New Perspectives on the Psychology of Human Motivation.* Hillsdale, N.J.: Lawrence Erlbaum Associates.

Levenson-Estrada, Deborah. 1994. *Trade Unionists Against Terror: Guatemala City, 1954–1985.* Chapel Hill: University of North Carolina.

Lewis, David K. 1969. *Conventions: A Philosophical Study.* Cambridge: Harvard University Press.

Lievens, Karin. 1988. *El quinto piso de la alegría: Tres años con la guerrilla: El Salvador.* N.p.: Ediciones Sistema Radio Venceremos.

Lindo-Fuentes, Hector. 1990. *Weak Foundations: The Economy of El Salvador in the Nineteenth Century.* Berkeley and Los Angeles: University of California Press.

Loveman, Mara. 1998. High-Risk Collective Action: Defending Human Rights in Chile, Uruguay, and Argentina. *American Journal of Sociology* 104(2): 477–525.

Lungo Uclés, Mario. 1995. Building an Alternative: The Formation of a Popular Project. In *The New Politics of Survival: Grassroots Movements in Central America*, edited by Minor Sinclair, 153–79. New York: Monthly Review Press.

Lynch, Kevin. 1960. *The Image of the City*. Cambridge, Mass.: MIT Press and Harvard University Press.

Lynch, Kevin. 1985. Reconsidering *The Image of the City* (1985). From *Cities of the Mind*, edited by Lloyd Rodwin and Robert Hollister. Reprinted in *City Sense and City Design: Writings and Projects of Kevin Lynch*, edited by Tridib Banerjee and Michael Southworth. Cambridge, Mass.: MIT Press.

Lynch, Kevin, and Tridib Banerjee. 1976. Growing up in Cities. *New Society* 37 (722): 281–4. Reprinted in *City Sense and City Design: Writings and Projects of Kevin Lynch*, edited by Tridib Banerjee and Michael Southworth. Cambridge, Mass.: MIT Press.

Macdonald, Laura. 1997. *Supporting Civil Society. The Political Role of Non-governmental Organizations in Central America*. New York: St. Martin's Press.

Mansbridge, Jane. 2001. Complicating Oppositional Consciousness. In *Oppositional Consciousness: The Subjective Roots of Social Protest*, edited by Jane Mansbridge and Aldon Morris. Chicago: University of Chicago Press.

Markoff, John. 1996. *The Abolition of Feudalism: Peasants, Lords and Legislators in the French Revolution*. University Park: Pennsylvania State University Press.

Markus, Gregory B. 1986. Stability and Change in Political Attitudes: Observed, Recalled, and "Explained." *Political Behavior* 8(1): 21–44.

Martín-Baró, Ignacio. 1973. Psicología del campesino salvadoreño. *Estudios Centroamericanos* 28(297–8): 476–95.

Martín-Baró, Ignacio. 1988. La violencia en Centroamérica: Una visión psicosocial. *Revista Costarricense de Psicología* 12(13): 21–34. Reprinted as "Violence in Central America: A Social Psychological Perspective," in *Towards a Society That Serves Its People: The Intellectual Contributions of El Salvador's Murdered Jesuits*, edited by John Hassett and Hugh Lacey. Washington, D.C.: Georgetown University Press, 1991.

Mason, T. David, and Dale A. Krane. 1989. The Political Economy of Death Squads: Toward a Theory of the Impact of State-Sanctioned Terror. *International Studies Quarterly* 33(2): 175–98.

McAdam, Doug. 1982. *Political Process and the Development of Black Insurgency, 1930–1970*. Chicago: University of Chicago Press.

McAdam, Doug. 1988. Micromobilization Contexts and Recruitment to Activism. *International Social Movements Research* 1: 125–54.

McAdam, Doug, Sidney Tarrow, and Charles Tilly. 2001. *Dynamics of Contention*. Cambridge: Cambridge University Press.

McClintock, Cynthia. 1998. *Revolutionary Movements in Latin America: El Salvador's FMLN and Peru's Shining Path*. Washington, D.C.: United States Institute of Peace Press.

References

McClintock, Michael. 1985. *The American Connection: State Terror and Popular Resistance in El Salvador.* London: Zed Books.

McElhinny, Vincent J. 1999. Revolutionary Experience and the Empowerment of Rural Producers in El Salvador. Paper presented at the 1999 American Political Science Association Meeting in Atlanta, Ga., September 2–5.

McElhinny, Vincent J. n.d. Revolution, Coordination, Empowerment: The Politics of Decentralization in Post-War El Salvador. Ph.D. thesis, University of Pittsburgh, forthcoming.

McElinny, Vincent J. 2001. Facing Up or About Face: Agrarian Inequality and the Prospects for Rural Development in Post-War El Salvador. Paper presented at the 2001 Latin American Studies Association Meeting in Washington, D.C., September 6–8.

Miles, Sara, and Bob Ostertag. 1991. The FMLN: New Thinking. In *A Decade of War: El Salvador Confronts the Future,* edited by Anjali Sundaram and George Gelber. New York: Monthly Review Press.

Montes, Segundo. 1986. *El Agro Salvadoreño (1973–1980).* Colección: Estructuras Y Procesos, vol. 14. San Salvador, El Salvador: UCA Editores.

Montes, Segundo. 1987. Los limites y posibilidades que enfrenta la participación política en el campo salvadoreño. *Estudios Centroamericanos* 463–4: 305–22.

Montgomery, Tommie Sue. 1995. *Revolution in El Salvador: From Civil Strife to Civil Peace,* 2nd ed. Boulder, Colo.: Westview Press.

Montoya, Aquiles. 1992. *El sector agropecuario reformado y la nueva economia popular.* Universidad Centroamericana Jose Simeon Cañas. Typescript.

Moore, Barrington, Jr. 1966. *Social Origins of Dictatorships and Democracy.* Boston: Beacon Press.

Moore, Barrington, Jr. 1978. *Injustice: The Social Bases of Obedience and Revolt.* White Plains, N.Y.: M. E. Sharpe.

Morris, Aldon. 1984. *The Origins of the Civil Rights Movements: Black Communities Organizing for Social Change.* New York: Free Press.

Nordstrom, Carolyn. 1997. *A Different Kind of War Story.* Philadelphia: University of Pennsylvania Press.

Olick, Jeffrey K., and Joyce Robbins. 1998. Social Memory Studies: From 'Collective Memory' to the Historical Sociology of Mnemonic Practices. *Annual Review of Sociology* 24: 105–40.

Olson, Mancur. 1965. *The Logic of Collective Action: Public Goods and the Theory of Groups.* Cambridge, Mass.: Harvard University Press.

Orlove, Benjamin. 1991. Mapping Reeds and Reading Maps: The Politics of Representation in Lake Titicaca. *American Ethnologist* 181: 3–37.

Orlove, Benjamin. 1993. The Ethnography of Maps: The Cultural and Social Contexts of Cartographic Representation in Peru. *Cartographica* 30(1): 29–46.

Ostrom, Elinor. 1996. Crossing the Great Divide: Coproduction, Synergy, and Development. *World Development* 24(6): 1073–87.

Ostrom, Elinor. 1998. A Behavioral Approach to the Rational Choice Theory of Collective Action. *American Political Science Review* 92(1): 1–22.

Paige, Jeffrey M. 1975. *Agrarian Revolutions.* New York: Free Press.

Paige, Jeffrey M. 1987. Coffee and Politics in Central America. In *Crises in the Caribbean Basin*, edited by Richard Tardanico. Newbury Park, Calif.: Sage.

Paige, Jeffrey M. 1996. Land Reform and Agrarian Revolution in El Salvador. *Latin American Research Review* 31(2): 127–39.

Paige, Jeffrey M. 1997. *Coffee and Power: Revolution and the Rise of Democracy in Central America*. Cambridge, Mass., and London: Harvard University Press.

Pansters, Wil G. 1996. Citizens with Dignity: Opposition and Government in San Luis Potosí, 1938–93. In *Dismantling the Mexican State?*, edited by Rob Aitken, Nikki Craske, Gareth A. Jones, and David E. Stansfeld. New York: St. Martin's Press.

Partido Demócrata. 1997. Por qué Joaquín Villalobos, Ana Guadalupe Martínez, Eduardo Sancho y los otros dejamos el FMLN y nos unimos al Partido Demócrata. San Salvador, El Salvador. Mimeograph.

Passerini, Luisa. 1980. Italian Working Class Culture Between the Wars: Consensus to Fascism and Work Ideology. *International Journal of Oral History* 1(1): 4–27.

Passerini, Luisa. 1992. Introduction. In *Memory and Totalitarianism: International Yearbook of Oral History and Life Stories*, vol. 1. Oxford: Oxford University Press.

Paus, Eva. 1996. Exports and the Consolidation of Peace. In *Economic Policy for Building Peace: The Lessons of El Salvador*, edited by James K. Boyce. Boulder, Colo.: Lynne Rienner.

Pearce, Jenny. 1986. *Promised Land: Peasant Rebellion in Chalatenango, El Salvador*. London: Latin American Review.

Pearce, Jenny. 1998. From Civil War to "Civil Society": Has the End of the Cold War Brought Peace to Central America? *International Affairs* 74(3): 587–615.

Peceny, Mark. 1999. *Democracy at the Point of Bayonets*. University Park: Pennsylvania State University Press.

PERA (Programa para la Evaluación de la Reforma Agraria). 1989. *IX evaluación del proceso de la reforma agraria*. San Salvador, El Salvador: Ministerio de Agricultura y Ganadería, Oficina Sectorial de Planificación Agropecuaria, Proyecto Planificación y Evaluación de la Reforma Agraria.

PERA (Programa para la Evaluación de la Reforma Agraria). 1991. *XI evaluación del proceso de la reforma agraria*. San Salvador, El Salvador: Ministerio de Agricultura y Ganadería, Oficina Sectorial de Planificación Agropecuaria, Proyecto Planificación y Evaluación de la Reforma Agraria.

Petersen, Roger. n.d. *Emotion, Individual Memory and Community-Based Narrative: Reconstructing Life in Violent Eras*. St. Louis, Mo.: Washington University. Typescript.

Petersen, Roger D. 2001. *Resistance and Rebellion: Lessons from Eastern Europe*. Cambridge: Cambridge University Press.

Petersen, Roger D. 2002. *Understanding Ethnic Violence: Fear, Hatred, and Resentment in Twentieth-Century Eastern Europe*. Cambridge: Cambridge University Press.

Peterson, Anna L. 1997. *Martyrdom and the Politics of Religion: Progressive Catholicism in El Salvador's Civil War*. Albany: State University of New York Press.

Polletta, Francesca. 1998a. Contending Stories: Narrative in Social Movements. *Qualitative Sociology* 21(4): 419–46.

References

Polletta, Francesca. 1998b. "It Was Like a Fever ...": Narrative and Identity in Social Protest. *Social Problems* 45(2): 137–59.

Polletta, Francesca. 1999. "Free Spaces" in Collective Action. *Theory and Society* 28(1): 1–38.

Polletta, Francesca, and James J. Jasper. 2001. Collective Identity and Social Movements. *Annual Review of Sociology* 27: 283–305.

Popkin, Margaret. 2000. *Peace Without Justice: Obstacles to Building the Rule of Law in El Salvador.* University Park: Pennsylvania State University Press.

Popkin, Samuel. 1979. *The Rational Peasant.* Los Angeles and Berkeley: University of California Press.

Portelli, Alessandro. 1985. *Biografia di Una Città. Storia e Racconto: Terni 1830–1985.* Torino: Einaudi.

Portelli, Alessandro. 1991. *The Death of Luigi Trastulli and Other Stories: Form and Meaning in Oral History.* Albany: State University of New York Press.

Portelli, Alessandro. 1997. *The Battle of Valle Giulia: Oral History and the Art of Dialogue.* Madison: University of Wisconsin Press.

Prosterman, Roy L. 1982. The Unmaking of Land Reform. *The New Republic,* 9 August, pp. 21–25.

Przeworski, Adam. 1985. Proletariat into a Class: The Process of Class Formation. In *Capitalism and Social Democracy.* Cambridge: Cambridge University Press.

Pyes, Craig. 1983. Salvadoran Rightists: The Deadly Patriots. Collection of reprinted articles that originally appeared in The *Albuquerque Journal,* 18–22 December. Albuquerque, N.M.: *Albuquerque Journal.*

Raudales, Walter, and Juan Ramón Medrano. 1994. *Ni militar ni sacerdote (de seudónimo Balta).* San Salvador, El Salvador: Arcoiris.

El Rescate Human Rights Chronology. Various dates. Compilation of reports from Salvadoran newspapers, church organizations, and TV news reports concerning human rights violations in El Salvador. Electronic file.

Rich, Adrienne. 1986. Notes Toward a Politics of Location (1984). In *Blood, Bread, and Poetry: Selected Prose 1979–1985.* New York and London: W. W. Norton.

Rivera Damas, Arturo. 1977. Labor pastoral de la Arquidiócesis de San Salvador especialmente de las comunidades eclesiales de base en su proyección a la justicia. Dentro de este marco, la persecución. *Estudios Centroamericanos* 32: 805–14.

Roseberry, William. 1991. La Falta de Brazos: Land and Labor in the Coffee Economies of Nineteenth-Century Latin America. *Theory and Society* 20: 351–81.

Ross, Lee, and Richard E. Nisbett. 1991. *The Person and the Situation: Perspectives of Social Psychology.* Philadelphia: Temple University Press.

Rundstrom, Robert A. 1990. A Cultural Interpretation of Inuit Map Accuracy. *Geographical Review* 80: 155–68.

Schelling, Thomas C. 1978. *Micromotives and Macrobehavior.* New York: W. W. Norton.

Schirmir, Jennifer. 1998. *The Guatemalan Military Project: A Violence Called Democracy.* Philadelphia: University of Pennsylvania Press.

Schwarz, Benjamin C. 1991. *American Counterinsurgency Doctrine and El Salvador: The Frustrations of Reform and the Illusions of Nation Building*. Santa Monica, Calif.: Rand Corporation.

Scitovsky, Tibor. 1976. *The Joyless Economy*. New York: Oxford University Press.

Scott, James. 1976. *The Moral Economy of the Peasant: Rebellion and Subsistence in Southeast Asia*. New Haven, Conn.: Yale University Press.

Scott, James. 1985. *Weapons of the Weak: Everyday Forms of Peasant Resistance*. New Haven, Conn.: Yale University Press.

Scott, James. 1990. *Domination and the Arts of Resistance: Hidden Transcripts*. New Haven, Conn.: Yale University Press.

Seidman, Gay W. 1994. *Manufacturing Militance: Workers' Movements in Brazil and South Africa, 1970–1985*. Berkeley and Los Angeles: University of California Press.

Seligson, Mitchell. 1995. Thirty Years of Transformation in the Agrarian Structure of El Salvador. *Latin American Research Review* 30: 43–76.

Seligson, Mitchell, and Ricardo Córdova Macías. 1995. *De la guerra a la paz: Una cultura política en transición*. El Salvador: IDELA/University of Pittsburgh/ Funda Ungo.

Seligson, Mitchell, and Vincent McElhinny. 1996. Low-Intensity Warfare, High-Intensity Death: The Demographic Impact of the Wars in El Salvador and Nicaragua. *Canadian Journal of Latin American and Caribbean Studies* 21(42): 211–41.

Seligson, Mitchell, José Miguel Cruz, and Ricardo Córdova Macías. 2000. *Auditoria de la Democrácia: El Salvador 1999*. San Salvador, El Salvador: IUDOP/UCA, University of Pittsburgh, and FUNDAUNGO.

Seligson, Mitchell A., William Thiesenhusen, Malcolm Childress, and Roberto Vidales. 1993. *El Salvador Agricultural Policy Analysis and Land Tenure Study*. Agricultural Policy Analysis Project II, Technical Report No. 133. Cambridge Mass.: Abt Associates.

Sen, Amartya K. 1977. Rational Fools: A Critique of the Behavioral Foundations of Economic Theory. *Philosophy and Public Affairs* 6(4): 317–44.

Sevilla, Manuel. 1985. *La concentración económica en El Salvador*. Managua: Instituto de Investigaciones Económicas y Sociales.

Sewell, William H., Jr. 1992. A Theory of Structure: Duality Agency, and Transformation. *American Journal of Sociology* 98: 1–29

Simons, Marlise. 1985. Daughter of Duarte Is Released by Rebels in Complex Exchange. *New York Times*, 25 October, pp. A1, A9.

Skocpol, Theda. 1979. *States and Social Revolutions*. Cambridge: Cambridge University Press.

Skocpol, Theda. 1982. What Makes Peasants Revolutionary? *Comparative Politics* 14(3): 351–75.

Skocpol, Theda. 1996. Unraveling from Above. *American Prospects* 25: 20–25.

Sluka, Jeffrey A. 1995. Reflections on Managing Danger in Fieldwork: Dangerous Anthropology in Belfast. In *Fieldwork Under Fire: Contemporary Studies of Violence and Survival*, edited by Carolyn Nordstrom and Antonius C. G. M. Robben. Berkeley and Los Angeles: University of California Press.

References

Smith, Christian. 1991. *The Emergence of Liberation Theology: Radical Religion and Social Movement Theory.* Chicago: University of Chicago Press.

Smith, Christian. 1996. *Resisting Reagan: The U.S. Central America Peace Movement.* Chicago: University of Chicago Press.

Spence, Jack, Mike Lanchin, and Geoff Thale. 2001. *From Elections to Earthquakes: Reform and Participation in Post-War El Salvador.* Cambridge: Hemisphere Initiatives.

Stanley, William. 1996. *The Protection Racket State: Elite Politics, Military Extortion, and Civil War in El Salvador.* Philadelphia: Temple University Press.

Starn, Orin. 1999. *Nightwatch: The Politics of Protest in the Andes.* Durham and London: Duke University Press.

Stokes, Susan. 1995. *Cultures in Conflict.* Berkeley and Los Angeles: University of California Press.

Stoll, David. 1993. *Between Two Armies in the Ixil Towns of Guatemala.* New York: Columbia University Press.

Stoll, David. 1999. *Rigoberta Menchú and the Story of All Poor Guatemalans.* Boulder, Colo.: Westview Press.

Strasma, John, Peter Gore, Jeffrey Nash, and Refugio I. Rochin. 1983. *Agrarian Reform in El Salvador.* Washington, D.C.: Checchi.

Suárez-Orozco, Marcelo. 1992. Grammar of Terror: Psychological Responses to State Terrorism in the Dirty War and Post Dirty Argentina. In *The Paths to Domination, Resistance and Terror*, edited by Carolyn Nordstrom and JoAnn Martin. Berkeley and Los Angeles: University of California Press.

Taylor, Charles. 1985. Human Agency and Language. In *Philosophical Papers*, vol. 1. Cambridge: Cambridge University Press.

Taylor, Michael. 1988. Rationality and Revolutionary Collective Action. In *Rationality and Revolution*, edited by Michael Taylor. Cambridge: Cambridge University Press.

Thompson, Martha. 1995. Repopulated Communities in El Salvador. In *The New Politics of Survival: Grassroots Movements in Central America*, edited by Minor Sinclair. New York: Monthly Review Press.

Tilly, Charles. 1978. *From Mobilization to Revolution.* New York: McGraw-Hill.

Tilly, Charles. 1993. *European Revolutions, 1492–1992.* Cambridge: Blackwell.

Tilly, Charles. 1999. The Trouble with Stories. In *The Social Worlds of Higher Education: Handbook for Teaching in a New Century*, edited by Marco Giugni and Florence Passy. Thousand Oaks, Calif.: Pine Forge Press.

Truth Commission for El Salvador. 1993. From Madness to Hope: The 12 Year War in El Salvador. Report of the Truth Commission for El Salvador. Reprinted in *The United Nations and El Salvador, 1990–1995.* The United Nations Blue Books Series, vol. IV. New York: United Nations.

UCS-AIFLD (Unión Comunal Salvadoreña-American Institute for Free Labor Development). 1981. *El Salvador Land Reform Update. Executive Summary, Land to the Tiller Program.* El Salvador: Unión Comunal Salvadoreña.

USAID (United States Agency for International Development). 1987. *The National Plan.* San Salvador, El Salvador: USAID. Typescript.

References

Vázquez, Norma, Cristina Ibáñez, and Clara Murguialday. 1996. *Mujeres~Montaña. Vivencias de guerrilleras y colaboradoras del FMLN*. Madrid: Horas Y Horas.

Villalobos, Joaquín. 1986. El Estado Actual de la Guerra. *Estudios Centroamericanos* 449: 169–204.

Wade, Robert. 1988. *Village Republics: Economic Conditions of Collective Action in South India*. Cambridge: Cambridge University Press.

Walter, Knut, and Phillip J. Williams. 1993. The Military and Democratization in El Salvador. *Journal of Interamerican Studies and World Affairs* 35: 39–88.

Warren, Kay B. 1998. *Indigenous Movements and Their Critics: Pan-Maya Activism in Guatemala*. Princeton, N.J.: Princeton University Press.

Whitfield, Teresa. 1994. *Paying the Price: Ignacio Ellacuría and the Murdered Jesuits of El Salvador*. Philadelphia: Temple University Press.

Wickham-Crowley, Timothy P. 1987. The Rise (and Sometimes Fall) of Guerrilla Governments. *Sociological Forum* 2: 473–99.

Wickham-Crowley, Timothy P. 1989. Understanding Failed Revolution in El Salvador: A Comparative Analysis of Regime Types and Social Structures. *Politics and Society* 17(4): 511–37.

Wickham-Crowley, Timothy P. 1991. *Exploring Revolution: Essays on Latin American Insurgency and Revolutionary Theory*. Armonk, N.Y.: M. E. Sharpe.

Wickham-Crowley, Timothy P. 1992. *Guerrillas and Revolution in Latin America: A Comparative Study of Insurgents and Regimes Since 1956*. Princeton, N.J.: Princeton University Press.

Williams, Robert G. 1986. *Export Agriculture and the Crisis in Central America*. Chapel Hill: University of North Carolina Press.

Williams, Robert G. 1994. *States and Social Evolution: Coffee and the Rise of National Governments in Central America*. Chapel Hill: University of North Carolina Press.

Wipfler, William L. 1976. Statement by the Rev. William L. Wipfler before the Subcommittee on International Organizations of the Committee on International Relations of the House of Representatives of the United States Regarding the Status of Human Rights in El Salvador, Nicaragua, and Guatemala, June 9, 1976. Amnesty International Dossiers, 1975- . North and Latin America. Vol. Dominican Republic E3 – El Salvador E7, no. 14. Document E1. Microfilm.

Wise, Michael L. 1986. *Agrarian Reform in El Salvador: Process and Progress*. El Salvador: USAID. Typescript.

Witvliet, Charlotte van Oyen. 1997. Traumatic Intrusive Imagery as an Emotional Memory Phenomenon: A Review of Research and Explanatory Information Processing Theories. *Clinical Psychology Review* 17(5): 509–36.

Wood, Elisabeth J. 1995. Agrarian Social Relations and Democratization: The Negotiated Resolution of the Civil War in El Salvador. Ph.D. thesis, Stanford University.

Wood, Elisabeth J. 1996. The Peace Accords and Postwar Reconstruction. In *Economic Policy for Building Peace*, edited by James Boyce. Boulder, Colo.: Lynne Rienner.

Wood, Elisabeth Jean. 2000. *Forging Democracy from Below: Insurgent Transitions in South Africa and El Salvador*. Cambridge: Cambridge University Press.

References

Wood, Elisabeth J. 2003. Civil War, Reconstruction, and Reconciliation: The Repopulation of Tenancingo, El Salvador. In *Community, Politics, and the Nation-State in Twentieth-Century El Salvador*, edited by Leigh Binford and Aldo Lauria-Santiago. Pittsburgh, Pa.: University of Pittsburgh Press.

Wood, Elisabeth J. n.d. Challenges to Political Democracy in El Salvador. In *Advances and Setbacks in Democratization in Latin America*, edited by Frances Hagopian and Scott Mainwaring. Cambridge: Cambridge University Press, forthcoming.

Wood, Richard L. 2002. *Faith in Action: Religion, Race, and Democratic Organizing in America*. Chicago: University of Chicago Press.

Young, H. Peyton. 1996. The Economics of Convention. *Journal of Economic Perspectives* 10: 105–22.

Young, H. Peyton.1998. *Individual Strategy and Social Structure*. Princeton, N.J.: Princeton University Press.

Zamora, Rubén. 1991. The Popular Movement. In *A Decade of War: El Salvador Confronts the Future*, edited by Anjali Sundaram and George Gelber. New York: Monthly Review Press.

Zamora, Rubén. 1998. *El Salvador: Heridas que no cierran. Los partidos políticos en la post-guerra*. San Salvador, El Salvador: FLACSO.

Index

Adler, Glenn, 40, 41, 42
agrarian reform, 84, 181, 191–2, 228–9, 259; in 1976, 5, 26, 61, 93; in 1980, 2, 42, 60–2, 74, 230, 259; and cooperatives, 43, 74–7, 107, 110, 143, 152, 160–2, 177, 181, 193; first phase, 76, 106–7, 163–4; "New Options," 220, 222; third phase "land-to-the-tiller," 72, 74–7, 108–10, 166, 168–9, 220, 222; United States and, 27; in Usulután, 42, 62, 101, 106–11, 112, 161–6; in Western Jiquilisco, 60–2; *see also* CONFRAS; cooperativas; insurgent cooperatives
Aguilares, town of, 91–3, 100, 196, 241
Ajuluco, *cantón* of, 97
Alas brothers, José Ignacio and Higinio, 90–4
Alemán, Miguel, 62
Alianza Republicana Nacional, *see* ARENA
Americas Watch, 49; on government human rights violations, 53, 88, 109, 134; on FMLN violations, 156–7; on Tenancingo, 36, 98, 139–41
Amnesty International, 103, 131, 156
Anderson, Thomas P., 21
Anzora family, 198
Arce Battalion, 149–50

Archdiocese of San Salvador, 91, 109, 239; human rights agency of, 9, 36, 50, 149–50; National Debate (1988), 165; and Tenancingo accord, 136–7, 141–2, 144, 146
ARENA (National Republican Alliance), 27–30, 51, 88, 155, 163, 261–3
Argentina, 8, 23, 187, 207
Argüelo Sibrian, Petrona Josefina, 53, 136, 155
Atlacatl Battalion, 10, 29, 34, 38

Bacevich, A. J., 10, 127
Bajo Jocote Dulce, 209
Banfield, Edward C., 235
Barnes, William, 220
Batallón Belloso, 140
Batallón de Infantería de Marina, 179
Batallón Rafael Arce Zablah, 134
Beaver tribe, in British Columbia, 46
Berlín, town of, 63, 87, 108
Bermeo, Nancy Gina, 31, 85, 247
Bible study groups, *see under* liberation theology
Binford, Leigh, 35, 59, 103, 115, 126, 132, 144, 157, 177, 200; and Atlacatl Battalion at El Mozote, 34, 53; and liberation theology, 100–2, 120
Black, Jeremy, 45, 46, 49, 213, 214, 218

Index

collective identity, 13–5, 16, 20, 227, 238; by subordinate social actors, 20, 229, 246–51, 252; *see also* insurgent collective action

collective identity, 13–14, 19, 219, 236, 238, 247; in Guatemala, 250; *see also* insurgent collective action; political culture; social networks

Comandante "Miriam," 66

Commander Ana Guadalupe Martínez, 157

Communist Party, 21, 25, 66, 173, 195; *see also* FPL

Comunidad El Palmo, 206

Comunidad La Palma, 124

Comunidad Las Conchas, 65

Comunidades Unidas de Usulután, *see* COMUS

COMUS (United Communities of Usulután), 176–7, 178–90, 207, 220, 264; *see also* ERP; insurgent cooperatives; land

Confederación Nacional de Federaciones de la Reforma Agraria Salvadoreña, *see* CONFRAS

CONFRAS (National Confederation of Federations of the Salvadoran Agrarian Reform), 169, 173, 175, 178, 181, 190–2; support for insurgency, 161–6; *see also* insurgent cooperatives; land

Constituent Assembly, 88

Convention, 268

cooperatives: Bienaventurados, 76; California, 3–4, 128, 162, 181, 260; Candelaria, un Nuevo Amanecer, 67, 71, 154; El Carrizal, 87, 202; El Cuarumal, 76, 77; El Guayava, 76; El Jobalito, 151–2, 215, 217; El Palmo, 173; El Taurete, 76; El Tesoro, 76, 105; Escobares San Judas, 166; La Conciencia, 121, 169–70, 206; La Joya del Pilar, 78–9; La Luz en el Horizonte, 111, 168, 170; La Maroma, 62, 106, 161, 203, 207,

213; La Merced, 172; La Normandía, 4, 7, 62, 162, 178; La Salinera, 111; Las Conchas, 65, 215; Lempamar, 111; Loma Alegre, 168, 201, 203, 206; Los Ensayos, 201; Los Guardianos, 76; Mate de Piña, 178; Montecristo, 153, 225; Montemaría, 111; Nancuchiname, 106, 111, 162, 178–9, 203; San Judas Escobares, 205, 206; San Pedro Los Arenales, 66, 69, 206; Trece de Junio, 170–1, 182, 202, 204; *see also* insurgent cooperatives

Coordinadora para el Desarrollo de la Costa, *see* CODECOSTA

Coordinator for the Development of the Coast, *see* CODECOSTA

Córdova Macías, Ricardo, 223, 265

Corral Viejo, *cantón* of, 97, 139, 153

Costa Rica, 178

counterinsurgency, 52, 255; "hearts and minds" in, 28; insurgent response to, 28–9, 134, 190; National Plan (1983) and, 133; "prose of," 32; United States and, 131–2; *see also* agrarian reform

coup, 187; aborted (May 1980), 88, 187; history of in El Salvador, 29; October 1979, 26–7, 97, 164

Cristiani, President Alfredo, 28, 51, 74, 148

Cruz, José Miguel, 98, 175, 260, 265

Cuba, 122, 123

Cultural Revolution, 39

Cuscatlán, 17, 55, 85, 138, 150

Das, Veena, 35, 44

d'Aubuisson, Major Roberto, 26–8, 109, 163; *see also* death squads

death squads, 5, 26–7, 88, 109, 270; in Santiago de María, 73, 119; in Usulután, 58, 176; *see also* Regalado, Héctor Antonio

Deci, Edward L., 245, 246

Del'Pech family, 4, 74

Index

271; as a political party, 4, 175–6,
257, 261–5; basis of support for,
10–11, 52, 105, 116, 127, 154–9,
193–225; controlled zones, 53–4, 89,
121, 132, 134; "final offensive"
(1981), 27, 110; land conflict at war's
end, 178–89; in Las Marías, 65–6;
offensive (1989), 10, 28–30, 52, 122,
125, 135, 148, 168, 172, 175, 177,
183, 189; origins of (1980), 1–2, 27;
in Santiago de María, 73, 86, 88–9;
in San Francisco Javier, 77–8, 86,
123, 125; and Tenancingo bombing
(1983), 36–8; and Tenancingo
accord, 59, 135–47; in Western
Jiquilisco, 62; women in, 129–31;
see also civil war; ERP; FPL; human
rights; insurgent collective action;
insurgent cooperatives; insurgent
political culture; land; military
stalemate; peace agreement (1992);
Tenancingo; Usulután
Foley, Michael W., 187, 259
Foundation for Self-Development and
Solidarity for Salvadoran Workers,
186
FPL (Farabundo Martí Popular
Liberation Forces), 11, 56, 58, 92–7,
102–3, 112, 126, 133, 155–7, 186,
220; origins of (1970), 25; *see also*
ERP; FECCAS; FMLN; insurgent
collective action; liberation theology;
Tenancingo; Usulután
France, 139
Francisco Guirola, 3
Freedom Summer (1964), 10, 247
French Revolution, 239, 249, 265
Frente Farabundo Martí para la
Liberación Nacional, *see*
FMLN
Front for Popular Action, 92
Fuerzas Populares de Liberación
Farabundo Martí, *see* FPL
Fundación Salvadoreña de Desarrollo y
Vivienda Mínima, *see* FUNDASAL

FUNDASAL (Salvadoran Foundation
for Development and Low-Income
Housing), 135, 138–47; *see also*
Tenancingo

Güchter, Simon, 244, 245
Gibb, Tom, 88, 92, 93, 97, 103, 105,
123, 126, 131, 133, 135, 156, 204
Gintis, Herbert, 245
Goodwin, Jeff, 10, 13, 16, 116, 120,
200, 234, 240, 253, 254
Grande, Rutilio, 93
Green, Linda, 36, 37, 39, 40, 44, 207
Gruson, Lindsey, 88, 156
Guardado, Facundo, 11, 127
Guatemala, 27, 39, 40, 88, 95, 223, 250
Guazapa volcano, 55–56, 78, 80, 134,
140, 153, 208
Guha, Ranajit, 32, 249
Gutiérrez, Gustavo, 90

haciendas: California, 1–5, 62, 77, 102,
112, 128, 149–50, 171, 256;
Concordia, 4, 175, 186; La
Normandía, 4, 6, 74; Las Arañas,
187; Montemar, 188;
Nancuchiname, 77, 178; Nueva, 97,
118, 139; Santa Petrona, 148
Halbwachs, Maurice, 34
Hardin, Russell, 236, 252
Harley, J. Brian, 46, 47
Harnecker, Marta, 92, 134, 200
Hatfield, Mark O., 10
Hayden, Dolores, 47
Hernández Martínez, General
Maximiliano, 21
Hernández Romero, Pedro Juan, 162,
165
High Command, 131; and assassination
of Jesuit priests, 10, 29; and
Tenancingo accord, 140–1
Hirschman, Albert O., 252
Homberger family, 73, 88
Honduras, 24, 53, 77, 113, 134, 136,
211

301

Index

Index

Nicaragua, 16, 29, 30, 53, 113, 122, 178, 223
Nordstrom, Carolyn, 44
Northern Ireland, 41
Novoa, Enrique, 188
Nueva Esperanza, 178–9, 188
Nuevo Amanecer, 179, 188, 204, 225

oligarchy, 11, 21–2, 73, 82, 118, 164; see also land
Olson, Mancur, 12, 16, 240
Operation Phoenix, 134, 140
oral history, 34, 35, 39
ORDEN (Democratic Nationalist Organization), 95–6, 102, 110, 126, 127, 195–8, 208
Organización Democrática Nacionalista, see ORDEN
Ostertag, Bob, 134, 156, 157, 167
Ostrom, Elinor, 161, 243
Otorga family, 103
Ozatlán, 59, 108, 148

Paige, Jeffrey M., 11, 21, 22, 24, 28, 63, 197
Palomo family, 1–3, 77, 172
participation in insurgent collective action: agrarian class and, 195–200, 220–3, 227–8; campesino accounts of, 200–8; explanations for, 231, 232–3, 241, 246–7, 251; land distribution and, 194–5, 200–8, 220–4, 228; nonparticipant accounts of, 208–12; political affiliation and, 195–200; reasons for given in interviews, 193–225; see also emotional and moral reasons
Partido de Conciliación Nacional, 262
Partido Demócrata, 261, 264
Passerini, Luisa, 34, 50
path-dependency, 20, 231–2; patterns of insurgent support and, 237–41; see also insurgent collective action
peace agreement (1992), 3–4, 8, 29, 204, 224, 264; celebrations of, 51–2;

implementation of, 189, 257; interim agreements and, 3, 52, 185; land claims and, 63, 65, 67, 77, 83–6, 185–9, 258–9; and New York accord, 185; and ultimatum, 243–5; see also land
Pearce, Jenny, 13, 36, 58, 91, 92, 95, 126, 186
Peru, 39, 139, 249
Petersen, Roger D., 17, 33, 214, 232, 247, 252, 273
Peterson, Anna L., 100, 124, 203, 234
Philippines, 248
Poland, 161
political culture, 238; emergence of insurgent, 5, 195, 213–25, 230, 251; evolution of, 19, 20, 50, 241–3, 254; in Guatemala, 250–1; postwar, 18, 265; prewar, 14, 24–5; see also insurgent political culture
political liberalization, 25; see also democratization
political mobilization: comparison of with other cases, 157, 248; legacy of, 263–5; overview of, 20–30; postwar, 258–9; repression and, 230; in Tenancingo, 89–99, 119–20; in Usulután, 99–105, 119–20, 121, 237–8; see also Catholic Church; civil war; insurgent collective action; insurgent political culture; legacy of civil war; liberation theology; Tenancingo; Usulután
political modernization, 25
political opportunity structures, 227, 251–6; and cascade of occupations, 238–40; and danger of tautological explanations, 16; widening of as condition for social movement, 15–16, 20, 189, 200, 240; see also collective action; insurgent collective action
political parties, see ARENA; Christian Democratic Party; Communist Party; elections; Partido Demócrata

Index

San Vicente, 56, 58, 85, 111, 116, 126, 133, 148, 155, 220, 223
Sandinistas in Nicaragua, 16, 29
Santa Ana, 25, 85
Santa Anita, 93, 97, 139
Santa Cruz Michapa, 98
Santa Elena, 59, 65, 66, 102, 112, 114, 148, 155, 171, 182, 264
Santiago de María, 43, 59, 65, 110, 112, 114, 118, 162, 176, 182, 264; coffee in, 59, 72–4, 151; death squads in, 73, 87–9, 104–5, 119; oligarchic families of, 73, 148–9; overview of, 72–4; patterns of insurgent support in, 59, 86, 157–8, 190, 210, 230; *see also* insurgent collective action; insurgent cooperatives; land
Schelling, Thomas C., 236, 267
Schwarz, Benjamin C., 10, 127, 131, 132
Scott, James, 14, 15, 242
selective benefits: in *campesino* accounts, 203–4, 213, 219, 225; emotional and moral, 2, 18–20, 50, 231–41, 243, 246–56; material, 12–13, 19, 185, 193–4, 224, 227–8, 230, 240, 243, 267; in social science experiments, 243–6; *see also* collective action; insurgent collective action; preferences
Seligson, Mitchell, 8, 56, 194, 220–3, 259, 265
Siebentritt, Gretta Tovar, 53, 134, 136
Sixth Brigade, 4, 74, 88, 114, 148, 149, 170, 172, 179
Skocpol, Theda, 10, 11, 13, 161
Sluka, Jeffrey A., 41, 43
Smith, Christian, 28, 90, 131
Sobrino, Jon, 90
soccer war, 24, 77
social movements, 15, 18, 20, 26, 39, 52, 131, 253; *see also* insurgent collective action; social networks

social networks, 13–5, 20, 250, 251, 253; emergence of during mobilization, 238; generalized reciprocity of, 13; prewar weakness of, 14–15, 227; solidary communities and, 16; *see also* collective identity; insurgent collective action; insurgent political culture; insurgent social network
social science experiments, 243–6
South Africa, 41, 157, 161, 223, 250, 260
South Vietnam, 108
Spain, 139
stalemate, *see* military stalemate
Stanley, William, 20, 24, 25, 27, 77, 108, 132
Stoll, David, 35, 95, 159, 234, 255
Strasma, John, 109, 110
Suchitoto, 43, 90–4, 100, 196, 208–10
Sultanpuri, 35, 44
Sweden, 62

Tarrow, Sidney, 20, 251
Taylor, Charles, 14, 236, 240, 253
Tecoluca, 220, 223
Tenancingo: accord, 59, 136–47, 150, 191–2; agrarian reform in, 108–9; bombing of (1983), 36–8, 98, 134, 211–12, 248; Community Council, 141–6, 191–2; counterinsurgency in, 132–3; dual sovereignty in, 121–59; map of, 81; overview of, 55–6; patterns of land tenure in, 78–83; and political culture, 18; political mobilization in, 89–99, 119–20; postwar, 264–5; repopulation efforts in, 59, 126, 135–47, 230; *see also* insurgent collective action; insurgent cooperatives; insurgent political culture; liberation theology; military stalemate
Thompson, Martha, 132, 136, 137, 177
Tiananmen Square, 250

Scott Morgenstern and Benito Nacif, *Legislative Politics in Latin America*
Wolfgang C. Muller and Kaare Strom, *Policy, Office, or Votes?*
Ton Notermans, *Money, Markets, and the State: Social Democratic Economic Policies since 1918*
Paul Pierson, *Dismantling the Welfare State?: Reagan, Thatcher and the Politics of Retrenchment*
Marino Regini, *Uncertain Boundaries: The Social and Political Construction of European Economies*
Jefferey M. Sellers, *Governing from Below: Urban Regions and the Global Economy*
Yossi Shain and Juan Linz, eds., *Interim Governments and Democratic Transitions*
Theda Skocpol, *Social Revolutions in the Modern World*
Richard Snyder, *Politics after Neoliberalism: Reregulation in Mexico*
David Stark and László Bruszt, *Postsocialist Pathways: Transforming Politics and Property in East Central Europe*
Sven Steinmo, Kathleen Thelan, and Frank Longstreth, eds., *Structuring Politics: Historical Institutionalism in Comparative Analysis*
Duane Swank, *Global Capital, Political Institutions, and Policy Change in Developed Welfare States*
Sidney Tarrow, *Power in Movement: Social Movements and Contentious Politics*
Ashutosh Varshney, *Democracy, Development, and the Countryside*
Elisabeth Jean Wood, *Forging Democracy from Below: Insurgent Transitions in South Africa and El Salvador*